APARTHEID AND BEYOND

APARTHEID AND BEYOND

*South African Writers
and the Politics of Place*

Rita Barnard

OXFORD
UNIVERSITY PRESS

2007

OXFORD
UNIVERSITY PRESS

Oxford University Press, Inc., publishes works that further
Oxford University's objective of excellence
in research, scholarship, and education.

Oxford   New York
Auckland   Cape Town   Dar es Salaam   Hong Kong   Karachi
Kuala Lumpur   Madrid   Melbourne   Mexico City   Nairobi
New Delhi   Shanghai   Taipei   Toronto

With offices in
Argentina   Austria   Brazil   Chile   Czech Republic   France   Greece
Guatemala   Hungary   Italy   Japan   Poland   Portugal   Singapore
South Korea   Switzerland   Thailand   Turkey   Ukraine   Vietnam

Copyright © 2007 by Oxford University Press, Inc.

Published by Oxford University Press, Inc.
198 Madison Avenue, New York, New York 10016

www.oup.com

Oxford is a registered trademark of Oxford University Press

Library of Congress Cataloging-in-Publication Data
Barnard, Rita.
Apartheid and beyond : South African writers and the politics
of place / Rita Barnard.
p. cm.
Includes bibliographical references and index.
ISBN-13 978-0-19-511286-3

1. South African literature (English)—History and criticism. 2. Politics
and literature—South Africa—History—20th century. 3. Apartheid in literature.
4. Place (Philosophy) in literature. 5. South Africa—In literature.
6. South Africa—Politics and government—1994– I. Title.
PR9359.6.B37 2006
820.9'968—dc22   2006003812

3 5 7 9 8 6 4 2

Printed in the United States of America
on acid-free paper

ACKNOWLEDGMENTS

M y work on this project was funded by the Research Foundation of the University of Pennsylvania, which granted me a number of summer research fellowships to travel to South Africa, and also by the School of Arts and Sciences of the University of Pennsylvania, which awarded me its faculty research fellowship and enabled me to do some uninterrupted writing in 1996–97. I am grateful for this support.

Thanks are also due to audience members at various other institutions where I presented early versions of this work. The insightful comments of members of the academic community at Dartmouth College, Duke University, Edinburgh University, Oxford University, the University of KwaZulu-Natal, the University of Warwick, the University of the Western Cape, the University of the Witwatersrand, the University of York, and the Wesleyan Humanities Center made this a much better book than it would otherwise have been. I owe a great debt of gratitude to many friends and colleagues who supported me in difficult times, including Nina Albert, Roger Allen, Nancy Armstrong, Richard Begam, Lee Cassanelli, Joe Clarke, Eric Cheyfitz, Stuart Curran, Joan Dayan, Thadious Davis, Jane Drucker, JoAnne Dubil, Lars Engle, Jim English, Penny Fielding, Sanjay Krishnan, Henrika Kuklick, Ignacio Lopez, John Marx, Michael Valdez Moses, Lydie Moudileno, Molly Mullin, Jean-Michel Rabaté, Michèle Richman, Don Shojai, Paola Splendore, and the late, inimitable Paul Korshin. Without the advice and encouragement of a number of South African expatriates in the United States and Britain, I would have given up long ago. I think with great affection of all of them, especially Derek Attridge, Grant Farred, Jeremy Foster, Neil Lazarus, Carol Muller, Rob Nixon, Mark Sanders, Andrew van der Vlies, and, way back in my grad school days, Kay-Robert and Desirée Volkwyn. My friends and colleagues in the South African academy, including David Attwell, Kosie de Villiers, Kai Easton, Joan Hambidge, Michiel Heyns, Eva Hunter, Margaret Lenta, Freddie Marais, Achille Mbembe, David Medalie, Sarah Nuttall, Stan Ridge, Marilet van Reenen, and Ingrid Winterbach inspired me and helped to keep me more or less up to date with South African developments. Cherryl Walker generously shared some of her superb unpublished work on land reform with me. Cousin Dries van Heerden, the last Boer socialist, was always a source of hopeful insight into the new South Africa, as were my siblings, Sari, Mientjie, and Faan Barnard. The generosity, loyalty, and companionship of my uncle Barnie and my auntie Inge Barnard have brightened up my life for the past thirty years. They must share much of the credit for whatever I have managed to achieve since I arrived at Stellenbosch in 1976, eager for change.

My students at Penn and Brown, including Ijeoma Akunyili, Jeff Allred, Bindi Bhagat, Alice Brittan, Chris Dacus, Jon Eburne, Rob Faunce, Gregg Flaxman, Jennifer Glaser, Jonathan Goldman, Matthew Hart, Stephanie Harzewski, Stephen Hock, Chris Hunter, Darren Jaspan, Joshua Karetny, Carmen Lamas, Lars Larson, Jacob Leland, Matthew Merlino, Cindy Port, Monica Popescu, Thangam Ravindranathan, Mark Sample, Deborah Shapple, Sara Sjolund, Shivani Tibrewala, Jonah Willihnganz, and dozens of others equally talented and dear were my staunchest supporters and my liveliest companions over the past ten years. The brilliant members of the Mods and Latitudes research groups at Penn, where I presented my work-in-progress on Coetzee and Mda, were an especially valuable source of conversation and criticism. My research assistants Andrew Lynn and Ian Duncan were skilled, diligent, and patient beyond their years. I would also like to thank my three South African literature students at the Bread Loaf School in rainy, beautiful southeast Alaska: Ben Foley, Eder Williams, and Karen Reyes. I will always appreciate their imaginative reach and remember the time they "did a Toloki"— picked bunches of wildflowers from all over the city of Juneau—to celebrate the conclusion of our work together. *Dumela*, friends! The Women's Studies faculty and staff at Penn made sure that I got my last chapter done. Demie Kurz, Ania Loomba, Janice Madden, Ann Matter, Luz Marin, Anne Norton, Susan Sidlauskas, and many others gave my work-in-progress the finest critical attention and offered sisterly support in the final stages of writing this book. Thanks, finally, to Susan Chang, Elissa Morris, and Shannon McLachlan, editors at Oxford University Press, for their patience and professionalism.

Dana Phillips offered rigorous proofreading and stubborn love. Though I feared throughout the years of writing this book that we would end up in the poorhouse, I always knew that with him there the place would be neat and clean, and full of cool music and clever words.

I gratefully acknowledge permission to reprint, in revised form, the following articles:

"Dream Topographies: J. M. Coetzee and the South African Pastoral." *South Atlantic Quarterly* (Winter 1994): 33–59. © 1994 by Duke University Press.

"Coetzee's Country Ways." *Interventions* 4 (2002): 384–394. © 2002 by Taylor & Francis Ltd.

"*Disgrace* and the South African Pastoral." *Contemporary Literature* 44 (Summer 2003): 199–224. © 2003 by the University of Wisconsin Press.

Warm thanks and acknowledgments are also due to Duke University Press and to *Novel: A Forum on Fiction* for allowing me to incorporate brief parts of the following essays into chapter 6:

"The Place of Beauty: Reflections on Elaine Scarry and Zakes Mda," in *Beautiful/Ugly: African and Diaspora Aesthetics*, ed. Sarah Nuttall (Durham: Duke University Press, 2006), 102–121.

"On Laughter, the Grotesque, and the South African Transition: Zakes Mda's *Ways of Dying*." *Novel* 37 (Summer 2004): 278–304.

I am grateful, finally, to Craig Fraser for allowing me to use his beautiful photograph from *Shack Chic: Art and Innovation from South African Shack-Lands* (Cape Town: Quivertree, 2002) as the cover image for this book.

CONTENTS

EDITIONS CITED

Coetzee, J. M. *Dusklands*. New York: Penguin, 1985. Abbreviated DL.

———. *In the Heart of the Country*. New York: Penguin, 1982. Abbreviated HC.

———. *Waiting for the Barbarians*. New York: Penguin, 1982. Abbreviated WB.

———. *Life and Times of Michael K*. New York: Penguin, 1985. Abbreviated LT.

———. *Foe*. New York: Penguin, 1987. Abbreviated F.

———. *White Writing: On the Culture of Letters in South Africa*. New Haven: Yale University Press, 1988. Abbreviated WW.

———. *Age of Iron*. New York: Random House, 1990. Abbreviated AOI.

———. *Doubling the Point: Essays and Interviews*. Ed. David Attwell. Cambridge: Harvard University Press, 1992. Abbreviated DP.

———. *Boyhood: Scenes from Provincial Life*. New York: Penguin, 1997. Abbreviated B.

———. *Disgrace*. London: Secker and Warburg, 1999. Abbreviated D.

———. *Youth: Scenes from Provincial Life II*. New York: Viking Penguin, 2003. Abbreviated Y.

Dike, Fatima. *So What's New?* In *Black South African Women: An Anthology of Plays,* ed. Kathy A. Perkins. New York: Routledge, 1998, 23–46. Abbreviated SWN.

Fugard, Athol. *Tsotsi*. Johannesburg: Ad Donker, 1980. Abbreviated T.

———. *A Lesson from Aloes*. New York: Random House, 1981. Abbreviated LA.

———. *"Master Harold" . . . and the Boys*. New York: Knopf, 1982. Abbreviated MH.

———. *Notebooks: 1960–1977*. New York: Theatre Communications Group, 1984. Abbreviated N.

————. *Boesman and Lena*. In *Blood Knot and Other Plays*. New York: Theatre Communications Group, 1991, 141–197. Abbreviated BL.

————. *Cousins: A Memoir*. Johannesburg: Witwatersrand University Press, 1994. Abbreviated C.

Fugard, Athol, John Kani, and Winston Ntshona. *Statements: Sizwe Bansi Is Dead, The Island, Statements after an Arrest under the Immorality Act*. New York: Theater Communications Group, 1986. Abbreviated S.

Gordimer, Nadine. *The Lying Days*. New York: Simon and Schuster, 1953. Abbreviated LD.

————. *Livingstone's Companions*. New York: Viking, 1971. Abbreviated LC.

————. *The Conservationist*. Harmondsworth: Penguin, 1978. Abbreviated C.

————. *Soldier's Embrace*. London: Jonathan Cape, 1980. Abbreviated SE.

————. *Burger's Daughter*. Harmondsworth: Penguin, 1980. Abbreviated BD.

————. *July's People*. New York: Penguin, 1981. Abbreviated JP.

————. *Something Out There*. New York: Penguin, 1985. Abbreviated SOT.

————. *The Essential Gesture: Writing, Politics and Places*. Ed. Stephen Clingman. New York: Knopf, 1988. Abbreviated EG.

————. *My Son's Story*. New York: Penguin, 1991. Abbreviated MSS.

————. *Jump and Other Stories*. New York: Penguin, 1992. Abbreviated J.

————. *None to Accompany Me*. London: Bloomsbury, 1994. Abbreviated NTA.

————. *Writing and Being*. Cambridge: Harvard University Press, 1995. Abbreviated WB.

Magona, Sindiwe. *Mother to Mother*. Cape Town: David Philip, 1998.

Mda, Zakes. *When People Play: Development Communication through Theatre*. London: Zed, 1993. Abbreviated WPP.

————. *Ways of Dying*. Cape Town: Oxford University Press, 1995. Abbreviated WD.

————. *The Heart of Redness*. Cape Town: Oxford University Press, 2000. Abbreviated HR.

Tlali, Miriam. *Muriel at Metropolitan*. London: Longmans, 1979. Abbreviated MM.

————. *Mihloti*. Johannesburg: Skotaville, 1984. Abbreviated M.

————. *Soweto Stories*. London: Pandora, 1989. Abbreviated SS.

APARTHEID AND BEYOND

INTRODUCTION

A "place": a position whose contradictions
those who impose them don't see, and
from which will come a resolution they
haven't provided for.

—Nadine Gordimer, *Burger's Daughter*

Apartheid and Beyond is conceived, in the first instance, as a contribution to the
study of South African literature of the period between 1948 and 2000—the
years of the National Party's political domination, as well as the first few years of
the new democracy. In the broadest terms, this project may be described as an
effort to articulate the impact of apartheid on literary and cultural production
through readings of a number of important writers: J. M. Coetzee, Nadine Gordimer, Athol Fugard, Miriam Tlali, and Zakes Mda. More specifically, this study
examines the cultural and political significance of certain key places, including the
farm, the white suburban home, the black township, the shack settlement, and the
theater, in the light of theoretical work on the interconnections between spatial
relations, systems of power, and ideological and generic forms. It will be evident in
these chapters that I am not merely interested in questions of setting, in the matter
of the place represented *in* the text, but also in the place *of* the text. I will consider,
in other words, the situatedness of textual production and consumption—the way
in which writing for or from a particular location makes a difference in the form
and significance of a text.

At the heart of each of my readings (though variously configured) is a sociospatial dialectic—one that is most economically expressed in the phrase "knowing
one's place." The ambiguities of this cliché (referring both to one's standing in
the racist power structure and one's geographical situation) express the oppressive
conflation of the spatial and the political. Yet the idea of "knowing one's place," as

the geographer John Western has argued, contains a liberatory promise: "its wit-
ting ambiguity also implies that there is some pregnant meshing of the two meanings, and that from this meaning can arise a third meaning: to 'know one's place'
can imply an appreciation of its possibilities, to know its potential creativity for
social action."[1] This book is, therefore, concerned to explore the ideological and
dystopian aspects of South African social space, as well as the possibilities and the
emerging realities of its transformation. It is with respect to emergent social space
that literature, with its capacity to rewrite and reinvent new identities, new stories,
and new maps, has been and will be of particular interest.

There are, to date, surprisingly few critical works (other than single-author
studies and collections of essays) that consider South African literature in a broad
thematic way, and there are fewer still without the modifiers "black" or "white"
inserted in the title.[2] Despite the fact that two South African writers have been
awarded the Nobel Prize, South African literature is still in some ways an emerging field of inquiry, and one that continues to require redefinition in view of the
changed circumstances in the country. Yet its interest and relevance to current
concerns in the literary academy seems to me beyond dispute. In his book on
South African culture and the world beyond, Rob Nixon has argued that the
resistance struggle against apartheid was more fully globalized than any other
struggle for decolonization and that (though interpreted and represented in
locally specific ways) it served as a rallying point for several forms of resistance and
political groupings. The impact of the South African situation on North American popular and political culture was by no means negligible in the 1980s (one
thinks of the boycott of Sun City, of Hollywood films such as *A Dry White Season*
and *Cry Freedom*, and of the almost messianic visit of Nelson Mandela after his
release from prison). South African literature, likewise, has also been influential:
it has shaped, as Nixon argues, the prevailing image of both cultural persecution
and *écriture engagé*.[3] Even in the highbrow realm of theory, the country's racial
policy proved to be a galvanizing and sometimes contentious matter. It was, after
all, with reference to apartheid and in response to a provocation from Nixon
and Anne McClintock (then graduate students at Columbia) that Jacques Derrida offered what is perhaps his clearest statement on the political implications
of deconstruction: a powerful answer to those who would accuse his theoretical
work of an irresponsible evasiveness with regard to political matters. This critical
exchange was, as Lars Engle has pointed out, a "kind of tribute to the importance
of South Africa as a politically activating case."[4] The work of J. M. Coetzee, with
its critique of the Enlightenment project as manifested in colonial exploration, its
deconstruction of binary oppositions like "civilization" and "barbarity," its subversion of British canonical texts like *Robinson Crusoe*, and its rigorous investigation
of the ethics of representation, has proved an ideal testing ground for some of the
abiding preoccupations of metropolitan postcolonial theory.

It is true that with the demise of apartheid, the immediate and challenging ethical intensity of the South African situation has diminished; but given the
vitality of postcolonial studies in the academy, it seems unlikely that the interest
in the country's literature and culture will abate. South African literature, as J. M.
Coetzee observed back in 1983, touches a nerve everywhere in the West because

it offers such an "inexhaustibly fertile field for writers and journalists interrogating the colonizer-colonized relationship."[5] Now that the sometimes suspicious moral *frisson* that apartheid provided is a thing of the past, South Africa should become even more important in the interrogation of this relationship, especially since it might suggest—in practice, rather than merely in theory—new possibilities of transcending the Manichean opposition of colonizer and colonized, and of moving toward a new culturally hybrid democracy.

My focus on the ideological and political meaning of place and spatial relations has been guided, in part, by a conviction that it is in this area that a study of the South African situation will be of particular importance to cultural and social theory. During the last two decades or so, literary critics and theorists have increasingly turned to spatial metaphors ("exploration," "decentering," "mapping," and so forth) to describe their methodologies; and there has been a marked interest in a whole array of theoretical concepts that are fundamentally spatial or geographic: we might think, for instance, of Mikhail Bakhtin's "chronotope," Benedict Anderson's "imagined communities," Gloria Anzaldúa's "borderlands," Fredric Jameson's "cognitive mapping," and Gilles Deleuze and Félix Guattari's "deterritorialization."[6] Perhaps the most influential of all these spatially oriented theories (though it is focused on the more repressive and pessimistic aspects of social space) has been Michel Foucault's analysis of disciplinary architecture: his insistence that certain sites (specifically, prisons, barracks, schools, hospitals, and asylums) are essential to the exercise of power and the construction of the bourgeois subject. From the perspective suggested by Foucault's work, material structures are simultaneously ideological structures: buildings, cities, and the like may be grasped both as domains of knowledge (in that they embody a spatial ordering of categories) and domains of control (in that they effect an ordering of boundaries).

The reassertion of the spatial in critical social theory has been especially important in the study of imperialism, colonial discourse, and postcolonial theory. After all, maps, boundaries, the naming of places—indeed, the discipline of geography itself—is scarcely separable from the imperial project. Even Foucault's writing, which would seem so intently focused on France or, at most, on Europe, has in fact proven to be strikingly relevant to discussions of colonial geography and colonial power. Timothy Mitchell's work on Egypt, for example, has emphasized the fact that the panopticon itself was a colonial invention, and has argued that disciplinary power is inherently colonizing in nature.[7] It is thus significant, but not surprising, that Edward Said should describe his magisterial *Culture and Imperialism* as "a kind of geographical inquiry into historical experience," and that he should defend (in what are surely indisputable terms) the importance of this emphasis: "Just as none of us is outside or beyond geography, none of us is completely free of the struggle over geography."[8] History always *takes place*, as Said suggests, and nowhere is the question of land, of territory and power, as pertinent and contested as in the long and continuing history of imperialism.

Apartheid, though inseparable from this global phenomenon, clearly represents an extreme and therefore starkly illuminating instance of the territorialization of power. Social geographers who work on South Africa are fond of quoting the former prime minister B. J. Vorster's outrageous defense of his government's policy of "separate development": "If I were to wake up one morning and find myself a Black man, the only major difference would be geographical."[9] This devious piece of political rhetoric contains a grain of truth. For under apartheid, geography certainly did make a major difference. All the essential political features of South Africa's "pigmentocratic industrialized state" were fundamentally space-dependent: the classification of the population into distinct racial categories, the segregation of residential areas on the basis of race, the restriction of black urbanization, the system of migrant labor from rural areas to the towns, the emphasis on ethnicity and traditionalism, and the formidable apparatus of state surveillance and control.[10] Of all these features, there is not a single one that did not, in practice, rely on the power of space to separate individuals from each other, to direct and control their movements, and to reinforce social distinctions. Indeed, without such territorial devices as the black township and the bantustan, and the policing of these spaces by means of forced removals and the pass laws, apartheid would have been impossible to implement. The poet Jeremy Cronin, writing out his own experience of imprisonment, has given one of the most striking accounts of apartheid's oppressive but contradictory political geography:

> South Africa is a society of . . . insides, beyond high walls. Every day at 3.30 p.m., year in and out, after hours of hard labour or just plain loafing about, over 100,000 men and women are counted once, twice, and then locked up for the night. South Africa is said to have the highest prisoner to population ratio in the world. But this prison regime is merely one face of a countrywide grid of spatial controls. There are cordoned-off ethnic "group areas," bantustans, supposed independent countries the size of large farms, single-sex labour hostels, and mine compounds behind barbed wire. There are endless spaces within other spaces. It is no easy feat to maintain the indigenous and overwhelming majority as excluded "foreigners," while simultaneously including them for their much needed labour. Inside, outside, inside.[11]

Of all the elements in this grid of spatial controls, the black township is one of the most compelling, from a political, cultural, literary, and theoretical perspective, and it is a site I will frequently refer to in this study. From the point of view of its material structure, or "space syntax," the orthodox township designed by the apartheid regime would seem particularly amenable to a Foucauldian reading: it was, as the architect Glenn Mills has argued, "a strategic device by which a particular form of power-knowledge is realized."[12] Planned in the late 1940s and early 1950s, these notorious places of deprivation had a surprisingly respectable aesthetic and scientific genealogy. The National Building Research Institute, founded by the government in 1945, based their designs for a "scientific" and "modern" solution to the social problem of what was then called "native housing" on the models of Le Corbusier's *Ville Contemporaine* and *Ville Radieuse* and the workers' housing estates inspired by them.[13] These high-minded sources emphasize the intertwining of knowledge and power. The very design elements that the planners advocated for functional, scientific, and aesthetic reasons—the broad streets, the "green areas" between the cities and the townships, and the bold, graph-like patterns of the roads and houses—were simultaneously also strategic devices. The broad streets permitted access to armored vehicles (they were wide enough to allow a Saracen tank to make a turn); buffer zones and limited road access allowed the townships to be sealed off from the cities in times of unrest; and the orderly repetition of identical houses on a geometric grid facilitated surveillance by police and informers. The "modern" solution to a housing shortage amounted, in short, to a mechanism of control. From a more subjective point of view, moreover, the township's terrain would seem to be expressive of a society of division and fragmentation. It seemed designed to increase a sense of alienation and to prevent the individual from achieving any kind of cognitive map. "From the point of view of the moving individual," as Mills observes, the township environment "is difficult to 'read': it is hard to retrieve some description of how the parts relate to the whole."[14] In the face of all this, the history of the South African transition offers certain important political and theoretical lessons. The fact that the disciplinary space of the township became the crucial locus of resistance in the antiapartheid struggle suggests that we need to be suspicious of totalizing models of power, of descriptions of place that ignore the transformative and creative capacities of human beings.

If the township is perhaps an obvious example of an ideologically saturated and yet successfully contested place, we might briefly consider, as another example of the peculiar richness of the South African sociospatial text, a site that is more readily overlooked, namely, the train. Foucault once suggested that the train presents an "extraordinary bundle" of spatial relationships: "it is something through which one goes, it is also something by means of which one can go from one point to another, and then it is also something that goes by."[15] But under apartheid, the train accrued an even denser set of social meanings and possibilities than those listed here. From the point of view of black South Africans, the train was clearly a tool of oppression, indispensable to the maintenance of residential segregation and to the exploitation of labor. It brought day laborers from distant townships, as well as migrants from even more distant rural areas, to work in the white cities. It is no accident that the train has been the subject of many songs (e.g., "Stimela" ["Steam Train"]) and many stories and poems (e.g., Can Themba's "Dube Train," Mbulelo Mzamane's "Dube Train Revisited," Oswald Mtshali's "Amagoduka at Glencoe Station," Miriam Tlali's "Fud-u-u-a!" and Mtutuzeli Matshoba's "Three Days in the Land of a Dying Illusion"). Indeed, it is a measure of the train's cultural significance that the most important literary magazine to emerge from the Black Consciousness era should have been called *Staffrider*: the word for a daredevil commuter—a person who leaps onto a moving train and hangs at a precarious angle from the handrail at the door. With the intensified antiapartheid struggle of the 1980s, moreover, the train was transformed into much more than a functional vehicle in service of the apartheid economy. According to Matshoba, the powerful trade union COSATU was essentially built on commuter trains: they became "mobile meeting places" where people from different companies could talk about their aspirations and experiences at work, and where organizers could reach an audience without contravening the government's restrictions on public meetings.[16] The fundamental contradiction of apartheid's divide-and-rule policies, a contradiction that is expressed also in the case of the townships, is evident here: it lies in the fact that social segregation requires also a certain spatial aggregation—that imposed divisions open up the possibility of new communities, new identities, new affiliations.[17]

The local character of these preliminary readings of South African social space may already suggest something of my approach in the chapters that follow. While I recognize the danger of overemphasizing the exceptionality of apartheid—of regarding South Africa as "a world apart"—there is also, I feel, a danger in abandoning a sense of the specificity of its history, its geography, and its literary traditions in favor of more glamorous abstractions like "colonial space." While I am deeply interested in the global implications of these local readings, I do have certain reservations about the term "postcolonial" when used as a singular universal, reservations that are shared by other scholars working on South Africa. The country's postcolonial status was both dubious and strenuously contested during the apartheid years. For the Afrikaner minority, as Annamaria Carusi has pointed out, the country's postcolonial status was, in a sense, a *fait accompli*; they had been in control of an independent republic since 1961. This was not true for the black majority. But it nevertheless made more sense for them to think of the liberation struggle as aimed at a *postapartheid* rather than a *postcolonial* society.[18] To say this is not to deny that there are connections between the themes I have raised in my readings and those that have emerged, for example, in recent work on Canadian and Australian culture (where "place" has been something of a hot topic). The deconstruction of the mimetic claims of the Western map, the inadequacy of European landscape iconographies to the task of describing new colonial territories, and the production of new, locally defined and strategic identities: all of these "postcolonial" themes are to a greater or lesser degree relevant to my project. Yet I am more or less in accord with Vijay Mishra and Bob Hodge's call for those "smaller *récits*" that "must replace the *grand récits* of postcolonialism"—"smaller *récits*" in which "it may well be that the term 'postcolonial' is never used."[19]

Some recent studies of space and place have been structured in very inventive ways. Hilton Judin and Ivan Vladislavić's collection *Blank _____: Architecture, Apartheid, and After*, for example, is an enormously interesting compilation of work by South African architects, philosophers, geographers, anthropologists, creative writers, and photographers. The book offers not a table of contents but a map marking all the thematic territories to be explored (fortifications, promised lands, invasions, homelands, violence, segregation, and so forth) and providing the coordinates for each author's contribution rather than the conventional chapter and page numbers. Though this device does make it somewhat of a challenge to locate the pieces one would like to read, it has the advantage of giving one a visual sense of where the subject matter of each contribution is located in the broad field of inquiry and of how it relates to other contributions. Also imaginative is Ian Baucom's book *Out of Place: Englishness, Empire, and the Locations of Identity*, which is structured around a series of revealing chronotopes: Gothic architecture, Victoria Terminus in Bombay, the Anglo-Indian Mutiny pilgrimage, the cricket field, the country house, and the zone of urban riot. Compared to these studies, *Apartheid and Beyond* is entirely conventional in structure, organized as it is around a series of authors of whose work it offers a largely appreciative account. The six chapters that make up my book should be seen as free-standing but nevertheless interconnected essays. The interpretive and theoretical framework for each essay emerges from the literary texts under scrutiny, rather than from any a priori assumptions about space and place (other than the generally accepted understanding of "space" as the more inclusive and abstract term and of "place" as the more particular and qualitative term, referring to geographically situated locales that serve as physical settings for social activity). Consequently, the book's methodology is eclectic, although I do have an overarching interest in the idea of "cognitive mapping," as defined by Fredric Jameson, and the related notion of "intellectual space," as defined by Mamphela Ramphele. I take the liberty of adopting a shifting perspective on some of the complex social phenomena in question: for example, I consider the postapartheid city in its more oppressive aspects in connection to the work of Nadine Gordimer, and in its more fluid and liberatory aspects in connection to the work of Zakes Mda. I have, however, tried to organize these chapters so that cumulatively they provide a geographical history of South Africa, albeit one that is narrated in a fragmentary way: my readings of literary texts touch on such key topics as colonial settlement and landownership, apartheid's forced removals, the development of the black townships, the emergence of informal settlements at the urban fringes, and the gradual integration of the apartheid city. Since each chapter (except for the final one on Mda, whose novels have all been published since 1994) is concerned with one or more apartheid-era work but also extends its focus into the postapartheid era, a strictly chronological ordering of chapters was not feasible: each addresses a number of different historical moments. But it is nevertheless my hope that the book as a whole will yield a sense of the broad historical dynamics at stake and that it will be legible, at least in some measure, as an account of the sociospatial aspects of the transition from apartheid to democracy.

Chapter 1 is concerned with the work of J. M. Coetzee, who has offered, in both his fiction and his academic writing, an extraordinarily complex and passionate critical engagement with the South African pastoral. I adopt as a polemical starting point Stephen Gray's still useful if somewhat dated attempt to sketch out a South African literary history based on a shifting "sense of place": a history in which South African writers become increasingly independent of the metropolitan readership and increasingly committed to national concerns. Gray's scheme, I argue, is problematic for various reasons, most signally because it is based on a mimetic conception of the relationship between the literary text and its environment—as though scenic description were the defining issue in South African literature and, indeed, in the literature of all settler colonies. Gray's is clearly a scheme in which Coetzee's early work, with its antimimetic and demystificatory impulses, cannot be accommodated. My reading of Coetzee's (anti)pastoral fiction, therefore, starts out by considering the expression of these two impulses in his writing. I begin by meditating on the idea of "atopia" (which Teresa Dovey has used to describe the deconstructionist strategy of "drifting habitation" that shapes Coetzee's earlier works) and then focus on the idea of the "dream topography" (which allows for a more located sense of Coetzee's fiction and the political work it does, without returning us to a naïve empiricism). I demonstrate how the two major "dream topographies" that the South African pastoral projects on the land (that of the Afrikaans *plaasroman* and that of English-language landscape poetry) apply to Coetzee's fiction, especially to *In the Heart of the Country* and *Life and Times of Michael K*. My readings of these novels, as well as some of Coetzee's critical essays, suggest that the task of "geographical projection" or even geographical "prophecy" (in John Berger's phrase)—of bringing whatever is marginalized and occluded into view—is central to Coetzee's earlier work. In the case of the South African pastoral, the chief occluded element is, of course, the labor of the black worker, whose inscriptions of and claim to the land constitute, as Coetzee has argued, the genre's embarrassing blind spot. The final section of the chapter turns to Coetzee's postapartheid novel *Disgrace*. The novel is a pessimistic one, in which any sort of pastoral possibility is placed under tremendous new strains, not least of which are the demographic exigencies that drive rural people to informal settlements and threaten to collapse the old distinctions of country and city. While it does revisit and rewrite some of the themes of the earlier (anti)pastoral novels, *Disgrace* is, I argue, no longer concerned with demystification. The reversal of margin and center, or figure and ground, has become outmoded and unnecessary in the context of a wholesale reversal of roles and redefinition of social space. In its treatment of animals—especially dogs—*Disgrace* gestures toward strenuous new ethical obligations, which can no longer be made sense of in terms of the moral economy of the colonial or postcolonial pastoral.

Chapters 2 and 3 are concerned with the work of Nadine Gordimer, whose chief project during her long and productive career as a novelist has been, by her own admission, an effort to see or find "the link between people and the place that has bred them." The title of chapter 2, "Leaving the House of the White Race," is drawn from an early interview in which Gordimer described her own political awakening as a process of first leaving her "mother's house" and then "leaving the house of the white race." My strategy in this chapter is to take her metaphor at face value and to examine the way in which domestic space, especially the white suburban home, functions as an ideological apparatus for the reproduction of racial and gendered subjectivities in South Africa. My analysis focuses on a number of texts I think of as very loosely autobiographical (in that they have a female narrator or protagonist who either shares some of Gordimer's childhood experiences or is explicitly identified as an author), including *The Lying Days* and *July's People*. The latter novel is, in my reading, particularly revealing of the spatial dimension of Gordimer's political thinking. It explores the proposition that if political hegemony is experienced and reinforced territorially, the same must be true of revolution, which is therefore figured in the novel as an explosion of all established places, from the Union Buildings to the master bedroom in the suburban home, along with the social relations of deference and domination these places define. The chapter also explores an important counterimage to the hegemonic space of the bourgeois home, namely, the street, which features in Gordimer's work as the site where history "takes place": as a utopian public space of bodily contact and chance encounter and of the unpredictable polyglot sociopolitical life that apartheid's white suburban homes were designed to seal off.

In the conclusion to this chapter, I turn not only to Gordimer's major work of the transition, the 1994 novel *None to Accompany Me*, but also to a consideration of the complex actualities of contemporary Johannesburg, where new geographies of crime and privatized security seem to threaten the emergence of the liberated public space of which Gordimer always dreamed.

Chapter 3 is largely concerned with Gordimer's apartheid-era masterpiece *The Conservationist*, a novel that returns us to the relationship between the country and the city and permits an in-depth discussion of South Africa's master narrative about land: a mythic story of colonial dispossession and restitution that is captured in the African National Congress (ANC) slogan *Mayibuye iAfrika!*—to which Gordimer covertly refers at the end of the novel. Drawing on Achille Mbembe's notion of the "aesthetics of superfluity" and on Michel de Certeau's notion of the "concept city" (which produces the opposition to its own order in the form of "waste products"), I offer an account of apartheid's forced removals. I suggest that this sad history is marked in Gordimer's text by the recurrent images of "things of out of place," like litter and trespassers and, above all, the body of a dead city slicker that is found on the rich white protagonist's highveld farm. These "things out of place" constitute what De Certeau would call "the mark of the other," which threatens the "proper places" established and subtended by apartheid's oppressive gridding of the land. I suggest that Gordimer proposes in *The Conservationist* and in related interviews a hard-nosed and unsentimental view of conservation as an alibi for possessiveness: a regrettable view, ultimately, in a country where ecological issues will long remain of vital importance. My discussion of this matter enables us to draw comparisons between her work and Coetzee's. *The Conservationist* also looks forward, I suggest, to Zakes Mda's novel *The Heart of Redness*, in which ecological preservation reemerges as a contested matter. The chapter concludes with a consideration of the master narrative that animates *The Conservationist* from the more sobering vantage of postapartheid South Africa, where the practical task of negotiating the tension between the immense symbolic significance of land and the actual difficulties of farming in a largely semiarid terrain has proved difficult. Gordimer's postapartheid fiction retains an interest in the politics of land, but wisely eschews the revolutionary allegory that is dramatized with such poetic force in *The Conservationist*.

In chapter 4 I turn to the playwright Athol Fugard, whose thematic concerns (e.g., an interest in the relationship between domestic space and subjectivity) overlap in some measure with Gordimer's. In fact, Fugard's play *Boesman and Lena* anticipates the motif of rubbish that features so prominently in *The Conservationist*. Though I do not explore the institutions of South African theatre (even though these are relevant to the questions of space and the location of culture that have engaged me in this book), I do consider the specificities of dramatic performance, where "bodies in space" are not only a primary theme, as in Gordimer's work, but also the primary signifiers. Taking off from Una Chaudhuri's work on the "geography of drama," I consider Fugard's ambivalent engagement with the ideas of home and homelessness, exile and belonging: themes that are well suited to drama, given the capacity of the medium to make the audience aware of spatial confinement and, by extension, of the need for physical expansion and liberation.

I trace in works like *Tsotsi* and *Boesman and Lena* the development of Fugard's idea that poverty is best grasped as "the violence of immediacy"—as the absence of any kind of protective shield, whether it be a roof over one's head or the capacity for intellectual mediation and cognitive mapping. I extend this consideration of mediation and mapping into a consideration of translation. I define this multivalent concept, which in its application to Fugard has both a thematic and a performative dimension, as both the interpretive space that must be traversed between the real world and the "elsewhere" of drama, and the space of creative and critical mediation. I demonstrate in some detail how the idea of translation complicates our understanding of the underestimated play *A Lesson from Aloes*, which is often taken as a rather simplistic depiction of an Afrikaner's stubborn sense of filiation and rootedness, but which strikes me instead as a celebration of the human capacity for affiliation and cultural grafting. My reading of this play thus ends up validating not the nostalgic and regional Fugard, who, as he liked to put it, saw his creative task as that of loving the "little grey bushes" of the Eastern Cape, but the Brechtian Fugard, who affirms, especially in his metatheatrical moments, the artificiality of the stage as a figure for the constructedness—and therefore the changeability—of social relations. Despite his obvious attachment to the land, Fugard's crucial artistic interest, I argue, is not in landscape but in "scenery," with its ambiguous reference to both the natural world and the world of theater. The aphorism "A man's scenery is other men," found among the notebook entries concerning *A Lesson from Aloes*, thus anticipates the ethos articulated in Coetzee's Jerusalem Prize speech, which condemns white South Africans for using their love of the land as a kind of alibi for their denial of love—and liberty, fraternity, and equality—to those who share their national territory.

The central text in chapter 5 is Miriam Tlali's *Muriel at Metropolitan*, the first novel to be published in South Africa by a black South African woman. My reading of this novel is framed by a polemic regarding the politics and poetics of antiapartheid writing. I consider Tlali in relation to what Louise Bethlehem has described as "the rhetoric of urgency" in South African literature and criticism. Bethlehem demonstrates how many writers and critics, both black and white, favored an almost journalistic kind of realism, one associated with the documentation of physical surroundings in "stark, grim detail," along with "minute-to-minute sensations." They validate, in other words, a version of the Benjaminian "urban shock," an unmediated sensory overload, destructive of any sustained attempt at contemplation. My argument (which derives in part from Mamphela Ramphele's reflections on the politics of space in relation to the empowerment of South Africa's most deprived citizens) is that this (anti)aesthetic turns a symptom—a lack of physical and intellectual space—into a solution and an article of literary and political faith. Though Tlali herself has often made pronouncements that are entirely of a piece with the rhetoric of urgency and has commented on the deleterious effects of spatial constriction on black women's writing, I read *Muriel at Metropolitan* (perhaps somewhat perversely) as a text that works to create intellectual space and to avoid any kind of direct reporting of oppressive physical conditions, though it does analyze their effects. Since *Muriel at Metropolitan* is set in a shop selling radios and furniture to black customers, it is also a novel that permits reflection on the expressive function of modern commodities in the lives of South Africa's black urbanites. To aid these reflections, I investigate consumer culture not only in the apartheid era (via the conversations about the meaning of furniture and radio included in Tlali's novel) but also in postapartheid South Africa (via a fascinating text of 1990, Fatima Dike's play *So What's New?* in which three black women ritually gather to watch *The Bold and the Beautiful* on TV). This play, I argue, foregrounds the problematic relationship between empowerment and enhanced intellectual space on the one hand and the merely materialistic dreaming inspired by global capitalism on the other.

Chapter 6 turns to two postapartheid works by the novelist Zakes Mda. The first of these, *Ways of Dying*, looks back in some detail on the history of black urban space over the last three decades and looks forward to its transformation, along with the production of fluid urban subjectivities and the invention of a new kind of aesthetic education. Following the lead of urban anthropologists and geographers like AbdouMaliq Simone and Jennifer Robinson, I suggest that the transition to democracy has allowed us to view not just contemporary urban space but even apartheid's city of division in new ways. I attempt to demonstrate in my reading of *Ways of Dying* how the new directions in urban studies may productively inform literary studies, and vice versa. I conclude *Apartheid and Beyond* with a reading of Mda's ambitious novel of the year 2000, *The Heart of Redness*. This novel is perhaps a surprising candidate for inclusion, since in it Mda decisively brackets off the apartheid years as the "struggles of the middle generations" and focuses his attention on the nineteenth century (specifically on the tragic Xhosa Cattle Killing of the 1850s) and on the contemporary moment. Mda thus moves beyond the thematics of apartheid and the antiapartheid struggle in order to reflect on the broader story of colonial modernity and postmodernity. Yet this novel is still marked by a clear "commitment to territory" (to steal and redeploy a phrase from Es'kia Mphahlele), which is evident in its close attention to a grassroots struggle over the proposed development of a casino resort in an ecologically vulnerable and historically important rural village. Such disputes, I argue, cannot be understood without considering the rather complicated ways in which what Arjun Appadurai has described as the "traffic in criteria" for judging aesthetic value operates on the local, national, and global levels. In attending to these questions of taste and belonging, Mda's novel seems to me to sketch out a new conception of the location of culture in postapartheid South Africa and to refocus our attention not only on the matter of ecological conservation but on the emerging landscapes of tourism and leisure: the landscapes by which postapartheid South Africa will be represented and marketed in the world at large for some time to come. I therefore close by reflecting, along with Njabulo Ndebele and Jean and John Comaroff, on the predicament of South Africa as a nation of the second postcolonial era (following the fall of the Soviet Union and the new hegemony of a neoliberal global economy) and on the way South African cultural heritage and national belonging are being redefined, especially in relation to the African continent and to the world economy at large.

Which brings me, I suppose, to my own position. I decided to write this book after the peculiar experience of having to cast my vote in the 1994 South

African election at the Philadelphia Civic Center, a few blocks away from my office in Bennett Hall at the University of Pennsylvania. It was in an experience that combined a sense of national belonging with a profound sense of distance and dislocation: while my countrymen and -women were lining up together in their thousands to cast their ballots and to share for the first time their collective hope for a peaceful nation, I walked back alone to the English Department's dingy building feeling both elated and a little silly with my small ANC flag in my hand. Thinking of the massive changes that would follow the historic election, it occurred to me that I only had a small window of opportunity to write about the land of my birth with some sense of familiarity, and resolved then and there to set aside all other projects and pursue this one.

Of course, my telling of this story involves something of a myth of origins. But I tell it as a way of suggesting the extent to which this book is one replete with personal emotions—with a desire to finally understand the country I have often despaired for and even hated, as well as a yearning for a new country, full of fresh political, cultural, and experiential possibilities. I have been "writing across a rift," in Achille Mbembe's phrase: a rift that can only partially be bridged by visits home, by reading, and by discussions with South African friends and colleagues.[20] While my work has surely benefited from the broader perspective and from the admittedly nostalgic passions being an expatriate has brought me, it has no doubt also been marred by these strong feelings in ways I cannot even see, and even more so by my arguably inadequate experience of the quotidian textures of place, which I consider to be crucially important. It is not easy to engage in what Sarah Nuttall has called the challenge of "writing the 'now'" in South Africa, or even to track the slow emergence of the "now" in the literature and history of the apartheid era, when one is thousands of miles away.[21] And South Africa–based scholars can be—rightly or wrongly—suspicious of such an enterprise. I recall all too vividly how a South African academic reacted to my description of my project and its (in her view) far too narrow canonization by saying, "Oh, we don't write like that any more," and how a critic for the e-journal LitNet excoriated me for (1) writing about South Africa while living in Pennsylvania, (2) writing about European theorists like Roland Barthes while living in Pennsylvania, and (3) writing about anything at all, since in days long past I was once the carnival queen of the University of Stellenbosch. To the latter objections I will offer no defense, but to the former, I would respond simply by inviting other scholars to fill the gaps left open in this book by writing about the many cultural figures I could have included but did not. (Ivan Vladislavić, Marlene van Niekerk, Breyten Breytenbach, and Phaswane Mpe all seem like excellent candidates for analysis.) I can only hope that this book does something to demonstrate my conviction that the long-distance view might be a productive one to adopt in a world where the local may not be erased (as I show in the Mda chapter) but where it is increasingly penetrated and shaped by influences and interests from far away.

DREAM TOPOGRAPHIES

W er den Dichter will verstehen/Muß in Dichters Lande gehen."The implications of this quotation from Goethe, which serves as the epigraph to
J. M. Coetzee's 2002 memoir *Youth*, are ambivalent. We may choose to read these
lines as the motto of the aspirant author, John, who has traveled to the gray city
of London to better understand and emulate his idols, the poets Ezra Pound and
T. S. Eliot. But we may also choose to read these lines as offering guidance to
Coetzee's readers: the epigraph may be an oblique confession on his part that,
despite his rejection of the designation "South African writer," his fiction has to
be understood in some sort of relation to his native country.[1] This is not to say
that Coetzee's readers have to become literary tourists, or that the South African
settings of (some of) his major novels hold the key to his challenging and enigmatic work. It is telling, after all, that *Youth*, which is subtitled "Scenes from Provincial Life II" in its U.S. editions, does not set out to represent provincial scenes,
but rather the provincial presuppositions of its protagonist during his years in the
metropolis. The indirection of the subtitle should alert the canny reader to the
fact that *Youth* is actually a meditation on the relationship between literature and
place: a good portion of the text is made up of an ironic recounting of the young
author's callow notions about the comparative merits of cities like London, Paris,
and Vienna as staging grounds for poetic genius and the comparative romantic
allure of women from countries like France, Italy, and Sweden.

The Country of the Novelist

At first reading, *Youth* may strike one as the glum tale of its protagonist's failure to become a poet. But the book is equally and more rewardingly legible as the story of his gradual commitment to prose—of his growing understanding that, unlike the poet, the fiction writer is, however reluctantly and ambivalently, a located creature, perhaps even "a person unable to live without a country" (Y 137). All the happy moments in *Youth* (as when John reads Beckett's *Watt* and finds himself rolling on the floor with laughter) are ones in which we see him edging toward his true vocation. And all the fresh insights he stumbles on—the ones that rupture the memoir's rehearsal of his disabling truisms about poetic life—reveal something about the craft of fiction and prefigure the work Coetzee was eventually to write. The most crucial of these insights arises from John's initial venture into fiction: a short story about a young man who discovers by the subtlest of signs that his love has been unfaithful to him. Much to the young author's dismay, the story turns out to be set in South Africa. It takes place on a beach, which is not, as we are led to understand, described in any detail, since John's conscious interest in the piece lies in creating a quasi-Jamesian drama of psychological recognition. Nevertheless, the setting seems obscurely important to him: English people, he feels, will not understand the story, because for them the word "beach" would bring to mind a "few pebbles lapped by wavelets" rather than breakers crashing against a rugged cliff and seabirds shrieking as they fight the wind. The story, he sadly concludes, is unpublishable. But the experience of writing it yields the understanding that while "poetry may take place everywhere and nowhere," prose seems "naggingly to demand a specific setting" (Y 63).

This insight is at first an unwelcome one, since it compromises John's attempts to transcend his inauspicious nationality. It is only when he reads the travel narratives of the early explorers of the Cape—Peter Kolbe, Anders Sparrman, John Barrow, and William Burchell—in the British Library that he is able to claim his colonial identity with a sense of exhilaration rather than humiliation. The very strangeness of encountering South African place names in a book awakens him to the imaginative possibilities of writing about places that are not yet "wrapped in centuries of words," as English places are (Y 137). In the vast and trackless Cape frontier, John discovers "the country of his heart": not the "new South Africa" of apartheid, whose horrors are daily laid bare in the *Manchester Guardian*, but an older South Africa in which "Eden was still possible" (Y 137), a world whose geographical openness suggests its openness to hypothetical histories yet to be devised. With this discovery, scenic description ceases to strike John as merely the shibboleth that will reveal him as a sorry colonial and becomes instead an urgent challenge: "If to make his book convincing, there needs to be a grease-pot swinging under the bed of the wagon as it bumps across the stones of the Karoo, he will do the grease-pot. If there have to be cicadas trilling in the tree under which they stop at noon, he will do the cicadas" (Y 138). Thus the youth who arrives in London eager to remake himself as a literary cosmopolitan ends up discovering the geographical and generic territory he is to claim for his own, however ironically, in his first novella, "The Narrative of Jacobus Coetzee."

Later on in his life, as an established author steeped in the traditions of South African literature, Coetzee was to address the task of describing South African places in a less enchanted manner. He comments in a 1992 interview on the predictable catalogue of details by means of which "the Karoo has been done to death in a century of writing and overwriting (drab bushes, stunted trees, heat-stunned flats, shrilling cicadas, and so forth)" (DP 142). But it is nevertheless significant that Coetzee's portrait of the artist as a young man should trace the origins of his literary career back to his acceptance of the inescapably chronotopic nature of all fiction.

That it should do so makes considerable sense in light of his subsequent oeuvre: both his criticism and fiction are shaped by a fascination with such geographically or topographically defined genres as the exploration narrative and the pastoral, as well as with such politically significant spaces as the imperial border, the labor camp, and the torture chamber. The titles of his first two novels, *Dusklands* and *In the Heart of the Country*, hint at this fascination, referring as they do to strangely elusive yet symbolically resonant places. It is possible that the structuralist orientation of Coetzee's academic training (he has a Ph.D. in linguistics) might have something to do with his interest in spatial organization. But his interest in place and space also has an experiential and personal dimension, evident in a skeptically and rigorously examined attachment to the South African landscape. Coetzee once remarked, after all, that a person can only be in love with one landscape in his or her lifetime.[2]

The increasing discomfort one notes in Coetzee's work of the 1980s with the dominance of a Marxist historicism in South African academic circles can also be attributed—at least in part—to his concern with the spatial. I say "in part" since, as the polemical essay "The Novel Today" (1988) reveals, Coetzee's impatience with the all-swallowing tendency of historical master narratives derives in the first instance from his sense of himself as a novelist. This identification with his craft quite obviously lies behind his discomfort at the thought that, in times of political pressure, the novel becomes reduced to a mere supplement to or illustration of the discourse of the historical "real."[3] But it is important to note that other contemporary social theorists engaged in the critical analysis of space and place have, like Coetzee, challenged the explanatory privilege of historicism. The geographer Edward Soja, for one, has polemicized vigorously against the marginalization of space by the historical discourse of Western Marxism and has posited that in contemporary forms of capitalism, spatial relations have become just as mystified as the commodity form once seemed to Marx—and that they therefore require renewed attention. This argument compels us to consider the degree to which the erasure of the conditions of labor in today's world depends on the geography of late capitalism (which some scholars have come to refer to as "global apartheid"). The impoverished workers who produce our glossy commodities tend to live far out of sight, beyond the experiential realm of the privileged, in Mexico, the Philippines, or a South African township, and their invisibility perpetuates the illusion of historical progress in the world's economic centers.[4] I think that we can say, without falling into the trap of "swallowing up" Coetzee's novels in the discourse of critical human geography, that this line of thought resonates with certain moments in his writing, both academic and fictional: that his work, as I will suggest in this chapter, is concerned with how people inhabit, how they imagine, and how they represent the physical terrain that surrounds them.

The literary possibilities of a critical geography are suggested in an intriguing passage from the novelist John Berger (a passage that Soja cites in his opening chapter): "Prophecy now involves a geographical rather than historical projection; it is space and not time that hides consequences from us. To prophesy today it is only necessary to know men [and women] as they are throughout the whole world in all their inequality. Any contemporary narrative which ignores the urgency of this dimension is incomplete and acquires the oversimplified character of a fable."[5] The notion that it is space that now hides inequalities from us brings to mind Coetzee's sardonic denunciation of the political geography of apartheid in a 1986 essay:

> If people are starving, let them starve far away in the bush, where their thin bodies will not be a reproach. If they have no work, if they migrate to the cities, let there be roadblocks, let there be curfews, let there be laws against vagrancy, begging, and squatting, and let offenders be locked away so that no one has to hear or see them. If the black townships are in flames, let cameras be banned from them. . . . Certainly there are many lands where prisons are used as dumping-places for people who smell wrong and look unsightly and do not have the decency to hide themselves away. In South Africa the law sees to it as far as it can that not only such people, but also the prisons in which they are held, become invisible. (DP 361)

These ideas have significant implications, even now, for those who strive to understand and redress the inequality of South African men and women.[6] For apartheid, as Coetzee so clearly understands, operated from day to day as a means of distributing people in space and thereby of controlling the way they saw the world. The system strove to perpetuate itself by decreeing that certain spaces must be invisible: homelands, prisons, torture chambers, and black cities were deliberately hidden, removed from view. The beneficiaries of apartheid were not necessarily sadistic; but like all those who live at the expense of others, they/we preferred not to see those "consequences" of which Berger speaks. Their ideal, and to an extent also their actual social topography, is the one described by a perceptive vagrant in Coetzee's *Life and Times of Michael K*: a camp placed hundreds of miles away, in the middle of the Koup or some such arid waste, from which workers could "come on tiptoe in the middle of the night like fairies and do their work, dig their gardens, wash their pots, and be gone in the morning leaving everything nice and clean" (MK 82).

I will return to this passage again at the very end of this book. For now, I would like to suggest (though Coetzee would certainly balk at the notion) that in moments like this one, his writing offers us something of that demystifying "geographical projection" or "prophecy" of which Berger speaks. Coetzee's work often renders visible the places the system would rather keep out of sight and mind and thus reminds us to consider not only "presences" but also the "ghosts" who, as he suggests in a powerful passage from *Age of Iron*, haunt all official representations, "lean against the edge" of the snapshot of privileged lives, "bending it, bursting in" (AOI 111). At other times, Coetzee's examination of the spatial and topographical is more literary, as in his critique (most prominently, but not exclusively, in *White Writing*) of the codes that have shaped the representation of the South African landscape, from the familiar descriptive catalogues, like the one I cited earlier, to the recurrent ideological preoccupations of the farm novel and landscape poetry. Perhaps most importantly, Coetzee's work—and I am thinking specifically of the Jerusalem Prize address of 1989—requires us to examine our automatic responses to places (especially, in the case of white South Africans like myself, our oft-proclaimed love of the country's vast landscapes) and forces us to ask what political and imaginative failures such passions might conceal. With this last difficult task in mind, I will consider Coetzee's fictional and literary critical engagement with the tradition of the South African pastoral in the pages that follow.

A Sense of Place

It may be useful to consider, as a polemical starting point, the way Coetzee's work fits—or, rather, fails to fit—into an influential early account of the meaning of "place" in South African writing: Stephen Gray's essay "A Sense of Place in the New Literatures in English, Particularly South African," first delivered in 1982 as an address at Macquarie University in Australia. The fact that this informal and occasional piece should have been described as a "central text of contemporary South African literary historiography" is a measure of the thinness, even to date, of South African investigations of this matter: we still have nothing (outside of Coetzee's own work and some of the fine essays in Hilton Judin and Ivan Vladislavić's collection *Blank _____: Architecture, Apartheid, and After*) that can compare in its suggestiveness for literary scholarship with, say, the Australian Paul Carter's imaginative work on colonial geographies.[7] However, in his essay, Gray demonstrates that the notion of "a sense of place"—no matter how vague and obfuscatory it may be—can be used to generate a serviceable scheme of the successive phases of a South African (and more broadly postcolonial) literary historiography.[8] He outlines this history as follows.

In the first phase, the colony offers what Richard Rive has called a "Scenic Special": the exotic appeal of a remote place with strange physical and human scenery. In this body of writing, the colonial landscape is presented to readers in the centers of power as different: it supplies a novel entertainment for the armchair traveler back "home." The effect is a sort of verbal safari, entirely Eurocentric in its assumptions. Though its historical origins lie in the Renaissance, as Gray points out, this kind of discourse remains influential. It includes not only the work of early travel writers, like the ones Coetzee discovered in the British Library, but also that of their myriad successors: writers like Lawrence Durrell and Laurens van der Post, along with (we might add) the producers of travel magazines, TV documentaries, and feature films, like Jamie Uys's popular movie *The Gods Must Be Crazy*, or the Disney vehicle *A Far-off Place*. Today, as South Africa tries to refashion itself into a tourist paradise, this kind of cultural product is unlikely to disappear: indeed, one might see such kitschy phenomena as the Lost City Resort, advertised as the site of an ancient African civilization miraculously discovered by the resort's developers, as a material manifestation of this exoticizing genre. Gray's first category, in other words, is both historically specific and perennial; it is defined not only by qualities inherent in the texts themselves but also by the location and manner of their reception.

The second phase in his scheme is distinctively and assertively colonial. It consists of works that assert a new sense of place and belonging, which is tied, for Gray, to the emergence of a "defecting patriotism."[9] This phase is initiated by Olive Schreiner: a unique figure in the South African context, but one who has Australian and Canadian counterparts in Miles Franklin and Suzanna Moodie, respectively. In such isolated and singular texts as *Story of an African Farm*, "phase two" literature reacts to the cultural tourism of the first phase by asserting an inescapable rootedness in the landscape and the emotional horizon of the colony. In Schreiner's case, that setting is the stony desert of the Great Karoo, a landscape that, as Gray puts it, becomes "the spiritual core of the work."[10] It is ironic, there-fore, that this literature was received in the metropolitan center, where Schreiner had to find her readers, as indistinguishable from "phase one" writing: *Story of an African Farm* was largely seen as bringing an entertainingly novel "sense of place" to English literature. Schreiner's critique of the aridity of European ideas and val-ues, offered from her forbidding, marginal vantage in the South African desert, was readily overlooked.

In its third phase, South African writing becomes, for Gray, much less vulner-able to such Eurocentric misreading, since it is associated not only with a full-fledged sense of national identity but also with the emergence of a cultural nexus that supports a national literature: a publishing industry, a community of local readers and critics, and a self-referring use of language, norms, and values. Place remains, or so Gray's argument goes, a defining feature, but it is no longer—as it was with "phase two" writers—a cultural battlefield on which the rights to an indigenous identity must be won from the imperial power. It emerges, rather, as a set of familiar experiential localities, in which literary figures as different as Athol Fugard, writing from the scruffy city of Port Elizabeth, and Sipho Sepamla, writ-ing from the explosive Soweto scene, can stage their distinct literary projects.[11]

Now, there are clearly a number of problems with this outline.[12] Given the extent to which postapartheid culture has been shaped by the forces of global-ization, the contemporary critic may well want to ask how autonomous the national literary market place associated with Gray's "phase three" writing really was, and whether the linear narrative of a liberation of colonial literatures from the influence of metropolitan and exoticized consumption is entirely tenable.[13] After all, Gray himself observed in a 2001 interview that the simultaneous arrival of national liberation and neoliberal economic forces has meant that literature remains out of reach for most South Africans, for whom the cost of books is pro-hibitive. It would seem, in retrospect, that the national (English) literary scene was sustained in good measure by the liberation struggle, and that both its financial basis and its coherence began to fragment in the wake of the 1994 election.[14] But even if we view Gray's scheme in its own historical moment, it is vulnerable to criticism. It is clearly open to the objection that it is reductive in its definition of "place" as the "single variable" that generates the distinctiveness of the so-called new literatures and in its claim that "the elements of plot, character, action, use of dialogue, rhythm, and all the other techniques of making literature, remain the same" as those of British literature.[15] This presupposition ignores the extent to which indigenous forms (especially styles of oral performance in the South African case) have shaped cultural production. But the most important weakness vexing Gray's schema is the fact that he relies on an all too empirically conceived notion of "place." The implicit notion of artistic representation, consequently, is straightforwardly mimetic and bears the implication that South African literature must perforce represent South African scenes.[16]

It is, therefore, not surprising that Gray makes no reference to the work of J. M. Coetzee. After all, the first part of *Dusklands* and *Waiting for the Barbarians* (two works that had already appeared and had generated much discussion by the time of Gray's talk) are not set in South Africa at all. This omission is symptomatic: Gray's historiographic scheme could not accommodate Coetzee's sophisticated investigations of questions of place (and the Bakhtinian term "chronotope," which intimately links setting with genre, plot, and temporality, is in any case a better word to describe Coetzee's object of interest). As Stephen Watson once observed, Coetzee's novels "float free of time and place, even in the act of alluding to a time and place which is specifically South African."[17] At stake in his work is not place as an empirical and inert object of mimesis, but rather the discursive, generic, and ultimately political codes that inform our understanding, knowledge, and representations of place. There is, consequently, a deliberate unsettledness in Coetzee's novels. His early experimental fiction undermines and defamiliarizes the chronotopic dimension of fiction, but does so precisely to draw our attention to it, and to make it available for critical scrutiny. His work, therefore, cannot fit into any given South African tradition or reflect any historically progressive "sense of place," because it sets out to dismantle and analyze such matters.

Atopia

The unsettled character of Coetzee's fiction is emphasized by Teresa Dovey (the author of the first book-length study of his work) when she selects, as one of the keywords of her analysis, Roland Barthes's notion of "atopia" or "drifting habitation."[18] "Atopia" evokes, in appropriately spatial (or perhaps antispatial) terms, the deconstructive and writerly quality of Coetzee's texts: especially his formal shiftiness, as evident in the fact that his early novels, like hermit crabs, inhabit—but only to abandon—the shells of various fictional genres such as the narrative of exploration and the pastoral.[19] "Atopia" thus identifies Coetzee's project as one of displacement. It entails a refusal to settle in any space that is conventionally and ideologically given: a critical gesture that Dovey explains (in the Lacanian terminology she privileges) as "a constant deferral of the position available to the subject in language." While I shall eventually take issue with

Dovey's readings, the idea of "atopia" does provide a useful initial rubric under which we may consider one way Coetzee problematizes the notion of a "sense of place": by subjecting his novelistic topographies to a peculiarly shifty metafictional treatment.

The idea of "atopia," or rather "drifting habitation," is most applicable to Coetzee's second novel, *In the Heart of the Country*. This is, of course, a novel whose problematic temporality strikes us immediately. We are never allowed to be certain about when the events described in the novel take place (the narrator is never sure if she is in a time of donkey carts or bicycles or airplanes). Nor are we sure what "really happens"—the sequence and the effects of events are always in doubt. The same is true of the novel's ostensible setting—despite all the realistic details of the whitewashed homestead, the gravelly yard, the chickens, the dust, and the gleaming copperware. The title itself initiates a kind of ironic instability: it appears to allude to a symbolically significant location, but the narrative, with its rapid succession of often self-canceling segments, seems really to have nothing at its "heart." The text continually reminds us that the farm is entirely fictive, that there is no "stone desert" but only a "stony monologue" (HC 12). Magda, the narrator of this monologue, repeatedly and regretfully insists that the panorama before her depends entirely upon her consciousness and her words: "Seated here I hold the goats and stones, the entire farm and even its environs, as far as I know them, suspended in this cool, alienating medium of mine, exchanging them item by item for my word counters. A hot gust lifts and drops a flap of ochre dust. The landscape recomposes itself and settles" (HC 26). Yet it would also be incorrect—and too safe—to think of this consciousness as in any way settled or "central." Magda thinks of herself as a void, a hole (HC 41), and she frequently seems on the verge of dissolving into complete insubstantiality: "a ghost or a vapour," she muses, "floating at the intersection of a certain latitude and a certain longitude" (HC 17)—an intersection that remains a purely hypothetical location. The farm is, one might say, an excuse for a savagely comic meditation on the fate of the marginal intellectual. It is not located in the proverbial "middle of nowhere" (such remoteness would accord with the realist notion of the vastness of the Karoo), it *is* nowhere, "on the road from no A to no B in the world, if such a fate is topologically possible" (HC 19). Indeed, it is figured, at times, as a kind of antispace: "a turbulence, a vortex, a black hole" (HC 39), a swallowing up of any presence.

Considering all this, what seems curious is the extent to which the novel remains visual in its effect and how much it is concerned with description. Even the highly self-reflexive passage cited above seems—just for a moment, when a gust of wind raising the dust appears to disturb the "suspended" verbal landscape—to flirt with a more conventional realism. And there are certainly moments when the narrative imparts, however ironically or hypothetically, a conventional South African "sense of place." We might think, for instance, of the description of the impoverished settlement, Armoede, where the servant, Hendrik, goes to fetch his bride. It is offered in the form of a list the slightly weary tone of which emphasizes the familiarity and typicality of the details: "the bleak windswept hill, the iron shanties with hessian in the doorways, the chickens, doomed, scratching in the dust, the cold snot-nosed children toiling back from the dam with buckets of water, the same chickens scattering now before the donkey cart" (HC 17). But despite the vividness of detail, the context does not permit this dash of local color to achieve much in the way of a mimetic effect. For the narrator merely imagines this scene, admitting that she has never been to Armoede. Indeed, she "seem[s] never to have been anywhere": a fate that would explain the curiously improvisational quality of her descriptions even of her own home turf—her ignorance, for instance, of whether or not she happens to have any neighbors. The place name "Armoede" also seems to work in a complicated and contradictory way, undermining, as it were, its own suggestion of referentiality. To anyone familiar with South Africa, the name "Armoede" ("Poverty") seems "realistically" typical, calling to mind any number of those curiously morbid place names that dot the country's map: Lydenburg (Town of Suffering), Misgund (Begrudged), Verlatenheid (Desolation), Weenen (Weeping)—the list could be extended. But this reality effect is undercut, one feels, by the all too perfect and all too allegorical match between the name and the scene. The settlement's appellation seems to bear the mark of the literary and to draw attention to itself as linguistic label: as Magda laments, it is all a matter of "names, names, names" (HC 17).

In the absence of any resistance to the process of naming and of the linguistic reciprocity of which Magda dreams (HC 101), everything becomes solipsistic and improvisational. The landscape is clearly a figment of Magda's narratorial consciousness, her "speculative . . . geography" (HC 19); but at the same time her consciousness seems equally determined by the ostensibly fictive, composed landscape. Magda's "speculative bias" (HC 20), her radical though somehow insubstantial freedom, has its origin, she tells us, in the vast distances of the land into which she must stare: "I make it all up in order that it shall make me up" (HC 73). Such are the unstable, shifting operations, the "lapidary paradoxes" (HC 19) that make up this fiction.

It is easy to see why *In the Heart of the Country* in particular has provided grounds for the Lacanian reading offered by Dovey. Her association of the narrating self with the hermit crab, scuttling from shell to shell, or code to code, or signifier to signifier, is in many ways compelling and accurate. But it seems to me that in the matter of genre, which is central to Dovey's understanding of what she rightly calls Coetzee's "fiction-as-criticism," her deconstructive reading has certain limitations.[20] It is true, of course, that generic instability is perhaps the most telling characteristic of self-reflexive fiction. Coetzee himself notes that what clearly distinguishes the postmodern text from the realist novels of, say, Daniel Defoe or Thomas Hardy, is that Moll Flanders and Jude never pause to ponder what kind of text it is they seem to be inhabiting (DP 63). And *In the Heart of the Country* is no exception to this postmodern tendency: Magda constantly questions what kind of action or event might justify her insubstantial presence in the elusive heart of the country: not Greek tragedy, despite the imagined ax-murder and the surrounding "theatre of stone" (HC 3); or Gothic romance, despite her brief fantasy of waiting for "a castle to crumble into the tarn" (HC 17); or even the colonial idyll, with its dreary possibilities of marriage to a neighbor's second son or dalliance with an itinerant schoolmaster.

Yet the seductions of the more lyrical aspects of the pastoral are ever-present in the novel, and they are not so easily dismissed.[21] When Magda asserts that she would not be herself if she did not "feel the seductions of the cool stone house, the comfortable old ways, the antique feudal language," it is still possible to take the remark as just another momentary, self-canceling speculation. But by the end of the novel, the tone seems to have shifted. Magda's monologue concludes on a note that suggests that Coetzee's fictional strategies are not fully explained by an atopic reading. This lyrical finale, however self-consciously announced as "closing plangencies," expresses a desire that seems rather more specific and local in its implications than the universal linguistic condition of desire and deferral figured for Dovey by the hermit crab:

> There are poems, I am sure, about the heart that aches for Verlore Vlakte, about the melancholy of the sunset over the koppies, the sheep beginning to huddle against the first evening chill, the faraway boom of the windmill, the first chirrup of the first cricket, the last twitterings of the birds in the thorn-trees, the stones of the farmhouse wall still holding the sun's warmth, the kitchen lamp glowing steady. They are poems I could write myself. It takes generations of life in the cities to drive that nostalgia for country ways from the heart. I will never live it down, nor do I want to. I am corrupted to the bone with the beauty of this forsaken world. . . . I have chosen at every moment my own destiny, which is to die here in the petrified garden, behind locked gates, near my father's bones, in a space echoing with hymns I could have written but did not because (I thought) it was too easy. (HC 138–139)

Magda's imagined poems about Verlore Vlakte (Lost Plains) are not parodied in these lyrical lines. But, while allowing the reader to indulge—for a brief moment—in the nostalgic beauty of "country ways," the narrative voice never fully endorses her own sunset idyll: these are poems that "could have been written" but never will be.

And just as Magda resists the "easy" pastoral poetry to which she is drawn, Coetzee himself resists the easy option of "that heady expansion into the as-if" (HC 4) mentioned earlier in the novel. His apartheid-era fiction is marked by a reluctant abnegation of certain artistic forms: a gesture that is explained in his comments on the situation of the contemporary author in one of the interviews from *Doubling the Point*. He speaks of "the pathos—in the humdrum sense of the word—of our position": writers today are "like children shut in the playroom, the room of textual play, looking out wistfully through the bars at the exciting world of the grownups, one that we have been instructed to think of as the mere phantasmal world of *realism* but that we stubbornly can't help thinking of as the *real*" (DP 63). This intriguing comment suggests that Coetzee is not fully enamored of the antimimetic and deconstructive techniques that he himself deploys: he speaks of the "impasse of anti-illusionism" while recognizing—almost regretfully—the necessity for such techniques. In the history of the novel, he argues, metafiction is a "marking of time." It is surely no coincidence that this condition of marking time—of waiting—is the same morbid condition so often associated with white

South Africans living in the uncertain age of what Nadine Gordimer (following Gramsci) has described as the "interregnum."[22] Thus, while acknowledging the paradoxical nature of such a move, we may localize Coetzee's atopic strategies and recognize not only a historical but also an ethical impulse behind his anti-illusionism. For it was specifically as a white South African under apartheid that Coetzee felt he should refrain from pastoral indulgences; and it was as a novelist writing within a particular troubling historical configuration that he felt he should avoid producing what he describes in an essay on Beckett as the "daydream gratification of fiction" (DP 49).

The problem with Teresa Dovey's reading of Coetzee's work (a reading that did much to set the tone for the somewhat hypertheoretical Coetzee industry that has followed in its wake) is that it is not balanced by a consciousness of the contingency and historicity of cultural forms. Most notably, there is no sense in her work that the psychoanalytic and deconstructive theories she deploys may themselves be destabilized: that they may acquire different nuances and create different meanings when they are invoked in different contexts or deployed at some remove from their source.[23] This critique has been suggested in general terms by David Attwell, who notes that in Dovey's discussion of *In the Heart of the Country* the Hegelian master-slave dialectic is entirely stripped of its historical and political aspect—that is, of the implication that such goals as freedom and self-realization are attainable only in a just society.[24] The problem becomes even clearer if one looks closely at some of Dovey's curiously reductive readings of passages from Coetzee's early work. An example is her gloss of a key moment in *Life and Times of Michael K*—the passage in which the starving Michael K meditates on the minimal and ahistorical way he would like to live on the land: "I am not building a house out here by the dam to pass on to other generations. What I make ought to be careless, makeshift, a shelter to be abandoned without a tugging at the heart-strings. . . . The worst mistake, he told himself, would be to try to found a new house, a rival line, on his small beginnings out at the dam" (MK 101–109).

Dovey's reading of this rather touching passage renders it almost mechanically self-referential. Michael K's improvised dwelling place becomes nothing but an allegory for the operations of Coetzee's novel: "This text in particular must not be too close to Coetzee's own meanings; he must be able to abandon it, without a tugging at the heartstrings, to the successive meanings which new readings will generate."[25] For all its apparent openness, this allegorical reading is one that discourages any more specific interpretation. But even if we do take K's invisible, traceless, self-erasing mode of living on the land as a figure for a certain mode of writing, we must remember that K himself recognizes that it is the context of war, the times of Michael K, if you will, that demands this strategy: "What a pity that to live in times like these a man must be ready to live like a beast. A man who wants to live cannot live in a house with lights in the window. He must live in a hole and hide by day. A man must live so that he leaves no trace of his living. That is what it has come to" (MK 99). "Drifting habitation" as a literary strategy must likewise be seen in relation to a particular historical condition.

A similar point can be made in relation to Dovey's reading of another important meditation in *Life and Times of Michael K*, which occurs when, after a vicious assault on the Jakkalsdrif labor camp, K ponders the relationship between parasite and host:

> Parasite was the word the police captain had used: the camp at Jakkalsdrif, a nest of parasites hanging from the neat sunlit town, eating its substance, giving no nourishment back. Yet to K lying idle in his bed, thinking without passion (What is it to me, after all? he thought), it was no longer obvious which was host and which parasite, camp or town. . . . What if the hosts were far outnumbered by the parasites, the parasites of idleness and the other secret parasites in the army and the police force and the schools and factories and offices, the parasites of the heart? Could the parasites then still be called parasites? Parasites too had flesh and substance; parasites too could be preyed upon. Perhaps in truth whether the camp was declared a parasite on the town or the town a parasite on the camp depended on no more than on who made his voice heard loudest. (MK 116)

Dovey relates this passage, predictably, to J. Hillis Miller's argument in "The Critic as Host." "The term 'para-site,'" she ventures, "comes to signify as a locus of substitution and refers to the way in which Coetzee's novel, which is parasitic in relation to the previous texts which it deconstructs, will in turn become the host to successive parasitic readings."[26] While it is certainly possible to understand acts of reading and interpretation—thematized in the second section of the novel, where the medical officer "reads," or invents, the story of Michael K—in terms of the relationship of host and parasite, I find myself wanting to insist that atopic reading, the punning etymology which turns the "parasite" into a "locus of substitution," misses something. It universalizes the term's reference, and in so doing flattens out the operations of a text that seems to ask questions with urgent ethical implications for South Africa in particular: Who eats whom? Who lives off whom? Who lives in the town, and who in the worker's camp? Who lives in the white city, and who in its shadow township? The host-parasite opposition, in other words, has a local meaning and potency: atopic slippage, the "endlessness of textuality," as Attwell puts it, is halted by "the brute facticity of power" (DP 11).

White Mapping

I would now like to move from the concept of "atopia" to that of the "dream topography"—a more productive concept, which enables us to give the ethical and political dimensions of Coetzee's novels their due without recourse to naïve empiricism. The term emerges from Coetzee's discussion of the South African pastoral in *White Writing* (1988), where literary genre is treated as not so much a metafictional strategy, or temporary home for the writerly hermit crab, as a kind of social dream work, expressing wishes and maintaining silences that are political in origin. The idea of the generically and ideologically determined "dream topography" offers us a spatial concept that is both more stable and more historically responsive than "drifting habitation." It avoids, moreover, the vague appeal to personal experience that inevitably adheres to the notion of a "sense of place," and underscores instead the importance of discursive codes and cultural maps.

The essays in *White Writing* are mainly concerned with two rival dream topographies, two rival versions of the pastoral tradition in South Africa. They are, if you will, the maps—the ideological blueprints—this genre has projected on the land. Both of these projections are already sketched out in Coetzee's 1977 review of Ross Devenish and Athol Fugard's *The Guest,* a film based on a painful period in the life of the Afrikaans poet and morphine addict Eugène Marais, during which he was ordered by his doctor to go cold turkey on a remote Transvaal farm. To the dismay of the film's director, who no doubt expected wholehearted support from intellectuals for his contribution to the very short list of art films produced in apartheid South Africa, Coetzee's comments were acerbic. He observed that the film's representations of the white man's relation to the land were patched together from flattering myths designed—however unconsciously—to keep certain irresolvable inconsistencies from view.[27] Marais's hosts, the Meyers of Steenkampskraal, are presented via a visually seductive *mise en scène* of whitewashed walls, dark vertical frames of doors and windows, a dinner table in the glow of lamplight: by interiors reminiscent of the classic Dutch painters, and by settings that gleam with Rembrandt browns and golds. This visual coding, Coetzee points out, serves to imply that the Meyers are no "rootless colonials" but, simultaneously, "rude children of the African soil and heirs to a venerable European tradition" (DP 118). The limited contexts in which we see the family, moreover, make it difficult to raise certain troubling questions about the running of this African farm. Coetzee spells these questions out: "If the Meyers run a cattle farm, why do they never talk about cattle?" "Where do the African-farm laborers who materialize out of nowhere for a single fifteen-second sequence live?" "How do the Meyer men spend their time when they are not eating?" (DP 118) The film, Coetzee implies, confines itself to the terrain permitted by the ideological horizons of the Afrikaans pastoral, within which the Meyers and their farm stand as emblems of goodness, simplicity, and permanence.

As far as the film's presentation of the poet goes, Coetzee argues that yet another myth applies: that of the Genius in Africa, the man for whom consciousness is pain, and for whom the African landscape is a murderous mother-goddess, who silently rejects the alienated poet-supplicant, though he tragically adores her stony bosom. Marais's glamorously dystopian relationship with the land is, of course, no less ideologically fraught than the rough-hewn arcadia of the ordinary Afrikaners. In fact, it allows Coetzee to articulate for the first time an idea that will become one of the crucial arguments of *White Writing*: for the majority of South Africans, people "for whom Africa is a mother who has nourished them and their forebears for millions of years," a poetic stoicism makes no sense at all: "South Africa, mother of pain, can have meaning only to people who can find it meaningful to ascribe their 'pain' ('alienation' is here a better word) to the failure of Africa to love them enough" (DP 117). An aesthetic preoccupation with the land, however restrained or even tragic, thus masks a resistance to thinking about South Africa in sociopolitical terms.

In *White Writing*, these two sets of codes or mythic maps of Africa—the one arcadian, the other dystopian—are examined in more elaborate and more generally (or generically) applicable ways. Coetzee describes the first dream topography as follows: "a network of boundaries crisscrossing the surface of the land, marking off thousands of farms, each a separate kingdom ruled over by a benign patriarch with, beneath him, a pyramid of contented and industrious children, grandchildren, and serfs" (DP 6). In this conception of South African territory, the farm—the very soil, in fact—is imagined as a wife to the fathers and sons, who all merge into a single mythic husband-man. This dream topography may be identified with the *plaasroman*, and with the more nostalgic and romantic aspects of the Afrikaner *volkskultuur* generally speaking (though the English writer Pauline Smith may also be seen as contributing to this tradition).[28] It is the mythic space not only of novelists like Van Bruggen or Van den Heever (whom Coetzee discusses) but also of countless movies, stories from popular magazines like *Huisgenoot*, old soap operas on Springbok radio, and so forth.[29] What is key to Coetzee's conception, however, is the fact that this imagined topography involves a mode of writing of the most material sort: the furrows of the plow assume the character of a signature, a letter of ownership, a title to the land (WW 85). In the optic proposed by the *plaasroman*, the pastoral activities of plowing, digging, building, fence-making—even the construction of those Cape Dutch houses in the classic shape of the letter H, a shape Magda tries to read in *In the Heart of the Country* (HC 3)—are all to be regarded as acts of inscription.

The second and rival dream topography Coetzee describes is one in which South Africa is imagined as "a vast, empty, and silent space, older than man, older than the dinosaurs whose bones lie bedded in its rocks, and destined to be vast, empty, and unchanged long after man has passed from its face." In this conception of Africa as the oldest and most daunting of continents, "the task of the human imagination is to conceive not a social order capable of domesticating the landscape, but any kind of relation at all that consciousness can have with it" (WW 7). Such a conception generates a poetry of empty space: a failed but stoic lyricism. The literary tradition associated with this disheartening topography originates with Schreiner's negative pastoral *Story of an African Farm* (the classic of "phase two" literature in Stephen Gray's scheme) and is then continued by a succession of English-language poets. Although its key tropes are absence, silence, and the failure of language, this topography of desolation must also be apprehended as a form of writing. Though it does not inscribe the land with the obvious signatures of culture and cultivation, it does project on it an inscrutable blankness. In this blankness—much the same blankness that fascinated Conrad's Marlow in *Heart of Darkness* when he pored over maps as a boy—Coetzee sees evidence of the exercise of a certain historical will: a desire "to see as silent and empty, a land that has been, if not full of human figures, not empty of them either; that is arid and infertile, perhaps, but not inhospitable to human life, and certainly not uninhabited" (WW 177). This topography, the product of a particular version of the sublime, thus relies on an act of erasure. The silence the solitary poet encounters in the empty landscape, or so Coetzee reminds us, bears an uncomfortable resemblance to the myth purveyed by apartheid-era historiographers, who claimed that the land settled by the Voortrekker pioneers in the nineteenth century was open, empty, and unpeopled.

The crucial point of *White Writing*, then, is that in both of the dominant literary versions of the pastoral in South Africa—the Afrikaner novelist's patriarchal idyll, as well as the English poet's naturalistic lyricism—the black person, whether as the farmer of an earlier age or as the agricultural worker or even just as human presence, is obscured. Coetzee's meditations in this book, like his earlier meditations on *The Guest*, thus lead to a series of uncomfortable questions that strike at the heart of the South African political system. Does the poet's inevitable failure to hear the language of the stones "stand for, or stand in the place of, another failure, by no means inevitable: a failure to imagine a peopled landscape . . . to conceive a society in South Africa in which there is a place for the self?" (WW 9). Still more pointedly: "Was there no time before the time of the forefathers, and whose was the land then? Do white hands truly pick the fruit, reap the grain, milk the cows, shear the sheep in these bucolic retreats? Who truly creates wealth?" (WW 11). These questions reveal the fundamental blindness of the white man's dream about the land: its "blindness to the colour black" (WW 5). They also reveal Coetzee's characteristic critical procedure in the first half of his career: he does not read the "writing" so much as ask what the writing occludes, and he does not seek the truth in direct utterances so much as in evasions and omissions.[30]

The themes and methods deployed in *White Writing* are also evident in Coetzee's fiction.[31] *Life and Times of Michael K*, for instance, is both a meditation on the ideological function of the pastoral and an example of the critical strategy of subverting the dominant discourse and listening to its silences. That there should be connections between *White Writing* and *Life and Times of Michael K* is hardly surprising, since the novel was written concurrently with some of the essays in the critical study. Even the lines from Ovid's *Metamorphoses* that serve as the epigraph to *White Writing* indicate the two books' overlapping concerns. These lines serve to underscore the difficulties that beset the life of Michael K, the gardener, and that have historically beset South Africa, the troubled garden colony:

Cadmus agit grates peregrinaeque oscula terrae
Figet et ignotos montes agrosque salutat
   . . . superas delapsa per auras
Pallas adest montaeque iubet supponere terrae
viperos dentes, populi incrementa futuri

Pressing his lips to foreign soil, greeting the unfamiliar mountain and plains,
Cadmus gave thanks . . . Descending from above, Pallas told him to plow and sow
the earth with the serpent's teeth, which would grow into a future nation.

The epigraph suggests that the settler's pastoral efforts have been synonymous with war and strife from the very beginning. The context in which Michael K finds himself likewise conflates the ideas of gardening and war, or rather forces gardening and war into an oxymoronic embrace: after all, this a novel in which people dig into the earth to plant mines, and march about in prison camps with spades rather than rifles over their shoulders. There is even an element of pastoral burlesque in the idea of Michael K leaving the war-torn city, not like the epic hero of old carrying his father on his back, but pushing his mother in a wheelbarrow. Michael K sets out for the Karoo with a desire to escape the war and realize a pastoral dream: "a whitewashed cottage in the broad veld with smoke curling from its chimney" (MK 9). But his experiences soon reveal to him that the country is mapped and gridded in such a way that any pastoral fantasy, or just a simple rural life, is proscribed for a person who is officially classed as "coloured," or more exactly as "CM-40-NFA-Unemployed" (MK 70). He can live freely in this terrain only by becoming simultaneously a trespasser and an escapee (MK 97).

The protagonist's racial status is, of course, essential to the novel's demystificatory operations. Adopting K's perspective allows Coetzee to reveal the dystopian dimensions of the Afrikaner's dream topography of beloved farms and fences: the enclosures by which the Visagies of the novel have staked out their "miles and miles of silence" to "bequeath to their children and grandchildren in perpetuity" (MK 47). The novel's allegorical strategies entail representing this topography as in a photographic negative and, in so doing, revealing its homology with the Foucauldian carceral archipelago. K's South Africa is a place where one can only dream of "forgotten corners and angles and corridors between the fences, land that belonged to no one yet" (MK 47). What one actually experiences is a proliferation of "camps": "Camps for children whose parents run away, camps for people who kick and foam at the mouth, camps for people with big heads and people with little heads, camps for people with no visible means of support, camps for people chased off the land, camps for people they find living in storm-water drains" (MK 182). The map of the Afrikaner's pastoral idyll thus merges with the map of a vast prison made up of innumerable cells—a social topography in which everybody is either fenced in or guarding a gate.

The scandalous force of this merger can only be grasped only if one recalls the conventional association of the vast South African landscape with notions of freedom, a commonplace of innumerable poems and even patriotic songs, such as "Die Lied van Jong Suid-Afrika" ("The Song of Young South Africa"), the nationalistic bombast of which I found quite stirring when I first was taught to sing it as a child:

> Die hoogland is ons woning, die land van son en veld,
> Waar woeste vryheidswinde waai oor graf van menig' held.
> Die ruimtes het ons siel gevoed, ons kan geen slawe wees,
> Want vryer as die arendsvlug is die vlugte van ons gees.

> The high country is our dwelling place, the land of sun and veld
> Where wild winds of freedom blow over many graves of heroes.
> The open space has fed our souls, we cannot ever be slaves,
> For freer than the eagle's flight are the flights of our spirit.

The lines bring to mind one of the more profound insights expressed by Magda in *In the Heart of the Country*: one can be imprisoned just as readily in a large place as in a small (HC 122). And the release from this large prison, as Coetzee suggests in his Jerusalem Prize speech, cannot come without the sacrifice of privilege and power: liberty always "comes in a package" with equality and fraternity. It is therefore inevitable that South Africa's literature of vastness should have undertones "of entrapment, entrapment in infinitude" (DP 97–98): undertones Coetzee turns into the dominant tones of *Life and Times of Michael K.*

In light of these reflections on fences and prisons, it seems all the more significant that we should discover in Coetzee's fictional meditations on the South African pastoral the one scene that must remain hidden if the Afrikaner's dream topography is to be sustained in its mythical virtue. This scene appears in *In the Heart of the Country* as part of Magda's "speculative history," or "speculative geography," in which she imagines the fate of her servants' ancestors:

> Hendrik's forebears in the olden days crisscrossed the desert with their flocks and their chattels, heading from A to B or from X to Y, sniffing for water, abandoning stragglers, making forced marches. Then one day fences began to go up and from shadowed faces issued invitations to stop and settle that might also have been orders and might have been threats, one does not know, and so one became a herdsman, and one's children after one and one's women took in washing. (HC 18–19)

The lines remind us that the history of agricultural enclosure, as Raymond Williams demonstrates so well in *The Country and the City*, is a history not just of settlement but of displacement and exclusion. In this case, the first herder-farmers are turned into temporary sojourners, or, like Robert and Michael in *Life and Times of Michael K*, into persons of "no fixed abode." This displacement is the secret historical precondition of the Afrikaner's idyllic map of rural homesteading: the old tracings from A to B are the submerged and erased text that challenges the settlers' elaborately inscribed title to the land. The logic of the dream topography imposed on this originary script requires, of course, that the black man's subsequent inscriptive acts of digging and plowing should leave no trace, that they should be legally and culturally invisible. This idea is a recurrent one in *Life and Times of Michael K*, and it finds its most frightening expression in a passage where K imagines that all the dispossessed might be sent off to dig, not in order to plant anything, but to erase themselves: to scoop out a mass grave into which their own bodies can be thrown (MK 94).

The brilliance of the survival strategy Michael K devises is that he finds a way to reclaim displacement and tracklessness as a form of freedom. He turns the social condition prescribed for him—that of having to work the land without owning or inscribing it—into something else, something to be desired. The significance of his solution is prefigured in a memory he retains from his school days: "One of the teachers used to make the class sit with their hands on their heads, their lips pressed tightly together and their eyes closed, while he patrolled the rows with his long ruler. In time, to K, the posture grew to lose its meaning as punishment and became an avenue of reverie" (MK 68). K's mode of farming rewrites, both despite and because of its invisibility, the rules of the game of the

South African pastoral. He preserves the idea of plenty through starvation, the idea of self-affirmation through self-erasure, the idea of rural dwelling and settlement through "drifting habitation." In this way he keeps alive "the idea of gardening" (MK 109) in a time of war.

Something similar can be said of Coetzee's artistic practice, since the capacity for changing the rules of the game is precisely what he values most in a work of art.[32] Like K, he proceeds by negation and, if needs be, "invisibly." The latter possibility is delicately suggested in one of the interviews from *Doubling the Point*, where David Attwell and Coetzee discuss a quotation from Rilke, which Coetzee cited in a 1974 essay on Nabokov: "It is our task to imprint this provisional, perishable earth so deeply, so patiently and passionately in ourselves that its reality shall arise in us again 'invisibly.' *We are the bees of the invisible*" (DP 27). The impulse here is strikingly lyrical, but Coetzee responds to it cautiously, commenting on the nostalgic qualities of Nabokov's desire for the past and observing (in words that seem to foretell the project of *Boyhood*) that one must look at the past with a cruel enough eye to see what made its joy and innocence possible. This observation applies not only to the past, of course, but also to the pastoral—and to the poetry of empty space that celebrates South Africa's vast landscapes. The perspective that emerges is nuanced, even paradoxical. As Coetzee implies both in *White Writing* and in his Jerusalem Prize acceptance speech, it is not permissible to love a colonized land with an unreflective sincerity: a poetics of love for mountains, stones, trees, and flowers is ethically foreclosed for the settler. And yet Coetzee suggests that one must continue to "imprint" the "provisional, perishable earth" in oneself in the manner suggested by Rilke—so that, as Michael K says in one of his naively wise meditations, "the thread that binds man to the earth" may not be entirely broken (MK 109).

Utopia

It is appropriate, therefore, that critics such as Attwell and Neil Lazarus should have associated Coetzee's writing not with the playful practices of postmodern metafiction but with the ethical seriousness of high modernism, and more specifically, with the negative dialectics of Theodor Adorno. Coetzee's apartheid-era novels are works that, in the words of Adorno's essay on commitment, "point to a practice from which they abstain: the creation of a just life."[33] The connection with Adorno suggests the following question: if Coetzee's fiction is in the main antipastoral and dystopian, then is it not our task as critics (following his own example) to read dialectically, to subvert the dominant, to discover in his work the utopian possibility, or pastoral impulse that cannot be expressed directly? One of the most remarkable and virtuosic passages in *White Writing* suggests that this approach is exactly what is called for, at least for the reader of Coetzee's earlier work. In this passage, Coetzee seems to address his fellow critics directly: "Our craft," he says, "is all in reading the other: gaps, inverses, undersides; the veiled; the dark; the buried, the feminine; alterities." But then he poses the following question: "Is it a version of utopianism (or pastoralism) to look forward (or backward) to the day when the truth will be (or was) what is said, not what is not said, when we will hear (or heard) music as sound upon silence, not silence between sounds?" (WW 81).[34]

These wistful lines bring to mind the conclusion of *In the Heart of the Country*: one detects, in both instances, a regretful, minimalist lyricism, a muted yearning to come right out and sing "the beauty of this forsaken world" (HC 139). But we should not underestimate the cautiousness of Coetzee's language (a language that, as Peter Strauss once put it, is "forever on guard against itself").[35] The passage from *White Writing* admits to pastoral or utopian desires only in the form of a rhetorical question and indicates a strong awareness of the untimeliness of such desires. It asserts, in a fashion reminiscent of Adorno, the necessarily negative stance imposed on the apartheid-era writer, the refusal of easy "daydream gratification," precisely so that our utopian impulses may be preserved for a later, less bleak time.[36]

It is, therefore, not only possible but also necessary to trace the utopian possibilities in Coetzee's bleak fiction. Like the Magistrate in *Waiting for the Barbarians* who in a dream urges the barbarian girl to put people in the empty city she builds out of snow, Coetzee's earlier works seem to demand, in their very silences, a landscape replete with the sounds of humanity and a society based on reciprocity and fraternity. Their implicit ethos is explicitly expressed in the essay "Into the Dark Chamber." Coetzee here comments on a crisis moment in Nadine Gordimer's novel *Burger's Daughter*. The protagonist, Rosa Burger, unable to intervene when she sees a poor man cruelly flogging a horse, finds herself waiting for "a time when humanity will be restored across the face of society, and therefore when all human acts, including the flogging of an animal, will be returned to the gambit of moral judgment." In such a place and in such a time, Coetzee observes, the novel would once again be able to "take as its province the whole of life" (DP 368). In such a place and in such a time, the novel would also be able to describe even the secretive space of the torture chamber without becoming complicit in promoting its dark glamour, since it too could be "accorded a place in the design." We could easily extend this logic still further and say that in such a place and in such a time the novel could again be able to evoke—not ironically but lyrically—the country ways of the pastoral.

The Postapartheid Pastoral

The question of whether postapartheid South Africa will in fact allow an untroubled pastoralism to emerge animates Coetzee's 1999 novel *Disgrace*, and the answer it seems to give is no. Even "not yet" seems too optimistic. The temporality of this work is no longer that of waiting, and its critical impulse is no longer antirealist, metafictional, or deconstructive. A new era has arrived, and it is an era not just of political reform and land restitution (a reformed Land Bank now assists black peasants to become landowners) but also of revenge. And though *Disgrace* does not lack the dimension of sociopolitical critique common to Coetzee's earlier novels (it has been read as articulating an opposition to the utilitarian, functionalist, and homogenizing ideologies of globalization), its approach is no longer that of demystification—the reversal of margin and center, or of figure and ground.[37] Such critique has become outmoded and unnecessary in the context of a wholesale reversal of roles.

Disgrace is, in other words, a very different kind of book from *In the Heart of the Country* and *Life and Times of Michael K*. But it nevertheless revisits many of the issues raised in these earlier engagements with the pastoral. It is useful, in fact, to compare *Disgrace* and *Life and Times of Michael K* in some detail. As we have seen, the earlier work presents, albeit in anorexic and unsustainable form, a utopian vision: a dream of rural life without patriarchal or colonial domination. In *Disgrace*, Coetzee seems to have relinquished this dream. In the "new South Africa" of the novel, the maternal, antifoundational pastoral of Michael K seems entirely untenable. The urge to stake one's claim, to own, and to procreate is forcefully present. Hunger and denial are displaced by desire, and desire is figured—appropriately, since the plot concerns prostitution, sexual harassment, and rape—by way of phallic tropes: arrows, snakes, and the like. In contrast to Michael K, who strives to be trackless, David Lurie, the disgraced professor of Romantic poetry who is the novel's protagonist, worries about what he will leave behind when he dies. And when we first encounter his daughter, Lucy, she stands sturdily on her patch of land, "her toes grip[ping] the red earth, leaving clear prints" (D 62). The novel's new black farmer—eager to shed the humble roles of "gardener" and "dog-man" (D 64)—is in every way a patriarch: a man who, in the course of the novel, builds himself a new house that "casts a long shadow" (D 197) and who schemes to ensure that his line will not only survive but dominate. It is surely no accident that this man should bear the name "Petrus," the same name as the humble foreman in Nadine Gordimer's story "Six Feet of the Country," in which a group of black farm workers are denied the right to give a proper burial to a family member. Ambitious, resourceful, and, above all, aware that the political tables have turned, "this new Petrus" (D 151), as Lurie at one point calls him, is readily grasped as the postapartheid counterpart to Gordimer's character, ready to claim his six feet of the country—and more.

The traditional pastoral sensibilities—the love of "the old, *ländliche* way of life" (D 113)—are placed under brutal new pressures in *Disgrace*, and they are different pressures from those at work in *Life and Times of Michael K*. The opposition between country and city, still in place in the earlier novel, is on the verge of being effaced by the demographic exigencies of the new South Africa. "The country is coming to the city," Lurie thinks, as he observes a child herding a cow in one of the proliferating squatter settlements on the fringes of Cape Town. "Soon there will be cattle again on Rondebosch Common" (D 175). The time-honored associations attached to the terms "country" and "city" are consequently destabilized: the idea of the country as a place of moral simplicity, from which a critique of the city may be staged, is rendered untenable. Nor is it possible any longer to view the city as the locus of progress and the country as the locus of the "backward, nostalgic glance" of the pastoral mode (WW 4). The new black peasantry, grasping and scheming, is efficient and modern—"unlike Africa" (D 151) in Lurie's stereotypical conception. Petrus, with his Land Bank grant and founder's ambitions, savors the term "forward-looking" (D 136). Most importantly, the old South African relations of "baas en Klaas" (D 116), of "boys" doing the labor for white landowners, have been abolished. Indeed, they now seem so archaic that Petrus can play with the term "boy" in the same way, Lurie thinks, that Marie Antoinette once played at being a milkmaid (D 152). The notion of the country as refuge, moreover, is decisively challenged in the course of the novel: the crime that takes place on the farm to which Lurie retreats in disgrace only plunges him further into that abject state. But it is not only the binary pair of country and city that is undermined in the novel: all established oppositions and boundaries seem to be under threat of collapse, especially the opposition between stranger and kin, confounded as it is by the act of rape—that "god of chaos and mixture, violator of seclusions" (D 105). A crisis of definitions, relationships, and responsibilities thus lies at the heart of *Disgrace*.

This crisis is investigated on the level of fundamental linguistic structures—both grammatical and lexical. The novel's free indirect narration conveys a curious sense that its word choices are imperfect and still in the process of being made: words are handled with a meticulous and even burdensome awareness of their morphological, semantic, and cultural complexities. The word "friend," for instance, appears along with its full etymology ("Modern English *friend* from Old English *freond*, from *freon*, to love" [C102]): information that estranges both the word itself and the basic human bond it defines. A similarly intense and destabilizing scrutiny seems to be demanded by the novel's many italicized foreign words. They are used with such deliberation that the reader cannot but pause to wonder whether these lexical strangers have any place in or purchase on the "new South Africa": whether the cultural values in which they are embedded are at all translatable. A striking case in point is *eingewurzelt* ("rooted in"), the adjective David Lurie reaches for when he tries to characterize Lucy's neighbor Ettinger, a surly "man of the earth," shotgun at his side, determined to stick it out on his parcel of the Eastern Cape (D 117). The word, redolent with notions of organic community and peasant tradition, is intended to affirm the man's tenacity. But the very fact that it is a German word effectively undermines its definition: Ettinger's origins, or so Lurie muses, may be too European for him to survive on the postapartheid platteland without a brood of sons. The lexicon of the novel thus seems to suggest a point frequently reiterated in Coetzee's scholarly writing: that meanings are not necessarily transferable from one language to another, and that full translation is impossible (DP 90, 182). It is a point that bears rather sinister implications if one views the novel in the way Zoë Wicomb does in her rich and troubling commentary on *Disgrace*—as a meditation not only on the process of translation, but also on what is (for Wicomb) the intimately related process of a historical transition from apartheid to democracy.[38]

The novel's many instances of linguistic erudition—the foreign words, the interest in etymology, and also the recurrent reflections on the perfective form of the verb—are, of course, in character: they serve as markers of David Lurie's academic and cosmopolitan mode of thought. But a foregrounding of linguistic matters has been a consistent feature of Coetzee's intervention in the tradition of the South African pastoral over the years, and an analysis of the pastoral aspects of *Disgrace* returns us, once more, to the two dream topographies mapped out in *White Writing*. In works like "The Narrative of Jacobus Coetzee," *In the Heart of the Country*, and *Boyhood*, Coetzee refers to certain sociolinguistic rules that have traditionally governed the speech and the conversational exchanges (and by extension also the subject positions and hierarchies) of the dream topography of the Afrikaans idyll. In "The Narrative of Jacobus Coetzee," the nationalistic historian who is the ostensible author of the second part of the novella reveals a suspect yearning for the "durable relations" that pertained on the old farms and recalls the way the speech of workers was still marked by a feature of the "Hottentot" language, in which one indicated assent by reechoing part of the previous phrase: "'Drive them to the north camp.' 'To the north camp, my master'" (DL 115). The historian's description of the master's and servant's "dance in slow parallel through time" is, of course, but an aestheticization of relations of power and submission, relations that reduce the "coloured" servant's voice to an echo of that of the white landowner.

In *In the Heart of the Country* and *Boyhood*, a different grammatical construct is foregrounded, but one that is no less expressive of social hierarchies: namely, the peculiar avoidance, in polite Afrikaans, of the second person singular when addressing a social superior. It is a usage that not only makes for curious syntactic redundancies but also expresses, at least in Coetzee's view, the speaking subject's entrapment in a grammar of deference and domination: a grammar that forecloses any dream of more reciprocal relations between young and old, black and white, colonizer and colonized. In Afrikaans, as Magda muses, there is little hope for "words of true exchange" (HC 101). *In the Heart of the Country* records at some length (and in Afrikaans, in the original edition) a conversation between Magda's father and the servant Hendrik:

> "Where are you from?"
> "From Armoede, my baas. But now I come from baas Kobus. Baas Kobus says the baas has work here."
> "Do you work for baas Kobus?"
> "No, I do not work for baas Kobus. I was there looking for work. Then baas Kobus said that the baas has work. So I came." (HOC 20)

The exchange not only illustrates the grammatical rule governing the second person (a rule that horrifies the young protagonist of *Boyhood*) but also demonstrates yet again, in the strictly codified flow of question and answer, the dance of master and servant that so charms the pious historian of "The Narrative of Jacobus Coetzee."[39]

In *Disgrace*, of course, these rules are cast aside by Petrus. His native tongue, not incidentally, is isiXhosa (an important reason for the novel being set in the Eastern Cape rather than in Coetzee's more familiar Karoo): it is unmarked by the echoes of assent that the nationalist historian would associate with the Hottentot tongue. Petrus's utterances, moreover, are in a nonstandard but functional English, a language that not only cuts across the old conversational grammars but is also stripped of all the historical and literary associations with which David

Lurie's highly polished English is laden. Petrus's English is an English without a past, an English with an African inflection: it is the colonizer's language reappropriated and deformed in order to express the black man's newly gained sense of mastery.[40]

If *Disgrace*, through the figure of Petrus, abolishes the linguistics and social relations of Coetzee's first dream topography, it also revisits and abolishes the codes that defined the second: the negative pastoral of the English landscape poet in Africa. It is no accident that David Lurie is a specialist in Romantic poetry, and not only in light of his association with Lord Byron, the seducer, "mad, bad, and dangerous to know" (D 77). He is also the author of a book entitled *Wordsworth and the Burden of the Past*, and it is in the course of describing Lurie's lectures on Wordsworth at the newly renamed Cape Technical University that Coetzee once more draws our attention to the old problem of the failure of European languages to describe the African landscape. In his discussion of the Mont Blanc section of *The Prelude*, Lurie tries, rather awkwardly, to explain the idea of the Romantic sublime to the young people of the new South Africa: this country, he ventures lamely, also has mountains where "we" may hope "for one of those revelatory Wordsworthian moments we have all heard about" (D 14). The students, however, remain uninspired. As cultural translation, Lurie's commentary moves in the wrong direction: the members of his audience, as Zoë Wicomb tartly points out, are not part of any "we" who climb mountains in the wake of the English poets.[41] It is only the *Europäische* Lurie who still needs to apprehend the African landscape in this fashion. The students' indifference reminds us of a point Coetzee first addressed in his review of *The Guest* and has returned to at various times subsequently: namely, that the problem of scenic description—the difficulty of finding a language in which to relate to the African landscape—is not one that afflicts the speakers of African vernaculars. David Lurie's despair at the viability of English in Africa—a despair that does not take into account Petrus's decisive appropriation of the new kinds of mastery the language offers him—may be viewed as a late and exceptionally pessimistic revisiting of one of the characteristic tropes of Coetzee's second dream topography: one in which (the English) language fails and where the (English) poet's voice is silenced by the realities of Africa, which have now come to assume a new but no more hospitable guise.[42]

But, as one might expect, *Disgrace* moves beyond this familiar form of failure. And it appears, at least in the novel's penultimate scene, that the aesthetic pleasures of the pastoral have not been completely erased. Indeed, this scene may be viewed as the last in a series of risky moments in Coetzee's work (including the ending of *In the Heart of the Country*, to which I have already attended) when he indulges, however briefly, in idyllic description. In this case, he presents a serene landscape—the gentle sun, the stillness of midafternoon, bees busy in a field of flowers (D 218)—in which a pregnant woman, Lucy Lurie, bends at her work. This picturesque, even mythic, vision of "field-labor; peasant tasks, immemorial" (D 217) is only slightly ironicized by the reminder that it owes much to the "ready-made images of Sargent and Bonnard," "city boys" like David Lurie, but capable nevertheless of having their breath taken away by rustic beauty (D 218).

The scene ends with father and daughter striking up, in a modest and ordinary sort of way, a new relationship:

> "Will you come in and have some tea?"
> She makes the offer as if he were a visitor. Good. Visitorship, visitation: a new footing, a new start. (D 218)

Needless to say, the idea of "visitorship" is a resonant one in this novel about strangers and kin. But the idea of "visitation," while not without its ambiguities, is clearly oriented to the future. With its religious overtones, it expresses the hope of some new arrival (one cannot help but recall Rilke's beautiful image of the "bees of the invisible"), perhaps even of an unexpected grace. It makes sense, then, that in these closing moments of the novel, David Lurie begins for the first time to muse in a positive way about the future: about whether he might yet be reeducated to better appreciate rural life, and, more importantly, about whether his daughter might not, with luck, "last a long time." Though the product of rape, her mixed-race child, or so Lurie thinks, will be "a child of this earth" (D 216).

If the ending of *Foe* invites us to imagine a place "where bodies are their own signs" (F 151), *Disgrace*'s penultimate scene may invite us to imagine the farm in the Eastern Cape as such a place, a place where the difficulties of cultural translation may be overcome, wordlessly, by bodily experiences: pregnancy, field labor, the materiality of dwelling on the land. The scene, in short, hints at a newness that still eludes the descriptive language of its observer, who continues to rely on outmoded, foreign phrases, as in the Goethean reference to "das Ewig Weibliche" (D 218).[43]

Payback Time?

Disgrace is far more pessimistic than *Life and Times of Michael K.* Its vision of a society in which all is reduced to the circulation of goods—of "cars, shoes, cigarettes," and women, too (D 98)—and to a language of the most functional sort is not an appealing one. Yet, it does not, to judge by the lyrical penultimate scene, entirely lack the earlier novel's muted and vulnerable utopian yearnings. But even if we read the penultimate scene of *Disgrace* in this redemptive way (as I think we are lured into doing by the sheer poetry of the writing), we are not allowed to forget the darker implications of this violent novel, which are by no means exorcized by a lyrical description of fields of flowers. And to see Lucy Lurie's pregnancy in the way I have just proposed is to some degree to accept her deeply troubling notion that the rape is the price that she has to pay in order to continue to live on the land. If this is indeed the implication of the novel, the protests of many critics, including Coetzee's fellow writers Zoë Wicomb and Athol Fugard, are surely justified.

A more complex interpretation, however, emerges if we attend to the novel's peculiar fascination with animals, and especially to its ethically and emotionally complicated final scene: one that surely deserves as much emphasis as the more appealing penultimate scene. At the animal clinic where he has ended up working,

David Lurie assists in euthanizing a particularly endearing and affectionate dog whose life he could have saved, at least for a little while. It is an act redolent of betrayal but also, one obscurely senses, of a profound love and responsibility. And given the pastoral concerns that have been the focus of this chapter, one cannot fail to note that the last words of the novel, "Yes, I am giving him up" (D 220), are reminiscent of the radical renunciation announced a few pages earlier by Lucy Lurie as a precondition for living on the land. The new South Africa, she argues, may require whites to start over with nothing, "like a dog": "with no cards, no weapons, no property, no rights, no dignity" (D 205).

To make some sense of the ethos that seems to be proposed in the novel's final scene, it may help to bear in mind the etymology of one of the most fundamental words in the tradition of the pastoral and in the history of settlement in South Africa as well, namely, the word "farm." It derives, as Ampie Coetzee reminds us in his essay on the *plaasroman* and the discourse of land, from the Medieval Latin *firma*, which means not only "the confirmation of a document, the signature" (a definition already implied in my discussion of the Afrikaner's dream topography) but also a "fixed payment."[44] Now: the idea of payment and the concomitant ethos of monetary exchange, debt, ownership, and the like, is an extraordinarily important motif in Coetzee's work, even though it has in large measure escaped critical notice. If *Youth*, as I have argued at the beginning of this chapter, draws our attention anew to the importance of the politics of place in Coetzee's work, it also underscores the importance of economic themes. It is, I think, not insignificant that *Youth* opens with an account of the young John's frugal economies, his small earnings and ascetic expenditures. The memoir is not only about finding a place where one might live the life of an artist but also about calculating what such a life, a life of ostensible freedom, might actually cost. Such economic concerns as these are frequently present in Coetzee's (anti)pastoral texts. (*In the Heart of the Country*, for instance, is moved along to its strange conclusion when Magda vainly sends Hendrik to the bank to try to withdraw the money for his wages.) And the idea of the "fixed payment" that might be required to legitimate the settler's aesthetic enjoyment and use of the land is explicitly emphasized in both *Boyhood* and the Jerusalem Prize address. In *Boyhood*, the young John reflects on the price that he may have to "knuckle down and pay" in order to live on his uncle's Karoo farm, "the only place in the world he wants to be." It is, as he obscurely understands, an exacting price: to belong on Voëlfontein, he would have to sacrifice English for Afrikaans. He would have to become an Afrikaner, which, as he sees it, would mean that he would have to "stop asking questions, obey all the *mustn'ts*, just do as he was told" (B 91). He would also have to sacrifice the possibility of living outside the rigid grammar of deference and domination, which, as the fledgling linguist intuits, is part of the very sociolinguistic structures of the Afrikaans language. In the Jerusalem Prize speech, the payment is fixed at an even higher rate, and the sacrifices are more demanding. One cannot, Coetzee insists, enjoy the pleasures of fraternity, of that reciprocated love that can underpin and justify one's aesthetic love for the landscape, "without paying for it." And the price—"the very lowest price"—is the destruction of "the unnatural structures of power that define the South African state" (DP 97).

In *Disgrace*, the novel that emerges from a South Africa in which the old structures of power are being dismantled, the ethos of payment is a dominant concern. The novel's beautiful penultimate scene does not get us around this ethos: it instead suggests ways of accepting and aestheticizing it. It is only in the novel's final scene that one may detect an emerging ethos that is based on something other than a settling of accounts and the paying of a price. In refusing to single out the special dog, Lurie is accepting, perhaps helplessly, perhaps resolutely, the claims of an infinite number of other creatures with whom he has no special connection—who are neither his "own kind" (D 194) nor his historical victims.[45] To understand this gesture we have to bear in mind the disturbing phrase from *Jude the Obscure* (a reference to the suicide note of Jude's eldest child, who hangs himself and two of his siblings) that occurs to Lurie in an earlier meditation on the fate of the clinic's dogs: "*we are too menny*" (D 146). The final scene seems to recognize the claims of the "menny"—too many—suffering others. They are all equally urgent, and they are by definition excessive and incalculable; yet we seem to be obscurely bound to these forgotten creatures, even if they happen to be, in Lucy Lurie's words, nowhere "on the list of the nation's priorities" (D 73). The impossible ethical obligations Coetzee seems to gesture toward in the novel's final scene have nothing whatsoever to do with kinship, labor, ownership, or debts—or anything else that can be made sense of in the moral economy of the colonial or postcolonial pastoral. But it is in this manner that he seems, ultimately, to respond to the "new South Africa," with its surface moral pieties and its deep-seated sense that payback time has at last arrived.

Though *Disgrace* does not entirely divest itself of the longing for rural life, it seems to move far beyond the concerns of Coetzee's earlier engagements with the pastoral. The closing gesture is not an expression of the same restrained and deferred utopian impulse that marked the lyrical ending of *In the Heart of the Country* and *Life and Times of Michael K.* It is rather one that projects us into a wholly new and discomfiting ethical frame. The new South Africa is no utopia: it is rather the site of a painful othering, whose conditions and terms will no longer, or so Coetzee seems to sense, be articulated adequately in relation to matters of land and rural life. *Disgrace*, therefore, marks, I will riskily predict, Coetzee's farewell to the genre that absorbed so much of his critical attention and creative energy in the first half of his career.

2

LEAVING THE HOUSE OF THE WHITE RACE

> The traditional residences we grew up in
> have grown intolerable: each trait of com-
> fort in them is paid for with a betrayal of
> knowledge, each vestige of shelter with the
> musty pact of family interests.
>
> —Theodor Adorno, *Minima Moralia*

> A woman relates, "As a girl I always wished
> that burglars would come."
>
> —Ernst Bloch, *The Principle of Hope*

The Transport of the Novel

Compared to the experimental and metafictional writing of her compatriots
J. M. Coetzee and Ivan Vladislavić, Nadine Gordimer's novels may seem straightforwardly realist—more so than they actually are. For there are frequent moments
in Gordimer's work when, without entirely breaking the realist frame, she engages
in a self-reflexive meditation on the meaning, form, and reception of fiction.[1]
One such moment occurs in the 1981 novel *July's People*, set in an imagined future
of revolution and civil war. It is a scene of reading—a scene that tells us much
about how we, in turn, may read the concerns that engage and the conditions that
shape Gordimer's writing. The novel's main character, Maureen Smales, who only
days before had been living the life of a comfortable Johannesburg suburbanite,
is sitting outside a hut in the impoverished African village to which she and her
family have hastily fled under the protection of their erstwhile servant, July. Surrounding Maureen is the bush, a terrain so vast and disorienting that she scarcely
dares to venture beyond a few landmarks, which are themselves disconcertingly
unfamiliar: a few huts, a goat kraal, a chicken coop made of dead branches and
twigs. To while away the time, Maureen has tried to interest herself in the thick
book she grabbed before leaving the city: Alessandro Manzoni's historical novel
I Promessi Sposi, in translation as *The Betrothed*. She discovers, however, that the act
of reading has somehow been emptied out as a result of her displacement: "The

transport of a novel, the false awareness of being within another time, place, and life that was the pleasure of reading, for her, was not possible. She was in another time, place, consciousness; it pressed upon her and filled her as someone's breath fills a balloon's shape. She was already not what she was. No fiction could compete with what she was finding she did not know, could not have imagined or discovered through imagination" (JP 29). Fiction, as this passage suggests, is profoundly intermeshed with questions of location. Maureen's condition, caught as she is in a kind of ontological and epistemological no-man's-land between "back there" and "out here," is also the condition of the novel—especially if that novel is, as in this case, a historical novel being read in translation.

The keyword here is "transport," and the passage plays on both its literal and figurative senses. Literally, Manzoni's book has been transported remarkably well from Milan and across the centuries to wind up in Maureen's hands amid the chickens and the thorn trees. But the figurative transports of literature are presented as much less mobile. (In this respect, the passage could be read as an ironic comment on those popular speculations about which favorite book or record one would like to have along if one were to be shipwrecked on a desert island.) The novel's meaning and value prove to be as unstable as the meaning and value of the brass "BOSS BOY" armband from the gold mines that Maureen discovers in an abandoned hut. The achievement these objects represent does not necessarily make sense in different circumstances. Maureen's own geographical translation makes the imaginative effort required by reading—by that "false awareness of being in another place"—seem puny in comparison to the effort required by the mere cognition of the here and now. The ordinary and unconscious act of mapping the world (which we could describe, in Althusser's famous formula, as "the representation of the subject's Imaginary relationship to his or her Real conditions of existence") has suddenly become a conscious and difficult task.[2] In Maureen's circumstances, novel reading becomes impossible because two even more fundamental fictions—ideology and subjectivity—have been revealed as geographically contingent. Indeed, the influence of place is conceived here in a surprisingly direct way: "who one is," Gordimer suggests, is shaped by one's physical and social environment in the same way that air pressure determines the shape of a balloon.

There is a certain logic, consistent with a substantial body of Gordimer's writing, in the fact that the passage I have cited should flow seamlessly into a description of the disturbing poverty Maureen discovers in the village women's huts. For Gordimer's work frequently suggests that the act of reading—not to mention the subjectivity of the reader—is grounded in domestic space, in one's conception of what is "normal" and one's sense of "home" or "here." She has often observed that for someone growing up in a South African mining town (someone like Maureen Smales in *July's People* or Helen Shaw in *The Lying Days*, or, for that matter, Gordimer herself), the most ordinary English domestic fiction, with its references to nannies and nurseries and Christmas in winter, involves no less of a "transport . . . into an unattainable world of the imagination" than do "princes that changed into frogs" or "legendary castles" or "houses that could be eaten like gingerbread" (LD 10).[3] Though Maureen's experience in the wake of a revolution presents an extreme situation, it emphasizes a central theme in Gordimer's work: the situatedness of consciousness and culture, or, to borrow a phrase from the geographer John Western, "the dialectic of person and place."[4] In fact, Gordimer herself once described her most enduring intellectual preoccupation as an effort to see or find "the link between people and the place that has bred them" (EG 9).

In recent years, critics like Dominic Head and Johan Jacobs have begun to trace out some of the connections between Gordimer's work and new trends in critical human geography, and have productively related her novels to Michel Foucault's notion of the heterotopia and J. Hillis Miller's reflections on "figurative mapping."[5] Her work has also inspired one of the canonical essays in postcolonial theory: it is in response to her 1991 novel *My Son's Story* that Homi Bhabha formulates his conception of the "location of culture"—of the aesthetic as the site where the opposition between the private and the historical world is undone— and proposes a comparative methodology that would speak to the "unhomely condition of the modern world."[6] Earlier Gordimer critics, however, tended to treat the question of "place" in her work in fairly conventional terms, by focusing largely on the matter of landscape or "landscape iconography." Such approaches have tended to generate either overly romantic or overly prescriptive readings of the novels, as though the issue for Gordimer were a matter of whether or not a character can "identify" with an African landscape, or of whether or not the land-scape in which a given novel is set is described without recourse to European descriptive *topoi*.[7] The first of these notions is particularly problematic, it seems to me, in that it disregards the fact that the very idea of character is in Gordimer's work often a function of place: while Gordimer might speak fairly loosely in her interviews about landscape, or even a "sense of place," her fiction tends to trans-late such notions into a closely detailed, micropolitical exploration of sociospatial relations.[8] It is striking how deliberately and critically the various meanings of the word "place" are examined in her novels. In *Burger's Daughter*, for example, where the word is frequently emphasized by scare quotes, the protagonist observes that black South Africans tend not to use the expressions "my house" or "my home" but speak instead of "my place." "A 'place,'" or so Rosa Burger reflects, is "some-where to belong, but also something that establishes one's lot and sets aside much to which one doesn't belong" (BD 149). Even the casual usage of the word—as in "Fats's Place" or "Marisa's Place" (BD 149)—points to crucial political questions of identity, of inclusion and exclusion. It is fitting, then, that in a retrospective lec-ture of 1995 Gordimer should have described her cultural and political project as an effort to be "part of the *transformation of [her] place* in order for it to know [her]" (WB 130, Gordimer's italics). Her long career as a writer constitutes, in her own assessment, a continuous struggle to achieve a situation in which the self and her social space can be brought into a harmonious ethical alignment.

In *July's People*, the ambiguities of "place" are explicitly addressed. At one point in the novel, July tells Maureen that she should no longer go out to gather food in the veld with the women of village: "This is their place," he says, and she must not "work for them in their place" (JP 97). Maureen is baffled as to whether his objection relates to the matter of "territory" (as though she were staking a claim to land that is not hers) or to the matter of "role," of identity and conduct. The point is, of course, that these distinctions cannot really be drawn. "Role" and "territory" are inextricably conflated in the daily exercise of power, a conflation that is neatly expressed in an oppressive cliché: "One must know one's place." (Or in Afrikaans, where it seems even more quintessentially South African, " 'n mens moet sy plek ken.") Places are not just metaphorically expressive in Gordimer's work (as they almost always are in realist novels) but are also conceived of as ideologically productive: the ordinary enclosures in which we live shape, as much as they represent, dominant social relations.

My readings in this chapter are centered on one of the key sites for Gordimer's analysis of social space: the house or, more specifically, the white suburban home. This approach somewhat revises what is still, arguably, the dominant approach to Gordimer's work, which is to see it in terms of a linear "history from the inside": a narrative of political evolution from a liberal humanist optimism and confidence in the ability of individuals to "only connect" to a recognition of the ineffectuality of this position and, finally, to an identification with more revolutionary forms of political struggle.[9] But to read Gordimer's work with an interest in the spatial is to discover salient connections between texts and a persistent fascination with certain significant sites that have been underplayed in the diachronic conception of her work as responsive to the progression of historical events. These continuities and connections are particularly evident in Gordimer's semiautobiographical fiction: in novels like *The Lying Days* and *July's People* (the two texts I will discuss at greatest length in this chapter) and short stories like "The Termitary" and "Once Upon a Time." I use the term "semiautobiographical" rather loosely, to indicate texts with a female narrator or protagonist who either shares some of Gordimer's childhood experiences or who is explicitly identified as an author. My account of these texts will also return us to some metafictional questions about character, *Bildung*, genre, and the "transport" or locatedness of the text and the reader. All of these literary matters are affected, I will argue, by Gordimer's interest in the peculiarities of South Africa's political geography.

The Map of Human Relations

I would like to approach the matter of domestic space by contextualizing it historically and theoretically: with a brief discussion, first, of Gordimer's conception of public space, and second, of the broader geographical and cultural conditions that help to define her artistic practice. The 1963 essay "Great Problems in the Street" offers some key insights into her understanding of apartheid's effect on social space, and thus presents a useful starting point. The essay is in part a celebration of the idea of the street as the site of a certain democratic possibility. This is not to say that the South African city itself is imagined positively: Gordimer makes it perfectly clear that the city is a place where "fear regulate[s] every move and glance" (EG 54) and where laws forbid blacks from entering libraries, hotels, theaters, and other public buildings. Yet, because of these restraints, the street becomes politically potent: it is the one place where blacks and whites still move together. As such (and according to the aphorism by Nietzsche alluded to in the title of the essay) it is the place where "great problems" are to be confronted: the street is, one might say, where history takes place.

Such a confrontation, in Gordimer's view, occurred in the late 1950s and early 1960s, when the prohibitions and boundaries of the political system were challenged in a series of protest marches, the last of which was a demonstration against the banning of demonstrations. She describes the street where these marches were staged as a meeting place of opposites: "black and white, office cleaners and executives, young students from the University and old bums from the Library Gardens" (EG 55) are all brought together in a common cause. One may detect here what Irene Gorak has described as a libidinal investment in the idea of physical closeness—of diverse, jostling, "interpenetrating" bodies.[10] But a specifically political investment is also clear. For the street is also imagined as a discursive space, a space of debate, where the indifferent—those who only wish to go on "living pleasantly" in the sun (EG 52)—are compelled to engage with the committed, if only by glancing at a protest poster or overhearing snatches of a speaker's words. The street is thus a space of heterogeneous and heteroglossic encounter. It holds, in Gordimer's curiously theological phrase, "both the flesh and the word" (EG 54), a kind of utopian promise: a merging of bodies and political expression in a potent collective presence.

But "Great Problems in the Street," though it articulates this ideal, is in fact about its absence: it is an elegy of sorts for the disappearance of public space. At the time of its writing, there was already "silence in the streets," as Gordimer tell us at the end of the essay (EG 57). The government's draconian crackdown on resistance after the Sharpeville massacre, the banning, gagging, or house arrest of activists, and the passage of laws forbidding public meetings had effectively ensured that "great problems" would henceforth not be debated but "dropped into the dark cupboard" (EG 54)—forgotten and repressed. The streets, of course, still exist, but they are no longer imagined as collective: there is now a separation between body and word, between real and imagined social space. A white person, as Gordimer points out, might still be jostled by people who are different, but would be able to say that "they have nothing whatever to do with me." Instead of the expressive closeness of bodies, there is now an imposed division between the committed and the indifferent, between black and white, which Gordimer expresses in a compelling spatial metaphor: "a Sahara whose faint trails, followed by the mind's eye only, fade out in sand." Since this vast desert—extending, as she imagines it, right up to the edge of the "pretty suburban garden"—is not on "the map of human relations," most of South African social space comes to seem uncharted, almost nonexistent (EG 53).

There is, of course, a kind of potency in this trackless terrain, which we might regard as the site of much of Gordimer's fiction. (One thinks, for instance, of the early story "Is There Nowhere Else We Can Meet?" which describes a violent but strangely intimate encounter between a white woman and a black man in a deserted stretch of veld, just off a main road.)[11] Indeed, the idea of such unmapped territory recurs with great symbolic force some twelve years after the "Great Problems" essay in *Burger's Daughter*, when Rosa Burger encounters a man brutally whipping his donkey in a byway "that doesn't appear on the road-maps and provides access to 'places' that don't appear on any plan of city environs" (BD 207). But the point that I would underscore is that Gordimer conceives of her task as an effort to name and map those areas of the social topography that under apartheid became "points without name." It is significant that her own comments on the violent scene from *Burger's Daughter* suggest that the meaning of this encounter lies for her in the fact that through this experience, Rosa comes "to realize where she stands in her life": it forces her to locate herself in a politically meaningful way, precisely in relation to those places and those people the government would rather relegate to invisibility.[12]

The aesthetic project implicit here may be connected to the notion of cognitive mapping (an idea I will return to also in my reflections on Fugard). This term has gained critical currency primarily through Fredric Jameson's work on postmodernism, but it can usefully be applied in other contexts as well. "Cognitive mapping," as Jameson has disarmingly observed, is a term that many readers have found quite mysterious. This puzzlement is at least partly attributable to the fact that, as far as the postmodern world goes, Jameson offers no example of the practice, except implicitly his own work. But in abstract terms and as a kind of pedagogical and aesthetic desideratum, "cognitive mapping" is readily described: it is an attempt to name the system—to offer some kind of representation that might help individuals situate themselves with regard to the vast multinational networks of global capital.[13] I should specify straight away that "mapping" should not be taken too literally as a cartographic matter; nor is it necessarily mimetic. It gestures, rather, toward a mode of politically enabling interpretation. Indeed, Jameson has admitted on occasion that "cognitive mapping" might be taken as a code word for class consciousness, and it is this resonance of the term that I would like us, above all, to keep in mind. Yet there are reasons why late capitalism requires the specifically geographical thinking suggested by the term: the loss of historicity, the disorienting experience of postmodern hyperspace, and the displacement of sites of production and exploitation (theoretically the places where class consciousness might arise) to the less visible margins of the global system.

In this last respect, there is a significant continuity between postmodernism, or the cultural logic of multinational capitalism, and modernism, which Jameson has boldly conceptualized as the cultural logic of imperialism. Imperialism, he argues, already has the effect of a spatial and epistemological disjunction (an effect he thinks through only with respect to the consciousness of the metropolitan subject).[14] "A significant segment of the economic system," he observes, "is now located elsewhere, beyond the metropolis, outside the daily life and existential experience of the home country—in places whose experience and life remains unknown and unimaginable for the subjects of the imperial power."[15] The operations of empire thus connect the metropolitan subject, whose quotidian routines may be confined to, say, a small section of London, with many invisible others—with people working in India or Jamaica or Hong Kong; but the exact meaning of that connection remains for most people entirely obscure. The nature of imperialism is such that the relevant social spaces and structures that affect the very quality and character of daily life cannot really be known any longer through personal experience: "the truth of that experience no longer coincides with the place in which it takes place."[16] Imperialism in this sense creates the political unconscious of modernism. Part of the social totality remains structurally inaccessible; and the strange new artistic forms we associate with modernism are, for Jameson, the result of an unconscious and stylistic compensation for this epistemological incompleteness. The postcolonial situation represents, then, an important change, in that the unknown and repressed "others" of imperialism begin to speak: they become, in other words, subjects, who must be consciously registered as a problem by the metropolitan powers.

Jameson's account of modernism is, of course, boldly polemical and vulnerable to criticism on several fronts. For one thing, it rests axiomatically on the unfashionable Lukácsian assumption that the work of art is characterized by an "intention towards totality," however covert and unconscious that intention may be.[17] But one can certainly see ways in which this account might speak to the South African situation and might be suggestive especially with regard to white writers. For apartheid can surely be grasped as a deliberate and anachronistic perpetuation or reinvention of the spatial and epistemological distortions of imperialism within one country's borders. Needless to say, this geographical contrivance could never quite work: the presence of black South Africans could never be totally erased, either in official political discourse or in literary forms, in the way that the colonial subject is erased (in Jameson's account) in the imperial consciousness. Apartheid, to put it in Freudian terms, operated not so much by the mechanisms of psychosis (occlusion) as by the mechanism of neurosis (repression). It makes sense, then, that the fiction of white South Africans has so often adopted the mode Lars Engle has described as the political uncanny: a mode of writing that is precisely neurotic, perpetually engaged in recording the return of the repressed, in seeking out what lies at the limits of its own epistemological frame. It is a literature hovering, as a result of its peculiar geopolitical situation, between the colonial and the postcolonial, and arguably between the modern and the postmodern as well.[18]

Gordimer's work seems to me enormously significant in light of these considerations. One would obviously not wish to equate her work with that of the European modernists Jameson analyzes (though it is interesting that he should take E. M. Forster, a novelist who has deeply influenced Gordimer, as one of his key examples); nor would one want to equate apartheid with European imperialism.[19] Yet the connection is evident when Gordimer speaks of people who live in South Africa with a "colonial consciousness," an outlook that permits the (privileged and white) individual to "float on the surface of the society" and ignore the most fundamental social fact, "which [is] the overwhelming presence of black people."[20] Such experience, one might say, fails to "coincide with the place in which it takes place." We might observe, also, that like Jameson, Gordimer is a deeply sympathetic though idiosyncratic reader of Lukács, and that she assumes, like both theorists, that fiction is characterized by "an intention towards totality." As she puts it in a 1982 essay, "the revolutionary sense, in artistic terms, is the sense of totality, the conception of a 'whole' world, where theory and action meet in the imagination" (EG 142). Like Jameson, moreover, her conception of totality has not only a historical but also a geographical dimension. When asked in a 1983 interview what the task of "the novel as history" might be, Gordimer answered in a way that suggests the need for a kind of spatial demystification: "If you are living during a time when one portion of the population is extremely affluent and the other is very poor, the historical importance of [your] work of fiction would be to show how that extremely affluent group managed to justify their existence to themselves, never mind the world, while round the corner they knew there was a starving mob, and in their houses they had the daughter of a starving family scrubbing floors."[21] The novel, in other words, takes on the task of bringing to consciousness what is "round the corner" or even "in their houses"—whatever is placed (socially and spatially) where it can conveniently be ignored.

The Lying Days

"Where the pretty suburban garden ends, the desert begins" (EG 53): the topography evoked in "Great Problems in the Street" suggests rather succinctly why domestic space should be so important in Gordimer's work. The statement implies that the official "map of human relations" decreed by apartheid is, in fact, confined to the white suburban home, the very site from which it is virtually impossible to engage with "great problems"—with the real conditions of existence in South Africa. It is no accident, then, that Gordimer should describe her own process of political awakening in relation to domestic space: "First . . . you leave your mother's house, and later you leave the house of the white race."[22] The house is represented in her work as the quintessential colonial space; the most intimate of South Africa's many ideological enclosures. A cursory glance at the titles of her short stories confirms the centrality of the figure ("Home," "Safe Houses," "Inkalamu's Place," "Open House," "The Intruder," "Inhabitants of the Last Tree House"). And it is surely worth pondering the fact that her last novel from the apartheid era should conclude with the burning down of the family home.

It might seem curious that a system of racial exploitation should be thought through in terms of a site as apparently benign as, say, "a modest house with a bungalow face made of two bow-window eyes on either side of a front-door mouth," to cite a characteristic description from the story "The Termitary" (SE 114).[23] The brutality of Coetzee's labor camps in *Life and Times of Michael K* or the creeping capitalism of Doris Lessing's general store in *The Grass Is Singing* might seem more appropriately emblematic. But the fact is that apartheid was, from its very inception, mobilized around the idea of housing—that is, of racially segregated housing. Dr. D. F. Malan's election campaign in 1948 was centrally concerned with the perceived need to protect the white home against the *swart gevaar* (black danger) and, in more practical terms, to find the means of accommodating and controlling the thousands of black people who had flooded into the cities during World War II. The solution was, of course, the construction of the planned subeconomic townships outside the "white" urban areas, those grim places Gordimer describes so well in *The Conservationist*: "ridge after ridge of the prototype shelter that is the first thing little children draw; a box with a door in the middle, a window on either side, smoke coming out of the chimney" (C 24). If, as Engle has suggested, the so-called architects of apartheid (Malan and especially Verwoerd) presented their policies as a way of making South Africa *heimlich* for the white person, this *Heimlichkeit* had its uncanny double from the very start.[24] The comfortable suburban house, in both a historical and socially symbolic sense, was inseparably connected to its prototypical and repressed other: to the house in the township, a place that has remained unseen (perhaps even now) by many, if not most, white South Africans. From this perspective, Gordimer's first novel, *The Lying Days*, seems particularly shrewd in the way it explores the effects of the 1948 election by focusing on questions of urban and domestic space: it records the lack of adequate houses for black workers, the active development of new suburbs and apartment blocks for whites, and, most sinisterly, the invasion of domestic privacy—of peoples' bedrooms—through the Prohibition of Mixed Marriages Act of 1949.

But there is another and even more fundamental sense in which Gordimer's understanding of domestic space is political. It is in the house where everyday life is defined, where, as she argues in a 1977 essay, it is made to seem a fact of nature that "the black does not enter through the white's front door."[25] Her houses, especially those evoked in the semiautobiographical writings I am largely concerned with here, are clearly conceived of as ideological apparatuses, in very much the Althusserian sense of the term. They are the means by which individuals are "interpellated" as subjects: the means by which individuals are trained so that they will "know their places" in the social hierarchy, and so that, from these "places," they in turn will help to reproduce its structures.[26]

This conception of domestic space seems to me to hold true throughout Gordimer's writing career; however, *The Lying Days* explores these ideas more deliberately than any of her other texts (with the possible exception of *July's People*). It does so, moreover, in a way that forces us to rethink certain dismissive critical assessments of its political stance (as naïvely liberal in its views on race and as constrained in its historical engagement as a result of its emphasis on the protagonist's inner development).[27] The narrator Helen Shaw is aware, almost from the start of the novel, of the rather oppressive educational function of her family's home on the Atherton mining estate: "I too had my place," she observes, "the place of the Secretary's daughter . . . in the hierarchy" (LD 28–29). She notes also how concerned this social order is to reproduce itself: it is axiomatic on the mine estate that a girl's suitor must always be viewed against the "background of her own home," so that "if and by the time marriage resulted, he was already inculcated in the kind of life the girl's family had led and which, without question, he would be expected to lead with her, trooping off as ants go to set up another ant heap exactly like the one they have left" (LD 163). The family home in *The Lying Days* is clearly not designed to encourage autonomous development: it is, rather, a place where the "occupants" are somehow "subordinate" to the rooms (LD 179); a place where they do not exactly live, but where they are "presented to visitors as creatures without continuity . . . like actors placed in a stage-set" (LD 161)—and the significance of the word "place" and the idea of "roles" here should be evident.

Given the aim of social reproduction, moreover, it is intriguing that the houses in this novel are described in feminine terms: that their architectural flaws and excessive furnishings should be compared to women who try to hide their physical flaws behind makeup and curls (LD 110).[28] The house is imagined as an already-gendered mold that will form the female protagonist as a woman. More specifically, it seems designed to ensure that she will replicate her mother, a woman whose voice "come[s] out of the house like the voice of the walls" and whose views include stern notions about whom those walls should exclude: "natives," "Jews," all those who are "not our kind" (LD 17). It is significant, in this light, that in the very first chapter of *The Lying Days* we find Helen looking into the same mirror her mother often uses. She does so, however, not to reconfirm any sense of her own subjectivity; rather, she stares at her reflection until her face becomes "just a face like other people's faces met in the street" (LD 5). It is as though she deliberately seeks a kind of othering of the mother-like self she is compelled to adopt—as though she desires (unconsciously, at this point in the novel) to place herself outside the house and in what is always for Gordimer the archetypal public space.

The ideological interpellation effected by the suburban home, of course, is not entirely irresistible, and insofar as the novel's protagonist tries to "mak[e] [her] own life" in the city of Johannesburg instead of "taking it ready-made" (LD 173), *The Lying Days* is a *Bildungsroman* of sorts. But it is at least equally a critique of the form: Gordimer's conception of the spatial contingency of subjectivity—of the subordination of the self to walls, if you will—undermines the sense of accretive personal growth and cumulative development that is conventionally associated with the genre. As Judie Newman has observed, Helen's conception of "the real me" (LD 322) seems to shift depending on whether the narrator is at home with her parents on the mining estate or in Johannesburg with her lover; she even concludes her story by underscoring the fragmentariness of the "thousand different images" that have made up her life (LD 339).[29] It is possible to read this fragmentariness from a feminist point of view and argue, as Newman does, that the novel records the elusiveness of coherent individuality and autonomous development for a woman in patriarchal society. But also implicit in Newman's reading is the further idea that such development is impeded in the social world of this novel by the incommensurability of the different social spaces in which the narrator must operate—whether it be the mining estate with its marked divide between the dangerous work that goes on underground and the trivial social life aboveground, or the city with its vast gap between the liberated life around the university and the constraints of poverty in the outlying townships. *Bildung*, or so the novel seems to suggest, is hard to achieve in a country where a person's various roles and places are so remote from each other and are yet so powerfully determinant. Indeed, the fact that the novel is divided into three sections, "The Mine," "The Sea," and "The City," could be seen as structurally underscoring this point.

It makes sense, then, that Helen's final crisis, which leads to her resolve to go overseas, should be so oddly exteriorized. After witnessing the death of a protester in the township, she does nothing for weeks but sit on the balcony of her lover's apartment, watching the construction of a new apartment block on the next lot.

Once this building is completed, its framework filled with bricks and glass and paint, her decision is announced without the revelation of any inner motivation: "It came to me, quite simply, as if it had been there, all the time" (LD 307). This peculiarity is explicable in the light of the novel's rather pessimistic thematic engagement with the spatial contingency of subjectivity. In Gordimer's treatment of this crisis, the narrative of Helen's inner development appears to have been replaced by the more literal development of the apartment block; *Bildung* is displaced (the pun seems hinted at by the text) by a building.

The determinant relation between place and subjectivity is profoundly implicated also in the novel's treatment of racial inequality. These issues come to the fore most pointedly midway through the novel, when Helen is studying at the university and begins to take an interest in a fellow student, a black woman named Mary Seswayo. (This part of the narrative, I should note, takes place around 1947, before the passage of the ironically named Extension of University Education Act, which barred black students from most of the white universities.) Their first encounter, significantly, occurs in front of the mirror in the campus cloakroom, where Helen imagines that she sees in Mary a kind of recognition, if not a reflection, of herself: "What I saw on her face was what was on my own" (LD 89–90). This imagined identification, which Robin Visel has read as a misguided effort on the part of the colonizing woman to "self" the "other," is not immediately ironized in the text.[30] But it is certainly put into doubt by subsequent events— especially those relating to matters of social space. Helen becomes increasingly aware of the political constraints imposed on Mary's movements. She is perturbed, in particular, by what she imagines to be the difficulty of reading—as Mary must read—amid the "overwhelmingly physical life of the townships" (LD 168). How does one grasp the structure of a novel, the elegance of Shakespearean dialogue, or that ostensibly self-evident "meaning of meaning," she wonders, in a place where "the woman [is] making mealie porridge over the fire, the man [is] carefully preserving the dirty bit of paper that is his pass, the children [are] playing for a few years before they become nursegirls and houseboys" (LD 168)? The ironic contrast between the (literal) mobility of cultural texts and the lack of physical and social mobility of human beings is deliberately emphasized here.

Yet Helen's proposed remedy for Mary's situation is ill-considered and merely underscores the problem of sociospatial inequality. She asks her mother's permission to invite Mary to stay with them during the exam period so that she can have a quiet space to work; however, as a concession to her mother's racist views, she suggests that Mary could sleep in her old playroom—now a storage space—in the back yard. This embarrassingly patronizing suggestion (which her mother angrily rejects) forces a reevaluation of Helen's mirroring experience. As her friend, Joel Aaron, shrewdly guesses, Helen's fantasy identification with the black woman reveals a self-serving dimension: it has much to do with an effort to define her own difference from her mother: "to prove [her] enlightenment as opposed to [her mother's] darkness" (LD 107). The cloakroom incident, I would argue, already hints at the grounds for Gordimer's later suspiciousness of an easy universalizing feminism in the South African context of racial inequality. It suggests, moreover, the irrelevance of Helen's newly found liberal notions. For all her good intentions, she cannot individually provide the space in which Mary can actually move and live as her equal (and Mary, who is angry when she learns of this scheme, recognizes all too well that she would not be visiting as a friend in the house). If, as a white woman, Helen is constrained by the "nice little home" (LD 224) in which she is expected to end up, Mary is relegated, even by a well-meaning fellow student, to a makeshift enclosure outside of "normal" society: to "a place for things that had no place" (LD 168). The playroom-cum-storage-shed allegorizes the idea that there is no space provided, outside the servants' quarters, for the development of a woman like Mary.

Far more important, however, than this rather crudely symbolic site is that "other place": the black township (or the "location," as it was still called at the time of the novel). *The Lying Days*, like Gordimer's later novels, describes the townships in terms that correspond to a remarkable degree with Foucault's notion of the heterotopia. This term identifies certain peculiarly significant sites that, while they do exist in society (they are not utopian—"no place"—like the gingerbread houses and legendary castles of Helen's childhood reading), nonetheless have the curious property of "suspect[ing], neutraliz[ing], or invert[ing]" the set of relations that they happen to designate, mirror, or reflect."[31] The heterotopia, one might say, is simultaneously a representation and a contestation of the "normal" spaces of a given society. This kind of space is introduced in a crucial scene in which Helen and another companion take Mary Seswayo to her home in the location of Mariastad. As is characteristic in this novel, the emphasis is again on architectural structures and on domestic space. But what is particularly significant is the way the township is described as a compressed and disordered version of the white suburb or the mine estate; indeed, in the oldest part of the township, where Helen and her companion eventually get lost, the "closeness of the place, the breath-to-breath, wall-to-wall crowding" produces a disconcerting sense that "all bounds had disappeared" (LD 157). *The Lying Days*, it would seem, already presents the township in terms Gordimer would elaborate much later in *Burger's Daughter*: as a place "where definitions fail," "where functions lose their ordination and logic" (BD 149–150). The effect of this confusing and claustrophobic diminution is evident with regard to individual structures within the township as well. The tiny chapel, for instance, seems to be the "utter simplification" of all that has accreted through the ages around "the architectural idea of a church," and the houses—"each as big as a tool shed"—are so cramped that the conventional organization of domestic space seems to have been imploded (LD 155). Helen notes with naïve and shocked surprise how the lack of space results in a completely incongruous arrangement of furniture: dining chairs may be pressed up against a bed, and a piano may stand in the kitchen. This rearrangement of the home forces her to redefine her very concept of living ("living," that is, as shaped by familiar architectural structures, by the normative walls of her mother's house): "There were not enough rooms for each to serve one designation—dining room, bedroom, kitchen—they were all simply living rooms in the plainest sense, whether you must work, or cook, or sleep, or make love" (LD 156).

Helen tries, at first, to construct an image of Mary's house (which she never gets to see) from the minimalist details she observes around her, in the way that an archaeologist might recreate an "atmosphere" by restoring "arms, trinkets, drinking vessels to [an] excavated city" (LD 157). But this safe-making response to the otherness of poverty is shattered by the appearance of a single, strangely potent figure: a "neat girl with an ordinary white enamel jug fetching some water for herself" (LD 157) at a communal tap. If "Mary's house" becomes the domestic heterotopia (both the mirror image and the contradiction of the mother's house), the young girl seems to function as the mirror image and the contradiction of Helen herself. This figure reintroduces social space—"the everyday living out of our lives"—into the narrator's conception of this "other" city. The result is that she loses all her epistemological confidence: "At this the grasp of my imagination . . . let go. She, too, came with a jug for water to a tap in the mud. So in how many other commonplaces that I take for granted in my own life shall I be wrong in hers?" (LD 157). The effect of poverty on every aspect of quotidian existence ("the water that must be fetched from the tap in the street, the physical closeness of . . . the lives of others" [LD 157], and so forth) strikes Helen with such overwhelming force that the very idea of a universal "formula" of human emotions and belief, the essence of her newly liberal attitude, is destroyed. Now, when she thinks about Mary Seswayo, she imagines not a mirror in front of them, but a wall between them, over which she can only barely see her friend.

   The Lying Days thus already asserts the exactingly materialist perspective that resurfaces some thirty years later in *July's People*. The thematic core of the later novel—that the universal and "*absolute* nature" (Gordimer's italics) of even such basic human experiences as love or death is illusory, that experience and consciousness are radically altered by the subject's "place in the economy" (JP 65)—is already implicit in the Mariastad scene. It is "out of [our houses]," as Helen Shaw suggests, that we "love, want, and believe" (LD 157); and in an unjust society, these houses may be disturbingly different. This early awareness of the situatedness of consciousness—of the dialectic of person and place—in *The Lying Days* thus pushes Gordimer's work beyond a liberal humanist position from the very start. It also forces a redefinition of the idea of *Bildung*: the autonomous evolving subject seems a rather tenuous construct in the emerging apartheid society that is the context of Gordimer's first novel.

Breaking Open Daily Life

It is important, as my reading thus far would suggest, that we consider Gordimer's interest in the house and in domestic space in a fairly literal-minded way, in terms of a set of walls enclosing certain kinds of spaces, people, and objects. But the house also functions in her fiction, especially in some of her short stories, as what J. M. Coetzee calls a dream topography: the spatial expression of a certain wishful and often deceptive fiction about the world. We might again recall Lars Engle's theoretical description of apartheid in terms of the idea of the *heimlich*—an interpretative scheme that relies on strict spatial and conceptual boundaries, on inclusion and exclusion. The *Heim*, as he puts it "is a reminder, to those within it facing out, of their own security, fixity, stable meaning, knowledge of what matters."[32]

In Gordimer's fiction, the "house of the white race" is characteristically the place where "mother . . . like[s] to have 'everything nice'" (LD 161). The opening of the story "The Life of the Imagination," from the 1971 collection *Livingstone's Companions* develops this conception in wonderfully ironic detail.[33] The "comfortable, orderly house" in this story is "a place where whether the so-and-sos would fit in at dinner, and whose business it was to see that the plumber was called, and whether the car should be traded in or overhauled were the daily entries in a ledger of living"; it is a place where nightmares "never overstep the threshold of morning" and where sexuality (which, of course, might not be entirely "nice") is reduced to "good-night kisses as routine as the cleaning of teeth" (LC 107). The home is, most importantly, as the narrator of "The Termitary" puts it, the place "where nothing ever happens" (SE 114).[34] For Gordimer, such a hermetic enclosure of niceness is a dangerous political fantasy; the routines it ensures are the temporal equivalent of the geographical delusion that Joel Aaron identifies when he suggests that he lives "not in Africa" but at "129 Fourth Street Atherton" (LD 129). Her fiction, as Engle has argued, therefore performs a task comparable to that of psychoanalysis (a practice Freud himself associated with the uncanny). It renders the mind, or the home, or the polity uneasy—uncertain as to its own contents: *unheimlich*.

This point is expressed most directly in "Once Upon a Time," from *Jump*, Gordimer's collection of short fiction published during the turbulent time of the transition. The style of this satirical fairy tale is deliberately uncharacteristic: the opening of the story, narrated *in propria persona*, offers a retort to someone who kept asking Gordimer to write a story for children. But the narrative could be regarded as finally revealing the blueprint for her apartheid-era fiction. The "bed-time story," as she calls it, begins as follows:

> In a house, in a suburb, in a city, there were a man and his wife who loved each other very much and were living happily ever after. They had a little boy, and loved him very much. They had a cat and a dog that the little boy loved very much. They had a car and a caravan trailer for the holidays, and a swimming-pool which was fenced so that the little boy and his playmates would not fall in and drown. They had a housemaid who was absolutely trustworthy and an itinerant gardener who was highly recommended by the neighbours. (J 25)[35]

In "Once Upon a Time," however, the state of vacant domestic happiness is sealed off from unpleasant and unpredictable things—from those things, precisely, that mark the turbulent historical context of this apparently timeless fantasy: loafers and *tsotsis*, buses being burned, cars being stoned, and children being shot down by policemen. The home, we learn, is diligently guarded by insurance policies, medical benefits, neighborhood watches, burglar alarms, and finally by a vicious-looking razor-wire fence, installed by those ultimate purveyors to the paranoid: "DRAGON'S TEETH: The People for Total Security" (J 29). The company's name, which calls to mind Coetzee's epigraph to *White Writing*, aptly expresses the idea that the quest for "security" only produces further instability and violence.

This idea is made explicit in the narrative when the little boy, inspired by the storybook he got for Christmas, imagines himself to be Prince Charming making his way through the thorns and manages to get himself torn to shreds in the metallic thicket of coils atop the garden wall. This painful outcome is certainly legible as a sardonic comment on the inappropriateness of imported cultural forms—of those utopian, "no-place" fictions that, as Gordimer often implies, offer a poor guide to living in Africa. But the idea of the fairy tale (as I will suggest again later) seems to rise up in Gordimer's work whenever the assumptions of a spatially defined normality are put to the test. And in this case, the narrative conventions of the fairy tale serve to underscore Gordimer's most salient satirical point: it is impossible to live "happily ever after" because this is, after all, the formula of (en)closure, beyond which nothing happens. The apparently innocuous title "Once Upon a Time," the phrase that traditionally sets events in motion, foredooms the nice home—the final holdout of a "colonial consciousness." "Once Upon a Time," in this sense, reduces Gordimer's many narratives about invaders and intruders (e.g., "An Intruder," "The Life of the Imagination," "Correspondence Course," "Open House," and, most importantly, *The Conservationist*) to their most basic formula. There is no literal intruder here; instead, the intruder is narrative itself: the irruption of the unpredictable and the diachronic—the invasion of an ostensibly risk-proofed private space by history. We may now grasp the reason for the recurrence (with only slight variations) of a simple but extremely significant phrase in Gordimer's work: "Something has happened," the young narrator rejoices when her home life is disrupted in "The Termitary" (SE 114); "We think something is happen," announces a farm worker at the final crisis of *The Conservationist* (C 260); "I am the place in which something has occurred," declares the epigraph to *Burger's Daughter*; and "When it all happened" elliptically captures the moment of revolution in *July's People* (JP 9).

The narrative formula I have discussed would suggest that Gordimer, like many radical thinkers, tends to privilege history over geography, time over space: that the former is associated for her with change and life, and the latter with immobility and fixedness. But there are also moments in her work when change, even revolutionary change, is figured or experienced as a new kind of spatial practice.[36] "The Termitary," from the collection *Soldier's Embrace*, strikes me as a case in point. Published shortly before *July's People* and strongly reminiscent of Gordimer's essays on her childhood and of *The Lying Days*, the story begins with a series of memories about the repairmen who would visit the "modest bungalow" described earlier. It recalls, in particular, a crew of rather seedy exterminators called in to get rid of a termite colony whose underground habitation is undermining the foundations of the house. It is no accident that the exterminators should be the most interesting intruders, more so than the painters or the plumbers or the doctor. Their visit is singular, unprecedented; and their search for the hidden queen under the floorboards of the living room reveals the subterranean secrets of the home, the strange tunnels and passages that are "buried" by the house. The narrator presents these disruptive archeological activities as exciting and welcome; the revelation of the dark African earth under Axminster is experienced as a kind of liberation. The carefully crafted opening paragraph emphasizes, moreover, how spatial changes can disrupt the behaviors and appearances of everyday life:

> When you live in a small town far from the world you read about in municipal library books, the advent of repair men in the house is a festival. Daily life is gaily broken open, improvisation takes over. The livingroom masquerades as a bedroom while the smell of paint in the bedroom makes it uninhabitable. The secret backs of confident objects (matchwood draped with cobwebs thickened by dust) are given away when furniture is pulled to the centre of the room. Meals are picnics at which table manners are suspended because the first principle of deportment drummed into children by their mother—sitting down at table—is missing: there is nowhere to sit. People are excused eccentricities of dress because no one can find anything in its place. (SE 114)

The key to this passage surely lies in the idea of the festival, which in the work of such theorists as Henri Lefebvre and Mikhail Bakhtin evokes an alternative social order and a rupture of normal social and spatial relations.

It would be heavy-handed to read this story as a political allegory *tout court*, though there is a suggestion of collective and subversive action in the termites' "million jaws" devouring the very "timber that supports our unchanging routines" (SE 116). But "The Termitary" is reminiscent of other moments in Gordimer's work where the political intent is more obvious. The most striking connection, perhaps, is with the apparently autobiographical opening of "Once Upon a Time." Here Gordimer (or the narrator) is startled in the middle of the night by the creaking of the floorboards of her house. It is not an intruder, as she at first fears, but the house itself buckling and shifting. Her home, she reminds herself, is undermined, not by insects, but by men: by black men working the gold reefs thousands of feet below the bed, the floor, and the house's foundations—the repressed economic base on which the privileged enclosures of the suburbs precariously stand. Another kind of breaking open of daily life is hinted at in "The Termitary" by the references to the termite colony's mysterious nuptial flight, which comes to fascinate the narrator. (She even gets the Afrikaans poet Eugène Marais's classic study *The Soul of the White Ant* out from the library.) This rare, sudden, and unpredictable bursting forth of what was hidden in underground tunnels is also evoked as a kind of festival, "another event"; and, once again, the intertextual connections suggest a possible political subtext to what appears to be in "The Termitary" a simple childhood recollection. In *The Conservationist* "the winged ants floating out of the ground" (C 203), mentioned briefly in one of the novel's most lyrical passages, could be seen as one in a series of symbolically charged events or images that prophetically challenge the white farmer's hold on the African soil. (The most important of these, as we shall see in the next chapter, is the dead body of a black trespasser that portentously floats up out of the ground at the novel's climax.) While we must be careful not to overinterpret this intriguing entomological detail (lest we parody the idea of a micropolitics), it would appear that the white ant's nuptial flight hints for Gordimer at the possibility of a revolutionary rupture of the status quo: a dramatic (re)emergence of what was buried brought forth by a combination of circumstances for which "no one knows the formula" (C 203).

July's Place

The possibilities and difficulties of a radical reconfiguration of the quotidian are explored more fully and rigorously in *July's People*. This novel, as several of Gordimer's critics have noted, examines with a rather hard-nosed unsentimentality the proposition that the most fundamental experiences of life—love, death, sex, the acquisition of a sense of identity—are economically determined. But what has not yet been fully described is the sustained fashion in which the novel represents economic power and social hierarchy in spatial terms.[37] The novel's premise, a logical extension of the ideas I have examined thus far, could be articulated as follows: if political hegemony is experienced and reinforced territorially, then the same would be true of revolution—an event that the novel figures very precisely as the destruction of all established places. "An explosion of roles," the protagonist reflects at one point, "that's what the blowing up of the Union Building and the burning of master bedrooms is" (JP 117). Revolution is conceptualized in *July's People* as an architectural matter: it is the exchange of a seven-roomed suburban house with a swimming pool for a thatched hut with mud walls. Though this enterprise might seem slightly absurd (especially in my oversimplified formulation), it is appropriate that Gordimer should explore both the beginning of the apartheid era (in *The Lying Days*) and its imagined end (in *July's People*) in terms of domestic space. We must remember, moreover, that for Gordimer quotidian spaces define the very fabric of people's lives: "place," as she puts it in the novel, "alters the way of dealing with [an] experience; and so the experience itself" (JP 65). The emphasis on built structures and spatial relations that characterizes *July's People* should, therefore, not be regarded as reified, or contrary to historicist thinking. Historicization (a word Bertolt Brecht regarded as a synonym for "estrangement") is not so much a matter of representing the past (or, in this case, the future) as of perceiving the present as history. It involves, first and foremost, a defamiliarization—effected in Gordimer's novel through a geographical displacement—that allows one to see the quotidian practice of class society as unnatural and unjust.[38]

July's People's oft-cited epigraph from Gramsci's *Prison Notebooks* (which defines revolution temporally as an "interregnum" in which "the old is dying and the new cannot be born") is perhaps best regarded as something of a red herring. For the novel's examination of revolution in terms of a spatial defamiliarization seems much more Benjaminian than Gramscian—especially if we recall Benjamin's famous definition of revolution as the pulling of the emergency brake. Revolution is, from this perspective, an end to the "catastrophic" fact that "things just keep on going"—a derailing of the so-called progress of civilization from the routine tracks of ordinary bourgeois life.[39] Such a radical disruption of the everyday is precisely what occurs in the lives of the Smales family, whose translation from their familiar geography is so abrupt that their sense of time is thrown into disarray. Their flight, Gordimer tells us, takes them so far beyond "the norm of a present" that they are "jolted out of chronology" (JP 3–4). This experience finds an evocative emblem in one of the significant objects (others are a book, a gun, and a truck) that the family brings along with them to the bush: a little boy's toy racing car, which without any electricity can no longer speed along its fancy system of tracks.

The effects of this sudden rearrangement of a "habitual set of circumstances" (JP 6) are dramatized in the novel's opening scene, in which July brings the Smales family their breakfast tea on the first morning after their flight to his village. The description turns around the repeated phrase "a knock on the door." It is a phrase with a certain apocalyptic and biblical resonance, suggestive of a decisive moment of change; but in this passage, the knock is associated instead with the old and only recently defunct routines. The arrival of a morning tea tray held in black hands would "normally" (a word this novel puts under erasure) have announced the hour of seven all over white South Africa: in "governor's residences, commercial hotels, shift bosses' company bungalows, master bedrooms en suite" (JP 1). In these rooms, which metonymically represent the spheres of government, commerce, industry, and private life, the knock on the door is entirely unremarkable. It merely reinforces the conventional and political determinations of who should be inside and who outside, or—to put it in the terms suggested by the novel's opening sentence—of whose "kind" does what for whose "kind." But when these places and the power structure they define are destroyed, when there is no longer a dividing door on which to knock (the hut has only "an aperture in mud walls" [JP 1]), these old determinations seem to fall away. July's position and identity ("their servant, their host" [JP 1]) is suddenly indefinable. It is this change that *July's People* grasps as revolutionary, even if it is accompanied not by gunfire or rockets but, as in this scene, by the "gentleness, ordinariness" (JP 2) of the faint cheeping of chicks.

A related point is made in one of the novel's most intriguing flashbacks, one that returns us to the topography of the generic Transvaal gold-mining town that figures so prominently in Gordimer's memories of her own childhood. Maureen Smales recalls the experience of discovering, in a *Life* coffee-table book about South Africa and its racial policies, a photograph of herself as a child standing at an intersection with her family's maid, Lydia. By implicitly presenting this image of "the white school girl and the black woman with the girl's school case on her head" as typical of "white herrenvolk attitudes and lifestyles" (JP 33), the book reduces the complexity of what seems to be an affectionately conspiratorial relationship between the two. Yet the sudden encounter with this disconnected fragment of her life in the estranging context of an overseas publication enables Maureen to ask a simple question that had somehow not occurred to her before: "Why had Lydia carried her case?" (JP 32–33). Though the point is not made directly, the novel's detailed description of the trajectory of their habitual walk (from the bus stop, through the intersections at the local shops, to the house in the married quarters behind the recreation hall) suggests that there is something about the very familiarity of this terrain that has obscured certain truths about their relationship. It makes perfect sense, then, that Maureen should recall the experience of discovering the photograph as she struggles to reinvent her life in an entirely unfamiliar context. The question she asks herself about Lydia prefigures the many disconcerting questions about places and roles that suddenly arise in July's village, a place so distant and "other" that the Smales's old cognitive maps no longer seem adequate.

This defamiliarization of bourgeois domesticity is an experience that the novel's readers (and Gordimer always writes for an educated international audience) are at certain moments in the text made to share. The shifting point of view allows the reader to be privy to the thoughts of villagers—notably July's wife, Martha—from whose perspective the spaciousness and privacy of the suburban house appears unimaginable, if not laughable:

> A room to sleep in, another room to eat in, a room with books (she had a Bible), I don't know how many times you told me, a room with how many books. . . . Hundreds I think. And hot water that is made like the lights we see in the street at Vosloosdorp. All these things I've never seen, my children have never seen— the room for bathing—and even you [July], there in the yard had a room for yourself for bathing, and you didn't even wash your clothes in there, there was a machine in some other room for that. (JP 19)

The passage recalls and decisively inverts the Mariastad scene from *The Lying Days* in which the white narrator views the cramped spaces of the township's subeconomic homes, where there are no rooms set aside for specific activities, with an equally ignorant astonishment. Both passages are concerned with spatial definitions of ordinary life; but in *July's People*, despite the fact that the novel is largely written from Maureen's point of view, the white suburban definition of ordinariness is no longer exclusive or normative. The importance of this passage (which, incidentally, works on exactly the same principles as do the Russian Formalists' classic examples of defamiliarization in the fiction of Tolstoy) should not be underestimated. It demonstrates the novel's broad thematic preoccupation with a radical decentering—an epistemological unhousing—of white South Africa.[40]

July's People, then, like "The Termitary," is concerned with the idea of breaking open daily life and, through this rupture, it enables us to see the way relations of power and privilege are inscribed in the apparently innocent spatiality of the quotidian. But there is also a crucial difference between these texts' treatment of the idea: a difference that is sharply revealed by their shared imagery. In "The Termitary," the furniture is shifted around and the bedrooms are temporarily rendered uninhabitable; but in *July's People*, all the familiar "furniture of life" (JP 3) has been abandoned. The master bedroom (along with the position of social and interpretative mastery it represents) is no longer there. The novel, moreover, confronts the fact that, while revolution may be allegorized as a holiday or a festival, it is, in fact, neither: fundamental social change cannot be thought through merely in terms of a break or a rupture. The Smaleses, after all, are not entirely lacking in experience of the African bush where they have been stranded: Maureen has slept in a hut during family vacations in the Kruger Park; Bam has been out in the bush for hunting trips; and the family has eaten coarsely ground mealie meal bought at a health food shop. But the assumption underpinning these earlier experiences is that they are special, a change of routine, since "at the end of the holiday you packed up and went back to town" (JP 147). The permanent break, however, is an aporia of sorts: a contradiction that cannot really be imagined as long as one holds to any norm of everyday life or of "home."

These ideas are pointedly raised in a conversation between Maureen and her husband Bam, in the course of which she admits that she had once entertained the fanciful notion that the family might one day take a trip to see where July lived—as a kind of safari-style holiday. The contrast between her imagined visit and her actual experience at July's place is striking—and it is not just a matter of the real villagers' failure to stand in line and clap their hands, as they obligingly do in the imagined scenario. The very idea of a "visit," as the passage in question suggests, already equips one in a certain way: not just with the convenience of the "camping stuff" and "portable fridge" but also with the comfort of a tourist's interpretative framework. Thus Maureen imagines herself explaining to her children: "This is his home, this is how he lives. See how cleverly July builds a house for himself" (JP 38). The patronizing and self-congratulatory tolerance of difference expressed in this little lecture clearly relies on a secure sense of self—of "our" place versus "his" place. The visit is fun only because it is framed by the social space of bourgeois life; and it is no wonder that the point of Maureen's fantasy seems to have lain in talking about it, afterward, "to everybody at home" (JP 38).

The ironies set up by this passage are resonant. Not least of these is the fact that, once they actually have to live in the house that July (so cleverly) built, the Smaleses no longer seem able to use the pronoun "we": "Us and them," Bam Smales thinks at one point, "Who is us, now, and who them?" (JP 117).[41] Maureen, moreover, has profound difficulties in adjusting to the new domestic "normality" of July's place. Like Helen Shaw in *The Lying Days*, she seems at first to adopt something of an archeologist's or anthropologist's point of view in the face of this otherness: she associates an arrangement of beads where someone had been working in a special uninhabited hut with a tableau produced for "dioramas of primitive civilizations in a natural history museum" (JP 24). But when it comes to the places where people actually sleep and live, her cognitive and imaginative failure is evident (and it is underscored by the telling detail that her eyes take a long time to adjust to the darkness of the women's huts). Like the matchbox houses of Mariastad, these dwellings have a disturbing and potent doubleness as both the "prototype" (JP 2) and the negation of Maureen's concept of home.[42] Except for the small mirrors on their walls, "snapping at stray beams of light like hungry fish" (JP 30), they seem entirely devoid of what the white woman would regard as "the furniture of life"; and even these mirrors, which recall to mind the important mirroring scenes in *The Lying Days*, are scarcely reassuring.[43] The fact that they "reflect nothing" expresses a state of destitution unimaginable and devastating to Maureen, who before her transportation could not even imagine a circumstance in which a woman could not use the gift of a nightgown or a handbag (JP 16). More implicitly, the mirror's vacant surfaces also express Maureen's condition: they fail to reflect the observer back to herself in any whole and reassuring way, leaving her with the uncomfortably paradoxical realization that she "was no longer what she was." The women's dwelling places, in short, are key sites in the process of unhousing that is traced in the novel. What happens at July's home, one might say, is that the utopia or "no-place" of the imaginary trip (and also the "no-place" of novel reading I discussed at the beginning of this chapter) is supplanted by the disturbing heterotopia of rural poverty. Figured in the novel as a "country whose dispossession nothing reaches" (JP 141), poverty is precisely—to recall the terms of Foucault's definition of such "other spaces"—a site that "stands outside of all places" yet inverts and challenges the stable categories of the bourgeois world. The predicament of actually living in a place that has been constructed (and is still experienced) as a heterotopia is similar to that of experiencing the permanent break: it is an impossible cognitive situation, utterly corrosive of a stable sense of self.

An Explosion of Roles

If subjectivity, as I have suggested all along, is dialectically connected to physical enclosures in Gordimer's work, the environment in which *July's People* is set would seem particularly conducive to and expressive of its dismantling. The manmade structures at July's village and at his chief's all seem on the verge of disintegration: the branches that once formed the rickety cattle pens are being devoured by ants; the earth is gradually being washed away around the roof supports of even the solider buildings; the ramshackle hamlets look ready to be "removed at the sweep of a bulldozer or turned to ashes by a single match in the thatch" (JP 111–112). Even vehicles, which in consumer society are so often metonymic expressions or fantasies of the self, will here simply "rust and be stripped to a hulk" (JP 14). The description of the surrounding bushveld is similarly evocative of transience:

> Like clouds, the savannah bush formed and re-formed under the changes of light, moved or gave the impression of being moved past the travelling eye; silent and ashy green as mould, spread and always spreading, rolling out under the sky before [Maureen]. There were hundreds of tracks used since ancient migrations (never ended; her family's was the latest), not seen. There were people, wavering circles of habitation marked by euphorbia and brush hedges, like this one, fungoid fairy rings on grass—not seen. There were cattle cracking through the undergrowth and the stillness of wild animals—all not to be seen. Space; so confining in its immensity her children did not know it was there. (JP 26)

The insistent association of this wide terrain with mutability and motion—its constant "form[ing] and re-form[ing]," its "spreading," "rolling," and "wavering"—challenges the static, pictorial quality of conventional landscape. Though the savannah here seems to spread out before Maureen, its properties are, as the passage repeatedly emphasizes, not visual: "not to be seen." This insistent undercutting of a purely scenic, panoramic effect is entirely appropriate, considering the novel's thematic concerns. The conceptual vantage required for the observation or depiction of landscape (no less than that required to read a novel) implies a mastery, a confident locatedness, unavailable to someone like Maureen, who "[knows] only where to place her feet, precariously on the solid ground of footholds" (JP 40).[44] It is significant, moreover, that this description rather deftly leaves open the question of whether the sense of transience we have noted is a property of the bush, an effect of the shifting light, or a projection of the "travelling eye" of the observer, or even, on a more literary level, a kind of objective correlative for the spatial experience of generations of migrants. Without contradicting the idea that space exerts a potent, even "confining," effect on experience, the passage eliminates any secure sense that either space or consciousness, object or subject, is determining. Neither, it seems, is foundational. We are confronted instead with a kind of radical openness, an impression of flux.

This unstable environment (frequently figured in the novel in terms of ruins, makeshift enclosures, broken appliances, and the like) seems to have a devastating effect on Bam Smales, who is, significantly, an architect. Indeed, one senses an authorial vindictiveness in the treatment of this character, the designer, if you will, of "the house of the white race": a man who used to bid for government contracts, who designed shopping malls, and who presumed to publish an article, "Needs and Means in Rural Architecture" (JP 108), on the very places in which he himself seems to find it impossible to live. Bam's name—suggestive of a small, insignificant explosion—also seems to register Gordimer's irony. His fate, nevertheless, raises more general thematic and formal questions, especially regarding the convention of realist character, questions with which I would like to conclude this discussion of the novel.

The expressive function of the architect figure in this narrative is perhaps most pointedly revealed through the small building projects he undertakes in order to while away the time at July's place. Bam seems to understand, theoretically, the adaptations he would need to make to live and work out in the bush: the meagerness of resources, for instance, would require a kind of *bricolage*—a building by "rearranging," by "letting the walls of mud sink back to mud and then using that mud for new walls" (JP 26). Yet the busywork in which he engages is of a piece with his persistence in looking at his watch, long after it has become clear to his wife that the old modes of order have become irrelevant in their new, open-ended living space (JP 43). Bam's efforts suggest a covert desire to restore the old arrangements, whether it is by "mak[ing] a place" for things such as a water tank from "back there," or by finding a fixed role for himself, such as that of a builder or a "provider of meat" (JP 77), or, as one critic suggests, as a one-man "Third World development agency."[45] It is significant, then, that the scene describing Bam's repairs to the water tank should be followed immediately by the description of the fluid savannah I quoted earlier: the juxtaposition seems to ironize his efforts at material and psychological reconstruction. For Bam, the man of structures, the instability of "places" (and the dual sense of the word is once again pertinent) finally becomes intolerable. Indeed, as he is dislodged in the course of the novel from his accustomed position of privilege and power, he seems to undergo a demolition of his life experience: a retreat from maturity. His entire life until the age of forty comes to seem like "another kind of childhood" (JP 77), and he comes to think of himself as "a boy with a peashooter" (JP 41), an image that clearly plays on his name: *Bam!* Incapable of coping with the revolutionary "explosion of roles," Bam's thoughts recurrently turn to what one might describe as public spaces of crisis: a hospital waiting room (JP 48), the corridor outside an operating theater (JP 114), and a prison cell (JP 88). There is, for him, no sense of release from the limitations of private space, no sense of new possibility. Though at the end of the novel his actual location is very deliberately indicated—he is "an architect lying on a bed in a mud hut" (JP 98)—his wife recognizes that "he" is in some sense not "there." His name, Maureen thinks, has become a marker for an absence: "she had gone on a long trip and left him behind in the master bedroom" (JP 98). The coherent narrative of self, dependent on a temporal continuity that might span the two significant spaces, the hut and the master bedroom, is miss- ing. In this symbolic sense, as well as in the literal one (July has appropriated his truck), Bam has become "a man without a vehicle": he cannot be transported to what is after all not just an uncomfortable rural backwater but also, if we grasp the novel's spatial allegory, the possibility of a new postapartheid life. His subjectivity, so attached to the places and containers that once defined him—his house, his car, his professional status—is revealed as no more than a "botched imagining" (JP 98), fit for a world that no longer exists.

The treatment of this character, in short, involves an inversion and critique of novelistic *Bildung*—a deliberate exposure of the very idea of a coherent sub- jectivity (on which the conventions of realistic character are based) as a spa- tially contingent fiction. Though it remains a fairly conventional realist novel, *July's People* reveals in this respect its metafictional dimension, and returns us to concerns first raised in *The Lying Days*. It is no accident that the events that set the narrative in motion (the effects of the state's failure to "contain" the revolutionary uprising) should be described—quite explicitly—in terms of "the transformations of myth and religious parable": the bank accountant who warns the Smaleses to flee is cast in the role of "the legendary warning hornbill of African folk-tales," and July, the servant, who provides the white family with a place to go, assumes the role of the "frog prince" of European fairy tales (JP 9). But these intriguing references to the radical metamorphoses of other narrative forms should not be seen as offering an interpretive key to the novel: *July's People* is not legible as a fairy tale.[46] Indeed, Gordimer, ever suspicious of such forms, notes explicitly at the end of the novel that the "real fantasies of the bush delude far more inventively than the romantic forests of Grimm and Disney" (JP 160). Yet her references to fairy tales do suggest a self-consciousness about the way the novel's abrupt transformations exert critical pressure on a conventional, overly psychological conception of character—especially its gradual, accretive develop- ment through time. Toward the end of the novel (and, significantly, after Mau- reen's final attempt to read *The Betrothed*) such an awareness is again indicated in the recurrent image of ruins. The suggestion here is that not only the pres- ent tense of habit but also the past tense of narrative and chronology have been blasted to bits. Maureen imagines herself standing in the "rubble" of her inform- ing and intimate spaces (of "20, Married Quarters Western Areas," the space that defined her as a child, and of "the architect-designed master bedroom," the space that defined her as a woman) without having any sense of which place came first. She feels incapable of "recogniz[ing] her own sequence" (JP 139).That her thoughts should turn to the remembered detail of the brick-shaped breads Lydia once baked is almost allegorically appropriate: the old spatial and temporal constructs, the old ideological and fictional forms, are reduced in this figure to the most basic of building blocks.

This said, it is nevertheless important to recognize that Gordimer's implicit reflections on the conventions of the novel are never allowed to become strictly technical (which would surely have generated a more experimental novel). The meaning of the dismantling of Bam or Maureen's subjectivity must finally be grasped politically—and in relation to the elusive figure of July. It is surely significant that the situation Bam has to confront and finds so devastating is one that July has long had to cope with: he, too, has lived in a mud hut, he, too, has been "a man without a vehicle," and he, too, has had to be both "boy" and "big man" at the same time (JP 72). If Bam, as we have seen, is incapable of following Maureen on her "long trip," the same is true, in a more literal way, for the families of migrants like July, who have never known the luxury of a permanent family home. July's wife, who acknowledges "his other life, his other self" (JP 22), has had to experience—and accept—his absence and intermittent presence for years: a unified subjectivity, in short, is the effect of privacy and privilege. It is tempting, of course, to emphasize July's transformation in the course of the novel, from one who at first expresses his servile status in his very bearing but who eventually begins to walk around the village with a gaze "like a foreman's inspecting his workshop, or a farmer's noting work to be done on the lands" (JP 78). But to read his altered comportment simply as a sign of "character development" is to underplay the fact that July has always had a multiple identity: a condition emphasized in his wife's meditations and in the fact that he has two names, one of which—Mwawate—remains unknown to his "city people" almost until the end of the novel. It is significant that the white couple, trained as they are to read novels, "could not read him" (JP 60).And no wonder, since the very language in which they have spoken to him for fifteen years has construed his "character" as suitable only for spaces of labor and servitude: "kitchens, factories, and mines" (JP 96).

Leaving the House of the White Race

It is in its emphasis on the difference that class or one's "place in the economy" makes that the novel's critique of character, its explosion of roles and places, becomes a form of cognitive mapping.The narrative describes a discovery on the part of the privileged of the hidden identities and hidden places that lie beyond the comfortable topographies of their own daily lives.The reader of July's People is also drawn into this discovery, especially at those moments in the text that implicitly raise the question of his or her own locatedness, his or her own place in the geography of power. (One thinks, for instance, of the description of Maureen's reading of Manzoni, or the description, from the point of view of July's wife, of the astonishing wealth of an ordinary suburban home full of books.) The novel, which presents itself like a message in a bottle from a very distant space, also seems to ironize certain potential modes of its own reception. It ends with a curious valedictory description of July's village, evoked, for once, in picturesque and sentimental terms, as it might appear in a photograph made for international consumption: an image of "the single community of man-and-nature-in-Africa reproduced by skilled photogravure processes in Holland and Switzerland" (JP 156). This image functions, I would argue, as a cautionary example of precisely the kind of facile and voyeuristic negotiation of difference discredited by the novel's earlier references to the coffee-table book on South Africa's racial policies and, even more sardonically, to those photographic exhibitions in affluent South African shopping malls "whose favoured subject was black township life" (JP 125). The novel thus implies a challenge to its international audience: that they should devise a mode of sociospatial mapping that goes beyond a complacent "learning about foreign parts" (JP 125) and toward a recognition of the often ugly relationships between these forgotten and distant "parts" of the world economy and their own.

To say this is not to suggest that any sociospatial totality is actually represented in the novel. As far as the characters in *July's People* are concerned, there is no ready-made chart to replace the outdated antique map of the world printed on July's hand-me-down bedspread back in the abandoned servant's quarters (JP 66–67). But it is, I think, an aspect of the novel's rigor that it does not present a glamorized version of African pastoralism as a satisfactory postrevolutionary conceptual scheme (for whatever cognitive mapping may be—and it is perhaps in the nature of the notion that it will always remain a desideratum rather than a method—it is neither nostalgic nor narrowly local). There is little that is enabling or enviable, as Gordimer makes clear, about the worldview of July's chief, who can only understand the postrevolutionary world in terms of petty local conflicts, or in that of the impoverished women of the village, for whom "overseas" is a strange, almost contentless word and for whom the intercontinental planes that fly overhead signify a mobility and an expansive geography in which they have no part or place (JP 20). Nor does it seem that Maureen Smales, the most important of the novel's white characters, gains any new sense of social or geographical locatedness. Her surroundings remain a "boundlessness" in which she cannot even walk so far as to take the dog around the block. The best she can do is to improvise a very local sense of direction by mentally "sticking a pin where there was no map" (JP 27, 49). Yet her disorientation must, I think, be grasped dialectically. When Maureen finally realizes that she never really knew July, that "his measure as a man was taken elsewhere" (JP 141), she confronts at last the connections between knowledge, power, and social place that ideally she should have seen long ago. Painful as it may be, it is surely necessary for her to confront these connections and to abandon apartheid's distorted map of human relations: a map that, as we have seen, extended no further than the suburban garden, and was deceptive even about that which its fences enclosed. The much-debated final scene of the novel is, then, profoundly ambiguous but not altogether hopeless. Maureen runs toward the sound of a mysterious helicopter, lured, we are told, by the illusory promise of "a kitchen, a house just the other side of the next tree" (JP 160). In this regard her running is a retreat. But it is also true that her dash toward the helicopter dissolves all of her old attachments. Unlike Bam, left behind in the hut, and left behind, in a different sense, in the master bedroom, Maureen is in motion: her flight is a final abandonment of the house of the white race and the relations of affection and power that it once guaranteed. The novel thus eschews any final (en)closure and seems to affirm an open-ended, transient, and migratory existence, a mode of being that is perhaps peculiarly African and also (as has been argued) typically postcolonial.

"Home" the Streets

"First you leave your mother's house, then you leave the house of the white race." The logic of Gordimer's early formulation of the acquisition of political consciousness finds its most radical transmutation in the 1989 novel *My Son's Story*. In this novel, produced during the final years of the apartheid era, it is not the daughter, or even the son, who leaves the mother's house, but the mother herself. Aila, the compelling character whom Homi Bhabha describes, almost reverentially, as the silent possessor of the "strange house" of fiction, of the home-in-the-world and the world-in-the-home, becomes a revolutionary, goes into exile, and finally to prison.[47] And as if to eliminate any lingering possibility of a return of the old domestic relations, the "coloured" family's newly acquired house in a slowly integrating suburb burns to the ground.

It is also in *My Son's Story* that we encounter Gordimer's most affirmative evocation of public space: an ideal that had, as it were, gone underground since the publication of her essay "Great Problems in the Street" in 1963. The passage in question describes a mass demonstration at a funeral in Alexandra, and does so in a way that can only be appreciated fully if one recognizes in it a transformation of the topographic blueprints traced out in this chapter. The crowded scene in the township street is evoked in terms that simultaneously suggest both the home and the world, both belonging and liberation: "Everyone home: 'home' the streets; a habitation without barriers, the house's breached walls spilling inmates" (MSS 107). The passage climaxes with a vision of the closeness of bodies, an expressive collectivity in which blacks and whites are organically united and class differences (figured by the French perfume of a rich woman and the sweat of a drunk) seem to be transcended: "One ultimate body of bodies was inhaling and exhaling in the single diastole and systole and above was the freedom of the great open afternoon sky" (MSS 110). This is one of the very rare instances in Gordimer's oeuvre (another may be the conclusion of *A Sport of Nature*, with its fantasized inauguration of a black president) in which she eschews the discomfiting poetics of the "political uncanny" in favor of the more assertive poetics of the "revolutionary sublime."[48] It is a vulnerable moment, to be sure, for the sublime always strains at our credulity and our notions of proportion and good taste—and it has struck some of Gordimer's more skeptical critics as clichéd.[49] But the street scene in *My Son's Story* is nevertheless, as Dominic Head rightly observes, the "effective culmination" of Gordimer's rigorous and sustained examination of South Africa's social geography in her apartheid-era fiction. "Willful symbolism," though it may be, the evocation of the street as home in *My Son's Story* offers a sensual encapsulation of her most persistent intellectual concerns and political desiderata.[50]

But, while granting Gordimer a moment of utopian indulgence, we should also consider to what extent the development of urban space in the postapartheid era has lived up to her ideal of a truly public domain where racial and class divisions have been abolished. It is fair to say that the postapartheid city—though it will be affected for many years to come by the material legacy of the old racialized urban planning—has since 1994 been the site of much creative ferment and many new forms of life, ranging from the terrifying to the heartening. It has inspired (as we will see in chapter 6) a number of innovative and optimistic meditations on urban space as a nexus of crossings and fluid subjectivities rather than a grid of rigid structural divisions and inflexible identities. But it has also seemed to many scholars that the suburbs and even the streets of the new South African city have developed, though haphazardly and through speculation and short-term economic necessity rather than centralized planning, in ways that impede the ideal of a polyglot site of bodily closeness and chance encounter. The novelist Marlene van Niekerk has half-ironically proposed that the newly popular gyms could be seen as exemplary sites where, under the aegis of profitable franchises, black and white bodies may commingle in a new kind of deodorized, members-only collectivity.[51] But if we leave the air-conditioned gym behind and contemplate the broader relations between inner city, suburb, and township, it can be increasingly difficult to find evidence that the old geographies of division have been erased. It is rather the case that old divisions are now articulated and justified in new terms.

In a cogent analysis of the spatial dynamics of postapartheid Johannesburg, the architect Lindsay Bremner has described the effects of a surprisingly rapid dismantling of the interlocking technologies of race, public health, and law that originally provided the logic for the city's development and their equally rapid replacement with the interlocking forces of speculation, necessity, and crime. These forces are, in Bremner's account, no less divisive than the earlier technologies that underpinned apartheid. Crime, in particular, along with its proliferating counterdiscourses of security, militarization, and privatization, is extremely potent in its capacity to redefine positions of privilege and deprivation, inclusion and exclusion, and identity and otherness. It is true, Bremner concedes, that the inner city is once again full of life: pavements are crowded with hawkers from all over Africa; tailors and hairdressers and barbers are plying their trade; streets are congested with taxis; and city parks, formerly the tidy preserves of whites, are open to all and filled with the braziers and campfires of the homeless.[52] But if streets and public spaces are now "in the hands of the people," who are rapidly filling up the interstices of the old urban grid, most of the valuable center-city property remains in the hands of big business, if not in those of the same old white monopolies. "Between these groups," Bremner observes, "lies a gulf, filled to a large extent by ignorance, fear, paranoia, entitlement, resentment, and socio-economic inequality": a gulf that is vigorously maintained by all manner of privatized security operatives. The result is that city dwellers pass like tourists rather than fellow citizens through each other's still very disparate worlds.[53] In the suburbs, this situation is exacerbated: gated communities have proliferated; streets are blocked off from the public domain and guarded by barriers, alarms, and militaristic guards. If these security areas have regained a certain communality—to the extent that gates can be left open, children can play in the streets, and neighbors can move confidently between one another's houses—it is purchased, as Bremner points out, at the expense of broader mobility and freedom of movement: precisely the kind of chance contact that Gordimer privileges in her "Great Problems in the Street" essay. "Separations deepen," as Bremner puts it, "and a sense of shared space is lost."[54]

If Gordimer, as I argued earlier, sensed in the old white homes of the 1940s a kind of structural alienation from Africa, a way of hiding the continent's very soil under the Axminster carpets, that alienation has not disappeared in South Africa's neoliberal democracy. Indeed one might argue that it has been rather vigorously marketed, and in surprising new ways. The exuberant prose of real estate developers, Bremner notes, now "conjures up images and creates aspirations for lifestyles divorced entirely from reality—Victorian, Tudor, Mediterranean, Medieval, Modern." It is as if style has become "a vehicle for denying the violent context of the city and creating the image of a preferred life style." "If you can't emigrate," Bremner sardonically observes, "you can at least dig in with style."[55] We are witnessing, in other words, a highly commercial, phantasmagoric re-creation of the epistemological disjunctions of colonial modernity, in which experience fails (as Jameson puts it) to "coincide with the place in which it takes place." Or perhaps the situation is more challenging and novel. We may be called upon to recognize that the whole notion of an authentically African "place" (to which Gordimer, with symbolic interest in the African soil and its many palimpsestic layers of cultural inscription, has always been attracted) is itself being transformed. In the new urban landscape of Tuscan villas and reggae restaurants, we are not so much revisiting the disjunctions of colonial modernism as witnessing its intensification in the new, disconcerting, and outrageously uneven geography of global postmodernity. Shaped by these sweeping forces, the South African city runs the risk becoming a "giant theme park, an assemblage of fortified and stylized enclaves, residential, commercial, retail, or leisure, to which access is guarded and selectively granted."[56]

Gordimer's major assessment of the transformation of urban space in South Africa, her 1995 novel *None to Accompany Me*, addresses the period right before the 1994 elections, and therefore cannot represent the theme park city of the new century: a terrain of which Ivan Vladislavić has become the rightful bard.[57] Though it records the rise of a new commercial ethos, Gordimer's novel does not record the stylish "digging in" of the privileged but rather their fear and flight during the violence of the transition: the empty homes of émigrés are described, perhaps in another instance of willful symbolism, as residual sites, "suburban museums, exhibiting a white way of life that has ended" (NTA 243). But these relics of the old world are, as the novel demonstrates, increasingly being inhabited in new ways: the "homeground of the present" mapped out in *None to Accompany Me* is one of immense sociogeographic fluidity. The novel evokes precariously emergent versions of domesticity, as black residents move into apartments and homes once reserved for whites, and as new identities and family structures begin to emerge. This flux finds its culminating expression at the novel's conclusion, when the protagonist Vera Stark sells her 1940s-era house and becomes a tenant in the backyard cottage of a rising black entrepreneur: a synecdoche for the shifting relations of ownership and domicile in the new nation.[58]

Despite the fact that it addresses the results of a negotiated settlement rather than a revolution, the novel retains several of the tropes and concerns of *July's People*: once again, not all of Gordimer's characters are able to fully inhabit the labile present and the ever-shifting "here." Both Ben Stark, a sculptor turned marketer of exclusive luggage, and Didymus Maqoma, freedom fighter turned party historian, never quite arrive in the new South Africa. The latter, Gordimer notes at one point, might be present in "some version of himself," but—as was the case with Bam Smales—a part of Maqoma remains elsewhere, left behind in an earlier era (NTA 135). And if certain psychological qualities can prevent one from "moving with the times," so, too, can poverty and the threat of crime. It is telling, therefore, that the street does not really feature in this postapartheid novel, as the affirmative moments of *My Son's Story* might lead us to expect. The more privileged characters are, instead, trapped in "the car's isolation, air-conditioning, locked doors, and closed windows" (NTA 250), in fearful retreat from the vengeful advocates of "taking everything you haven't got from those who appear to have everything" (NTA 110).

Instead of the political sublime of utopian encounter, therefore, the novel offers an updated version of the familiar uncanny encounter with black dwelling places. It evokes the confusing mishmash of styles and materials that shape an informal settlement at the city's edge: "Now on the horizon, a vast unloading of scrap without any recognizable profile of human habitations, now at the roadside, the jagged tin and tattered plastic sheets that are the architecture of the late twentieth century as marble was the materials of the Renaissance, glass and steel that of Mies van de Rohe; the squatter camps, the real Post Modernism: of the homeless" (NTA 81). It is only after its destruction (by a mob of white vigilantes) that Vera Stark is truly able to recognize this place—the heterotopic prefiguration of the theme park city—as "home." Gordimer's first postapartheid novel, thus, reverts to her time-honored strategy of ungrounding any notion of domestic normality and, in so doing, emphasizing the vastly disjunct geographies of everyday life that continue to characterize South African society.

3

OF TRESPASSERS AND TRASH

Every "proper" place is altered by the mark
others have left on it.

—Michel de Certeau,
The Practice of Everyday Life

Motho ga a lathlwe. (You can't throw a person away.)

—Setswana saying

Forced Removals and the South African Pastoral

Of all South African novels, Nadine Gordimer's *The Conservationist* is the most
deeply invested in the nation's master narrative about land: a stirring, half-mythic
story of colonial dispossession and restitution.[1] This investment is especially evident if we read the novel in New Historicist fashion, by juxtaposing it with a
revealing minor document of the period from which it arises. I will, therefore,
begin my reading of *The Conservationist*, which remains Gordimer's most impres-
sive achievement and brings into play some themes crucial to any investigation of
the politics of place in South Africa, with just such a juxtaposition.

In 1974, the very year of the novel's publication and the high point of apartheid's "dynamic third decade," the Farmers' Association of Ladysmith in Natal
addressed a letter to officials of the apartheid government asking them to give
top priority in their so-called Resettlement Program to the elimination of a certain "black spot," the freehold settlement of Roosboom just south of the town.[2]
In addition to what they termed "ordinary 'border farmer' problems," such as
dogs, fences, veld fires, stray cattle, theft of grazing, stock poisoning, hunting, and
"vindictiveness," the farmers' letter listed several reasons for regarding this site as
uniquely troublesome. Roosboom, they felt, lay too close to the national road; it
was not only the cause of many traffic accidents but also much too visible in all
its squalor—presenting "a golden opportunity" to such "hostile overseas jour-

nalists and photographers" as might pass by. Moreover, the settlement's location, with easy access to Johannesburg and Durban by both road and railway, made it a strategic site from the point of view of terrorists. (The farmers noted anxiously that the notorious Nelson Mandela had addressed several meetings there in 1963.) Roosboom's removal, finally, was in the interest of conservation: the settlement's "uncontrolled intensive human population" caused the highly erodable soil in the area to silt up the white farmers' dams.[3]

The farmers' letter was effective. Two years later, Roosboom was gone. The people of the community were loaded onto trucks and dumped at Ezakheni, twenty-five miles away in the eroded hills of the Kwazulu bantustan. Neither the poetic resonance of the freehold's inoffensive name (which means "rose tree") nor the weightier argument that its residents had long and legally owned the land could stand up against the self-serving reasoning of the white farmers, backed up as it was by the sweeping land laws of grand apartheid. One of the former land-owners, Eliot Mngadi, later commented bitterly: "When our fathers bought the land, they were given these documents which gave them the right to own the place forever and ever, amen."[4]

The Roosboom story is not unique. It is one among hundreds of similarly dismal narratives recorded in the early 1980s by the Surplus People's Project as part of a nationwide study of forced removals in South Africa. Between 1960 and 1983, or so the project's researchers estimated, at least three and a half million people were evicted from their residences and shunted off either to desolate areas officially designated as "homelands" or to makeshift relocation camps called "closer settlements." Several of the latter bore uncannily appropriate names— Morsgat (Wastehole), Weenen (Weeping), Ledig (Idle), Klipgat (Stonehole), Stink-water—names that even M. C. Botha, then Minister of Bantu Administration and Development, had to admit were "unfortunate."[5] These names record a calculated immiseration of human life from which South Africa has not yet recovered— though it is true that many of the displaced communities have, since the 1970s and 1980s, found ways of adapting themselves to their formerly despised dumping grounds.[6] Interwoven as they were with almost every aspect of apartheid, includ-ing the maintenance of white economic power, urban influx control, ethnic strati-fication, and other divide-and-conquer tactics, the effects of forced removals were wide-ranging. But for my purpose here (that of sketching out the discursive con-text of Gordimer's novel), it seems most useful to emphasize the way this history exposes two contradictory and even delusional aspects of apartheid's ideology.

First: the forced removals exposed the peculiar mendacity of the apartheid government's efforts to present its land policies as a high-minded project of decolonization—of furthering "the black man's" striving to achieve national and ethnic identity.[7] They were, of course, quite the opposite. In fact, the National-ist government's brutal efforts to tidy up what it described as the "chessboard pattern" of black and white settlement may be grasped as the final and perhaps most hubristic moment of European colonialism on the African continent. The clearance of "black spots," as the activist priest Cosmas Desmond once put it, represented the belated "completion of the process of White takeover and settle-ment in South Africa."[8] From 1970 on, such operations received formal political sanction in a law rightly described as apartheid's "ultimate fantasy": the Bantu Homeland Citizenship Act, which at a stroke of the pen declared all blacks to be citizens of one of ten economically dependent ministates.[9] If the Land Act of 1913, in Solomon Plaatje's famous phrase, turned Africans into "pariah[s] in the land of [their] birth," the Bantu Homeland Citizenship Act turned them into aliens.[10] It was by the contrivance of this act that the apartheid government sought to avoid the charge that it was denying its black population's civil rights. The act would turn all black South Africans into migrant laborers, their status little different from, say, that of Turkish *Gastarbeiters* in Germany. It would also effectively divest the government of any responsibility for the welfare of the "surplus" people once they were dumped and for living conditions in the places to which they were exiled. Forced removals could therefore be equated with the "normal" deportation of undesirable foreign nationals. Like so much of apartheid's theory and practice, the Bantu Homeland Citizenship Act rested on a denial and repression of the facts. The minister of information, Connie Mulder, went to far as to predict the day when there would be no black South Africans at all—contrary to the evidence of the black faces still encountered every day in South Africa's cities, towns, and farms.[11] Mulder's legalistic fantasy, of course, takes no account of the experience of the thousands of people whose lives and communities were destroyed by the activities of the men driving the notorious "GG" (government garage) bulldozers.

Second: the forced removals exposed the self-serving ways the apartheid government deployed pastoral ideologies and sentiments. As I showed in my discussion of Coetzee's "dream topographies," the Afrikaners traditionally based their sense of cultural identity as *boerenasie* on the idea of the family farm. The National Party, consequently, was ever-mindful of the importance of a rural constituency in its political rhetoric. But, in practice, apartheid was urbanistic.[12] It created what Michel de Certeau describes in *The Politics of Everyday Life* as a "concept-city," that is, a political strategy that deployed its power territorially and operated by defining "proper places for all people and activities," from which the "surrounding exteriority" could be surveyed and policed."[13] It is entirely in keeping with the disciplinary, panoptic character of the "concept-city" that apartheid's land policies should have tended to foster more controllable, more visible, and more consolidated units (and we may recall here the idea of cleaning up the demographic "chessboard pattern"). The effect of these policies was identical in this respect to that which attended the capitalization—or "urbanization"—of agriculture elsewhere in the world: the displacement of a rural peasantry.[14] Apartheid's forced removals, though dreamed up by the descendants of Boers, brought an end to the old pastoral ways of black freehold farmers, tenants, and "redundant" agricultural workers alike. To be sure, the homelands and relocation camps to which the surplus people were moved could not be called "urban" in our ordinary understanding of the word. (Indeed, the cruelest aspect of the rural removals in South Africa may have been the fact that the displaced peasantry was officially barred from the city, the time-honored refuge for the landless.) But farming was seldom a viable way of life in these new settlements, where there was a chronic lack of arable land, water, and pasture.[15] Apartheid's territorial strategies thus involved if not exactly an enforced urbanization then at least an enforced villagization of thousands of people who formerly, in some way or another, had lived off the land.

Even if the removals did not constitute a complete rupture of older economies and customs, the emotional impact of this experience (which cannot be ignored in any cultural or literary analysis) was enormous. Victims of resettlement again and again conveyed a devastating sense of loss to the researchers of the Surplus People's Project.[16] For example, the elders of Babanango in Natal, evicted from land that had belonged to their ancestors since the time of Senzanghakhona, the father of Shaka, lamented to Father Desmond that the government's policies left them unable to live like "men with sensitive souls."[17] "We lead the life of a bird," declared a displaced woman at Glenmore. "We will never get used to one place."[18]

When one reads statements like these, one cannot help feeling that a remarkable degree of callousness or self-delusion is evidenced in the pronouncements of Nationalist officials such as M. C. Botha, who once declared that the victims of resettlement "liked" such dusty, dismal places as Stinkwater.[19] Implicit in Botha's remark is a denial of the fact that black South Africans also have a pastoral tradition—that they too have a sense of place and an attachment to ancestral land. It is a denial that may seem particularly counterintuitive and heartless on the part of a ruling class that so strenuously claimed pastoral virtues for itself.[20] But it is important to recognize that the function of pastoral ideology in South Africa (sentimentally expressed in *Blut und Boden* songs like "O Boereplaas, geboortegrond!") was not so much to assert positive values like rootedness, simplicity, and tradition as to signify racial difference. The idea that "the Native is not a farmer and never will be a farmer" or that "he would ruin every bit of land that was placed at his disposal" was a standard item in the Afrikaans and often also in the English-speaking farmer's dictionary of received ideas.[21] It is not difficult to see how this particular version of pastoralism—which celebrates the rural heritage of some people, while ignoring that of others—might serve the urbanistic strategies of the Nationalist Party's ambitious and devastating geographical schemes.

In light of all these considerations, the representative character of the Roosboom story should now be all the more evident. In emphasizing their concern for soil conservation in their case against the black freeholders, the farmers of Ladysmith were repressing the fact that overgrazing, deforestation, and erosion were much more likely to be a factor in the homelands or resettlement camps than on a freehold farm. And in bemoaning the squalor and inefficiency of Roosboom, the farmers were deploying, albeit unwittingly, one of the most time-honored rationales for colonial expansion: the justification of territorial expropriation on the basis of pastoral values like efficient land use or more prudent stewardship of the earth. The argument is a self-interested and self-perpetuating one: assume, first, that black people are indeed not farmers; next, take away their land; then, read in the dust and poverty where they have been dumped the incontrovertible evidence that black people are not proper farmers. This cruel and circular logic underwrites in the name of conservation (or strategic planning, or beautification) a history of waste and of poverty deliberately created in a country officially prosperous and at peace.

The story, however, does not end with the swirl of a dust devil. We cannot forget—especially since we now view this oppressive history from the perspective of a changed South Africa—that the creation of waste always contains the possibility of a dialectical revenge. My point is powerfully, if somewhat crudely, expressed in a poem published in the "poetry corner" of the *Natal Witness* during the terrible violence of the late eighties. "Are the garbage bins of parliament / Exploding with the squeezed-in voices of my people?" the poem asks, and it closes with the prediction that the "silent voice" of the oppressed will eventually "remove the stubborn lids."[22] Political garbage, as the imagery here suggests, is not readily disposed of and retains an explosive potential. This potential is fully acknowledged in De Certeau's discussion of the concept-city: all strategic forms of power, he insists, produce opposition to their own order in the form of "waste products." The "profit system," for instance, produces an unofficial loss, an unaccounted-for "expenditure," in the "multiple forms of wretchedness and poverty" it generates on its margins. Thus the concept-city inevitably struggles to maintain itself, as De Certeau rather poetically puts it, in "a world bewitched by the invisible powers of the other." Hence its characteristic paranoia—the fact that its discourse is always based on the "hypothesis of its own destruction."[23]

De Certeau's ideas are, again, readily applied to the South African situation—and his emphasis on the deep-seated paranoia of strategic operations speaks particularly clearly to the "total onslaught" rhetoric that the government began to deploy in the early 1970s. Since then, however, the explosiveness of waste, of human beings treated as rubbish, has become all too clear. (It is telling that one of the most imaginative recent accounts of the political logic of apartheid should explore the "aesthetic of superfluity" and waste, which is legible, even today, on almost every level of South African life.)[24] For despite all of the government's strategic house cleaning and despite all the security regulations banning "hostile overseas journalists and photographers" from squatter camps, the people victimized by apartheid's territorial schemes accrued a visibility and generated a degree of resistance that in the end became irrepressible. One thinks, for instance, of the struggle at the Crossroads settlement, of the bodily stubbornness of its many courageous residents who refused to be moved, and of the dramatic ways in which this inauspicious place became an international symbol of the resistance against apartheid. With cases like these, the history of forced removals reminds us once more of the interpretive force in the South African context of what Lars Engle has termed the "political uncanny": the return of the repressed, of the discarded, of those who "have been thrown away."[25]

The Tattooed Desert

The issues raised by the forced removals lie at the heart of Gordimer's Booker Prize–winning novel *The Conservationist*, a challenging text that, as I suggested earlier, derives its poetic power from the master narrative of the dispossession and restitution of the land—the chief mobilizing myth of the antiapartheid struggle and, for better or worse, of the new nation. Indeed, the novel includes in its intricate narrative weave many details reminiscent of the Roosboom case. The novel's protagonist, a rich mining executive and part-time farmer called Mehring is, like the Ladysmith farmers, beset with worries about veld fires, fences, and soil erosion. He also frets about dogs, traffic (especially the buses and taxis that come hurtling out of a nearby location), and the unsightliness of black people's dwellings. But the novel is chiefly concerned with the broad political issues in light of which all these details signify: it is preoccupied with the overarching question of the legitimate ownership of the land.[26] That Gordimer was deeply disturbed by the land policies of grand apartheid is evident in several of her essays from the 1970s and especially in her foreword to Father Desmond's 1971 study *The Discarded People*. This essay is intended as a consciousness-raising piece for an overseas audience and exposes the hollowness of the usual justifications of the forced removals—for example, that they represent an effort at "development," or that the fundamental inhumanity of the policy can be explained away by the cultural relativity of standards of living. In its more impassioned moments, the essay addresses some of the recurrent preoccupations of Gordimer's fiction and prefigures the way her thinking about the forced removals came to be refracted in *The Conservationist*.

The foreword begins by homing in on the sense of disorientation suffered by the "surplus people" and relates it to one of Gordimer's fundamental assumptions as a writer: the belief that subjectivity is profoundly shaped by spatial relations. This conviction is powerfully asserted toward the end of the essay: "Every human life, however humble it has been, has a context meshed of familiar experience—social relationships, patterns of activity in relation to environment. Call it 'home,' if you like. To be transported out of this on a Government truck one morning and put down in an uninhabitable place is to be asked to build not only your shelter, but your whole life over again, from scratch."[27] The removals thus signify for Gordimer a violation of the intimate and constitutive dialectic between person and place.

The foreword also extends Gordimer's perennial critique of liberalism by emphasizing the repression or blindness inherent in the way that even well-meaning white citizens respond to systemic injustice. She recounts how, in response to an appeal from the *Rand Daily Mail*, the people of Johannesburg made generous donations of food and blankets to the victims of removals starving in the "tent-and-hovel towns" where they had been dumped. In this gesture of sympathy, Gordimer detects a contradiction, one reminiscent of Blake's aphorism that "pity would be no more, if we did not make any one poor." By serving as a moral alibi, acts of charity enable the privileged to avoid a full consciousness of their complicity in the system that produces suffering. "How is it," Gordimer asks, that people "manage to close their minds to the implications of the resettlement policy while at the same time 'opening their hearts' to its inevitable results?"[28] Gordimer's appeal is for a more fundamental solution and a greater readiness to consider the social totality: to think through the exploitative and parasitical relationships that are involved in apartheid and, indeed, in the global capitalist system in which her overseas readers are implicated.[29]

The Conservationist explores themes similar to those addressed in the foreword, and in compelling ways. The novel's geographical and spatial concerns are first revealed in its epigraph, taken from a poem by Richard Shelton entitled "The Tattooed Desert." The poem offers a surreal evocation of the misadventures of a colonial do-gooder who heads out for the tropics on his bicycle, armed with cures for nonexistent diseases. He ends up discovering nothing but geographical and emotional disorientation. "Tell me who moved the river," the cyclist-explorer shouts at the end of the poem, "where can I find a good place to drown." His plight predicts the fate of Gordimer's protagonist—his failure to be a "good" colonialist (or, as he likes to put it, "no ordinary pig-iron dealer" [C 41]) and to maintain control of his African farm. The poem's title, "The Tattooed Desert," also introduces at the very start of the novel the idea of a mapped territory and the inscription of colonial space. It thus underscores what Achille Mbembe has identified as the privileging of *graphism* in apartheid's territorializing strategies.[30] The narrative that follows consistently represents the social and physical terrain in which it is set as "tattooed," or inscribed by fixed codes of behavior, movement, and speech—whether it be the "fine criss-cross of grooves" (C 58) that determine the conversational patterns between master and servant or the trajectory of Mehring's car "scoring a groove over and over again, ineradicable" (C 222), as it traces its habitual route along the new freeways to Johannesburg. The novel records, in other words, what Gordimer calls "patterns of activity in relation to environment" and the way such individual tracings come to constitute and express the larger geographical and political context of apartheid South Africa.

The Conservationist is also concerned with the pathological results, for both the individual and society, of a refusal to face up to fundamental social injustices. Curiously, Gordimer allows her protagonist, a man who represses much that is unpleasant and compromising, to recognize the limitations of any kind of piecemeal or therapeutic solution to South Africa's ills. "Charity's a waste of time, towards man or beast," he reflects, "it only patches up a little bit of pain here and there.... Everything needs changing" (C 199). When his mistress, Antonia, admits to a nostalgic impulse to "change the world but keep bits of it the way [she] like[s] it," Mehring quickly diagnoses the psychological and political dangers of such simplicity. "Who wouldn't make the world over if it were as easy as that," he thinks. "To keep anything the way you like it for yourself, you have to have the stomach to ignore—dead and hidden—whatever intrudes" (C 71, 79). This insight is a crucial one, since it alludes to the novel's controlling image: the corpse of a black stranger, hastily buried by the police in Mehring's pasture.

The trope of the buried black body, a figure for all that is repressed by the racist mind, first appears in Gordimer's work in The Lying Days, when the narrator, Helen Shaw, describes the privileged life led by white South Africans as "a picnic in a beautiful graveyard where people are buried alive under your feet" (LD 331). "I always think locations are like that," she explains, "dreary, smoking Hells out of Dante, peopled with live men and women" (LD 331). In The Conservationist, however, the trope is given a revolutionary valence.[31] The body insistently floats up to the surface of the soil and to the surface of Mehring's consciousness, allegorizing the idea of the return of the repressed and reasserting the long-denied claim of dispossessed South Africans to the land of their birth. This reemergence of what was hidden also expresses the possibility of a more complete social knowledge, of what Gordimer has called the "revolutionary sense of totality, the conception of a 'whole' world" (EG 142). And "totality," for Gordimer, has a territorial correlate in the ANC's longstanding political ideal of a unitary, undivided South Africa—a land free of such places as homelands and segregated "locations," where men and women have, in effect, been buried.[32]

If, as J. M. Coetzee has argued, the pastoral mode always stands for a local and partial solution to social problems, Gordimer's compelling farm novel, with its allegorical advocacy of totality and of the erasure of apartheid's boundaries, is resolutely antipastoral.[33] This observation may appear counterintuitive, for with its fragmentary structure and modernist techniques, *The Conservationist* is certainly not "whole" in any formal sense. It is not a novel that Lukács, the great theorist of totality, would have liked. Indeed, it is curiously—perhaps even deliberately—reminiscent of that most notoriously fractured and multivoiced of modernist texts, *The Waste Land*.[34] Like Eliot's poem, Gordimer's novel is woven out of overlapping perspectives and voices; it reiterates a similar set of leitmotifs, including the burial of the dead, the idea of prophecy, and the well-being of the land; and its imagistic patterns are based on the elements of earth, fire, and, finally, water. Both texts hint, moreover, at the possible emergence of a mythic order: *The Waste Land*'s submerged traces of the Grail legends and ancient fertility myths have an analogue in Gordimer's references (in a series of interruptive citations from the Reverend Henry Callaway's anthropological study *The Religious Systems of the Amazulu*) to the African ancestral spirits: "the Amatongo, they who are beneath" (C 163). Despite these hints at a new/old cultural order, both texts remain to some degree riddling and oracular. If, in the case of *The Waste Land*, the reader needs to be a kind of sibyl to spell out a coherent meaning in the handful of dust the poem flings at us, in the case of *The Conservationist,* the reader must be something of a literary *sangoma*, a diviner who can make sense of the novel's fractured conversations and memories, and of the array of curiously intriguing objects it foregrounds: scraps of paper, cigarette butts, shoes, eggs, and the like.[35]

It is not surprising, then, that Gordimer's more prescriptive critics should have faulted the novel from what is essentially a Lukácsian perspective. Abdul JanMohamed, for instance, has criticized the novel's focus on the subjectivity of the protagonist "at the expense of an adequate portrayal of social conditions and process."[36] Irene Gorak, similarly, has questioned the efficacy of "using modernism" (which for her is inherently quietistic and strangely conflated with the pastoral) to "foster revolution." Like JanMohamed, she complains that *The Conservationist* attends too closely to individual pathologies: it "squanders attention on a single character that most political novels divide among several characters."[37] This notion of what constitutes a "political novel" is, of course, limited (surely all novels are political in some way or another); but what is symptomatic and therefore interesting about Gorak's approach, with its strong emphasis on "historically determined revolutionary commitment," is the way it denies the political importance of the spatial. Her argument rests on the assumption that a writer who is "more aware of bodies in space rather than ideas unfolding across time" will not be adequate to the task of describing "a society in the throes of revolutionary transformation."[38]

This critique is not so much inaccurate as dogmatic. For in a country where the distribution of bodies in space has been so brutally policed, an interest in such matters is far from negligible. It is, after all, through a body—the buried body in Mehring's pasture—that the idea of a rediscovered historical awareness is figured in the novel. Gordimer's own comments on *The Conservationist*, moreover, suggest that she was perfectly aware of her vulnerability to this kind of antimodernist critique. In one of her interviews, she comments on the fragmentary character of the text and relates this formal device to the key issues of repression and reification. She explains that she deliberately left out any explanatory description of the novel's political context, of the specific "laws that bring about certain morbid forms of behaviour." The novel's experimental form is thus motivated for her on mimetic grounds: it is expressive of Mehring's "disjointed consciousness," of his incapacity to grasp the full social irony of his delight in those "simple things in life that poorer men can no longer afford" (C 22). But Gordimer also hopes to invite readers of *The Conservationist* to make interpretive leaps: they must fill in the significant silences if they are to "achieve an understanding of the effects of the colour-bar laws, if not the letter of the law itself."[39] While the pastoral idea of the local solution is certainly expressed in the novel, the overarching artistic and ethical purpose of the text—one in which the reader is invited to participate—is to construct a new whole, by discovering the relationship between things: between person and place, between subjectivity and material conditions, between country and city, and, as Gordimer hints, between the text of the novel and the text of laws like the Group Areas Act and the Bantu Citizenship Act.

The Conservationist's focus on the spatial, far from being static or quietistic, rests on a conception of antagonistic social practices not unlike those described by De Certeau. Indeed, his brief discussion of the colonization of Latin America by the Spanish seems almost uncannily pertinent: he imagines the colony as a contested terrain, as simultaneously a "desert"—a tattooed desert, if you will—and a "jungle." The territorial rhetoric of power—a panoptic grid projected on the land, which the colonizer treats as a "desert where nothing equally articulate exists"—also serves as the framework for the guileful, everyday resistance of the colonized. The grid becomes entangled in "a jungle" of "invisible tactics," which are in fact the daily practices of ordinary people and their multifarious, fertile, often invisible acts of resistance (poaching, trespassing, squatting, and so forth). Such acts of resistance, founded, as De Certeau puts it, "on a memory tattooed by oppression," are recorded in *The Conservationist*.[40] It is through this record of the quotidian politics of "bodies in space" that the novel stages its critique, not only of the white pastoral but also of apartheid's geographical schemes and their ultimately superficial inscription of African soil.

Apartheid's Grid

Given its poetics of omission, we cannot expect *The Conservationist* to narrate the history of forced removals in any direct way. In fact, the one time such an event is referred to, it occurs on the borders of South Africa and on the margins of the central character's consciousness. Midway through the novel, Mehring receives a letter from his son Terry, who is on vacation near Swakopmund in South West Africa. The letter reports, among other things, that all the Damara people living around Khan Canyon have been "'removed' to make way for a uranium mine and herded into a Reserve somewhere, the entire population" (C 100). This news does not seem to be of great interest to Mehring, who briefly recalls his childhood memories of the Damaras (as people who lived in the dry hills "like the stones") and muses for a moment about Terry's self-conscious use of scare quotes around the word "removed." Yet the fact that the industrialist-farmer's thoughts immediately turn to the matter of his son's inheritance ("who else is a farm for but a son") is significant. Even more telling is the way this incident reemerges some fifty pages later, when we find Mehring thinking about how much a rich uranium deposit could do to raise the gross national product of a developing country: it would put shoes on peoples' feet, he tells himself (C 147). These thoughts arise in order to allay a feeling of guilt and complicity in the expropriation, which involves the very industry in which he has made his money.

The incident Terry recounts, as well as the history of forced removals it synecdochically invokes, thus brings an indirect but pervasive pressure to bear on Mehring's dream of rural rootedness. Though the rich white man's meditations are often at center stage, *The Conservationist* provides glimpses of a political context that ironizes his efforts to enjoy a pastoral idyll—to live, one might say, like a man "with a sensitive soul." The novel describes, for instance, the constant struggle of the Indian shopkeepers to forestall their removal under the Group Areas Act; it mentions the problems of a displaced farm laborer who has to wheel and deal for a nasty job at the abattoir; and it tells us of an illegal migrant who carefully guards his yellowed recommendation letters ("Bearer, Witbooi, is a good boy" [C 33]), in the hope that these papers might some day meet with official validation. More rarely, an authorial comment explicitly alerts us to the effects of apartheid's land laws, as when we are told that black South Africans have to carry "papers that made them temporary sojourners where they were born" (C 114). The land policies of apartheid's third decade, in sum, are insistently if peripherally marked in the text—in much the same way that the black township near Mehring's farm always seems to mark the edges of his idyllic views with a smudge of smoky air.

Gordimer's preoccupation with the political geography of South Africa is evident in the careful description in the novel's opening pages of the terrain surrounding Mehring's farm. This highveld landscape is scarcely pristine. It is threatened by the encroaching city: mealie fields have been replaced by factories and landscaped corporate campuses, and towns have been taken over by steakhouses and discount outlets. It is subject, moreover, to the whims of apartheid's planners. Just behind the farm (which serves, Gordimer ironically notes, as a sign that the proprietor has "remained fully human" [C 22]), there is a vast black "location" fenced off with barbed wire; a squatter camp; and a dump where poor people scavenge. There are also rumors of blueprints for a "coloured" township to be built in the vicinity, a development that would encroach on Mehring's pastoral retreat. Much as they might deplore such "ghastly" planning, this geography of division ultimately benefits Mehring and other members of his class: people who have financial interests in such "development" schemes as the Sishen-Saldanha railroad and the platinum holdings in the Bantustans (C 30, 191). Apartheid's redrawing of the map thus holds little threat for Mehring: he even jokes that his only success in farming would occur if the government were to expropriate his farm so that he could sell out at a profit. Unlike so many of his poorer contemporaries, who might be bundled summarily onto trucks and dumped in uninhabitable places, his ability to maintain his way of life is, at the beginning of the novel, entirely secure.

Mehring's power and privilege is expressed also in those unconscious gestures, interactions, and movements that constitute everyday life—the kind of thing that De Certeau would describe as a rhetoric of spatial practices, and that Gordimer refers to as "topograph[ies] of activity" (C 75) or, in the foreword to *The Discarded People*, as "patterns of activity in relation to environment." The first description of a conversation between Mehring and his foreman already indicates the importance in this novel of "bodies in space." In this scene, both men are eager to talk. Mehring wants to complain to Jacobus about the farm children stealing guinea fowl eggs, and Jacobus wants to tell his boss that a corpse has been discovered in his third pasture. But despite this urgency, social conventions are not forgotten: Jacobus stands ten feet away from Mehring, "as if there were a line drawn there," and when a kind of conversational "collision" threatens, it is "of course" Jacobus who cedes "the right of way to the farmer" (C 11). The implicit metaphor of traffic is appropriate, for, as Raymond Williams has observed, "traffic is not only a technique, it is a form of consciousness and a form of social relations."[41] In *The Conservationist* traffic becomes a figure for all habitual practices—for all responses to social situations that are so unquestioned and so profoundly naturalized that Gordimer, at one point, compares them to a biological phenomenon: "those circuits created when electrical impulses in the brain connecting complex links of comprehension have been stimulated so often that a pathway of learning has been reestablished" (C 221).

The idea of traffic is connected in the novel to the recurrent image of the grid, that social tattoo on whose engraved lines are "laid down many automatic responses to everyday situations" (C 184). This metaphor has a specific significance in Gordimer's political rhetoric. In one of her essays from the late 1970s, she uses it to describe the ideological assumptions of apartheid (e.g., the conviction that a single power group has the right to define what "culture" is). Such beliefs, she argues, are a "grid on which, like the most functional of contemporary business premises, all manner of interior open-space arrangements may be made to suit the tenant" (EG 257).[42] The grid, one might say, is a figure for the ideological apparatuses of daily life, the nexus of practices in which relations of power are expressed and by which they are again and again reaffirmed—"grooved over and over again" (C 222). The significance of the novel's recurrent grid-like imagery is illuminated by De Certeau's conception of space. In *The Practice of Everyday Life* he presents the randomness of spatial "tactics," the trajectories of an individual's movements, as antithetical to the gridded structure of "place"—the territorial "strategies" of those in power.[43] In Mehring's case, this distinction ordinarily seems negligible: his "topography of activity" coincides comfortably with the grid of apartheid's social and geographical arrangements, just as his Mercedes glides smoothly along on the new highway system "like a mechanical hare on its track" (C 154). His habitual movements "from the flat to the car to the office, from tables to beds, from airports to hotels, from city to country" describe the "closed system" into which he is interpellated (C 75). Though he is what De Certeau calls a "subject with will and power," Mehring "inhabits—by filling—the place prepared for him"(C 205).[44]

This is not to say that the farmer-industrialist does not have contrary impulses. His yearning for an alternative spatial and therefore also social and epistemological experience is evidenced, for instance, in his enjoyment of a kind of "fugitive" status (C 156) one night when he secretly returns to his farm; it is expressed in his desire to see his farm "as it is when he is not there" (C 161); and it is revealed, most significantly, in what seems to be a curious kind of burial wish, which turns his thoughts—and his movements—again and again to the body buried under the soil of his pasture. Even so, the novel repeatedly suggests that the apparatus of the grid—the rule of the road, if you will—is finally indispensable to Mehring: it is constitutive of his subjectivity. The political dimension of this interpellation is exposed with particular clarity on the final occasion on which Mehring drives his Mercedes back to the city (after the disconcerting reemergence of the buried corpse). Behind the steering wheel, in the flow of traffic, he finds (temporarily, as it turns out) the "commonplace and ordinary reassurance of what are the realities of life" (C 251). But these "realities" reveal their self-deluding character when Mehring's meditations turn to a set of commonplace justifications of the South African system: "the white working man knows he couldn't live as well anywhere else in the world, and the blacks want shoes on their feet—where else in Africa will you see so many well-shod blacks as on this road?" (C 252). The mention of the shoes here is symptomatic, a trace of Mehring's earlier repression of the state's injustice in Namibia; and the received ideas he rehearses are entirely homologous to the patterns of movement that constitute his reassuring social traffic. Both serve, finally, to cover up the fundamental South African injustice: the fact of territorial dispossession, which is marked metaphorically (as historical allegory) by the buried black body, and metonymically (as contemporary geography) by the displaced Damaras.

Mehring's "patterns of activity in relation to an environment" serve—at least initially and in theory—to keep certain unpleasant facts, especially other bodies, at bay and out of sight. The attraction of the highway and the rules of the road clearly lies in the fact that they enable him to avoid random social "collisions." The point is illustrated by an incident one morning on the farm when, on the way to his car, Mehring suddenly finds himself in the midst of a group of day laborers who have been hired to do some weeding. His inability to go forward or retreat, surrounded as he is by this "ragged army" of people, some of whom look at him knowingly and some of whom move "blindly not seeming to know what they are making for" (C 182), represents a disconcerting loss of authority: for once, the human traffic does not flow in a way that assures his usual bodily autonomy. It is no accident, then, that Mehring is so often enclosed in the hermetically sealed space of his car or in an airplane. Even in the city, his habitual trajectory indicates his desire both to control and repress. He is seldom exposed to the street (which Gordimer has elsewhere posited as a utopian space of social interaction) but instead drives from one underground parking bay to the other (C 187), where gates are opened for him by black attendants.[45]

This mobility, the "closed system" of Mehring's global travels, does not necessarily involve a sense of freedom, but it is clearly desired and recognized as a form of power by those who lack it. Jacobus, for one, realizes all too well that the planes that fly over Mehring's bit of highveld signify privilege and a command of space. "They are always going to those countries white people go to," he reflects. "The whole world is theirs" (C 266). It is significant, in this light, that the black children on the farm should fashion for themselves cars out of wire in imitation of Mehring's, and that later in the novel, the woman who believes herself to be called by the ancestral spirits should dream that she has achieved a kind of magical mobility and a prophetic, panoramic view. "There was not," in this vision, "a single place in the whole country that she did not know because she went over it all, farther than Johannesburg and Durban, all in her sleep" (C 166).[46]

A Proper Place

If Mehring's habitual movements and his psychological investment in a kind of spatial repression suggest that he is, however unconsciously, identified with apartheid and its politics of division and separation, the same is true with regard to his very conscious efforts at "conservation." Gordimer treats these as politically suspect. Despite the fact that Mehring's farm—the vlei, the grass, the eucalyptus trees, the reeds—seems to have astonishing regenerative capacities, his efforts at conservation always have something of a paranoid, apocalyptic quality. This contradiction suggests that Mehring's concern for nature actually stands for something else: a possessiveness he would rather repress, or at least aestheticize. This point is underscored with particular force when he rather proudly shows his son the new signpost that he has erected, or so he believes, out of "concern for the land." But what the sign really announces—in English, Afrikaans, and Zulu—is Mehring's proprietorship. It addresses all trespassers, that "constant parade cutting up through the farm to [the] shanty town," with an unambiguous message (C 140):

NO THOROUGHFARE
GEEN TOEGANG
AKUNANDLELA LAPHA

Mehring's conservation is inseparable from his desire to police the boundaries of his property. In practice, "time for conservation" on the farm means that there are "buildings to be repaired, fire-breaks cleared," and especially "fences" that must be "seen to" (C 74). It means the maintenance of the map by which the proprietor defines his farm as special, as distinct from the location, the garbage dump, and the city.

Mehring's elaborate plans for the eventual layout of his farm also reveal a political subtext. He resembles in many ways the "improving" landlord from the eighteenth century, whose ideology, as Raymond Williams has argued, finds a twentieth-century and global avatar in the notion of "development."[47] Mehring envisions a spread with a pair of huge indigenous trees in a "defining position," a dignified approach, a curved road leading to a complex of outbuildings, and a "real Transvaal farmhouse" with a shady stoep "presid[ing]" over the land (225). Though this design is more in keeping with Pierneef, the painter of Transvaal landscapes, than Capability Brown, it is no less expressive of social relations: even the language—"presiding," "defining"—is suggestive of power and privilege. This suggestion is reiterated when Mehring purchases two expensive European chest-nut trees and his meditations again turn to the topography of his farm. He makes a mental note that the farm workers' compound—dreary gray cement-block houses surrounded by lean-tos of wire and tin—will have to be rebuilt "decently" (C 202). But his train of thought soon reveals that his notion of decency has little to do with the living conditions of the workers. It is rather a matter of the place-ment of their dwellings—they should be kept out of sight, clear of the river front-age, in a place where "their mess and fowls and cooking" will be safely hidden away (C 202).

In Mehring's highveld idyll, then, the workers are placed in a difficult, if not impossible, position. As his language reveals so clearly, their habitation will always be temporary for Mehring—and more or less illegitimate. He recognizes that Jacobus and "his kind" have been on the farm long before him. Indeed, he has picked up the stone hand-axes of "their ancestors" in his fields (C 184). But their residency, since it does not recognize the same map as he does—"boundaries," he notes, "mean little to them, when they say 'here'"(C 206)—can conveniently be labeled as "squatting." Jacobus and "his kind" are therefore not allowed to be seen, let alone to "preside over a view." Yet they are constantly blamed for their lack of aesthetic sensitivity and ecological consciousness, evidenced, for Mehring, in their regrettable tendency to be more interested in the well-being of cattle and crops than in that of birds, lilies, and willow trees.

Gordimer's lyrical descriptions of the landscape should therefore not obscure her fundamental suspicion of the aesthetic impulse.[48] The basis of her critique, which is allegorically presented in The Conservationist, is made explicit in her interviews and writings in the decade or so after the novel's publication. Like J. M. Coetzee, Gordimer sees in white South Africans' tendency toward an aesthetic mystification of the land a strange, antisocial displacement of affection. (One might recall here that in The Conservationist, Antonia mocks Mehring for having invented "a new kind" of love: "A superior kind, without people" [C 178].) But whereas Coetzee, in his Jerusalem Prize address of 1987, emphasizes the impor-tance of fraternity and the irony inherent in white South Africans' affection for rocks and stones and plants (things that cannot, like fellow human beings, ever return that love), Gordimer, in interviews dating from 1986 and 1987, offers a more hard-nosed critique, one devoid of Coetzee's muted pastoral nostalgia. She argues that the discourse of conservation readily serves as an ideological cover-up, especially in a country where the question of the ownership of the land is so fraught. A "concern about the natural environment in which we live," she notes, can become "something unpleasant and almost evil," since it is so often connected with a "lack of concern for human beings." The very "beauties of South Africa" thus become "one of the most ugly things about it." She even suggests that it would be better if the pristine beaches and manicured parks were dirtier, strewn with discarded ice-cream cups and the like: this would at least be a sign that the "great mass of people" were using and enjoying the land.[49]

The mundane detail of the ice-cream cups is not insignificant: at the heart of Gordimer's antipastoralism is a decoding of the social meaning of rubbish. White South Africans' desire to keep the country clean and beautiful masks, for Gordimer, their desire to preserve South Africa as a "private domain," as a "kind of exclusive club for white people."[50] Trash thus functions in the manner of Barthesian myth: it is something everyone "naturally" opposes and dislikes. But since it is implicitly associated with black people, the discourse of rubbish becomes what Barthes calls a form of "depoliticized speech": a way of justifying exclusion without seeming to say anything about race, or apartheid, or any such ugly topic.[51] One of the vignettes in Gordimer's 1984 novella *Something Out There* demonstrates the functioning of this myth. After a momentary and uncanny glimpse of what turns out to be a baboon in the bushes at the Houghton Golf Club, a society doctor assumes that the dark intruder must be a "black out-of-work." "Wasn't it true they were a problem for the groundsmen, no fence seemed to keep them and their litter out?" (SOT 26).

The rhetorical question is revealing and seems applicable, in hindsight, to *The Conservationist*. For Mehring's farm, which he calls "a fair and lovely place," is nothing if not a "proper place" in De Certeau's sense of the term. In fact, the novel seems to play on both of the meanings the word *propre* carries in French: the "propriety" of the farm relates to both "ownership" and "cleanliness." The connection between these two meanings is readily grasped from a spatial perspective and in terms suggested by the discussion of boundaries in Mary Douglas's anthropological investigations of cleanliness and pollution. In *Purity and Danger*, Douglas offers a definition of dirt as "things out of place." The clean and the proper, conversely, refer to whatever is kept within socially accepted boundaries. Both trespassers and trash are "things out of place." As such, they represent the dialectical antithesis of conservation, an antithesis that (while never explicitly named) is legible in Gordimer's novel as revolution—as the revenge implicit in the idea of waste.[52]

It is thus symbolically appropriate that Mehring should be obsessed with keeping his land litter-free and keeping trespassers off his property. It is as if he reads in these "things out of place" a challenge to the topography that makes sense of his bodily and political experience. His meticulousness—he won't "even leave a cigarette butt lying about to deface the farm" (C 43)—might seem laudable, except that his meditations soon reveal his automatic associations: "It's they—up at the compound," we find him thinking, "who discard plastic bags and put tins beside tree-stumps. He's forever cleaning up after them" (C 43). The political subtext of his pastoral housekeeping is also suggested by Gordimer's ironic juxtapositions of scenes. In an important early chapter, for instance, Mehring receives a letter from his son (this one addressing the matter of military service). He tears it up, and then obsessively collects every little scrap of paper in his hand rather than litter his pasture. The incident is followed immediately by the first extended description of the black township and the garbage dump that lie on the verge of Mehring's farm. The contrast is precise and surely deliberate:

> Thousands of pieces of paper take to the air and are plastered against the location fence when August winds come. The assortment of covering worn by the children and old people who scavenge the rubbish dump is moulded against their bodies or bloated away from them. Sometimes the wind is strong enough to cart-wheel sheets of board and send boxes slamming over and over until they slither across the road and meet the obstacle of the fence, or are flattened like the bodies of cats or dogs under the wheels of the traffic. The newspaper, ash, bones and smashed bottles come from the location; the boxes and board and straw come from the factories and warehouses not far across the veld where many of the location people work. (C 84)

The "location" occupies the same place in *The Conservationist* as the Valley of Ashes does in *The Great Gatsby*: an unpredictable, liminal place, midway between the city and the (pseudo)pastoral retreat, officially marginal yet symbolically compelling. Its ominous potency in Mehring's imagination is revealed through the revolutionary allegory of trash: if the white man's farm is "clean," the location, which the farm children perceive as rather "like the dump," is "dirty"—a place where people wait for taxis amid "beer cartons and orange peel" (C 39). As Mehring's thoughts become increasingly agitated in the course of the novel, the association of black people with trash is intensified. They come to resemble windswept rubbish: "They're used to anything, they survive, swallowing dust, walking in droves through the rain, and blown, in August, like newspapers to the shelter of any wall" (C 248). The simile confirms the idea that Mehring's constant tidying up is ultimately a way of signaling his difference from "them and their mess," and of erasing the signs of their presence.

These efforts are ultimately futile, as Mehring knows all along—hence the paranoid, apocalyptic character of his thinking. When the black children on the farm play with his precious guinea fowl eggs, he tallies the cost as follows: "Eleven. Soon there will be nothing left. In the country. The continent. The oceans, the sky" (C 11). The trespassers, he recognizes, will never be stopped: "the endless Sunday traffic from compound to compound, every farm is a thoroughfare for them, nothing can be done about it" (C 56). Mehring's attempt to use his farm as a sign that he is "no ordinary pig-iron dealer" (C 41) is stymied by the habits of ordinary men who leave gates open, make holes in the fence at the location, and take shortcuts across property lines. Like all such strategies, as De Certeau argues, the colonizer's attempt to set up a "proper place" is undermined and resisted: it is challenged by the very movements and bodies of the excluded. The disturbing sight of trespassers and trash—of "things out of place"—thus foretells Mehring's and apartheid's failure. The scraps of paper are particularly threatening and uncanny. They are not only what De Certeau would call the "marks and sign of the other" (that "other" who must bear papers that turn him or her into a "temporary sojourner") but also disconcertingly familiar. They recall Mehring's own essential piece of paper, his deed of ownership, which can just as easily be reduced to rubbish. His thinking is constantly haunted by his mistress's taunt: "That bit of paper you bought for yourself from the deeds office isn't going to be valid for as long as another generation. It'll be worth about as much as those our grandfathers gave the blacks when they took the land from them. The blacks will tear up your bit of paper. No one'll remember where you are buried" (C 177). There is, then, not so much a difference as a threatening sameness at stake in the allegory of things out of place. Both Mehring's deed of sale and the documents that make Africans "temporary sojourners" are finally of the same substance: they are paper—mutable, readily scrapped, shredded, and turned into trash. The difference between trespassing and legitimate occupation is equally slight—especially since the white man's occupation of the land, based as it is on conquest and dispossession, is in the larger historical frame also a trespass.

The instability of the latter distinction is expressed, I would like to suggest, via the punning that occasionally surfaces in the novel. The section in which Mehring meditates on his black "squatters" ends on a peculiar note, which makes sense only if we see it as an instance of ironic wordplay. Mehring, who has slept outside on a beautiful night, awakes with a strange sense of elation. High on the idea that "absolutely no one" can see him on "his own place," he decides to shit outside and produces—not "without pleasure," Gordimer tells us—"a steaming turd" (C 210). The point of all this, unless we are willing to go along with Mehring's view that the act is a sign of healthy animality, is surely that he too, when all is said and done, "squats" on the land. The very word "squatter" thus turns against the landlord and colonizer in a disconcerting and embarrassing way.[53]

The Mark of the Other

The Conservationist does not have a plot in the strict sense of the word. It sets up, instead, what Stephen Clingman has described as a "symbolic synchrony," a reiterative portending of Mehring's destiny.[54] I would argue, more specifically, that its symbolic sequences dramatize, again and again, the idea that the "proper place" of the white man's colonial idyll is, in De Certeau's phrase, "bewitched" by the mark of the other. The four most important and, for the protagonist, most disturbing incidents in the novel (the discovery of the body in the pasture, the veld fire, the flood, and the final scene, in which Mehring finds himself caught in embarrassing circumstances with a female hitchhiker at an abandoned mine dump) all hinge on the conflict of spatial practices I have sketched out: they are all legible in terms of the revolutionary allegory of things out of place.

The first of these events, the discovery and hasty burial of the stranger's corpse on the farm, establishes the controlling pattern of the entire novel. It is replayed both in the incident involving the laborer Solomon, who is found half-dead in the fields after he has been mugged, and, more obviously, in the rediscovery of the stranger's corpse at the end of the novel, after it is washed out of its shallow grave and is finally laid to rest with due ceremony. Critics have noted that the idea of the burial and reemergence of the body is also reiterated or paralleled in the formal structure of the novel. Motifs that are first introduced in oracular fashion by the interspersed citations from Callaway's *Religious Systems of the Amazulu* (e.g., those of the flood and the return of the ancestors) are played out with increasing explicitness in the narrative sections of the novel, thus enacting the idea of the return of the repressed on the level of form: the buried African subtext comes to control the surface narrative and takes possession of the text as a whole.[55]

The novel's form thus underscores the allegorical importance of its central image. But it is also important for a political decoding of the text to note exactly how the corpse is described in the first scene. The dead man's significance lies not only in the fact that he is black, or in the fact that he is found on a farm: the two salient details, for instance, in Coetzee's reading of the body as a subversion of the South African pastoral's symptomatic repression of the fact of black labor (WW 11). Equally important, I would argue, are his secondhand suit, his fancy shoes, and his fake snakeskin belt, which mark the dead man as "a city slicker" (C 15). He is "out of place" in the pastoral scene—an "intruder" (C 13), the most potent and the most persistent of all the many trespassers in the novel. Even Jacobus, who, according to Mehring, has only the vaguest sense of official boundaries, insists when the body is first discovered that "this is people from there— there—He points that same accusing finger away in the direction of the farm's southern boundary" (C 16). Moreover, as something discarded on someone else's land, the corpse is also, in a sense, rubbish. The farmer's annoyance at the stranger's unceremonious burial by the police stems not from any great humanity or moral sensitivity (Mehring is no Antigone) but from his insistence that his "proper place" must not become a "dumping ground" or a "public cemetery" (C 27). The corpse's doubly transgressive and illegitimate presence thus raises crucial political questions about the boundaries to and the ownership of Mehring's land. The dead stranger's bodily presence represents a destabilization of boundaries and the "symbolic synchrony" that it initiates allegorizes—paradoxically—the intrusion of the diachronic, of South Africa's repressed history, in Mehring's idyll.

The veld fire, the second defining event in the novel, involves neither other people nor bodies, but it is also revealing of *The Conservationist*'s spatial and racial configurations. The fire does not touch the crops, so there are no losses, Mehring thinks, to be recorded on the income tax forms. Yet it evokes in him an intense distress, which he attributes to his interest in conservation: the damage, he notes, extends all the way to the vlei next to the river, and he fears that the loss of the reeds that anchor the soil may lead to erosion in the rainy season (C 97). But the patterns of metaphor and association recorded in his internal monologue suggest that, on an unconscious and allegorical level, his distress has a political dimension. The fire is consistently described in military and cartographic terms: it is an "invader" that has taken control of a certain territory overnight, and its path is marked in blackened grass over "inlets, promontories, beach-heads," so that it redraws the outlines of Mehring's property with "new boundaries of black" (C 95). Like the "ordinary border farmers" of Ladysmith, Mehring seems immediately and unreflectively to associate the blackness left by the veld fire with black people. He notices other burnt patches near the bus stop where squatters wait for the bus and on cold mornings burn handfuls of grass to keep themselves warm and, for a moment, thinks that the veld fire must have entered the compound of his workers, darkened as it is by the heat of their braziers, ash, and smoke. He even recalls how his mistress used to favor African ceramics, marked in black by the fire of the kiln. The visual image of the new black map created by the fire suggests the tenuousness of the social inscriptions by which Mehring's ownership is marked on the land. It is no accident that his concern about the fire should turn his thoughts to other "disputed territor[ies]" (C 101)—to his altercations with Antonia about the country where he was born and how it should be named on the map: " 'South West Africa.' 'Mandatory territory' "—or, the name that troubles Mehring, since it represents political change, " 'Namibia' " (C 101). The fire symbolically amplifies the threat represented to Mehring by trespassers and trash: it is the mark of otherness and, as such, threatens to erase the boundaries that safeguard his pastoral dream.

The same can be said of the tropical storm that precipitates the novel's crisis. Sweeping in from the Mozambique Channel, it represents a radical challenge to the white man's topography of power. It has become something of a critical commonplace to see the storm as predictive of the fall of the colonial government in Mozambique in 1974, an event that was to rekindle revolutionary energies all over Southern Africa.[56] But even if one is reluctant to ascribe sibylline powers to Gordimer, the political resonances of the storm's transformations are undeniable. The deluge defamiliarizes the landscape the reader has come to know through the various descriptions of Mehring's commute to and from the farm and thus signals a kind of epistemological break. Not only are the familiar factories and the roadway no longer visible in their old places: the entire landscape has turned into its uncharted other—a seascape. "The sense of perspective," Gordimer tells us, "was changed as out on an ocean where, by the very qualification of their designation, no landmarks are recognizable" (C 233). This spatial "rearrange[ment]" (C 246) alters those habitual practices—the "topographies of activity"—that define the ideological grid of everyday experience. The highway is flooded; traffic grinds to a halt.

The political meaning of the storm is also expressed through a shift in the novel's allegory of trash. The black people from the farm and the location, who protect themselves from the rain under old fertilizer bags and scavenged sheets of plastic, may still seem to resemble the rubbish with which Mehring has equated them all along. But it soon becomes clear that the racist distinctions on which this habitual association rests no longer apply in the changed landscape. The description of the most sensational accident resulting from the storm hints at a significant reversal: a small culvert, usually dry and—as Mehring would not fail to note—full of "beer cartons thrown in by the blacks" (C 235), suddenly becomes a torrent, and its relentless force sweeps away a car driven by an Afrikaans couple. These two white people are symbolically discarded and turned into rubbish by the transformative forces of the storm: their car is found in a pit between the mine dumps—in a trash heap of sorts, "a graveyard for wrecked cars and other obstinate imperishable objects" (C 236). By dislocating the familiar topography, the storm symbolically disrupts apartheid's invidious boundaries, its distinctions between "us" and "them."

It is no surprise, then, that when Mehring is finally able to return to his farm, his first impulse is to reestablish his proprietorship: a desire expressed in his irrepressible urge to begin picking up even the organic debris the storm has left behind. He is anxious to find "the proper place, the proper slope" (C 245), to start digging drainage canals and eager to restore the farm's structures (the porch, for instance, where some sacks of fertilizer had been temporarily shielded from the rain) to their proper uses. But Mehring's absorption in "tidily looking" over the farm (to borrow Gordimer's odd yet appropriate phrase) comes to an abrupt end when the corpse of the buried stranger, washed up by the floodwaters, reemerges in the third pasture (C 246). For Mehring this confrontation is profoundly disturbing. The decaying body, he intuits, represents not only a trespass on his land but also an invasion of his most private space: his internal monologues. He realizes, on some level, that his most secret thoughts have been addressed all along (as the alert reader has already recognized) to this most intimate of intruders—this one piece of "organic debris" that will not yield to his conservationist efforts.

The strange "psychodrama" (as John Cooke calls it) of the novel's penultimate scene, which depicts Mehring's encounter with a tarty hitchhiker, can also be read in terms of the revolutionary allegory of trespassing and trash.[57] The place where the woman takes Mehring for a seductive picnic of sorts is just off the highway, near an abandoned mine dump. It is, not insignificantly, the same kind of place where the Afrikaner victims of the flood are washed up. Indeed, Mehring imagines himself in their position: "The Mercedes swept over the road into the culvert" (C 260). Despite its trees, its silence, and its initially inviting appearance, the spot soon assumes for Mehring a disquieting aspect. It is dirty, he notes, with "bits of rusty tin and an old enamel pot lying near by" and "a porridge of papers splattered against the trunk of one of the trees" (C 258). The place is overdetermined as a place of waste: the site of everything the aesthetically sensitive conservationist would rather repress. It is situated next to the mounds of cyanide waste dumped by Mehring's own mining industry and, on closer inspection, appears to be nothing more than an "overgrown rubbish dump." The accumulated garbage presents itself to Mehring as a disconcerting sign of "Others: That mess of wet paper, cigarette packs" (C 259), he thinks. "Others . . . have already fouled the place . . . witness that disgusting mess against the tree" (C 263). Most sinisterly, or so Mehring thinks, it seems like "a place where people might dump a body" (C 260).

This last observation suggests the key factor in Mehring's breakdown. His sense of his own power and distinctiveness, so profoundly invested in his ownership and appreciation of his four hundred acres, is dismantled by a subliminal awareness that this waste ground where he finds himself is not really all that different from his farm. After all, the farm has already been the dumping ground for a dead body, and it has also been marked by the signs of "others"—whether in the form of the litter of the workers or in the form of the Stone Age hand axes Mehring so proudly picks up in his fields. Even the aura of seedy sexual assignations that pervades this wooded place is troublingly familiar to him. Mehring's beautiful farm was also, when he first bought it, intended as a site for seduction, and the tag he applies to it early on in the novel—"a place to bring a woman" (C 42)—is ironically echoed in the hitchhiker's lewd scolding: "What you bring me here for then, man!" (C 261). The "industrial rusticity" of the roadside spot, moreover, underscores the vulnerability of Mehring's own pastoral pocket, which is also situated near the garbage dump, the black township, and the highway. Mehring's horror at the squalid picnic spot thus parallels his earlier feeling of dismay when he recognizes the hitchhiker as a distasteful double of Antonia: "a cheap mass-production of the original bare face he likes in a woman" (C 252). The "dirty place" comes to seem like the cheap double of his "fair and lovely place." It confronts him with precisely the kind of dislocating experience Lars Engle has associated with the political uncanny: a rising up of the familiar in the unfamiliar, of the self in the other—an experience that "leaves one unable to continue living one's life as before."[58] In Mehring's case, the experience represents the abrogation of his special relation to the African soil, by which he has so carefully tried to preserve his own distinctiveness. This is especially clear when at the end of the scene Mehring succumbs to a particularly stale version of white South African paranoia. He imagines that he will be caught *in flagrante delicto* with a "coloured" and that his face will appear "distorted, decayed, but just recognizable" (C 264) in a picture on the back of the Sunday newspapers.[59]

The rising up of this all too common nightmare emphasizes yet again the collapse of Mehring's carefully constructed boundaries and self-definitions: he comes to seem like a very "ordinary" white South African indeed. Moreover, in the "dirty" semipublic place, marked by the trace of others, Mehring seems stripped of his power to control his own territory. When a watching policeman (or thug) reprimands him for trespassing ("What d'you think you're doing in this place?") his loss of subjectivity and agency is complete. Mehring has, in effect, become identical to the man found dead in his pasture: he, too, is a "city slicker," out of place on a piece of African soil. The novel's penultimate scene ends with Mehring, the man who has been so careful to "command a view," as the one being looked at, as the object of surveillance and the scrutiny of others. His internal monologue closes with a strange invitation, expressive of his final fragmentation: "Come and look. . . . It's Mehring down there" (C 265). And the fact that he immediately decides to sell his farm signals his own forced removal from the land, perhaps even his own dumping on the trash heap of history.

Mayibuye!

The Conservationist, as I noted earlier, ends with a coda in which the farm laborers lay the murdered trespasser to rest as if he were one of their own. It is a scene that has contributed to the novel's characterization (by hostile critics like Gorak) as a retreat to the local solution of the pastoral: a mere replacement of the white pastoral by its black counterpart (C 56).[60] This is not a negligible charge, since the scene includes a full complement of pastoral props: hayrack, tractor, and simple people singing in "thin but perfect harmony" (C 267). However, in terms of the spatial allegory I have uncovered, the scene has a broader political meaning. It does not

merely endorse the values of a rural community. On the contrary, the farm workers' acceptance of the dead stranger as an ancestor, as "one of them," undoes the
opposition between country and city.[61] The burial is both a symbolic reintegra-
tion and a revolutionary prophecy; the stranger's body is returned not just to the
dust in the usual ritual sense but to the whole land—a land in which boundaries
no longer count. It is in this sense that "he ha[s] come back" (C 267)—a phrase
that echoes the ANC's rallying cry: *Mayibuye iAfrika!* (Come back, Africa!)—and
has taken "possession of the earth."[62]

But in view of the changed situation in postapartheid South Africa, my
reading of the novel's ending also requires a coda, and one that returns us to
the topic of apartheid's forced removals and their cultural resonance. With the
unbanning and subsequent electoral victory of the ANC—the return of the
underground resistance movements into the national and global public sphere—
it seemed as though the long history of territorial dispossession in South Africa
might gradually be reversed, and that the South African pastoral might therefore
be reimagined. The master narrative of dispossession and restitution seemed to
reach its climax in 1994, in the heady atmosphere of the first democratic election.
This moment marked the return of thousands of people to their land (among
them the people of Roosboom), who were able to reclaim their farms under a
special Presidential Lead Project—an initiative guided not only by the urgency
of this kind of redress but also by a recognition of its symbolic significance at
the dawn of the new democracy.[63] A sense of the elation of this moment can be
gleaned from the book *Back to the Land*, a verbal and visual record of the stories
of a dozen communities, including Roosboom, whose fate best adheres to the
outlines of the master narrative of colonial dispossession and subsequent restitution. In keeping with this stirring story, *Back to the Land* juxtaposes familiar
apartheid-era images of the dispossessed being carted off in government trucks,
of their grim protest meetings and vigils, and so forth with joyous images of their
return: with pictures of people laughing and crying, shaking hands with Derek
Hanekom, the new minister of Land Affairs, plowing their first furrows, rebuild-
ing their demolished homes, and so forth.[64] The spirit of the moment is also
revealed—and in a way that seems metaphorically apt—in the fact that the first
chief land claims commissioner, Joe Seremane, adopted the humane Setswana
saying "Motho ga a lathlwe" ("You can't dump a person") as an inspirational
motto.[65] Even after Seremane's departure from his post, the conciliatory attitudes
expressed by his motto and fostered by the negotiated settlement dictated that
neither blacks nor whites should be uprooted in the new democracy. The 1997
White Paper on South African Land Policy, though focused on the alleviation of
poverty and the redress of past injustices, is surprisingly moderate in its attitude
toward white landowners—far more moderate, in fact, than Gordimer's novel, in
which the wealthy protagonist is psychologically destroyed and forced to abandon his beloved patch of African earth. Alert to the symbolic meaning of land,
the White Paper asserts the right to private property and secure domicile for
landowners, workers, and tenants alike. And it is strikingly conciliatory on a rhetorical level, eschewing, "as far as semantically possible, racial or ethnic demarca-
tion in its vision of reform."[66]

But the judgment is still out on whether the land reform program will deliver on its promises. It certainly seems dubious that the reversal of the notoriously unjust 87-percent-to-13-percent allocation of land to the white minority and the black majority, respectively, will ever be realized.[67] The ANC, moreover, remains caught between its populist rhetoric of redress and the pragmatic demands of its neoliberal macroeconomic policy—and the disastrous fallout of the Zimbabwean land seizures has not made things any easier. Though the government has repeatedly announced its intention to accelerate land reform and redistribution, its latest policies favor black commercial farmers (the rural wing of the new national bourgeoisie, if you will) rather than the simple agricultural workers evoked in Gordimer's poetic conclusion. Most important, the desire to return to the land has proven, in many ways, to be symbolic, rather than expressive of any real inclination to farm. South Africa, we should recognize, has never been easy soil to till. The children of the displaced communities are not always keen to leave the more urban areas to which their families were removed, and a majority of claimants settle for cash rather than the old paternal acres: a measure of the increasing commodification of South African—and global—social space in the thirty years since Gordimer's novel was written.[68] It is a sign of the times to find Cherryl Walker, the tireless researcher for the Surplus People's Project in the 1980s, calling for a revision of the myth of dispossession and return in favor of a more forward-looking (and less pastoral) myth for the nation as a whole: a myth that would include "notions of citizenship, of plurality, of limited choices and public interest, but without abandoning the central themes of redress, of justice with reconciliation." The master narrative, she declares, "valorizes the past. What we need now is a narrative that orients us more successfully to the future."[69]

Gordimer's own postapartheid treatment of pastoral questions has been thoughtful—and rather muted. The optative and prophetic mode of *The Conservationist*'s coda does not set the tone for her major novel of the transition years, *None to Accompany Me*. This novel, while it does not match the stylistic achievement of *The Conservationist*, nevertheless offers a rich account of the labile social landscape of the early 1990s and gives ample evidence of Gordimer's ongoing interest in questions of land and land reform. Its main focus, as I showed in chapter 2, is the transformation of sexual and domestic arrangements during the years of the transition, and the emergence of a gradually integrating and increasingly commodified urban scene. But the professional life of the chief protagonist, Vera Stark, a lawyer for a charitable foundation for land rights, allows Gordimer to keep the impact of the transition on the lives of the rural poor in focus as well. Indeed, the novel's various dramas of personal transformation are staged against the panoramic backdrop of the struggle for the redress of apartheid's geographical schemes. The reader learns, in the course of the novel, about land invasions by homeless people, reclamations of ancestral grave sites, violent tensions between evicted tenant-laborers and white farmers, and even the struggle to prevent Robben Island from being leased to a resort developer. Though the concept-city of apartheid—along with "the Act that put the Idea into practice"—is formally abolished, and though evicted people can now "present the case for having restored to them . . . *their place*, which was taken away and allotted to whites" (NTA 13), the problem of land, of its ownership and its symbolic meaning, is far from resolved. It is significant that the first section of the novel is entitled "Baggage." The word clearly refers to the victims of forced removals, who were treated, as we are told in the first pages of the novel, as so much "baggage" by the apartheid state. But it also alludes to the dead weight of the past that is inevitably carried over into the transition, and the effects of which are still palpable both in individual psyches and in social space. If the characteristic temporality of the transition is that of anachronism, its characteristic geography is one of jarring juxtapositions. Thus the novel contrasts new middle-class developments that are being put up in the bare veld and their "sudden illusion of suburbia" (NTA 83) with the nightmarish phantasmagoria of squatter settlements located right next to them. It also opposes the precarious mobility of a young black clerk, who is finally able to occupy an ordinary city apartment, with the unmitigated destitution of his wife, who is left behind, like so many rural women, in mud-brick houses, those "scatterings of habitation, out-cropped along with the trashpits of white towns" (NTA 193).

As this descriptive line suggests, the new metaphor of baggage does not entirely displace the older rhetoric of trash. The novel's villain, a white farmer named Tertius Odendaal, is someone who—rightly and wrongly—believes that he "move[s] with the times" (NTA 22). When his land is invaded by landless squatters, he tries to have it declared a private township from which he can extract rent and, if need be, evict all those residents who cannot pay. But while his attempt to "diversify resources" is quite in keeping with the rampant commercialism of the new order, his attitudes toward his possible tenants are still readily expressed in the familiar apartheid-era epithets: they are "nothing," "trespassers," "vuilgoed," their homes and possessions the merest "rubbish" (NTA 24). The South Africa of the novel remains a place where citizens live in separate experiential worlds: to some people, the concept of land reform means the loss of a weekend fishing retreat, while to others, it means the loss of a livelihood, of the "mealies and millet they have worked the land for, every day, for generations" (NTA 163). But while recording the volatility of the transition in appropriately ambivalent fashion, *None to Accompany Me* does suggest an ethic that might draw citizens closer as part of the same nation. It is, ironically, Didymus Maqoma, the exiled guerilla who himself fails to adapt to the "now" of the emerging nation, who articulates it best. The challenge at hand, he thinks, is that of "not occupying the past, not moving into, but remaking our habitation, our country, to let us live within the needs and space of decency our country can afford" (NTA 184). It is an ethic of creative frugality (antithetical to the wasteful economies of De Certeau's concept-city), one that makes demands both on blacks, who are increasingly lured into thinking about consumer choices rather than basic rights, and on whites, who must begin to real-ize that "luxury's a debt they can't pay" (NTA 184).[70]

The difficulty of this task is never underestimated in *None to Accompany Me* or in Gordimer's remarkable short fiction of the transition period, to which I would like turn for a poetically apt conclusion to the meditations of this chapter. The 1992 story "Amnesty" concerns the arrest, imprisonment, and early release of a black political activist. But it is not exactly a happy story. Narrated as it is from the point of view of the activist's lover, a young woman who lives and works on a remote farm, it is also a tale of poverty and waiting. It constantly emphasizes the difficulties presented by rural isolation: traveling, keeping in touch with family members who have migrated to the cities, knowing where to find permits to visit a political prisoner, reaching out to aid organizations—all of these things are almost impossibly difficult, simply because "the farm is so far from town" (J 251). The activist's return home from prison, dressed in town clothes and fancy shoes and surrounded by an entourage of comrades, exacerbates rather than resolves the narrator's experience of social distances and divisions. Though the man insists that his work is "for all of us, on the farms as well as the towns" (J 248), it immediately takes him back to the cities and away from the narrator and their child. He shows little interest in the fact that she is again pregnant—that is "women's business" (J 255)—and his comrades, though they intently discuss strategies for organizing farm workers, never speak to her. It is also telling that the story should open with the young woman scratching herself on a barbed wire fence as she runs over to the next farm to tell "our people there" of the good news of the amnesty.

This detail suggests that the old oppositions and boundaries of the pastoral still exist: the divide between city and country, between men and women, between landowners and squatters remains in place. At the story's end, the young woman looks across the broad land on which "the farmers allow [her people] to squat," land that, she feels, rightly "belongs to nobody" and meditates on the fact that her man and, indeed, her life, has not been fully returned to her:

> Waiting for him to come back.
> Waiting.
> I am waiting to come back home. (J 257)

That Gordimer should express these thoughts in language that so clearly echoes the conclusion of *The Conservationist* is significant. "Amnesty" suggests that symbolic resolutions, like those offered in her powerful farm novel, will not be enough in the new nation announced with the release of Nelson Mandela and the undoing of the apartheid-era laws. It reminds us that the return to full citizenship, for the many South African women—and men—entrapped in rural poverty, cannot be celebrated prematurely.[71]

4

A MAN'S SCENERY

> This ugly little city....These are the ingre-
> dients: flesh and blood, sea, wind, and sky;
> dirty little streets; faces under streetlamps
> late at night; never rich and most times
> poor, poor enough for too much hope ...
> all that makes this earth my here and now.
>
> —Athol Fugard, *Notebooks, 1960–1977*

> Outside our human environment is the
> world of stones.
>
> —Athol Fugard, *Notebooks, 1960–1977*

Hotel Room, Park Bench, and Stage

In his essay "The Novel without the Police," Lars Engle categorizes the work
of J. M. Coetzee, Nadine Gordimer, and Athol Fugard according to Raymond
Williams's familiar triad of the dominant, emergent, and residual forces discernible
in any given cultural formation—including that of academic literary criticism.[1]
Coetzee's fiction represents what Engle sees as the dominant trend: an antipositiv-
ist, antihumanist practice of negative hermeneutics, suspicious of all essentialisms
and master narratives. Alert to the distortions of power, Coetzee challenges such
notions as self-identity, sincerity, and truth-telling, as do the European theorists
of whose work he is an incisive reader. Gordimer's fiction represents for Engle
certain emergent possibilities. Her novels, he points out, are concerned with characters who find themselves at the edge of their theories about themselves and
their world. This fascination with the unknown—with those moments when all
interpretive schemes collapse—allows Gordimer to transcend the negations of
contemporary theory. Her work, in Engle's strikingly positive assessment, emphasizes the utopian potential of epistemological disruption and projects her readers
into a future of as-yet-uncharted praxis. The residual figure in this scheme is the
playwright Athol Fugard: a writer who still believes in humanist commonalities,
individual self-affirmation, and the revelatory witness of the work of art. Though
Engle is cautious not to dismiss the adversarial potential of such ideals in apartheid

South Africa, Fugard nevertheless emerges in his account as the least interesting and most old-fashioned of the three major white South African writers—a judgment that may be borne out by the relative paucity and relative hostility of academic writing about his work.[2]

In this chapter I would like to complicate this conception of Fugard, since I believe that the impact of his major plays on South African culture is currently being underestimated and that even some of his neglected writings (including the play *A Lesson from Aloes*, which is the central but not exclusive focus of this chapter) are open to surprisingly unsettling interpretations. This play and other earlier works speak to a number of ongoing concerns in postcolonial studies, including the problem of national allegory and national belonging, the relation of the local and the global, the construction and representation of subaltern subjectivities, hybridity, and—that usefully multivalent concept—translation. This said, I must admit that the task I have set myself here is not an easy one. It is futile to deny that, compared to Coetzee and Gordimer, whose work consistently validates intellectual risk-taking, Fugard can seem downright sentimental. In recent years, he has frequently spoken of the story as a "safe place" for the teller, suggesting a rather comfortable view of art that Coetzee and Gordimer would seem unlikely to endorse.[3] In contrast to their scrupulous resistance to pastoral indulgences, Fugard seems positively to wallow in them. At times (as when he declares in his 1994 memoir *Cousins* that the bag of walnuts he harvests every year from the old walnut tree next to his windmill is more valuable to him than any theatre award he has received [C 24]), he sounds a bit like Gordimer's tycoon-farmer Mehring (in *The Conservationist*), savoring his rural refuge from worldly success. In his plays and public statements of the late 1980s and early 1990s, moreover, Fugard tends to reduce complicated political realities to homespun analogies. His simplistic comparison of the creation of a new South Africa to the reconstruction of his cottage in the Karoo hamlet of New Bethesda is a case in point.[4] So too are the reductive allegories of his plays of the transition period: especially *My Children, My Africa!* (which seems to hold that the liberation struggle should have proceeded with the orderliness of a well-run high school debate) and *Playland* (which imagines a new era of reconciliation between black and white in completely apolitical terms).[5]

In a notebook entry from 1990, Fugard blamed the international success of *A Lesson from Aloes* for initiating a decline in the intellectual intensity of his work: "Paging through the published notebooks yesterday I realized with a shock how the quality of my intellectual life has deteriorated over the past ten years. The decline has been insidious. . . . I doubt whether an original thought or image has found its way onto [these pages] for years" (528).[6] One wants to be charitable in the face of such candor. But it is difficult not to concur to some extent with this self-assessment, especially if one compares Fugard's thin intertextual engagement with Ovid's *Tristia* in his 2001 play *Sorrows and Rejoicings* to, say, David Malouf's reimagining of Ovid's banishment in *An Imaginary Life* (or, for that matter, to Fugard's own potent translation of Sophocles' *Antigone* in *The Island* [1973]). While Malouf explores the themes of exile, place, and language in a spirit of courageous encounter with otherness, Fugard seems nostalgic and comes perilously close to reiterating the old cliché about the way Afrikaans and Afrikaners are naturally fitted to the South African landscape. The sentimentality of *Sorrows and Rejoicings* is a particular disappointment, since it comes at a time when translation and transition—what Breyten Breytenbach would call "die Groot Andersmaak" (the great othering)—are such pressing issues for South Africans, and since the play seems to retreat from the complex dramatization of those very issues in Fugard's earlier works.[7]

One of Fugard's most troubling public statements from the point of view of the present study is an address he gave at Georgetown University in 1988, at the height of the antiapartheid struggle. The topic of the speech was Thoreau's *Walden*—a book one might have expected Fugard to be fond of given his deep interest in the natural world and his attachment to his own rural refuges at Schoenmakers Kop, Sardinia Bay, and New Bethesda. He selected a few passages from *Walden* for special attention, one of which he read twice to the assembled audience and glossed at some length: "I know of no more encouraging fact than the unquestionable ability of man to elevate his life by a conscious endeavor. It is something to be able to paint a particular picture, or to carve a statue, and so to make a few objects beautiful, but it is far more glorious to carve and paint the very atmosphere and medium through which we look, which morally we can do. To affect the quality of the day, that is the highest art."[8] The passage strikes me as the stuff of graduation speeches; but what I find fascinating is the way Fugard describes the context in which he first encountered these words. It was, he recounts, in a hotel room in Johannesburg on a particular night in 1985 when the violence of the South African political situation left him feeling depressed and desperate. Taking courage from Thoreau's words, Fugard made bold to apply them to both his own lot and to that of his less fortunate compatriots: "these words," he declares, "have got to be just as true to me in the safety and comfort of this hotel room, must be as true for a black man or woman, hungry, shivering out in the freezing cold of that Johannesburg winter's night, huddled on a park bench." He even adds, as if to persuade himself: "These words have got to be as true for you, black brother, in your misery as they are for me in my comfort."[9]

Now, one can scarcely blame Fugard for finding solace in a literary classic during the dark days of the emergency, and there is certainly something to his belief that "there are areas of life in which one is no-one's victim other than one's own."[10] But his epiphany comes troublingly close to a declaration of faith in what Herbert Marcuse termed the "affirmative character of culture": the (residual) conception of art and culture as a matter of the soul, as ennobling and universally compelling, if not compulsory. In such a vision, all material contingencies evaporate: hotel room and park bench are readily transcended in an equal opportunity of spiritual uplift.[11] This epiphany, of course, suggests a further point of comparison between Fugard and Gordimer. The latter's work, as I showed in chapter 2, is deeply concerned with the shifting meanings of traveling texts. The "transport of a novel," Gordimer suggests, is never constant or transcendent: aesthetic pleasure, relevance, subjectivity—all these matters are determined by the reader's social and geographical location. Fugard's account of his reading of *Walden*, by contrast, seems designed precisely to discourage such considerations.

And yet contingencies of place have been of key importance—on every conceivable level—to Fugard's own practice as a writer and especially as a dramatist. Whatever he might have said in his later years about the story as a "safe place" for the storyteller, his theater has seldom provided a safe place for his actors. It has been, rather, the site of psychological—and, at times, political—risk-taking and exposure. Moreover, some of the most challenging and productive improvisational exercises he has set for his actor-collaborators over the years have involved an exploration of spaces and spatial relationships. In 1974, for instance, Fugard gave John Kani and Winston Ntshona the following task: working with only a table and a chair as props, they had to explore the difference imposed on their interactions by the physical fact of whether they happened to be sitting or standing. How did the person seated in the chair react to the person waiting next to the chair, and vice versa?[12] This improvisation, the germ for the 1982 play "*Master Harold*" . . . *and the Boys*, provoked strong emotions in the actors. The one who was placed in the position of having to stand about and wait, in particular, felt resentful, dependent, and supernumerary. John Kani was moved, afterward, to meditate on "the mask and the face behind the mask" of servitude and on the ontological and existential questions that such real-life role-playing generates: "Who am I? Where am I? Who is Where?" and so forth (N 202). The actors' exercise allows us to pose a simple question to the later Fugard: if a single chair can have a perceptible impact on the way human beings relate to each other, why deny the difference that can be made by a comfortable bed in a warm room, or a park bench on a freezing night?

The answer is not hard to find: the insistent quality of the Georgetown address derives precisely from Fugard's awareness that he is going against the grain of his own earlier vision of "man as something that was made and determined by social factors and social circumstances."[13] Though this vision was seldom as unqualified and one-dimensional as he makes it seem in the speech, a backward glance at his oeuvre reveals that an interest in the politics of place—in such things as the "links between physical and mental geography" or "the relationships between ontological bewilderment and an insecure geographical position"—has informed his work from the very start.[14] In fact, Fugard's literary response to apartheid's geographical schemes often preceded and influenced Gordimer's work. Her introduction to Cosmas Desmond's study *The Discarded People*, as we have seen, offers a powerful description of the psychological effects of forced removals and their destruction of the web of relations people call "home."[15] But it was in Fugard's *Boesman and Lena* (1968), with its stark dramatization of the plight of two vagrants evicted from their makeshift shack, that the metaphor of rubbish suggested in Desmond's title was first put to literary use.[16] The crude question Lena asks toward the end of the play—"How do you throw away a dead *kaffir*?" (BL 190)—anticipates the central allegory of *The Conservationist*, in which the corpse of a black man is dumped like so much trash in a white farmer's pasture, refuses to stay buried, and comes to prefigure the erasure of all of apartheid's boundaries.

Moreover, Fugard's view of "home" is often surprisingly ambiguous.[17] It is true that, unlike Gordimer, he seldom imbues "things out of place" with an uncanny force, but this is because his plays are set not in "proper places" but on

the margins, amid the detritus of apartheid society. There are, however, moments
when his work seems to echo her ideological critique of domestic space. In several of the plays, "home-sweet-fucking-home" (as Hallie calls it in *"Master Harold"* . . . *and the Boys* [MH 50]) is presented as oppressive, since the memories it
safeguards are redolent of confinement, shame, and self-disgust. In *Cousins*, we
even find Fugard confessing to the "great and abiding pleasure" he derives from
an impersonal and empty hotel room (C 82): the kind of site one would be more
inclined to associate with Hillela, Gordimer's picaresque adventuress in *A Sport of
Nature*, than with the earthy resident of New Bethesda.

We should recognize, moreover, that as a dramatist Fugard's engagement with
matters of space and place is inevitably more complex and (literally) multidimensional than that of any novelist. It is, of course, possible to speak of space in a novel;
but what we are talking about in this case is "space mediated by words (or rather
by black marks on the page), scanned, then imagined and recreated by a reader."[18]
In drama, space is also mediated by words: the descriptive moments in the dialogue create a diegetic space for our imaginative habitation. But what defines
drama is mimetic space: to be enacted, a play must take place somewhere, and
this real space, the space of ostention, if you will, is the sine qua non of theatrical
performance.[19] This understanding is fundamental to Fugard's often-cited definition of the basic elements of "pure theater": "They are: the actor and the stage,
the actor on the stage. Around him is space, to be filled and defined by movement
and gesture; around him is also silence, to be filled with meaning, using words and
sounds, and at moments when all else fails him, including the words, the silence
itself" (S vii). These eloquent lines reveal what Fugard meant by the "Carnal Reality" of theater (N 171). Though dramatic space creates an "elsewhere," or a "possible world" (the chronotope of the play is not the chronotope in which we live),
that "elsewhere" is embodied, presented "*as if* in progress in the actual here and
now": dramatic space is iconic, indexical, encountered *in medias res*, as opposed to
the "elsewhere" of fiction, which is solely descriptive, a matter of "there," "that,"
"those," "then," and (most characteristically) the past tense.[20] Though we tend
to think of it in terms of voice and speech, dramatic performance must also be
grasped as an engagement with "the strange stillness that defines the present": a
stillness that, as Homi Bhabha puts it in his meditations on translation, "makes
graphic a moment of transition" wrested from the ordinary continuum of history.
In performance, as in translation, "the very *writing* of historical transformation"—
and Fugard, we must recall, has described his art as "writing *directly* into . . . space
and silence" (S xi)—may be made visible.[21]

If Gordimer's work is concerned with "bodies in space," so much more so
is Fugard's, in which "bodies in space" are not only the primary themes but also
the primary signifiers. Moreover, in the case of Fugard's drama (as in that of the
black resistance drama for which his work has been an undeniable stimulus),
theater has also been a material site of contestation. The attempts on the part of
South African playwrights to create an oppositional public sphere have led many
scholars interested in South African drama to focus their attention on the sites
and institutions of theatrical production, and Fugard's work is certainly open to
this kind of approach as well.[22] My purpose in this chapter, however, is not to tra-

verse this well-traveled ground but to consider what Una Chaudhuri has called the "geography of drama" in relation to the rhetoric, imagery, and characterology of Fugard's work, and to attend also (especially in my comments on *A Lesson from Aloes*) to what we may call the space of translation: a notion that, as will become clearer in the course of this chapter, has both a thematic and a performative dimension.[23] But even though the institutions of the theater and theatrical production are not my main concern here, we must not lose sight of the fact that, in order to pursue his career, Fugard had to confront the geographical constraints imposed by the apartheid government in very practical ways: he faced restrictions on rehearsal and performance space, the invalidation of his passport, the arrest and incarceration of cast members, and the like. This context is part of the meaning (at least in their initial reception) of Fugard's plays. Under apartheid, where oppression was so intimately linked with the policing of physical bodies and of geographical boundaries, the public arena of the stage—or even just the space filled by the body of a performer—had a particular potency. It was a site where surveillance could be turned into self-dramatization and discovery, exposure into self-affirmation: where truths were not revealed so much as given a public and symbolic dimension.[24]

We should also bear in mind that, more so than the novel or film (both of which forms may potentially represent the entire world), drama can make its audiences intensely aware of spatial confinement and, by implication, of the need for physical expansion and liberation. Fugard has always been extraordinarily conscious of this aspect of his medium. The figures in his plays, as the poet Don Maclennan observes, are always struggling to become characters in the proper sense of the word.[25] This struggle should not be seen solely as a matter of experimentation with conventional literary codes: it is also a reproach to a system that so often denied its subjects a material environment conducive to self-making. If, then, as J. M. Coetzee has argued, Fugard's work is animated by an ethic of love (DP 370), this ethic also implies an ethic of viable space: the crookedness, distortion, and "ugliness of the unloved thing" (N 91) is consistently associated in his writings with a lack of adequate physical protection and of the space and mediating distance requisite for any kind of empowering cognition.

The Violence of Immediacy

Though Fugard's contribution to our understanding of the politics of place in South Africa must ultimately be assessed in relation to his drama, his prose works—the early novel *Tsotsi*, the published notebooks, and the memoir *Cousins*—are also rich texts for anyone interested in apartheid's geographies of power. I would like to turn to these works very briefly, since they introduce some of Fugard's recurrent thematic preoccupations and also help us to grasp more clearly what is at stake when these themes are translated from printed text and into three-dimensional theatrical space.

Of the works I have mentioned, *Cousins* is perhaps the most explicitly about places. The memoir offers a portrait of the artist as a young man presented from a sidelong angle, via the author's recollections of his relationship with two older cousins, Jonny and Garth. But it is also an account of the social geography of the Eastern Cape and of the patterns of daily life imposed by that geography. Fugard describes the city of Pórt Elizabeth in terms of the antithetical lures of the municipal library, with its "hushed and civilized" atmosphere, and of the "rough and raw life" of Jetty Street, with its "brawls and beggars," sailors and hookers (C 46–47). He recalls the poor communities on the city's lamp-lit periphery, the afterglow of sunset on the mountains toward Uitenhage, the arid expanse of the Karoo, his family's various residences (from the Jubilee Hotel to the stifling suburban house in Newton Park), and his mother's one-time place of business, the St. George's Park Tearoom: the setting for *"Master Harold" . . . and the Boys.*

The connection between the memoir's personal and geographic impulses, however, is most strikingly foregrounded in a disturbing recollection involving Fugard's cousin Garth, who is presented as an anguished, unpredictable figure: an alcoholic, a compulsive liar, and a closeted homosexual. The memory revisits an evening in the Jubilee Hotel: Fugard, then known as Hallie, and his brother Royal are quietly doing their homework, when suddenly Garth, for no apparent reason, begins to taunt Royal with his lack of talent compared to Hallie. The torment culminates with Garth slapping the boy viciously, full in the face. This act is presented as unmotivated and mysterious: Garth's violence, as Hallie already seems to intuit, is the twisted indication of a secret, a sign that things are not as they appear. But what gives this undermining of appearances a symbolic potency is the nature of Hallie's homework. He has been drawing "a map of the Union of South Africa, showing the principal agricultural and industrial products of the various regions: gold in the Transvaal, maize in the Orange Free State, sugar in Natal and wine in the Cape." The map provides a satisfying sense of interpretive coherence and personal control: "I am very proud of my map," Fugard recalls, "the outline is clean and neat and for once without any smudges; the four provinces and protectorates have each been filled in with a different color and my printing of the names of the major cities—Durban, Cape Town, Bloemfontein, Johannesburg and Port Elizabeth—looks very official" (C 67). The significance of this remembered scene derives from the contrast Fugard implicitly draws between the representational clarity of the map—with its sharp outlines and its empowering, if reductive, knowledge of national geography—and the mysterious, psychologically murky quality of Garth's behavior. The act of violence is destructive on both an emotional and a cognitive level: it troubles the map's comforting mediation of Hallie's world.

This connection between violence and the breakdown of mediation (or "cognitive mapping") is a constant in Fugard's thinking. In 1966, as he was generating ideas for *Boesman and Lena,* he penned an apposite formula in his notebook: "Poverty = the violence of immediacy"/ Immediate (dictionary) = (of person or thing in its relation to another) not separated by any intervening medium" (N 132). The sensory evidence from which this equation derives is frequently recorded in the notebooks. In 1962, for example, Fugard described the appearance and behavior of poor whites in the waiting room of a Port Elizabeth hospital. In the room's stark, antiseptic light, he found that he could see the ways in which the poor are scarred by life more clearly than was possible in their "natural environment: a crowded, narrow world of rust, flaking paint, dark doorways, brown furniture" (N 64). Their bitter mouths and their alert, furtive eyes seemed to him to attest to their psychological and physical exposure: "Blows—fists and fate—fall quickly and unexpectedly. One must be constantly on the lookout—a drunk husband, a baby playing in the street, a thieving son at your handbag." Their bodies make you think, Fugard reflects, "of thorn-trees, of things planted and growing in a harsh world, in hard times" (N 64).

It is, however, in Fugard's neglected novel *Tsotsi* (written around 1960 and set in Sophiatown at the moment of the freehold township's destruction) that the theme of the violence of immediacy, along with its concomitant images of plants or bodies distorted by an insufficiently nurturing environment, is given its earliest literary elaboration. The novel's defining chronotope, a claustrophobic assemblage of partly demolished shacks that crowd in on the margins of the white city, would seem to condemn the characters to the condition that Es'kia Mphahlele describes as "the tyranny of place": they are assaulted from moment to moment by the sensory particulars of their impoverished urban surroundings. "Anything can get at us," a choric voice laments at one point in the novel, "fleas and flies in summer. Rain through the roof in winter, and the cold too, and things like policemen and death. It's the siege of our life, man" (T 115). *Tsotsi's* prose is thus appropriately replete with grim, naturalistic imagery—with details of the sort Georg Lukács would have excoriated as an abandonment of the novelist's task of representing the social totality, the dialectic of the objective and subjective world that constitutes historical progression.[26] But Tsotsi's broken images are in fact historically attuned. They offer an implicit condemnation of apartheid as an agent of reification, especially when it comes to those who are compelled to live on "the smallest unit[s] of the white man's money" (T 71) and of its destruction not only of people's dwellings but also of their capacity for coherent forms of reflection, or even for just for "count[ing] the days past and the hope for tomorrow" (T 8). The objective "raw ends and broken rubble" of Sophiatown's demolition, moreover, is dialectically related to the subjective fragmentation of the novel's characters. The callous inhumanity of Tsotsi, the gangster of the title, is the product of years of homelessness and abandonment. He recalls his past only in terms of a series of dislocated sensory impressions: the smell of musty newspapers, the sight of spiders, an injured dog, and so forth. He cannot "assemble himself into any coherent shape" or even remember his own name: "in front of a mirror he had not been able to put together the eyes and the nose and the mouth and the chin and make a man with meaning . . . he remembered no yesterdays and tomorrow existed only when it was the present, living moment, and his name was the name, in a way, of all men" (T 19).[27] Subjectivity, which Fugard clearly views as an effect of the cognitive mediation of memory, becomes fragile and insubstantial when it is too nakedly exposed—too subject, if you will, to a brutal social environment.[28]

A descriptive passage in the novel reveals one of the most important aspects of Fugard's conception of social space. Peering through the ruins of a bulldozed building, it seems to Tsotsi as though "the space itself, the intangible something defined by four walls and a roof, had been broken up and holes knocked in it"

(T 44). We may define this "intangible something" as the sense of "home": of an enclosure built to a scale commensurate with the human body, one that, in the poignant phrase from *Boesman and Lena*, will help to "make [the world] your own size" (BL 145). This notion of a humanized, proportionate space, large enough to ensure growth and intellectual expansion, but small enough to ensure adequate protection and self-definition, is a recurrent one throughout Fugard's career, though it eventually seems to lose its socially engaged and progressive dimension.[29] *Tsotsi*, however, makes it abundantly clear that inhabiting such a space tends to be the privilege of those with wealth and status. In one of the novel's most bitter scenes, a crippled beggar looks with resentment at the white people, warm in their "big cars" like "wonderful presents in their bright boxes" (T 67). The cozy, protective wrapping that the whites enjoy contrasts starkly with "the simple hand-worked fabric in which [Tsotsi] wrapped his existence" (T 45).

The moral, psychological, and physical distortions recorded in the novel are ultimately the result of a kind of spatial deprivation—of cramping, and, conversely, exposure:

> The world was an ugly place. It was the ugliness of things that had gone crooked and were now twisted out of all meaning. It was a deformity that began with houses that had been badly matched to the bodies they held, being too small, or too windy or cracked open to the rain like the careless laying of an egg on sharp rocks. Then there were the bodies themselves. In the cruel confinements of their lives they had grown awry. . . . It was true of all life. The only trees in the township, those around the cemetery, had expressed it in their stunted growth, drawing out the full meaning in their misshapen silhouettes seen against the windy sky. (T 78)

This passage—like the novel as a whole—insists on the importance of material conditions, especially adequate dwelling places, in the shaping of subjectivity and social identity. This message is strikingly expressed in the novel by the song of the mine workers, who lament spending their working lives in tunnels under the earth: "We are become moles. . . . We are become rats," they chant, reminding us of the ways living things can be stunted, or twisted into ugly and inhuman shapes, if no place is provided for them to grow and stand tall in (T 60).

With its various ruins and grotesques, then, *Tsotsi* is the ur-text for Fugard's literary investigations of the relationship between person and place. Though it languished for years in manuscript at the National English Literature Museum, it is a work that Fugard was to mine, however unconsciously, for motifs and dramatic ideas he would explore in his plays.[30] *Tsotsi* is most closely connected to *Boesman and Lena*, a play that translates the radical exposure captured in the novel's imagery into the semiotics of theater. As the play opens, the audience is confronted with an empty stage. This reduced setting, as Martin Orkin has observed, has a dual effect. It represents the extreme poverty and exposure of the play's two vagrants, whose shack has been bulldozed by the agents of the apartheid government. But it also gives the play an antirepresentational and experimental dimension: in the rigorous abstraction of its *mise en scène*, *Boesman and Lena* breaks away from the codes of naturalistic theater (especially in those productions where the actors donned their rags on stage in full view of the audience), in order to focus on the "potential of actress and actor as primary agents in the constitution of meaning."[31] By fore-grounding this potential, Fugard's dramatic space—even in this, his most austere play—is less determining and "tyrannical" and more affirmative than the grim chronotopes of his novel.

This affirmation, to be sure, is compromised and ambivalent. Exposed on an utterly bare and unaccommodating stage, the play's "two crooked *Hotnots*" (BL 188) act out a homelessness so radical that it may seem to resemble the meta-physical condition of Beckett's Didi and Gogo, were it not for the audience's rec-ognition (which changes, of course, as the time and place of performance changes) of the political context in which *Boesman and Lena* was originally embedded.[32] Like the leaky kettle, old mugs, and worn-out clothes with which they must make do, the bodies of Boesman and Lena are (to borrow a phrase from Fugard's stage direction) "cipher[s] of poverty" (BL 143)—and of a poverty imagined precisely as the "violence of immediacy." The two vagrants, however, are not equal in their destitution. The dramatic structure of the play is defined by the antithetical ways the two characters try to cope with their vulnerable psychological and socio-geographic position. For Boesman, the demolition of the shack offers, at least momentarily, a sense of freedom: freedom from the humiliating definition of self that such an inadequate dwelling space imposes. His phrase " 'n vrot ou huisie vir die vrot mens" ("a rotten little house for the rotten person" [BL 158]) offers one of the most abject expressions of the interrelationship of subjectivity and domes-tic space in all of South African literature. For Lena, by contrast, the demolition is cause for tears: it is yet another of life's constant blows frustrating her effort to piece together a coherent memory of her life of wandering. Her attempts to recall, in order, the names of all the places she and Boesman have wandered through, as they "helped write" the obscure "little paths on the veld" (BL 168), can be seen as a desperate desire for some kind of cognitive map. But even the most basic intellectual mediation (like the construction of identity) is hard to achieve for a figure like Lena, who has only "the sky for a roof" (BL 145) and who is constantly brought back to the painful here and now by her partner's fist in her face.

In its dramatization of two opposing attitudes toward home and homeless-ness, *Boesman and Lena* may seem to replay the quintessential dualities of mod-ern drama—dualities reaching all the way back to Ibsen, in whose work, as Una Chaudhuri has observed, "a crisis in the concept of home is staged as a collision of incommensurable desires: the desire for a stable container for identity and the desire to deterritorialize the self."[33] But the local and political implications of Fugard's play make it impossible to assimilate his work unproblematically with the European tradition: *Boesman and Lena* makes it perfectly clear that both of the desires identified by Chaudhuri are futile in the world of apartheid. Many crit-ics have therefore argued that *Boesman and Lena* recontains its utopian moments (such as Lena's comical song in which she names and celebrates the places of her life), and with good reason: the characters leave the stage as heavily burdened and yet just as unaccommodated as they were at first entry. But the play's end-ing also intensifies one's awareness of the affirmative dimensions of performance.

When Lena reluctantly follows Boesman, declaring that at least "somebody saw a little bit" (BL 197), her words attest to the meaningfulness of the theatrical event, even as her own "scenery" is once again reduced to "Boesman's back" (BL 147). Her parting words, in effect, interpellate each audience member as a witness, not just to her victimhood, but also to her courageous effort to define herself and her world. Boesman, by contrast, represents an antitheatrical principle, in that he does not wish his shame to be seen: "Musa khangela!" ("Don't look!" [BL 188]) he shouts at Outa, the dying wanderer who joins their company. But Boesman's appeal also applies to the spectators of the play, who in all likelihood do not avert their eyes, and are doubtless made to feel uncomfortably complicit in his exposure and humiliation. In these antithetical ways, Fugard alerts his audience, not only to the places represented or referred to in the dialogue (those poor communities—Veeplaas, Redhouse, Korsten, Coega—whose names seem to "litter" Fugard's writings [C 32]) but also to the space of theater itself. *Boesman and Lena*'s significance lies in this achievement: it is arguably the first South African play to focus such self-reflexive attention on the conditions of its own enactment—on the fact that the stage may function as a virtual public sphere, where subjunctive actions and agencies may be invented and tested out.[34]

Habitat: Algoa Park

Since *Boesman and Lena* has been given ample scholarly commentary, I would now like to turn my attention to *A Lesson from Aloes*, the play Fugard himself has identified as a crux in his career—and rightly so, since it revisits the settings and preoccupations of the earlier Port Elizabeth plays, even as it looks ahead to the plays of the early 1980s, which were increasingly absorbed with private themes and intended for international audiences. The play offers a dramatic meditation on the idea of geographical belonging and, as such, extends Fugard's interest in viable space beyond the home to the homeland. Focused on the imminent exile of the activist Steven Daniels, *A Lesson from Aloes* raises questions of national identity, indigeneity, rootedness, and displacement, questions that have beset not just South Africa but all colonies. The play asks, in effect, whether colonized land can seem like home to anyone, settler or native. (For, as the poet Jeremy Cronin observes, the experience of colonialism is precisely that of being made "to feel like a foreigner in the land of one's birth.")[35] It is telling, therefore, that in an early version of the play, the central character, Piet Bezuidenhout, an Afrikaner formerly active in the resistance movement, is obsessed with decorating an ornamental pond in his backyard with plastic animals. The decision to turn him, instead, into a collector of aloes seems to have been one of the factors that helped Fugard give dramatic shape to the numerous sketches about this character he had recorded in his notebooks for over a decade. As an indigenous plant, capable of surviving drought and transplantation, the aloe raises all of the questions I have listed and is a considerably more multivalent symbol than many of Fugard's critics, who have tended to view the play as a parable advocating a stubborn endurance on native soil, have recognized. If the aloe offers a "lesson about survival," this lesson strikes me as a rather indirect one (as I will argue more fully later on): the aloe should be grasped as a dialectical image of affirmation and critique, and needs to be considered alongside Fugard's other biological figures for the mutilating effects of a lack of viable space.

A pertinent example of one such figure can be found in a 1972 interview in which Fugard offered the following revealing comments about the adaptation of plants to a dry environment: "Thorn trees don't protest the endless drought of the Karoo. Those fantastic years that pass without a single bloody drop of rainfall. They just go on trying to grow. Just a basic survival informs the final mutilated, stunted protest." The contradiction one sees here (the thorn trees don't protest—and yet they do) is precisely to the point: like the stunted and misshapen trees of Tsotsi's township, the thorn trees of the Karoo are an instance of what Siegfried Kracauer once defined as the complex "protest action" of the grotesque (the equivalent, if you will, of Fugard's "ugliness of the unloved thing").[36] The same can be said of the aloe: it is a figure of defiant indigeneity and survival, but it also denounces, with its grotesque thorns, thick leaves, and waxy surfaces, the extreme conditions that have produced these protective traits. The critical aspect of the image of the aloe in fact seems foremost in the play. The aloes in jam tins that clutter up the stage are readily seen, in their hopeless tackiness (something they have in common with the earlier version's plastic animals), as a symbolic comment on the stifling confinement of suburban life: a confinement that is underscored in the drama's mimetic space, alternating as it does between a cramped backyard and an equally cramped bedroom. It is no accident, therefore, that Piet's wife Gladys, despite her obsession with privacy, should demand an ampler space for herself. ("God has not planted me in a jam tin!" she exclaims [LA 17].) Even the stoic Piet is upset when he sees the twisted roots of the plants tying "themselves into knots looking for the space creation intended for them" (LA 9).

The question of viable space is not only presented mimetically (by way of the props and the stage set) but also addressed diegetically, through the two Bezuidenhouts' antithetical meditations on the idea of "home." The play in effect stages an investigation of whether "home" and "belonging" should be conceptualized in terms of filiation, as a matter of bonds pertaining to the realm of nature and the given (such as family, nationality, and inherited cultural and linguistic forms), or in terms of affiliation, as a matter of bonds pertaining to the realm of culture and choice (such as political commitments, group identifications, and elective linguistic and cultural forms). The nuances of this investigation derive from Fugard's thoroughgoing awareness of the extent to which "home" is a discursive construct, a performative notion created by individuals through acts of memory, identification, and especially naming. Interviewed for a *New Yorker* profile in 1982, Fugard revealed his own need to name his world—a need that becomes problematic when it comes to aloes: "Aloes are capable of a high degree of hybridization, which makes identification a nightmare. I want to name the name," Fugard confesses. "It's a false attempt at an act of possession."[37] The aloe thus complicates the fundamental colonial act of naming: an act we might consider, along the lines suggested by Eric Cheyfitz in *The Politics of Imperialism*, to be an act of translation, intimately dependent on notions of ownership and place.

The idea that naming might make one "feel more at home in the world" (LA 4) is articulated by Piet Bezuidenhout, the play's vocal advocate of filiative bonds. In the very first scene of the play, he classifies himself as one would a plant: "For better or for worse, I will remain positively identified as Petrus Jacobus Bezuidenhout; Species, Afrikaner; Habitat, Algoa Park, Port Elizabeth" (LA 5). He wishes, in other words, to make his identity seem naturally determined: to turn his modest backyard at 27 Kraaibos Street into a "habitat." The same impulse is evident in his homespun philosophizing about language, which he sees, essentially, as the invention of a system of nomenclature. Piet's meditations are imaginatively grounded on the myth of Adam's task in the Garden of Eden: the task of inventing a language that would illuminate the essential characteristics of all the objects in the world. Piet's obsession with identifying the aloes in his collection by their scientific names can be seen as an attempt to imagine himself as a kind of Afrikaner Adam, at home in the Eastern Cape. He insists that names are "more than just labels" and meets opposing arguments with a forceful affirmation of his attachment to the soil. To the challenge implicit in one of his beloved quotations from English poetry, "What is in a name? That which we call a rose/ By any other name would smell as sweet" (LA 4), he responds with comic fervor: "'Then deny thy father and refuse thy name.' Hell! I don't know about those Italians, but that's a hard one for an Afrikaner" (LA 5). What Piet seeks, one might say, is the linguistic equivalent of biological rootedness: a motivated, inherently meaningful link between signifier and signified. He yearns for the sort of connection that his wife Gladys, at their first meeting, attached to the surname Bezuidenhout: a name, she says, with "a strong earthy sound" (LA 13).

But the Gladys Bezuidenhout we see in the play represents a very different attitude toward language and place. Traumatized by the intrusion of the security policemen who entered her bedroom and confiscated her diaries, she is left with a profound sense of dislocation. For her the word "home" has no natural meaning, no motivated referent: though born and bred in South Africa, she is, as she declares toward the end of the play, "more than prepared to call some other place that" (LA 68). Gladys has little sense of filiative connections (her mother's death leaves her cold) or geographical awareness: her memory of a childhood holiday is characteristically atopic: "I think it was Cape Town. Not that it made any difference where I was" (LA 7). From her perspective, words are just "labels," a point Fugard ironically underscores by giving her the maiden name of Adams. Unlike Piet, she has no interest in the names of plants, nor does she care much about the names of people. Those she manages to remember (like "Steven" and "Peter") she anglicizes, and thus renders more formal and more foreign. For all her surface politeness, her alienation is just as violent and, at times, just as crudely expressed as that of the abusive Boesman, who, as we have seen, tries to prevent Lena from naming her world. He tells Lena that a "drol" (turd) or a fart would be more meaningful than her words because at least "it stinks" (BL 150), while Gladys tells Piet that she would like to force him to eat her diaries and turn them into shit. It is as if she wants to force Piet to confess to his complicity in her violation in a stark, unmediated, and sublinguistic fashion.

If Piet's verbosity is naïve and vulnerable, Gladys's suspicion of any linguistic accommodation with the world is even less viable. It is telling that she should end up in a "mental home" (the euphemism is fitting) called Fort England—the actual name of an institution in Grahamstown, but, of course, a symbolically significant one. The location, as it were, sets Gladys outside the scope of national allegory. Yet she remains a forceful figure in the play. Her defiant assertion to Steve, Piet's former comrade in the resistance movement, that "black skins don't make the only victims in this country" (LA 78), protests against the tendency of the political struggle to occupy all available narrative terrain in apartheid South Africa: "I accept that I am just a white face on the outskirts of your terrible life, but I'm in the middle of mine and yours is just a brown face on the outskirts of that. . . . I've discovered hell for myself" (LA 78). Her point—that not all suffering is reducible to racial injustice—is by no means negligible, and it may be because of the emotional force of her torment that many critics have taken her views seriously, to the point where they apply her line about Piet to the play as a whole: "it's all got to do with him being an Afrikaner and this being home" (LA 68).

To do this, however, is to ignore the fact that the play actually undermines the old truism about the Afrikaner's closeness to African soil. Indeed, I would suggest that *A Lesson from Aloes* is responsive to Coetzee's sardonic criticism of Fugard's 1976 film *The Guest*: a film that, as Coetzee argues, does deal in some of the time-honored myths about Afrikaners and the land.[38] The play also complicates the simple opposition between Piet and Gladys that I have set up in the preceding paragraphs. It is evident early on that Piet's vehement insistence on his rootedness conceals a certain vulnerability, and by the second act the cause of this vulnerability is clear: Piet is an erstwhile farmer displaced from his land by drought. Much as a skeptical reader might like to see him as a version of the "imperial eye" that dominates by naming, his cultural and political position is not one of power. His efforts, as we see in the light of the play's revelations, are pitched against apartheid's pernicious and all too efficacious performatives. By means of such speech acts as naming a certain area white and then evicting its black inhabitants from their homes, apartheid makes it impossible for the person of conscience to belong in South Africa. It makes Piet's pastoral dream seem puny, if not self-deluding. This may be why Fugard presents him as a highly unoriginal name-giver: the fact that he looks up his aloes' names in a book (an important part of the stage "business" in act 1) equates his Adamic efforts with his comical habit of trying to match his experiences with purple passages borrowed from the English and American literary canons.

The few names Piet does manage to invent, moreover, are curiously un–South African. Though he proclaims his admiration for a name like "Willem Gerhardus Daniels," which seems to him to "belong to this world as surely as any one of those aloes" (LA 66), the names he chooses to bestow entirely lack this quality of indigeneity. We might think here of "Gladysiensis" (the name he wants to give the unidentified aloe he is preoccupied with at the opening and closing scenes of the play), "Xanadu" (the exotic name he gives his house), and "Gorki" (the Russian name he wants Steve Daniels to give his son). Piet's quotations, though they are supposed to provide an apt expression of his feelings and surroundings, also tend to make his world seem foreign, as when he describes the dry and sunny South African autumn as "our season of mists and mellow fruitfulness" (LA 6). Whatever Piet might say about language and belonging, the rhetoric he deploys is not grounded like the aloes of the veld but transplanted, like the aloes in jam tins. He is, we might say, engaged in translation—not translation as an expression of colonial mastery and possession but translation in the Benjaminian sense of a practice that makes the strange seem familiar and the familiar strange.[39]

It is worth recalling here the semantic connection between *translation* and *metaphor*. Both words entail, in their respective Latin and Greek etymologies, a connotation of distance, transport, or "carrying across," which commentators from Aristotle onward have linked to a rhetorical transference between the familiar and the alien, the native and the foreign, and the natural and the artificial.[40] Translation is a matter of grafting rather than of rootedness. It undermines the notion of culture as filiation and sets in its place the possibility of affiliation: something we see in the name "Gorki," which is expressive of Piet's elective solidarity with a distant revolutionary tradition. These simple considerations accrue significance in the South African context, where Afrikaans, which is Piet's—and Fugard's—mother tongue, has historically been viewed as more indigenous, hence more suited than English to the task of describing Africa. But, as J. M. Coetzee has pointed out, Afrikaans is "in every structural respect a European language" and is every bit as artificial in its relation to Africa as English.[41] If Afrikaans has come to assume a kind of "naturalness," a motivated, nonarbitrary relation to the land, it is owing entirely to the process Cheyfitz denounces as "easy translation": a rhetorical maneuver that hides its own rhetoricity and represses the inherent difficulty of cultural transactions in any colonial context. In a world shaped by imperialism, whether internal or external, we all exist in translation, or so Cheyfitz suggests: the erasure of the artificial, distancing quality of all language is simply a fiction of power.[42]

It is against this background that we may consider Piet's speech and, by extension, the language of all of Fugard's early plays, which (as he has often noted) are always-already in translation: they are works that exist in between languages, written in English, but with an ear to an (unwritten) Afrikaans original (C 9–10).[43] The fact that Fugard has Piet speak not in Afrikaans, the language that would seem to suit his professed sentiments best, but in an accented and quoted English, marks his efforts to name and humanize his world as difficult, extraordinary, and eccentric from the word go. In the light of Cheyfitz's account of the politics of translation, the roughness of Piet's pronunciations and the dubious applicability of his quotations may have a demystificatory force: they remind us of the unnaturalness—the artificiality and metaphoricity—of every language.[44]

This idea seems especially relevant if we consider Fugard's understanding of performance (which theorists as diverse as George Steiner and Patrice Pavis have connected with the idea of translation) and his belief that his progress as a dramatist was dependent, ultimately, on a "greater honesty about, and use of, the unreality of the stage" (N 172).[45] That this progress was ongoing during the writing of *A Lesson from Aloes* is clear from several entries in Fugard's notebooks during this period. For example, he records how, despite his desire to present Piet's predicament "without pretence," he is constantly brought up against the inevitable artifice of his medium and the necessary distance between the "possible world" of the theater and the world of the audience: "Here is the problem," he muses, "I have got three dimensions and silence. When my actor moves from point A to point B, I want my audience to see an actor cross the stage, and not try to bluff them that Piet had moved from the gardenia bush to the water tap. . . . I sit in the theatre, the house lights go out, the curtain rises, I see a stage"(N 141).

This simple situation of a body executing a movement across a stage may not reveal what is at stake in Fugard's emphasis on the "unreality" of theater as well as his metatheatrical moments do. A characteristic example of these is the opening scene of the second act of *A Lesson from Aloes,* when Steve finally arrives for an anticipated farewell dinner and the friends playfully adopt a series of roles:

STEVE: (*Respectfully, but with an exaggerated degree of authority*) Excuse me, sir! (*He flashes some sort of identity card*) Security Branch. I wonder if you could help me?

PIET: (*Playing along*) Yes, my good man. What can I do for you?

STEVE: I'm looking for a mad Afrikaner, who recites English poetry. He stays around here somewhere.

PIET: (*Pretending outrage*) A what?

STEVE: His name is Piet Bezuidenhout.

PIET: Did I hear you right? An Afrikaner, reciting English poetry! And a Bezuidenhout at that!

STEVE: I told you he was mad, sir.

PIET: It's worse than that my good man. There's a name for his sort. Why do you think we lost the Boer War? And what do you think is making your people so cheeky these days?

STEVE: (*Whips off his hat; is suddenly servile*) Sorry, sir.

PIET: Subversive elements like him. English poetry! If I was you I would choose my company more carefully in future.

STEVE: Is it all right if I visit you instead, then? (LA 47–48)

The scene clearly turns on the ideas of filiation and affiliation. Piet recognizes, however jokingly, that, by his attachment to English poetry, and more importantly, to the antiapartheid cause, he has in fact chosen to "deny his father and refuse his name." The unspoken "name for his sort" is *volksverraaier* (traitor). But in all its details, the scene celebrates rather than censures the principle of translation-as-betrayal. It is fitting that Steve should announce himself by playing the Marseillaise on his harmonica: a revolutionary song for the old comrades-in-arms, but a French rather than a South African one. It has been transported, like all of Piet's quotations, from its original place. The role-playing the scene introduces also transgresses given boundaries and subject positions. While the words affirm the roles and sentiments decreed by apartheid, the friends' exaggerated performance undermines their hegemonic significance: authority, servility, and race all become masks and gestures. The implicit message of the performance is the familiar Brechtian one: that the social order is constructed and that identities (unlike biological categories) are not inherited ready-made. The artificiality of theater, in other words, has a political correlate: "Our world," as Fugard put it in 1975, "is never a 'given' reality, but a 'made' one" (N 215).[46]

It is in this light that we should consider the line Fugard constantly returns to in his notebook entries about Piet, Gladys, and Steve: "A man's scenery is other men" (N 140–141). Though the line does not actually appear in the final text of the play, it remains fundamental to its conception. The dual significance of the word "scenery" (relating both to the landscape and to the theater) is, of course, crucial: the word's ambiguity encapsulates the tension between the natural and the artificial that lies at the heart of *A Lesson from Aloes*. It is fitting, considering Fugard's aphorism, that the one truly utopian moment described in his play is not set in nature—in, say the "open veld with purple mountains in the background" (LA 15), about which Piet waxes lyrical in the opening scene. It occurs, rather, in Cadles township, "that ugly Coloured Area with all the factories" (LA 35), where Piet impulsively decides to join a group of bus-boycotters listening to a speech by none other than Steve Daniels. Piet describes this moment ecstatically: "Next thing I know is they were cheering and laughing and slapping me on the back and making a place for me in the front row. . . . It was like rains after a long drought. Being welcomed by those people was the most moving thing that has ever happened to me. Feelings about life and people, which I thought had withered away like everything else on the farm, were alive again" (LA 36). The sentiment here is resolutely social: Piet Bezuidenhout finds his most profound sense of belonging in the "place" made for him by people whose lives might seem to be "none of [his] business" and whose cause he might easily dismiss as "having nothing to do with [him]" (LA 35). His ideal scenery is precisely "other men."

For all its "horticultural symbolism" (as Dennis Walder has somewhat impatiently called it), *A Lesson from Aloes* ultimately privileges the human capacity for affiliation: for chosen languages, adopted causes, and constructed solidarities.[47] The filiative and biological principle, by the same token, is implicitly denounced in one of the play's most painful lines, with which Steve Daniel's father comes to summarize his life. Broken by his failed resistance to the apartheid government, which decreed that he and his family should be shunted off to a dismal township for "coloureds" far away from the beach where he loves to fish, he concludes: "Ons geslag is verkeerd" (LA 67). Though Piet tries to get the meaning across in English ("Our generation . . . our race is a mistake"), his rendering of it is inadequate because of the dense associations of the word *geslag* in Afrikaans, which include not only "generation" and "race," but "line of descent" and "gender." The near untranslatability of the phrase is of a piece with the fatality of the natural inheritance it expresses.

The Transport of Performance

If one chooses to read *A Lesson from Aloes* as celebrating the social and artificial over the natural and biological, one must account for the play's apparently pessimistic ending. The action concludes with Piet's failure to salvage his friendship with Steve, and as the lights go down, the audience sees him sitting in silence, holding the same unidentified "aloe anonymous" that preoccupied him at the beginning of the play. Piet's silence—his refusal to defend himself against the charge of treason, or even to provide, at Steve's request, a "quotation for old time's sake" (LA 81)—would seem to signal a retreat from the progressive possibilities of translation and affiliation. The presence in this scene of the nameless aloe, explicitly mentioned in the final stage direction, may even strike readers and audience members familiar with the traditions of white writing in South Africa as reminiscent of the time-honored trope of "namelessness"—of the silence that English-language poets traditionally projected onto those African scenes and objects they failed to translate into verse. In such a reading, Piet's silence would be legible as an apartheid-era version of the "negative pastoral": a pseudosublime retreat from any engagement with Africa as a social space.[48] Piet's silence, moreover, would seem to endorse Gladys's rejection of any linguistic mediation of the world and to lend credence to her notion that in order to live in South Africa, one needs to adapt to a life of minimal human and social expectations: that one must adopt a survival mechanism like the aloe's thick leaves or its "thorns and bitterness" (LA 16). Interpreted this way, the "lesson from aloes" would seem to contradict the "lesson" Piet once learned from Steve: "An evil system isn't a natural disaster. There's nothing you can do to stop a drought, but bad laws and social injustice are man-made and can be unmade by men. It's as simple as that" (LA 37).

To counter this quietistic reading in which apartheid comes to seem like a climatic condition, it is useful to attend to Gayatri Spivak's essay on the politics of translation. This essay has been seen as offering also a politics of theater—and with good reason, since Spivak here defines the process of translation as an attempt to "enter or direct that staging as one directs a play, as an actor interprets a script."[49] It is a definition that is compatible in spirit with my own working definition of translation as it applies to Fugard's art: as a traversing of the interpretive space between the real world and the "elsewhere" of drama. Good translation, as Spivak sees it, inevitably has three dimensions: logic (the body of information to be rendered), rhetoric (the various linguistic slippages and strains that resist any simplistic, mechanical rendering of the information), and, most important of all, silence. The emphasis on silence is Spivak's way of honoring the irreducible differences that a poor translation will tend to plaster over and subject to homogenization.[50] Her view of translation, in other words, does not privilege strict fidelity. Translation, she suggests, is like friendship, in that it is most creatively and most ethically sustained not by an assumption of sameness (we do not necessarily say "she is my friend because she is just like me") but by a recognition of difference. For friendships, Spivak insists, have the potential of alerting us to the trace of the other in the self. The same, of course, can be said of translations (and quotations), including performative renderings of written texts: they should be tested, Spivak suggests, not solely by their similarity to an original script but also by the new and exploratory forms of agency that they might open up both in the text and in the world.

Spivak's meditations, I would argue, are relevant to *A Lesson from Aloes* in two ways. First of all, they incline us to regard the silence at the play's conclusion as resonant and complicated, as part of a "good translation" rather than its foreclosure. The point seems all the more valid if we bear in mind the fact that Piet's final silence is foreshadowed by an earlier and highly revealing occasion when he found himself with nothing to say. This first silence, as the play's rich second act reveals, occurred when Piet's laborers on Alwynlaagte asked him to say a few words at the funeral of a child who died of malnutrition during the drought that eventually cost Piet his farm. Their request leaves him utterly defeated. He is unable to perform the speech act that the black funeral orator in *Sizwe Bansi Is Dead* performs so eloquently: renaming (or translating) the grave as "home" (S 28). Yet, despite Piet's painful sense of linguistic and personal failure—the origin of his subsequent passion for finding appropriate quotations in poetry books—his silence would seem to be an entirely fitting response. He does not pretend to name the experience of others or to speak for them in their moment of suffering and loss, just as, by the play's end, he refuses to offer a quotation to sum up the meaning of his former comrade's betrayal and exile. This particular silence, in other words, does not replicate but moves us beyond the impasse of the negative pastoral: it allows us to see Fugard's ending in ways that are quite contrary to the colonial imposition of blankness on Africa and its people.

If Spivak's validation of silence as an aspect of translation and performance is suggestive in relation to *A Lesson from Aloes*, so, too, is her validation of the recognition of difference over sameness. The latter is especially the case with regard to Fugard's deployment of the central metaphor of the aloe: a metaphor that some critics have found all too readily decodable. It seems to me that, despite all his stoicism and vaunted indigeneity, Piet Bezuidenhout is not, as is often claimed, "like" the aloes in his collection, to which he turns in despair at the end of the play.[51] In fact, Fugard's introductory notes to the play steer us toward a different perception of its final moments. When he describes Piet as coming "face to face with the absurdity of himself, alone," he uses the word "absurd" in its philosophical and literary rather than its colloquial sense. For Camus, of whose work Fugard was an avid reader, the absurd is precisely the negation of ready-made meanings, languages, and codes: it is a condition that underscores, rather than denies, the need for constructing new languages. The absurd, moreover, is inseparable from the urgent ethical obligation of creating fellowship with other men. The aloe can perhaps teach a lesson of sorts about survival, but it is not a lesson that a man can follow. The final scene implies—by negation—that neither aloes nor anything else in the natural world can serve as a substitute for human fellowship and commitment. *A Lesson from Aloes* thus foreshadows the lesson Coetzee was to articulate so movingly in his Jerusalem Prize acceptance speech of 1987: the relationship of white South Africans to the land will be unethical and inadequate if it remains merely a relationship with stones and plants and beautiful scenes. To glamorize such a love is to repress the reality that Piet is confronted with: that (as Coetzee puts it) there is too little fraternity in South Africa, or that (as Fugard's aphorism would have it) "a man's scenery is other men."[52]

Like the ending of *Boesman and Lena*, the melancholy conclusion of *A Lesson from Aloes* does not recontain the work's affirmative possibilities, nor does it erase the impact of those key moments in which the Brechtian or artificial aspects of Fugard's theater are foregrounded. Indeed, we may return now with a sharper sense of its significance to one such moment: the performance-within-the-performance when Piet and Steve recite Longfellow's poem "The Slave's Dream." The poem, which is worth quoting at some length, returns us explicitly to some of the issues of space and place that have, of course, been implicit in the idea of translation throughout these reflections:

> Beside the ungathered rice he lay
> His sickle in his hand
> His breast was bare, his matted hair
> Was buried in the sand.
> Again, in the mist and shadow of sleep,
> He saw his Native Land.
>
> Wide through the landscape of his dreams
> The lordly Niger flowed;
> Beneath the palm-trees on the plain
> Once more a king he strode;
> And heard the tinkling caravans
> Descend the mountain road....
>
> And then at furious speed he rode
> Along the Niger's bank;
> His bridle-reins were golden chains,
> And with a martial clank,
> At each leap he could feel his scabbard of steel
> Smiting his stallion's flank.
>
> Before him, like a blood-red flag,
> The bright flamingoes flew;
> From morn till night he followed their flight,
> O'er plains where the tamarind grew,
> Till he saw the roofs of Caffre huts,
> And the ocean rose to view....
>
> The forests, with their myriad tongues,
> Shouted of liberty;
> And the Blast of the Desert cried aloud,
> With a voice so wild and free,
> That he started in his sleep and smiled
> At their tempestuous glee.
>
> He did not feel the driver's whip,
> Nor the burning heat of day;
> For Death had illumined the Land of Sleep,
> And his lifeless body lay.
> A worn-out fetter, that the soul
> Had broken and thrown away! (LA 51–52)

Like all of Piet's quotations, "The Slave's Dream" is not a natural fit in the context in which it is redeployed, although one could argue that the tension created in the poem between represented and imagined places—between the rice fields of America and the jungles of Africa—is reminiscent of the tension between the oppressive mimetic and expansive diegetic spaces characteristic of Fugard's drama. The jungles and deserts of the "native land" that Longfellow evokes are unlikely to bear much similarity to the birthplace of any actual American slave. And the poem's exotic terrain is certainly a far cry from the world of the Eastern Cape: the "home" of the poem matches the two South Africans' experience of "home" about as much as the name "Xanadu" matches Piet's humble domain in Algoa Park. Both in the poem and in its theatrical performance, we are dealing with a series of displacements, crosscultural translations, and, if you will, crossracial minstrelsies.

Yet we cannot dismiss these various stagings as false or futile. The fact that Steve has memorized the poem in its entirety suggests that despite its exoticism and fustian, "The Slave's Dream" speaks to him, or, more exactly, that he is able to speak through it of his own nostalgia and longings—especially, one imagines, when he utters those lines about the forests shouting of liberty. The poem's meaning is changed and enhanced when one encounters it in the form of this strangely disharmonious duet, performed by a white man and a "coloured" man, by a man who has lost his family farm and a man whose family has been forcibly removed from their home and who is about to go into exile. The characters translate or relocate "The Slave's Dream," and in the process create new, if only virtual, subject positions from which they (at least temporarily) reach out to each other. And the same may be said of the various actors who, at various points in time and on various stages around the world, enact these roles.

The fact that the stage direction specifies that the performance should be "both comical and moving" is also significant in the broader context of Fugard's work. It relates this neglected metatheatrical moment to what is arguably the most memorable scene in his entire oeuvre: the conclusion of *The Island*, when a black actor (Winston Ntshona in the original production) dressed like a woman, with a funny, mop-like wig and crudely fashioned breasts, attests in the person of Antigone to the value of resistance against an unjust and inhumane order. The message, in this case, is not only translated from the Greek to the English, from Athens to Robben Island (or wherever the play is performed), from female to male, from written text to the semiotics of the stage, and perhaps most significantly, from the absurd to the serious and meaningful. It is a scene one may think of (as did Fugard himself) as a powerful moment of witness—as a way of speaking out against the period's enforced silence about the island prison where South Africa's political leaders were incarcerated.[53] But it is also a scene that reminds us of the extent to which dramatic witness is always modified and mediated by the performative, citational qualities—by the artificiality, displacements, absences, and (mis)translations—that are part of the medium. If, as I suggested in chapter 2, the novel is a matter of transport, both in its circulation as object and as a vehicle for imaginative voyaging, then theater is even more obviously a traveling medium, and it is in such metatheatrical moments as I have focused on in this chapter that its constitutive and ever-changing artifice is most readily displayed.

Where Is Here?

To conclude this chapter, I would like to return to the ontological questions that occurred to John Kani during the improvisation with chairs and tables I described earlier: "Who am I? Where am I? Who is Where?" Kani's perplexity and dislocation is readily given a more theoretical resonance. In *The Bush Garden*, Northrop Frye reflects, in passing, on the relative importance of the questions "Who am I?" and "Where is here?" in relation to Canadian literary history. As he sees it, the former question, the animating question in such European genres as the *Bildungsroman*, is less important and less pressing in postcolonial countries than the latter question. "Where is here?" in fact both precedes and determines the answer to "Who am I?"—that "famous problem of identity," as Frye dryly terms it. And "Where is here?" is a difficult question to answer. In places like Canada (and we could add here other places, such as the United States in the nineteenth century, Australia, and South Africa), one is confronted not only with vast and challenging territories, and with the lack of traditional genres and vocabularies through which to articulate these spaces, but also—and here Frye seems very relevant to our contemporary global predicament—with the problematic relationship between regional or national geographies and the world at large. Even as one is struggling to define a sense of place and identity within the national borders of the (post)colony, new techniques of communication are, Frye observes, "annihilating the boundaries of that environment" and creating a global cultural marketplace.[54]

The relevance of Frye's meditations to Fugard's work is readily apparent. In a notebook entry from 1967, he wrote as follows: "'Here'—what better words to start a play with (with which to start a play)" (N 155). The observation emphasizes the primacy in his dramatic imagination of the sociospatial themes that have been my concern in this chapter, and demonstrates the acuity of Fugard's intuitions regarding his craft. Theatre semioticians have frequently commented on the fundamental importance of verbal indices, most crucially the promixal and spatial ones like "I" and "here," to dramatic form and performance. Deixis, as Keir Elam puts it, is "instituted at the origins of . . . drama as the necessary condition of a non-narrative world-creating discourse."[55] But the way Fugard's notebook entry is formulated is also revealing: it tells us something about his peculiar cultural position, especially in those years when he was still writing, as he once put it, "in the face of nothing" (N 89). The anxiety (or joke) about the placement of the preposition "with" and, by extension, about the rules of English grammar, is the mark of Fugard's (post)colonial marginality—of his sense that he was writing from an inauspicious cultural location, at a distance from the great tradition of English literature. For all his subsequent fame, Fugard's early oeuvre is still best grasped as a minor literature (in Deleuze and Guattari's sense): a literature in transit between official languages.

To the question "Who am I?" Fugard would surely have responded: a "mongrel son of white South Africa's two dominant cultures . . . Afrikaner and English speaking" (C 9). But the question "Where is here?" remains more challenging—and the fact that Fugard's writing presents so many descriptions of meticulously observed scenes from the Eastern Cape (such as the one I selected, almost at random, as the epigraph for this chapter) does not readily necessarily resolve those difficulties. "Here?" we may recall, is the first word of *Boesman and Lena*, where it has all the theatricality of, say, the riveting moment in act 4 of *Anthony and Cleopatra* when Anthony declares: "Here I am Anthony / Yet cannot hold this visible shape."[56] In terms of the "possible world" of the play, the answer to Lena's question "Here?" is of course the mouth of the Swartkops River, which she, too, tired and burdened to look up and around her, can identify by the (pretend) mud between her toes. But in performance, the question "Where is here?" becomes both easier to answer (the index is given a referent) and more open-ended: for theatrical space, as Michael Issacharoff argues, may be conceived of as a series of concentric circles, the smallest being the stage itself and the largest the country of performance.[57] When Lena, or rather when Yvonne Bryceland or Ruby Dee or Nomhle Nkoyeni (to name a few of the best actresses who have performed the part), says "Here?" she draws attention not only to her own physical presence, the location of her body on a particular stage, but also to the bodily presence of the audience facing her, immersed as they are in a particular cultural and histori-cal context.

Of the importance of the actor's physical presence, emphasized in this instance by the spatial pointer "Here," Fugard was, of course, profoundly aware. No other medium (except perhaps a dadaist collage), he once observed, "uses more of the actual substance of life" than theatre, which is made of "flesh and blood and sweat, the human voice, real pain, real time" (N 89). But he recognized simultaneously that it is in this realism that drama partakes of the ephemerality of all living things. "Here," after all, is not only a grammatical pointer but also a shifter. Like "I" and "you" or "then" and "now," its meaning is dependent on the context of enuncia-tion. It encapsulates not only dramatic presence but also absence: the labile elu-siveness of performance and its capacity for constant relocation.[58]

It stands to reason, then, that some of the best critical reflections to date on the location of South African culture in a global frame, among which I would list Loren Kruger's essay "Apartheid on Display" and Jeanne Colleran's "Athol Fugard and the Problematics of Liberal Critique," should have been provoked by the international reception of South African drama, and, in the latter case, by the reception of Fugard's work in particular. If a text travels, certain interpre-tive translations must be made in order to insert it into its new context—its new "here." These translations may very well be depoliticizing, whether they involve, as Loren Kruger argues, the hypostatization of South African history as a single moment—that of the Soweto riots—from which metropolitan audiences like to derive a vicarious sense of political urgency or, as Jeanne Colleran argues, a strip-ping away of the historical context, that renders the South African work legible in the moralistic and therapeutic terms in which (white) Americans especially tend to cast racial politics.[59] Such inquiries are enormously fertile, not least so in the postapartheid era. The meaning of *The Island*, for example, can today no longer reside in the direct political challenge it posed in its original production at the Space Theatre in 1971. It becomes legible, instead, as a small act of celebration in the larger drama of a triumphal nationalism and, in the various postapartheid restagings of the play with Kani and Ntshona in their old parts, as a celebration of the now famous actors themselves. The reception of Fugard's own plays thus demonstrates the wrongheadedness of his rejection, in the Georgetown speech, of the material and political contingencies that beset all texts: translation, with its gains and losses, its play of similarities and differences, is the very condition of the circulation and survival of his own dramatic work.

These considerations suggest a fresh take on Fugard's frequent invocation of the example of William Faulkner as a model and spur for his regionalism, for his decision, as he puts it, to love "the nameless deformed little grey bushes" of the Eastern Cape (N 172) rather than pursue a more glittering life and more glamorous subject matter elsewhere. We may note that the terms in which Faulkner characterizes his regionalism (and which Fugard often mentions)—as the discovery of his own "little postage stamp of native soil"—are actually quite complex and contradictory, and productively so. The image of the postage stamp not only suggests the small scope and value of the territory represented but also evokes the possibility of travel—the potentially global reach of the regional text.[60] "Where is here?" is then a question to which critics of South African literature in the present day—an era when the regional and the national have become newly marketable even as their boundaries are being erased—cannot hope to provide any definitive or stable answer. But it is nevertheless a question we must continue asking ourselves, in order to remain alert to the geographies of cultural exchange in which the production and reception of Fugard's work and all of postcolonial literature are currently imbedded.

BEYOND THE TYRANNY OF PLACE

> To be respected, to live in a big house
> with separate bedrooms, a room for sit-
> ting, another for eating and a room to be
> alone, for reading or thinking . . . a house
> in which children would not be sent out if
> someone wanted to take a bath, where we
> would not have to undress in the dark or
> under the blankets.
>
> —Bloke Modisane, *Blame Me on History*

The Contestation of Spaces

The third chapter of *Country of My Skull*, Antjie Krog's personal history of the South African Truth and Reconciliation Commission (TRC), records some of the most agonizing evidence that was put before this controversial body. It includes her account of the testimony of Nomonde Calata, the widow of one of the so-called Cradock Four, a group of young activists who were killed by the police after brutal torture. Characteristically, Krog introduces the reader to this witness and her testimony in such a way as to foreground problems of form, language, and narration. She describes how she sat deep into the night, pondering the impli-cations of Calata's appearance before the commission with a friend she refers to only as Professor Kondlo. In the course of their conversation, the professor comes up with the startling idea of telling the tale of Nomonde Calata in the form of a comic strip. "I will call it," he says, " 'The Contestation of Spaces' ":

> The first page of my comic will carry the headline "The Past," and it will have two drawings. In the one frame, I will write "Male Storyteller (Historian)" and draw a group of men sitting in the traditional *kgotla* or *kroro* or *motse*—whatever you want to call it, that glamorous space in which men and boys meet each other. Where stories are told of where you come from, who you are, the structure of the group's male ancestry, who your role model is. The tales which interpret

your world for you, and help the male teller to make decisions about econom-
ics, politics, history.

Frame two will have the caption "Female Storyteller (Socializer of Children)." This drawing will show a space where food is prepared. Children of both
genders sit and listen to the stories of make-believe. A flowing gallery of magical and bizarre moments that cut into everyday life. "Are you awake? Are you
listening?" asks the grandmother. The children must react and interact with the
multidimensional performance. Unlike the stories of the men where boundaries are set, these stories undermine boundaries: men turn into women and vice
versa, animals become people, women fall in love with animals, people eat each
other, dreams and hallucinations are played out.[1]

When Krog objects, as her readers may, too, that that the wife of Fort Calata hardly
fits the stereotype of the storytelling grandma at the *pappot* and the fire, the professor readily concurs. "Exactly," he exclaims, thumping his first on the table: "Over
these drawings, I rubberstamp: MIGRATION, URBANIZATION, FORCED
REMOVALS. And then starts the actual story of Nomonde Calata as a woman, sitting in the male space of the British colonial city hall of East London and relating
a story as part of the official history of this country. It's bloody amazing."[2]

Though this conception is appealing in the way it hints at the capacity of
discourses to create spaces and vice versa, the verbatim transcription of the testimony that follows (the reader is asked to imagine that Professor Kondlo has
switched on Krog's tape recording of the hearings) leaves one in doubt as to
whether the comic-strip narrative will adequately capture the meaning of the
event. Nomonde Calata's testimony seems to return her to a traumatic experience
of unwording and unworlding—to the radical geographical and linguistic dissolu-
tion that Elaine Scarry explores in *The Body in Pain*. When called upon to narrate
the dreadful way in which she became aware of her husband's death (one of their
children saw a picture of his burnt-out car in the newspaper), Calata starts to cry
so painfully that the hearings are adjourned and resumed only after Archbishop
Tutu leads the assembly in singing the hymn "Senzeni na, senzeni na . . ." ("What
have we done, what have we done? Our only sin is the color of our skin . . . ").
Experiences like Calata's may, as Krog puts it, "surpass all fiction" and lie beyond
the reach of language and representation.[3]

But we need not go this far—to the point where we have to consider the
inadequacy of language in the very face of death—to see some problems with
Professor Kondlo's imagined comic strip. His aim seems to be to sublate the traditional opposition between men's and women's stories and spaces as presented
in the first two frames. But the energy with which he describes these opening
images suggests that he remains invested in gender distinctions. The representations of traditional life with its strict hierarchical oppositions will remain quite
visible under the marks of the rubber stamps that signify the apartheid era and its
cruel geographical schemes. One cannot help noticing, moreover, that the possibility of gender-bending—of men changing into women and women changing
into men—is mentioned along with cannibalism in a list of grotesque fantasies.
And other questions remain. Could a single appearance by a woman in an offi-

cially male space—no matter how symbolically potent—reverse a whole history of gender discrimination and racial apartheid? Could such an appearance redeem the woman's devastating experience of unworlding violence and loss? And should the public event in the East London magistrate's court, which seems to capture Kondlo's imagination, be the one by which Calata's participation in the contestation of space in South Africa is best represented? What of the remarkable incident, which Krog seems to find the most compelling part of the testimony, when the police invade the Calatas' house to intimidate Nomonde and she orders an officer to get up from her bed where he has sat down—an incident in which the micropolitics of space is dramatically played out and in which she is revealed as a woman of stunning self-possession and courage?[4]

But personal space and personal redemption do not seem to be the theme of Professor Kondlo's imagined comic. "The Contestation of Spaces" seems intended, rather, to construct and celebrate a narrative of national reconciliation. In this narrative, women do have a place (the TRC hearings, Kondlo insists, allow Nomonde Calata "the space to become a . . . custodian of history despite her gender").[5] They will tell stories and give witness. But one suspects that they will continue to speak and to be spoken of as mothers and grandmothers, widows and victims.[6] Given the uncomplicated triumphalist plot the professor has in mind, it is perhaps no wonder that he should be drawn to a highly schematic form and one that renders social space in a succession of two-dimensional squares.

Intellectual Space and Empowerment

Unsatisfactory though this particular account of the "contestation of spaces" may be, the idea remains a crucial one, both during the apartheid era and during the South African transition to democracy. It is a pervasive theme in the fiction of the 1990s and in a number of academic studies, including of one of the most important scholarly works to be published to date by a black South African woman: *A Bed Called Home: Life in the Migrant Hostels of Cape Town*, by the physician and anthropologist Mamphela Ramphele.[7] In this work, Ramphele (who, incidentally, is herself perpetually cast in the role of "political widow") addresses "the contestation of spaces" with a full recognition of the complexity of such a process.[8] She is especially mindful of the ambiguous ways in which conventional gender relations and traditional custom come into play in the replication, as well as the transformation, of real, symbolic, and imagined geographies. Ramphele argues that space is always multidimensional and must be examined on at least four levels, the physical, the psychosocial, the political-economic, the ideological-intellectual. Not one of these aspects of space is readily described on its own terms: they are inextricably connected, both in Ramphele's writing about them and in daily practice. Even so, a brief definition of each term—and especially of the concept of intellectual space—is useful for my purpose in this chapter, which is to bring a new critical perspective to bear on the writing of a few black South African women.[9]

Physical space, the first and most self-explanatory of Ramphele's four terms, may be examined in architectural and in broader geographical terms. Both on the micro level (that of buildings, rooms, the arrangement of furniture, and so forth) and the macro level (that of national territory), physical space defines an individual's location in the world. It delimits the area one may legitimately occupy. It establishes points of access to this area and thereby the capacity to admit and exclude others. By setting certain areas aside for certain purposes, it shapes social activities (such as eating and sleeping), as well as temporal routines. It is for good reason, therefore, that Ramphele starts *A Bed Called Home* by describing in considerable detail the architectural design, interior arrangements, and sensory impact of the oppressive migrant worker hostels that are the immediate object of her study: physical space is for her the most fundamental level of analysis, especially since it profoundly affects all other aspects of spatiality.

Psychosocial space may be thought of as "inhabited space." The term refers to the sites of interpellation, which determine an individual's "place" in the social and hierarchical sense of the word and thereby his or her expectations and aspirations. In the course of *A Bed Called Home*, Ramphele argues that psychosocial space may function in both liberating and limiting ways. She cites with obvious appreciation the words of a remarkable resident of the *favelas* of Rio de Janeiro on the transformative capacities of human creativity: "One has to be an artist to survive as a poor person . . . you have to imagine space where there is none."[10] But Ramphele recognizes equally that "people who have had to 'shrink' to fit the limited space they found themselves in" may subsequently find it difficult "to stand up and walk tall."[11] It stands to reason that squalid and cramped quarters will diminish a person's sense of dignity and that overcrowded or permeable structures will curtail his or her sense of autonomy (and we might bring to mind here Fugard's idea of the "violence of immediacy"). Psychological or inhabited space can shape identity in profound and enduring ways and, in Ramphele's view, will remain a factor to deal with for years to come in a democratic South Africa.

Political-economic space may be defined as "that aspect of social relations concerned with the capacity to marshal authoritative and allocative resources."[12] It refers to the terrain of state power and that of the larger and increasingly global economic system within which the power of the state is either bolstered or delimited. It is on this level of analysis that one may consider the effects of apartheid's notorious barrage of laws circumscribing individuals' mobility, places of work and domicile, freedom of assembly, rights of association, and so forth. But political-economic space, in Ramphele's conception, also provides a rubric under which one may consider the struggle of resistance movements to create, contest, and appropriate "room for strategic maneuver."[13] It is this dimension of space, she observes, that was dramatically and permanently enlarged by President De Klerk's historic speech of 2 February 1990, when he unbanned the antiapartheid movements and allowed them to operate openly in the national and international public sphere. Even if geographical transformation of the country will remain a slow process, it can at least proceed in ways that were not imaginable under the previous regime.

Ideological-intellectual space, the most abstract of all of the dimensions of spatiality Ramphele asks us to consider, is also the most important to her conception of her work and its potential political efficacy. Intellectual space, she argues, relates to the symbolic, cultural, linguistic, and discursive framework within which social interaction is conducted. Intellectual space may be defined as an individual's imaginary geography and conceptual horizons: it brings into play an individual's capacity for critical awareness of his or her environment and of the position he or she occupies in the power structure of his or her society. Adequate intellectual space enables a person to take a panoramic view, to make comparisons, and take calculated risks: it helps individuals identify the real sources of their oppression. In so doing, it enables them to devise strategies for true liberation, rather than short-term coping strategies (among which Ramphele counts a nostalgic adherence to traditional custom, conservative gender roles, and even a passive "victim status"), which may enable individuals to survive in constrained and oppressive circumstances but are likely to have retrograde effects in the long term. Intellectual space is the key idea put forward in *A Bed Called Home*: it is clearly, in Ramphele's view, something to strive for and cherish.

But it is important to remember, as Ramphele was forced to do again and again in the course of her investigations, that there is an almost direct correlation between limited physical space and limited intellectual space. Thus individuals who suffer the most severe deprivation and have the greatest need for transformation may be among the least capable of imagining change and of taking the risks that are inevitably involved in the crossing of any borders, whether physical, linguistic, or cultural. In Ramphele's judgment, the deliberate intellectual impoverishment of black South Africans under apartheid—the result of Verwoerd's policy of denying "the Bantu child" access to "greener" and ampler intellectual pastures—will prove quite as devastating a historical legacy as the denial of proper shelter and wages.[14] And the two forms of oppression are intimately related. Empowerment, in the emerging South African democracy, will therefore have to involve not only an improvement of living conditions but also a significant broadening of intellectual space: it will involve "making risk-taking affordable to people by expanding their perceptions of the space around them as well as actually expanding that space."[15]

Now, the word "empowerment" may strike many readers as a suspicious one, especially given the problematic ways in which "black economic empowerment" has come to be associated in the postapartheid era with the creation of a materialistic national bourgeoisie and with the ANC's all too docile relationship to the International Monetary Fund and the World Bank (of which Ramphele herself is currently the managing director). I will therefore be using the word in somewhat gingerly fashion in this chapter. But it does seem to me that we may retain some of its liberatory possibilities if we associate these ideas with what Arjun Appadurai, in his work with homeless people in Mumbai, has described as "the capacity to aspire." This term refers to the expansive and navigational aspects of culture (navigational in the sense that it involves a rudimentary sort of cognitive map, by which a person may find a way of linking the more and the less immediate objects of desire and striving). It is in the capacity to aspire, or so Appadurai asserts, that the future-oriented logic of development may find a natural ally, so that "the poor can find the resources required to contest and alter the conditions of their own poverty" and change "the terms of recognition" under which they function in their society.[16] These are clearly cultural resources that one can ill ignore in a place like South Africa, and it is for this reason that Ramphele is so outspoken about what she sees as the shortsighted anti-intellectualism of many South African radicals, shaped by the urgencies of the antiapartheid struggle, with its demand for "Freedom Now and Education Tomorrow!" Such an attitude, she feels, can only reduce any navigational capacity and impede efforts to broaden the intellectual space of South Africa's now officially liberated citizens.

The Rhetoric of Urgency

With its unflinching assessment of the consequences of oppression and its optimistic validation of creativity and empowerment, *A Bed Called Home* is a Janus-faced work and one that is characteristic of the South African transition. It would be easy to trace its thematic connections to the fiction of the period, especially to Zakes Mda's *Ways of Dying*, which (as I will show in chapter 6) is also concerned with the geographical legacy of apartheid and with the capacity of the poor for its creative transformation. But I propose instead to relate Ramphele's reflections on space to the literary culture of an earlier period. *A Bed Called Home* seems to me to provide a fresh vantage point—we may think of it as newly cleared "intellectual space"—from which we may reassess the nature and value of black South African writing from the apartheid era, as well as the critical discourse that, for good or for ill, accompanied its emergence.

This critical discourse, as Louise Bethlehem has argued in a wide-ranging and largely persuasive essay, was one that overwhelmingly favored realism—a realism of the most "stenographic" and documentary kind.[17] The most vigorous and polemic proponents of this antiaesthetic literary practice were often black writers (though white writers and academics of both liberal and radical persuasions also participated in this pervasive discursive regime). Mothobi Mutloatse, for example, roundly declared in a 1981 interview: "We need a writing that records exactly the situation we live in and any writing which ignores the urgency of political events will be irrelevant."[18] "We have not got the time," asserted Oswald Mtshali, "to embellish this urgent message with unnecessary and cumbersome ornaments like rhyme, iambic pentameter, abstract figures of speech, and an ornate and lofty style. We will indulge in these luxuries which we can ill afford at the moment when we are free people."[19] In the new black poetry, Mbulelo Mzamane claimed, "no barrier separates [the text] from social and political reality."[20] This strenuous investment in the idea of "the real" derives, or so Bethlehem argues, from a not entirely warranted assumption that telling the truth about apartheid would somehow help to bring about its end—that "revelation," as she puts it, "befits revolution."[21] Thus a style that seems to serve no aesthetic function, but only a reproduction of the "real" circumstances, became a sign of commitment to the antiapartheid struggle.

The pervasiveness of this rhetoric of urgency and immediacy derived, in Bethlehem's view, from a distinctly ideological agenda. By underplaying the necessarily mediated and tropological nature of all literary representation, the writers of the apartheid era (and, more vicariously, the critics who celebrated them) were able to invest their work with a sense of ethical seriousness and to claim for themselves a certain symbolic power. Only a few black voices were raised against this hegemonic rhetoric, the most prominent among them being the acerbic voice of Lewis Nkosi, who frequently denounced black South African fiction as imaginatively and intellectually impoverished—as "journalistic fact parading outrageously as imaginative literature."[22] In a 1986 essay, "South African Fiction Writers at the Barricades," he declared that the "naïve realism" of writers like Sipho Sepamla, Lauretta Ngcobo, and Miriam Tlali "owe[s] a great deal to a frustrated desire to abolish any space between literature and the horrible reality of life under apartheid." These writers, he charges, "attempt to reproduce or re-enact in their writings what is happening in the streets, as if language is ever capable of consuming reality, of digesting it, then of finally regurgitating it to us exactly as it was given without essentially changing it."[23] Nkosi's bodily rhetoric here might strike one as excessive, but it is also deployed in the critical and literary writing he opposes, and with none of his sense of irony and hyperbole. The oppressive environment of urban apartheid is at times invested with the capacity of "digesting" the observer rather than vice versa, in order to emphasize the complete lack of space between the word, the writer, and the world. Thus André Brink (in a passage that appropriates the psychogeographic vulnerabilities of black South Africans for the white protagonist of *A Dry White Season*) describes Soweto at night as "an enormous gullet that forced one further down, with peristaltic motions to be digested or excreted in the dark."[24] Brink's grotesque and nightmarish description, to be sure, is highly figurative, but its expressive function is to emphasize the overwhelming "reality" of apartheid's places of deprivation and the way the objective world consumes any subjective mediation.

Brink's fantasy finds its closest critical correlative in the work of Es'kia Mphahlele, who presents this short-circuiting of mediation, the erasure of the gap between the world and the text, as the very hallmark of black writing. In an influential but highly problematic essay, Mphahlele describes the oppressive and devouring urgency of material life as "the tyranny of place." The black writer, he insists, "tends to document his physical and human setting in stark, grim detail, to document minute-to-minute experience. There is a specifically African drama in the ghettoes that the writer cannot ignore. . . . He must come to terms with the tyranny of place or grapple with it, because he must have place, because his writing depends on his commitment to territory."[25] What Mphahlele articulates here could be grasped as an extreme case of what Walter Benjamin called "urban shock": an unmediated sensory overload, destructive of any sustained contemplation. Even temporality is fractured under the impact of apartheid's brutal version of urban modernity. The writer, as Mphahlele puts it elsewhere, produces "a response to the immediate, to the instant, a direct confrontation with the dominant political morality."[26]

The documentation of oppressive surroundings may at times assume a certain poetic force in the work of writers like Mongane Serote and Alex La Guma (and Nkosi always honorably exempts the latter from his denunciations). It is not mere journalism, especially when it implies a self-reflexive analysis of the way in which depressing and intrusive environments affect the writer's own psychological processes.[27] Even *A Bed Called Home*, written for the most part in perfectly unremarkable academese, seems to acquire an expressionist intensity in the passages where Ramphele describes the "overwhelming" impact of the physical space of the migrant hostels: the billowing dust, the overpowering smells, the flying bits of plastic litter (the "flowers of the Cape Flats"), and the dogs sleeping in the shade of wrecked cars. But Ramphele also notes that this sensory overload is cognitively disabling. In the midst of the noise and teeming activity of the migrant worker hostels, she comes to share something of their lack of intellectual space: it becomes difficult, she confesses, to "begin to make sense of a haphazard world which seems to defy all rules of order and logic, but which is 'home' for many thousands of people."[28]

The drift of my polemic should by now be clear. Bethlehem is, I think, quite right in criticizing the dominant literary discourse of the apartheid era (especially from the mid-1970s on) for its repression of the inevitable encodedness of all literary representation. She is right, too, in refusing to take the ethical claims of this dominant critical rhetoric on its own terms: the "trope-of-truth" and transparency is itself thoroughly rhetorical and should really be viewed as a trope masquerading as truth.[29] But I would add the following: what we are dealing with here is a symptom (of a lack of physical and intellectual space) posing as a solution and as an article of literary faith. The rhetoric of urgency posits as a value something that must, from the point of view of empowerment and the capacity to aspire, be grasped as a tremendous deficit. It is perhaps no accident that Mphahlele resorts to such a peculiarly distasteful term as "the *tyranny* of place" in order to describe and advocate what is for him crucial in black South African art: it is as if he dimly recognizes his conception as placing an irksome constraint on the generic and imaginative freedom of the black writer. I would suggest, further, that the definition of black writing produced under the aegis of the rhetoric of urgency is somewhat misleading. Many literary works by black writers in fact do considerably more than—or at least something rather different from—realistic documentation, and such writers are now ripe for rereading. I will therefore turn to the work of Miriam Tlali, the first black woman to write a novel in South Africa under apartheid, to suggest that one may discover in some of her writings a project that is as compatible with a forward-looking project of empowerment as it is with a project of urgent reportage.[30] Tlali's task, as she herself once put it, is to create a "platform" for herself and her readers: a project of literary and linguistic mediation in the interest of expanding intellectual space.[31]

"Fud-u-u-a!"

In antiapartheid literary criticism—to recap briefly—such matters as immediacy, temporal fragmentation (the "minute-by-minute" sensations), spatial constriction ("the tyranny of place"), and permeability (the radical exposure to the hurly-burly of one's surroundings) are often claimed as positive values for resistant literary production. In feminist literary criticism, by contrast, the very same matters have traditionally been identified as outright liabilities and as obstacles to women's creativity. Virginia Woolf writes in *A Room of One's Own* of the benefits for a writer of the sensory insulation one might experience in the courts and quadrangles of Oxford or Cambridge: "Strolling through those colleges past those ancient halls, the roughness of the present seemed smoothed away; the body seemed contained in a miraculous glass cabinet through which no sound could penetrate, and the mind, freed from any contact with facts . . . was at liberty to settle down upon whatever meditation was in harmony with the moment."[32] For poor women (and women, says Woolf, "have always been poor, not for two hundred years merely, but from the beginning of time") this kind of intellectual freedom, for which that private "room of one's own" is the minimal requirement, has of course been unavailable.[33] The same goes for private, uninterrupted time. As Tillie Olsen observes in *Silences*, motherhood has tended to mean that one is "instantly interruptible, responsive, responsible": "Children need one now. . . . The very fact that these are needs of love, not duty, that one feels them as one's self; that there is no one else to be responsible for these needs, gives them primacy. It is distraction, not meditation that becomes habitual; interruption, not continuity; spasmodic, not constant toil. Work interrupted, deferred, postponed makes blockage—at best, lesser accomplishment. Unused capacities atrophy, cease to be."[34]

If all this is true in the case of relatively privileged white Western European and American women writers, it is so much more so in the case of black South African women, who, as Tlali notes, have been "hemmed in on all sides by the political system."[35] One might be tempted to suggest (especially in light of Professor Kondlo's proposed comic strip on "The Contestation of Spaces"), that African women have traditionally been valued as storytellers, even if they have not been able to flourish as writers. But by Tlali's account, questions of space and privacy have affected these forms of women's expression as well. She points out that the time-honored practice of storytelling was enabled by very particular domestic arrangements. In traditional compounds, grandmothers would have their own huts, and the telling of stories would occur those nights when children would stay over in these older women's quarters. The constriction of domestic space in black urban areas, such as Sophiatown, where Tlali herself grew up, was "not as conducive to story telling": given the stress of urban life, grandmothers might well be tired at night, and even if they were up to their traditional task, "the breadwinner would want to go to sleep and perhaps there would be only one room and no space for this story telling."[36]

The distracting, demanding, and culturally impoverished nature of black urban life is a constant theme in Tlali's interviews about her career as a writer. "There's the financial problem, there's the problem of space," she explained in 1989 to Raoul Granqvist and John Stotesbury: "I write in my kitchen, not out of choice, but because there is nowhere else where I can write. You have seen the matchboxes, haven't you? We live in those matchboxes! And of course it is a problem, a very tangible one: I want to speak to these aspiring writers, and my husband has got visitors in the other room, and then in another room my stepfather or my grandfather is sleeping, and so on."[37] In other interviews, Tlali reveals her early determination to save enough money to have her family's township house

electrified so that she could have light to read by, and she recalls as small but significant victories her acquisition of a secondhand refrigerator and a toaster from
the furniture and electronics shop where she worked for some years.[38] But the
modicum of intellectual space Tlali managed to glean in this way seems to have
been compromised again as the political struggle intensified. During the states of
emergency of the 1980s, or so Tlali observes in an essay for the *Index on Censorship*,
she would have been unable find solace in a study, even if she had one:

> I would have to abandon it for the dusty streets—the real battlefield. The tear-
> gas, the resounding loud gunshots, the ever-hovering helicopters, the sirens, the
> dust; the cries of unending agony, the eager footsteps of the fleeing youths in
> school uniforms, forever scaling over the wire fences to escape from the pursuing
> army trucks and the casspirs. The utter lack of peace and quiet would extricate
> even the most stubborn bluestocking from her desk.[39]

It is no surprise, then, that Tlali should recurrently describe Soweto as a "quagmire" or as "quicksand" and that she should frequently make pronouncements
that seem entirely of a piece with the rhetoric of urgency: "Black women," as she
once told Mineke Schipper, "do not have the time to dream."[40]

South African critics—to varying degrees under the influence of the same
rhetoric—have therefore found ways to read Tlali's work in the usual ways: as
"depictions of community," antiaesthetic testimonies of political commitment,
validations of motherhood, and so forth. They have also focused for the most
part on her works that most closely resemble the fiction of other black writers.
Thus her novel *Amandla!*—which focuses on township life in the period of the
Soweto riots—tends to be discussed along with other novels on the same subject,
like Sipho Sepamla's *A Ride on the Whirlwind*, Mongane Serote's *To Every Birth Its
Blood*, and Mbulelo Mzamane's *Children of Soweto*.[41] The more unusual aspects of
her oeuvre, however, such as the early novel *Muriel at Metropolitan* (written before
the utilitarian realist modes of protest writing were fully established and theo-
rized) and even some of the interviews and travelogues included in the collection
Mihloti have received insufficient attention to date. It is in these works that Tlali's
project is revealed as not so much a "stenographic" record of political urgencies as
a kind of broadening of her own intellectual space and that of her readership. The
brief story "Fud-u-u-a!" strikes me as a key text: as a kind of blueprint for Tlali's
oeuvre in the same way "Once Upon a Time" is for Gordimer's oeuvre. Tlali
here describes the crowded circumstances on the trains that bring black workers
back and forth from the townships to the cities and the dangers that these conditions pose to women, who often find themselves subject to sexual harassment by
men who are jammed up next to them in the crowded carriages. The title is an
onomatopoeic rendering of the sound the commuting women make when they
press out against the people crowding in on them, letting out their breath, wrig-
gling, pushing with their chests and elbows, in order to claim a little more space
for themselves. It is under this odd, but affecting rubric—"Fud-u-u-a!"—that I
would like us to reconsider Tlali's writing.

A useful, if sidelong, starting point for such a reading is Tlali's interview with Lilian Ngoyi, the president of the ANC Women's League and the Federation of South African Woman in the 1950s, collected in *Mihloti*. While Tlali emphasizes Ngoyi's status as a mother (indeed, she makes much of the fact that the activist, when given an opportunity to study in China, chose to return home to her husband and children), she is clearly fascinated by the international perspective that Ngoyi's travels abroad allowed her to bring to bear on the South African political scene: by the inspiration, for instance, that Ngoyi derived from her encounter with the "tolerant, humane . . . structures" of socialist countries (M 54). Tlali's descriptions of her own travels emphasize a similar craving for broader comparative perspectives. The account of her trip to Egypt, for example, puts a whole new spin on the usual tropes of urban shock so prevalent in black South African writing. Tlali describes the intrusive clamor of Cairo street life: "I was awakened by the deafening sounds of hooting cars, by the loud voices, the whistling, bustling thousands of people outside. Bells were ringing or clanging and there was a continuous discordant chorus of all kinds of 'musical instruments' pealing away endlessly. . . . The noise penetrated through the layers of blankets, sheets, and counterpane" (M 94). From this experience of sensory overload, at first merely "alarming" and exotic, Tlali derives a broader interpretive insight. It becomes the source for what we may see as a peculiar gesture of belonging: "I listened for a while and laughed loudly. Such a thing would never happen in any of the towns I had been to in Europe, I thought. All that noise pollution! Whole populations would cry out in protest. Imagine that kind of encroachment into the lives of the respectable citizens unable to enjoy the peace and quiet of their apartments. I realized that I was now in 'familiar' ground. I was in Africa; dear beloved, deprived, marauded Africa" (M 94). Given the intellectual space to make a comparison between Cairo and Soweto, between Africa and Europe, Tlali is able to invent a more capacious and, if you will, postcolonial identity. She accepts the "tyranny of place" as one of her themes, but not necessarily as the formal or determinant condition of her work.

Metropolitan Furniture and Radio

A related but more complex case in point is Tlali's first work, *Muriel at Metropolitan*, written in 1968–69, when grand apartheid was still fully in place and the resistance temporarily driven underground. The novel is based on personal experience: it derives from the period in Tlali's life when she worked as a typist and bookkeeper for a shop called Mayfair Furniture and Appliances. Because of its autobiographical origins, critics have tended to read the novel as a documentary, and a rather formless one at that.[42] But *Muriel at Metropolitan* is actually quite strictly patterned and generically inventive. It is a political sitcom of sorts. In saying this, I am not suggesting that Tlali is consciously imitating the sitcom form, which she had probably never encountered: South African television broadcasts only started in 1976, several years after the novel was written. But the analogy

nevertheless seems to me an apt and productive one. The novel offers an enter-
taining microanalysis of the relationships of a limited cast of characters in a fixed
social setting. All the chapters start out by staging a revealing interaction, and
they all rely for their humor and for the object lessons they deliver on the typical behavior and attitudes of the dramatis personae, just as sitcom programs do.
Tlali's chapter headings—"Waiting," "A Slap in the Face," "Mixed Encounters,"
"While the Boss Is Away," "The Mechanic Walks Out"—would all work well
as the titles of episodes. Apparently a German television company optioned the
novel for a series in the mid-1980s, and it is easy to see why they thought it had
potential.[43]

Tlali's decision to change the name of the shop from "Mayfair" to "Metropolitan" underscores the allegorical centrality of the novel's chronotope: we
are dealing here with a microcosm or a "stage," as Tlali once put it, rather than
strictly realistic representation.[44] The shop's physical layout is both an expression
and a mockery of the government's fixation on the idea of racial segregation. A
counter separates the owner and the salespeople from their black customers. Wire
mesh, steel bars, and filing cabinets separate the white workers from their black
colleagues. There is even a "whites only" coat rack. The archaic and cumbersome
office bureaucracy is also organized according to apartheid principles. The ledger
cards for "Europeans" are filed in one cabinet and "Non-Europeans" in another.
And as in South Africa at large, the "coloureds" create a quandary, since their
names are not readily distinguishable from those of whites: the filing clerk has to
guess at their racial identity on the basis of their addresses. The shop, moreover, is
set up to facilitate surveillance. (One of the most painful aspects of Muriel's job
is that she has to ask to see the black customers' passbooks like a policeman in
order to process their purchases.) The boss, Mr. Bloch, has no office but sits on
a chair placed at what Muriel thinks of as the shop's "strategic point" (MM 67),
at the corner where the shorter and longer arms of an L-shaped passage meet
up. From this vantage he can see every nook and cranny of the shop, except for
an upstairs workshop and a small area behind a stack of linoleum squares, where
the canny boss-boy, Adam, sits reading the horseracing columns in the morning
paper. As this last detail already suggests, the novel's microcosmic setting captures
not only apartheid's rigid inhumanity but also its inefficiencies and failures. For
all its physical barriers, Metropolitan Radio can only function through the intimate collaboration and negotiation of blacks and whites (and it is no accident that
Tlali constantly presents her characters as having to squeeze past each other in the
tight spaces of the shop). But their collaboration is marred by the whites' incessant efforts to police boundaries and to exploit and degrade their most valuable
colleagues and customers.

By confining most of the action to the premises of Metropolitan Radio,
Tlali's novel keeps apartheid's "ghettoes"—the sites privileged by the rhetoric of
urgency—at a distance. It may be for this reason that critics have tended to see
Muriel at Metropolitan as offering a muted and restrained critique of apartheid, as
compared to her second novel *Amandla!* set in Soweto during the year of fire following the riots. But the earlier work actually includes a number of revolutionary
messages for the alert reader to decode. Consider, for example, the chapter "Fri-

day." True to the novel's sitcom-like formula, this "episode" records the quotidian interactions in the shop, including many jokes on the part of the white characters about black customers' names. It closes with a more or less comic incident involving a customer called Return, who requires attention just as Muriel is about to leave the shop to go home. Mr. Bloch cannot resist one of his trademark witticisms: "So," he says to Muriel, "you return from the door to Return" (MM 115). The pun seems pointless, until we notice that it unintentionally echoes and amplifies an earlier remark by Lambert, Muriel's most politicized coworker, who vows that he will not shave his beard until the day the people's leaders return from Robben Island. The apparently inconclusive chapter ending thus plays on the ANC slogan *Mayibuye, iAfrika!* (Africa, Return!) and it connects the ordinary chitchat in the shop with the more explicitly political moments of the novel— most notably the moment in a chapter entitled "Sophiatown," in which Muriel recalls a group of protesters singing the hymn "Thina Sizwe" with its poignant demand for the return of the land stolen from the black nation:

Sikalela . . . Sikalela Izwe Lethu! (We weep for our country)
Elathatwa . . .
Elathatwa Ngambahlophe (which was taken by the whites)
Mabayeke . . .
Mabayak'umhlaba wethu!" (let them leave our land alone!) (MM 127)

I shall return to this important scene shortly. Suffice it to say for now that Tlali's novel allows us to reflect on the physical space both of the workplace and, more implicitly, of the nation, and that South Africa's grim urban landscapes, though kept "offstage," are nevertheless crucial to her novel's political and thematic concerns. Metropolitan Radio is connected to the townships, the maids' rooms, and the "locations in the sky" (the rooms on the roofs of apartment buildings where the cleaners are permitted to live) through the activities of its sales agents and repo men. The very raison d'être of the business, moreover, is provided by the growth of apartheid's segregated residential areas. The fact that "thousand and thousands of cheap, mushroom-like brick or concrete structures were being built on the outskirts of every town to house the ever-increasing and inexhaustible number of the 'town' Africans" (MM 116) means that Mr. Bloch has a market for his products. For him the flow of blacks to the city is pure opportunity. Despite his physical racism, which is revealed at several points in the novel (most obviously when he grabs a cushion off the desk chair where Muriel is about to sit down), he is more than willing to make a profit from the people he disparagingly refers to as *soggens* or *soggadikas* (MM 136). In fact, Mr. Bloch prefers to deal with blacks because, unschooled in the ways of commerce, they often fail to understand that he is charging them exorbitant rates of interest on their purchases. And he is not the only character to turn racist legislation into profit. Ben, the building's black caretaker, runs an even sleazier operation on the roof of Mr. Bloch's premises: he squeezes himself into the boiler room or even a stinking public toilet at night, so that he can rent out his room to illicit couples contravening the Immorality Act.

The restrictive setting of *Muriel at Metropolitan*, in sum, does not diminish the sharpness or the range of the novel's investigations of place and space. In fact, it provides Tlali with the necessary distance to analyze rather than simply record the sensory impact of apartheid's oppressive geographical schemes. The chronotope of the shop permits Tlali to dramatize the ways South Africa's capitalist economy and its racist ideologies work both in collusion and in tension with each other. By situating her narrative in a downtown workplace, rather than in a segregated dormitory township, she is able to suggest that apartheid—even at its height—could not entirely foreclose on the broad processes of modernization and creolization in South Africa: processes that, as she makes amply clear through Muriel's narration, are experienced by even the more fortunate blacks as painful, humiliating, and compromising.[45] Most importantly, the fact that Metropolitan happens to be a shop dealing in furniture and household appliances permits Tlali to examine the consumerist desires of the "town Africans" and, by extension, what Chabani Manganyi has described as the expressive "inner space" of township homes: a dimension of black experience that was largely ignored in the discourse of apartheid's urban planners, and in the more "spectacular" forms of South African literature as well.[46]

At the time of Tlali's writing, National Party ideologues were intensely suspicious of black participation in the market as consumers, since this participation could open up hybrid forms of self-expression that ran counter to apartheid's vision of unadulterated and distinct ethnic identities. One reason why the black townships were entirely devoid of businesses and shops (other than illegal shebeens) was the leaders' belief that access to consumer goods would foster material aspirations, which would inevitably entail political aspirations.[47] Grand apartheid's schemes depended on fixed notions of the "standard of living" appropriate to blacks and to whites (a topic that is hotly debated in Tlali's novel [MM 179]). Television, with its potential for enlarging consumerist appetites and expanding intellectual space, was therefore anathema to key figures in the party, as Rob Nixon's research has amply demonstrated. The medium's vaunted tendency to turn the world into a single global village—at a time when the Nationalists were "reinventing 'pure' Xhosa villages in Transkei, Zulu villages in KwaZulu, Ndebele villages in KwaNdebele, and so forth"—struck people like Albert Hertzog, the minister of telecommunications, and Piet Marais, the chairman of the South African Broadcasting Corporation (SABC) and the Broederbond, as a technological and social nightmare.[48]

Given this political context, the treatment of consumerism and mass-mediated culture in *Muriel at Metropolitan* is appropriately ambivalent. Muriel's observations make it perfectly clear that her boss's hire-purchase schemes are usurious and exploitative, and that her colleague Mrs. Kuhn is not entirely wrong when she marvels at the folly of mine workers who are willing to "go hungry and naked" for the sake of owning a radio (MM 32). The possibilities of the medium are therefore not presented in utopian fashion. Under apartheid, as Tlali was well aware, the potentially unconfined spatiality of the medium, with its extraordinary ability to link domestic space with the territory of the nation and the world at large, was not entirely a site of freedom.[49] The SABC's Radio Bantu service, which from 1960 on broadcasted programs in nine African languages, was specifically intended to bolster the apartheid regime's vision of ethnically authentic and separate cultural identities. The government even subsidized cheap FM radios to prevent black South Africans from tuning in to potentially insurrectionary shortwave broadcasts from independent African nations (especially from Radio Ghana and Radio Tanzania) and from Radio Moscow's international service.[50]

This situation is alluded to in a number of revealing interactions and conversations in *Muriel at Metropolitan*. One such interaction occurs when Mr. Bloch tries to deter a pair of white customers from buying an FM set: he tells them that the initials FM mean "For *Muntus*" (MM 113); white customers, he implies, deserve something better. Some of Metropolitan's black customers, unsure of just how radio works, are suspicious of the medium's ability to bridge vast distances. They fear that their sets will extend the shop owner's capacity for surveillance and that he will somehow be able to reach them—even miles away in the Transkei—if they failed to pay the bill. Mr. Bloch's joking remarks to a prospective buyer about how a particular set will "catch" not only "English station, Afrikaans station" but even "Police station" are therefore far from reassuring; they serve as unintentional reminders of radio's function as state apparatus (MM 107). It is no wonder that the politically aware Lambert should lament the fact that "the *Muntus* must pay [so] heavily for their indoctrination" (MM 113).

But despite all this, the novel never trivializes or condemns the black consumers who are drawn "like bees" (MM 30) to the wares on display at Metropolitan Radio. Their avid desire for "Manchester dining-room suites" (MM 53) and the like is presented as entirely understandable, given their lack of adequate physical space and political room for strategic maneuver. The ownership of furniture clearly serves as a substitute for real domestic security. In the face of apartheid's disdain of egalitarian consumer culture, the capacity of commodities to express personal tastes and to help create an alternate psychological space for an oppressed individual becomes an important, and all too seductive, resource.[51] Such forms of expression and creativity are at stake in the case of Anna Gxagxa, Mr. Bloch's best customer, who over the years has managed to furnish her entire house—sofas, carpets, curtains, and all—in maroon. Anna's tastes strike Muriel as comic and excessive, until she learns that maroon is the color Anna's religious group wears on ritual occasions and that the woman sees maroon as the color of dignity. Considering the period's draconian strictures on free speech and antigovernment activities, it is not altogether far-fetched to think that the desire for commodities like furniture and radios might (however unconsciously) be expressive of a degree of political resistance as well—especially if we consider the bizarre comments on furniture in one of Prime Minister H. F. Verwoerd's more ludicrous and patronizing speeches about the economic advantages of the bantustans:

As the towns in the Bantu areas develop, Bantu families will need furniture. The furniture used in European homes and which they purchase at present is not always right, for example, as regards size, for use in homes. Under the policy of separate development it thus becomes possible for the Bantu to create his own little furniture factory in the Bantu Areas. . . . Industries, however small, belonging to the Bantu themselves, in the Bantu areas, are also one of the fruits expected from separate development.[52]

Verwoerd's profound racism expresses itself here in the logic of scale: unwilling to contemplate the possibility that black peoples' houses may be expanded and enlarged so that they could live on the scale of "Europeans," he magnanimously grants the homeland residents a little factory for their own little furniture. His rhetoric here seems to express the hope, as Alice Brittan has suggested, that "the routine occupation of diminutive chairs might cause the body itself to shrink" and along with it, the "Bantu's" intellectual and political space.[53] The practice of cramming large items of furniture into a small township house (which researchers on black urban life have observed as early as the 1930s) is therefore not a case of colonial mimicry, which, in Homi Bhabha's reading, serves to destabilize and trouble white domination. It is rather, Brittan argues, a concrete expression of an intention to acquire that power and should be grasped as "the future tense in material form." The tiny, overfurnished homes of black South Africans are then anticipatory structures, models to be built to proper scale once political space is enlarged.[54]

The many conversations about the meaning of furniture in *Muriel at Metropolitan* seem all the more significant in light of these speculations. Reflecting on the various laws barring black homeownership, Anna, the woman who loves maroon, wearily declares: "Sometimes I wonder why we buy furniture at all." Muriel readily supplies a psychological explanation: "We need something firm to hold on to, even if it is only a piece of wood. It gives life a meaning, just to hurry home and sit and look at the furniture, even if it is ill suited for the brick boxes they build for us" (MM 169). But other customers seem aware of the sociopolitical aspirations that are expressed in the black consumers' passion for household goods: "These Boers," they reason, "are always envious when we buy better furniture than they do. They realize that even if they try to keep us down by not paying us anything when we work for them, we still try our best to buy good things. They feel that we are competing with them and they do not like it" (MM 38–39). However financially reckless they may be, the blacks' purchases thus represent a claim to equality—exactly what Dr. Verwoerd's obsession with differential scales and standards of living was designed to repress. It is perhaps no accident, then, that the discussions of furniture and domestic space in *Muriel at Metropolitan* should eventually lead us—again—to the broad topic of national territory and colonial occupation. "The land really belongs to *us*, mind you," Anna tells the black staff at Metropolitan. And while whites might find her tastes excessive and absurd, she thinks the same about their claims to ownership and domination: their political position strikes her as no less preposterous than if Africans were to invade Italy and try to keep themselves in power with election slogans like "Keep Black South Europe Black" (MM 169).

Between Two Worlds

The metonymic evocation of black domestic space in *Muriel at Metropolitan* is already a unique contribution on Tlali's part to black South Africa writing. But it is above all her meticulous interest in language—and by extension in ideological-intellectual space—that most clearly distinguishes her practice from the (largely hypothetical) version of black writing validated by the rhetoric of urgency, according to which the forms and codes of representation are supposedly transparent. Metropolitan Radio is consistently presented as a multilingual and therefore multidimensional site. While the white staff may set up physical barriers to protect and separate themselves from their black customers and colleagues, the blacks can easily retreat behind the linguistic barrier of their own languages, which the whites dismiss as the merest noise.[55] Thus even the lowly tea-boy Johannes can safely express his views about the white women, who are "so lazy" that it is no wonder their husbands will not pay *lobola* to marry them (MM 27). Several scenes in the novel explore the capacity of language to define space and to create an ideological world distinct from the immediate physical environment. A case in point is the chapter "Waiting," in which Tlali ponders the role of traditional custom in the political-economic space of apartheid South Africa (a topic that also engages Ramphele in *A Bed Called Home*). The scene in question starts with yet another little incident that would play out perfectly in a sitcom. On an ordinary busy workday, the repo man Agrippa comes into the shop and greets the salesman, William, with extreme formality, as though he were a chief: "S'bona wena, we Matanzima!" William responds in kind: "Ewe, Sobhuza!" The greetings, Muriel notes, are reminiscent of the days of yore, when Zulu warriors would salute King Shaka with the cry of "Bayete!" And for the two men that is, of course, the point: it is as if the one man is "entering a *kraal* and dressed in *amabheshu*" and the other is "sitting on a grass mat spread over a floor smeared with cowdung" (MM 42). They are, one might say, creating an imaginary geography for themselves, an ideological space in which they may momentarily assume different subject positions from those they occupy in the social space of the shop. By means of their archaic greeting they are able to distinguish themselves in a flattering way from their younger, Johannesburg-born-and-bred coworkers, whom they scornfully refer to as "children of the houses with numbers" (MM 42). But while Tlali is alert to the comforts provided by this linguistic coping strategy, she is quick to remind the reader, through the observations of Muriel and Lambert, of the broader political and economic context in which the performance is staged. Muriel calls on the old men to look around them and notice that they are not carrying shields, but stacks of portable radios: whether they like it or not, their world is the modern world and specifically the world of apartheid, where tribal chiefs are corrupt dummies and daily life is governed by the distinctly unglamorous superintendents of the Bantu Administration bureaucracy. Even the power of an independent king like Sobhuza of Swaziland, Muriel points out, is delimited and checked by the international capitalist system: Mr. Bloch owns a huge farm in the newly independent territory, over which he, and not King Sobhuza, holds sway.

This essentially comic scene, in short, demonstrates the surprisingly complex spatiality of Tlali's chronotope: it can expand to include not only the physical terrain of the shop's interior but also the political-economic space of the nation (and its neighboring territories), as well as the interpellative ideological spaces created by language and tradition. There is, however, one key incident in the novel (in addition to the final "severance scene," when Muriel finally leaves Mr. Bloch's employ) that takes place away from the usual *mise en scène* of Metropolitan Radio and therefore deserves our careful attention.[56] In the chapter "Sophiatown," Muriel and the driver Henry are instructed to give their Afrikaans-speaking colleague Mrs. Stein a ride to her home. As it so happens, Mrs. Stein lives in Triomf, the low-income white suburb built on the very ruins of the demolished freehold township of Sophiatown: one of the most important sites in South African urban history and literary culture. The chapter opens, true to the novel's sitcom-like structure, by describing one of the many misunderstandings that arise in the multilingual and multiracial workplace when Mrs. Stein, whose servant has been relocated to Rustenburg for a pass violation, tries to hire an unemployed customer as her new sleep-in domestic. When she tries to direct the prospective maid to her home, Mrs. Stein creates confusion by her reluctance to call the suburb by its former name, which the black woman would have understood instantly: her uncle, as it turns out, lived in Sophiatown for years. This small but significant repression of the past introduces a meditation on memory and redemption, which reveals yet another way in which Tlali's project in *Muriel at Metropolitan* exceeds the (anti)aesthetic of journalistic immediacy.

The historical Sophiatown, which Muriel fondly remembers from her student days as "the centre of the metropolis" (MM 123), is of enormous interest in any history of South African social space and urban culture. The township was a thorn in the flesh of the Nationalist government, not so much because of its putative slum conditions as because of the heterogeneous and creolized forms of urban life it fostered. In the "little Paris of the Transvaal," culture was both intensely local—as Tlali suggests through Miriam's nostalgic invocation of once-familiar place names like Toby Street, Tucker Street, Victoria Road, and Good Street (MM 125–126)—and a long-distance affair.[57] The townships' intellectuals—Bloke Modisane, Can Themba, Es'kia Mphahlele, Todd Matshikiza, and the young Lewis Nkosi—were attracted to American jazz and to international literary figures like James Joyce, John Osborne, and Langston Hughes. Its gangsters, known as "the Russians," "the Koreans," "the Berliners," and "the Americans," were aficionados of Hollywood gangster movies and addicted to brand-name fashions from London and New York: Florsheim shoes, Van Heusen shirts, and Borsolino hats.[58] These aesthetic and consumerist predilections enabled the Sophiatowners to "leapfrog over white South Africa" and to connect themselves to whatever seemed "interesting, attractive or superior in distant places."[59] If, as Ulf Hannerz has observed, the apartheid ideologues' conception of culture was an extreme version of the idea of a "global mosaic," in which each piece was bounded, discrete, and firmly located, Sophiatown's emerging culture was that of a "global ecumene," in which "meanings and symbolic forms of varying provenance" are distributed via an "open continuum, stretched out transnationally from center to periphery."[60] Sophiatown thus occupied a particularly rich and multivalent position in the cultural geography of global modernity (a similar position, in fact, to that of postapartheid Johannesburg): it stood midway between the centers of the industrialized nations and the extreme periphery of the rural areas to which it was connected by returning migrants and the commodities they carried with them—radios, gramophones, musical instruments, and new styles of dress. Sophiatown was, in fact, "a center with its own periphery," just as Muriel remembers it to be, and one that would strike the nationalist government, intent on stratifying and localizing cultural consumption, as a fundamental threat.[61]

Tlali's description of Muriel's return to the site of the freehold township does not fully exploit the contrast between the expansive imaginary geography of Sophiatown and the restrictive cultural landscape of the apartheid suburb. But the temporality of the passage in question is quite complicated and extends far beyond the moment of narration. Muriel's immediate sensory experience of the white suburb—the sounds of traffic and the shouts and laughter of white youngsters playing soccer—fades out and is replaced by a cityscape of memory. "I stood and looked into the past," Muriel tells us (MM 126). Her former life in Sophiatown is, as it were, brought into the present moment, but in ruinous fashion: the "hopes of redemption" (MM 126) that were a constitutive part of the remembered moments cannot be reexperienced. The rubble of the church where Muriel was married—still visible in white Triomf—leads her to reflect on the fact that without domestic security, marriage and family life can serve only to reproduce the condition of serfdom. But while it remains largely elegiac, the "Sophiatown" chapter introduces the possibility of liberation through the remembered words of the protest song "Thina Sizwe," which, as we have already seen, insists on the return of the land—the entire country—to the black nation. It suggests that the Afrikaners' "Triomf" ("triumph") may not endure forever. The very soil on which it is built, Muriel thinks, is still wet with the tears of black mothers and can thus provide only the shakiest foundation for the victorious "concept-city" of apartheid.[62]

If Muriel's reflections, while denying the possibility of personal redemption, hint at the return of the repressed, her colleague Henry's remarks assert that possibility considerably more powerfully and crudely. Denouncing the new suburb's vainglorious name, he thinks of "all those cockroaches and lice [the white people] have built their beautiful homes on." "Where is their pride," he asks: "All those nice gardens of theirs fertilized by the shit of black children who used to run about here naked and neglected while their mothers cared for white kids. All those buckets from the latrines they used to empty into the streets—where's all their white pride?" (MM 128). This vision of the apartheid city as an uncanny palimpsest (the same vision that Marlene van Niekerk exploits in her postapartheid novel *Triomf*, where the saga of a cretinous Afrikaner family's decay is initiated by the discovery of "kaffir bones" in their back yard) becomes all the more compelling if we consider the various instances in the novel where whites reveal their racist preconceptions of blacks as putative vectors of infection and disease. It is telling, in fact, that during the drive to Triomf with Muriel and Henry, Mrs. Stein keeps her face turned to the window and away from her black coworkers, because, as Muriel jokes, "she wants to breathe the 'free' air, and not the same air the kaffirs are breathing" (MM 125). The futility of such segregationist desires is sharply exposed by Henry's understanding that the whites cannot avoid being contaminated from the dirt and deprivation they themselves create—especially so in places like Triomf that supposedly symbolize the victory of apartheid's policies. The trope of shit (which is metonymically present in the novel's recurrent altercations about segregated toilet facilities) is dangerous and mobile in the discursive and geographical domain of apartheid: as "the sign of undifferentiation" or as "matter out of place"—simultaneously inside and outside, self and other—it symbolically undermines the very notion of boundaries. Especially when it is so clearly associated with a history of abjection, shit cannot but disturb a political order of rigidly separate identities and places.[63] Marked off from the other chapters in the novel by its setting, the "Sophiatown" chapter thus touches on the familiar colonial dynamics of infection and underscores the chief political insight of Tlali's novel: namely, that the urban Africans whom the government would try to wish away by such actions as the demolition of Sophiatown are not only omnipresent but indispensable. They "spend most of their days with the whites in their business places and their homes," "travel with them all day and night from place to place all over Southern Africa," and "toil side by side with all the other races in all walks of life to make [the] country the paradise it is said to be" (MM 11). An avoidance of physical contact, Muriel insists, will not immunize anyone: "the only way to ensure that the air that *they* breathe and food that *they* eat will not be 'contaminated' by the blacks is by raising their standard of living" (MM 89).

This vision of a unitary and creolized culture is, arguably, abandoned in the final chapter of the novel, when Muriel's attempt to land a new job with a business called Continental Scooters is thwarted by apartheid's petty regulations (there is no separate toilet for her at the new workplace, and her work permit can therefore not be approved) and she decides to resign from Metropolitan Radio anyway, never again to collaborate with whites. It is as if Tlali would like to remind us of the ways in which all aspects of spatiality are constrained by the political-economic space of the apartheid state. But the conclusion of *Muriel at Metropolitan* does not negate the importance of the subtler and, I would argue, quite effective forms of linguistic, cultural, and spatial contestation that are traced out in the text as a whole. Tlali originally considered giving the novel the title "Between Two Worlds," a phrase that appropriately draws attention to the ambivalent position the main character is forced to occupy. It is significant, in this regard, that Tlali does not present Muriel as a mother (we only learn that she has a child and a husband midway though the text) but focuses rather on the various roles she has to play at the workplace: of translator, interpreter, policeman, and spy. These roles afford her the privileges, as well as the disadvantages, of someone who is not confined to a given and well-established space but must operate at the intersections of conflicting cultures. Though this mediating role is painful—Muriel comes to view herself as a kind of "shock absorber" between blacks and whites (MM 140)—and is ultimately too compromising to sustain, it does provide scope for interpretative freedom or, if you will, intellectual space. By eavesdropping on conversations that are conducted on the "white" side of Metropolitan Radio,

Muriel is able to understand her own position and the boundaries that constrain her in a critical and perhaps ultimately liberatory fashion. Among other things, she is made aware of the limits imposed on her by culture and gender. While the white women order the tea-boy around and make him run errands to the pharmacy and the teashop, Muriel finds herself unable to do so: "according to our custom a woman does not send a man. We reserve a place, an elevated place for our men" (MM 27). But she also notices that the white women have no power: the shop is Mr. Bloch's domain, and he calls the shots. Muriel is also in a position to observe that while the black workers are constrained by their fear and their lack of power within the apartheid state, the whites are constrained by their fear and their lack of power in a changing international scene. Their constant bickering about the stupidity of the new African leaders, about the United Nations, and about America with its riots and racial strife reveals the vulnerability and smallness of their political and social world.[64]

Though, as Margaret Lenta has pointed out, the white women constantly try to put Muriel in the position of a maid and inferior by means of the language with which they address her, the final position of linguistic mastery is Muriel's—and that of the novelist.[65] By "analyzing situations" (which Tlali once described as her particular talent) and by inventing the microcosmic chronotope of the novel, she creates an intellectual space, or "platform," that elevates character, author, and ideal reader (who is consistently imagined as black) above the position of "serfdom" that Muriel fears might be her lot.[66] Tlali is consequently able to provide a critical perspective not only on the separate worlds of black and white South Africans but also on the terrain they share, and on the contemporary world at large. In this respect, Tlali's Metropolitan works rather like a radio (if I may invent another fanciful analogy): it is a small textual site in and from which a wide, even an international array, of signals and meanings are gathered, amplified, and broadcast.

So What's New?

Muriel at Metropolitan enables us to examine all of the dimensions of space outlined in Ramphele's useful study. The impact of physical space on social life can be traced in the novel's microanalysis of a single workspace and also in its less frequent, but nevertheless insightful, reflections on South Africa's emergent urban geographies and on the national territory at large. The dynamics of psychosocial space can be explored in the novel's revealing conversations about radios and furniture and its attention to black consumers' creative forms of self-invention, especially in the domestic sphere. The effects of political-economic space—a wholly confining terrain for black South Africans during the period in question—are exposed in the novel's treatment of the complex relationship between the capitalist marketplace and the oppressive racial legislation of apartheid. The importance of intellectual space, finally, is evident in the novel's detailed examination of the various forms of linguistic inclusion and exclusion in which all the characters engage. It is ultimately best demonstrated in the novel itself, which, as I have suggested, is itself a means of expanding critical awareness and (potentially at least) of fostering the black readership's capacity for taking a panoramic view, making comparisons, and identifying the sources of their oppression.

But what has happened to black women's writing in the supposedly freer time since the end of apartheid? Has any new fiction shown the benefits of an expanded intellectual space? Are there new writers whose fiction breaks with the hegemonic aesthetics of urgency and reportage favored during the days of the struggle? Are the stories of women writers distinguishable from male-sponsored national allegories of the sort I discussed at the very beginning of the chapter?[67] And if intellectual space has indeed been enlarged, what form does that enlargement take? Has "empowerment," or "the capacity to aspire" retained its liberatory qualities, or does it threaten to become indistinguishable from *embourgeoisement* and from ordinary consumerist desires for such commodities as CDs, televisions, cell phones, and computers—all of which serve to connect personal space with the vast terrain of a global economy?

These questions about cultural and literary expression, of course, raise further and more fundamental questions. Has the new South Africa, now more than decade old, really brought about a significant material improvement in the physical surroundings and mobility of the majority of women? To what extent is the intellectual space of those who have not managed to make it into the middle class still constrained by inadequate physical and personal space? A cartoon by the well-known political artist Zapiro offers a sobering answer, and one that is backed up by crime statistics. He depicts South African women as three little piggies in a snug little house—fashioned entirely of paper. The roof is made out of the Constitution and the Bill of Rights; one wall is made from a draft of the Women's Charter and another out of the Report of the Gender Commission, with sections on Equity and Women's Rights; and a restraining order serves as a slightly shaky pediment. The house clearly offers scant protection from the wolf depicted to the right of the frame: a slavering, *louche*-looking creature with the legend "Ongoing Male Violence" inscribed on his chest.[68] Zapiro's cartoon implies that the good intentions of the ANC government have not yet ensured a happy ending to the national story of the contestation of spaces. While political violence has diminished, the incidence of rape and other forms of violence against women remains frighteningly high. And while there may well be more black women with control over rooms of their own than there were under apartheid, privacy and security have not yet become ordinary expectations. Indeed, several scholars have argued that the neoliberal economic policies of the ANC government have only increased the unevenness and inequity of urban development. The Reconstruction and Development Programme (RDP) and other housing schemes have endeavored to make the new constitutional right to adequate housing a reality, but the design and construction of the houses have seemed so unsatisfactory to many of the poor that a new vocabulary of mocking names has arisen to describe them: the RDP houses are "Unos" (as in the name of the small Fiat), "Smarties" (as in the name of the multicolored sweets—RDP houses are often painted in different colors), and "Popcorn" (they pop up everywhere).[69] By a 2003 estimate, about three million people still need housing, seven and a half million lack access to running water, and about twenty-one million go without sanitation services.[70]

But to get a sense of some postapartheid developments that have in fact changed the personal lives of South African women, it may be helpful to shift from statistical to anecdotal evidence and to follow the veteran journalist Allister Sparks to the drearily named relocation settlement of Stinkwater, north of Pretoria. During the 1980s, Sparks met there with Sylvia Malala, a woman who lived in a wood-and-iron shack. Mrs. Malala described to him the details of her daily existence. She would spend a large part of her waking hours, summer and winter, exhausting herself in a daily quest for two of the most basic commodities of her family's subsistence: firewood and water. First, she would push a wheelbarrow for about six kilometers over the sandy dunes to collect stems and branches from an ever-diminishing thicket of scrub on a nearby farmer's land. Next, she would take an hour-long walk with a twenty-five-liter bucket balanced on her head to collect water from a reservoir outside the settlement. Only after these errands were done could she attend to her other chores: washing, cooking, cleaning, and the like.[71] This grueling routine, as Sparks notes, was far from exceptional in the old South Africa. According to Francis Wilson and Mamphela Ramphele's research in the early 1980s, the particular character of poverty under apartheid could be grasped by bringing to mind the image of a black woman walking across the veld with a load of firewood on her head, passing underneath a high-tension electrical line.[72] As an image of deprivation, such a figure is not particularly spectacular and might even strike the privileged viewer as picturesque. But when one considers, as Wilson, Ramphele, and Sparks all urge us to do, that the electrical line belonged to a state-funded company, capable of providing (relatively) clean and readily available energy to all the white towns and farmsteads in the nation—a company that could, in fact, produce enough energy to electrify every home in Africa south of the equator—the cruel absurdity of the system stands revealed. The image of the woman with her bundle of firewood perfectly captures the way black people's lives under apartheid were governed by what Achille Mbembe has described as a "logic of superfluity," in terms of which it was no great loss if a woman's life was wasted in unnecessary—and environmentally devastating—drudgery.[73]

Five years after the transition to democracy, Allister Sparks visited Mrs. Malala again. His account of the experience is worth citing in some detail, since its ambivalences may help us assess the lingering effects of the old, as well as the impact of the new:

> I found her relaxing on a settee watching television. She rose to switch on an electric kettle and offer me tea. The water came from a communal tap at the street corner, 100 meters from her home. She still had no job and she was still living in a rural slum, which still had the awful name Stinkwater. The dirt road was still rutted, there was still a pit lavatory in the garden and the family still had to bathe in a battered tin tub. In purely economic terms the ending of apartheid had brought Mrs. Malala nothing. But the provision of water and electricity had transformed her life. The daily drudgery was over. For the first time in her life

she had leisure. And entertainment. Her son, who has a good job in the city, had given her the TV set, as well as the kettle, an electric stove, an electric iron and a refrigerator. . . .

"I am nothing, I have nothing, I'm just an African mother," Mrs. Malala, who never went to school and whose husband abandoned her 13 years ago, murmured as she served me the tea. "But now I have got time to rest, and I've got more time for my church work on Sundays and Thursdays." Leisure, fellowship, entertainment. They may seem modest enough gains, but given the drudgery of the past they amount to a dramatic improvement in her quality of life.[74]

Sparks's pre- and postapartheid encounters with Mrs. Malala speak to the real (though far from uncontroversial) achievement of the ANC government in the more equitable provision of basic utilities to the population.[75] And they relate in profound ways to the spatial and cultural issues I have discussed in this chapter. Students of Tlali's work might note that Mrs. Malala describes herself with the very same phrase—"I am nothing"—that heads the manuscript version of *Muriel at Metropolitan*.[76] But what must detain all of us in Sparks's anecdote is the sharp understanding it affords of the changes that the ownership of commodities like a refrigerator or television can bring about in the daily life of the very poor, something that is easily forgotten by those of us who take such things entirely for granted. And while one cannot immediately equate the images of elsewhere that the television may bring to Sylvia Malala's shack with intellectual space (Ramphele, we must recall, is careful to associate that term with a capacity for political critique) it is reasonable to speculate that even the most inane TV program may occasionally provide opportunities for comparison and reflection, and may thereby make change and risk-taking more feasible than they are in situations of the most austere deprivation.[77]

With these reflections in mind, we may return to my original set of questions and consider what the end of apartheid has meant for the cultural production of black South African women (a category that will, of course, become increasingly useless as the experience of South Africa's citizens cease to be defined by the racial essentialisms of the past).[78] It is impossible to offer anything more than a sketchy outline of trends in this brief coda, but I would like to mention two writers whose work is particularly relevant to the nexus of themes addressed in this chapter. The first is Sindiwe Magona, a woman roughly of Ramphele's generation, who has been living in New York and working for the United Nations for the past fifteen years or so. Her 1999 novel *Mother to Mother* commands attention but is, in my view, a deeply troubling performance. It addresses a tragic international incident: the death of Amy Biehl, the American Fulbright scholar, who was killed by a mob of young men in the township of Guguletu shortly before the 1994 election. The novel is presented as a communication between the mother of one of the killers and the mother of Amy Biehl. Potentially, this narrative frame would seem to allow considerable intellectual space: it seems designed to encourage a consideration of the legacy of apartheid from a more global perspective, to invite revealing comparisons, and to devise new political and stylistic alternatives. But in these respects Magona's novel is, in my reading at least, disappointing. In major portions of *Mother to Mother*, she reverts to the poetics of imaginative confinement and urban shock implicit in the idea of "the tyranny of place"—and turns it into a full-blown determinism. Her description of the township of Guguletu offers a panorama of squalid and confining exteriors:

> As far as eye can see [*sic*]. Hundreds and hundreds of houses. Rows and rows, ceaselessly breathing on each other. Tiny houses huddled close together. Leaning against each other, pushing at each other. Sad small houses crowned with gray and flat unsmiling roofs. Low as though trained never to dream high dreams. Oppressed by all that surrounds them . . . by all that is stuffed into them . . . by the very manner of their conception. And, in turn, pressing down hard on those whom, shameless pretence stated, they were to protect and shelter.
>
> The streets are narrow, debris filled, full of gullies alive with flies, mosquitoes, and sundry vermin thriving in the pools of stagnant water that are about the only thing that never dries up and never vanishes in Guguletu.[79]

Like many of the other writers examined in this study, Magona here emphasizes the way physical space impinges on the psychological. But the overall message of *Mother to Mother* (whose title alone should perhaps give us pause, since the communication is predicated on conventional feminine roles) lacks the dialectical quality of the other analyses: Magona implies that the killers are purely victims of circumstance—the products of apartheid's soul-numbing ghettoes. The system, or so she asserts in her author's preface, is the only killer.[80]

More troublingly, the novel seems at times to suggest that Amy Biehl herself was to blame for her death: that she failed to see that the townships were not "her place" (a phrase sinisterly reminiscent of apartheid's logic of geographical segregation) and that her efforts to cross boundaries were ill-advised—a sign, in fact, of her privilege and unwarranted moral self-satisfaction. To judge by this novel, the confining legacy of the rhetoric of urgency is still quite palpable in postapartheid writing. But since Magona writes from a retrospective vantage and as an expatriate, her deployment of the old tropes of urban or rather "township shock" is really but a belated and synthetic performance of the old "stenographic" impulse of protest writing. *Mother to Mother* may derive its dubious ethos from the more claustrophobic and spectacular versions of antiapartheid writing. But one suspects that Magona may be relying on the old struggle rhetoric largely because it has come to suit the expectations and tastes of an international audience, familiar with images of political victimization from Africa and drawn to the redemptive allegory of militant nationalism with which the novel concludes.[81]

For a fresher sense of postapartheid narrative possibilities (and difficulties), I would now like to turn to an arresting text from 1990: Fatima Dike's play *So What's New?* The title cannot but bring to mind the "new South Africa," the emerging shape of which was still hotly debated at the moment of Dike's writing. But the question "So What's New?" relates most obviously to the ever-developing saga that absorbs her main characters, who tune in every afternoon to the latest installment of the American soap opera *The Bold and the Beautiful*. The action of the play, such as it is, is anchored by the three women's ritual gathering in front of the TV in Dee's house and by their expert commentary on the ever-vacillating relationships of the Forester family of Los Angeles: Ridge, Brooke, Clarke, Sally, Margot, Stephanie, Eric, and others.[82] We are, quite evidently, a world away from Mr. Bloch's exploited consumers in *Muriel at Metropolitan*, who had to make do with government-controlled FM broadcasts on their portable sets. But it is not only the ownership of a television set that marks the changes in the situation of Dike's characters, as compared to Tlali's: Pat's job, significantly, is to sell real estate in Soweto—something unthinkable in the age when the entire black population were essentially tenants of the state.

Dike's interviews reveal that she was well aware of the break between this play and her own apartheid-era writings: *So What's New?* represented "a celebration of [her] freedom," including the freedom to write "a fun play about black women in the township just having fun, watching soaps, looking for men and stuff."[83] But the innovation of the play lies not only in the fact that it eschews the old rhetoric of urgency. Dike is also the first black South African writer since the Sophiatown era to revisit the thematics of transnational cultural consumption. It is no accident that her characters are former members of the Chattanooga Sisters singing trio, who cherish fond memories of Sophiatown musicians like the hunky Nathan Mdledle of the Manhattan Brothers and the members of Alf Herbet's African Jazz. *So What's New?* is an attempt to investigate and to revive the once-stalled possibility of a heterogeneous black urban culture, with all its ambivalences and ironies. This is not to say that political violence is absent from the play, or that the characters' financial or domestic security is assured. The fact that Dee makes her living by running a shebeen and Thandi by dealing drugs indicates that they still have no proper place in the formal economy: their capacity to aspire, while far from negligible, is fragile and distorted—especially compared to the high ideals of the younger generation, represented in the play by Dee's daughter Mercedes, who is committed to matters like ending illiteracy and building a strong black nation (SWN 40). Even Pat's ostensibly solid occupation, we eventually learn, is not without an element of deceit and predation: she essentially manipulates the aspirations of black buyers who, some years down the road, may find themselves evicted or still living in bare rooms because they cannot afford to buy furniture along with paying the mortgage. One is reminded, moreover, by the offstage noises of drinkers, that Dee's home, in which she tries to create a good life for Mercedes, is also a rather unsavory workplace. And if Dee's situation is vulnerable, Thandi's is even worse. Since the matchbox house she lives in is registered with the Municipal Council in her no-good brother's name, she can be evicted if she makes any trouble for him—despite the fact that she pays the rent and has installed all manner of upscale conveniences, like a Jet Master fireplace, sliding doors, and Italian tiles (SWN 31).

The precarious domesticity of the female characters is most explicitly dramatized in a scene where a gun battle is waged right outside Dee's house. The TV goes blank, and they peek out in sheer terror at the armed men outside, who seem to be gangsters stealing their cars, but who could really be anyone, given the chaos of the times: "township residents fighting the hostel dwellers, or youth fighting the taxi drivers, or police doing a house to house search for dangerous weapons, or the hostel dwellers helping the defense force search the township for members of APLA, or white people in balaclavas helping the police and the army" (SWN 35). This ubiquitous violence stands in dramatic tension with the world of the soap opera. While the former Chattanooga Sisters have but a precarious toehold on the world of goods and leisure, the characters of the show have the material security that permits their exclusive preoccupation with things like romance, diamond bracelets, and trips to Hawaii. Even so, Dike never presents the Sisters' avid interest in *The Bold and the Beautiful* as reprehensible or even entirely escapist. Silly though it may be, the soap opera helps the women imagine a change in the terms of recognition by which they might operate in their society. In a comical scene early on in the play, Pat and Dee picture the latter's fickle boyfriend Willie in a submissive, conventionally feminine role. He irons, he scrubs, he rubs Dee's feet when she comes home from work, and he nevertheless gets kicked out of her house—not for failing to produce an heir, as might be the lot of an African woman, but for always demanding sex. "Willie," Dee imagines herself saying, "besides being a bad housekeeper, you're a bad cook and now you want to be a breeding machine. Unfortunately I can't let you do that here. Pack your bags and go home, tell your father I'll be coming to demand my lobola back, I'm sure there are many men out there who could do what you have failed to do" (SWN 27). This is, of course, a self-indulgent fantasy and "reverse sexism," as Dee acknowledges, but it does serve to identify a few of the traditional sources of male power, including the gendered division of labor and the institution of bride price, or *lobola* (SWN 28).

Even more comical is the soap opera–like scenario that all three of the Sisters create later on in the play, when they collectively imagine what might happen if the handsome Ridge were to step into South Africa and have an affair with Pat— that is to say, with "the patrician Pat Mahambebuza of the Mambebehlala Estate Agency" (SWN 33), who sells property in Saxonwold, advertises her business all over the country, and takes her lovers on erotic weekends to places like Sun City and the Wild Coast. In their dream, Dee's shebeen is gloriously magnified, with an Olympic-sized pool, a living room replete with marble and cushions, and a separate suite, complete with Jacuzzi, where drunken clients can recover from their *babelaas* the morning after. The excessiveness of their scenario is not lost on the Sisters: Dee repeatedly undercuts their collective fiction with her worries about how it would jibe with her real dream, which is to get Mercedes through high school and university. It is telling, in fact, that Dee and Thandi at first reject the notion of merging their own stories with that of the soap opera characters ("We're not rich enough," "We're not beautiful enough," they protest) but that the thought that amazing things might happen "in the future, in the new South Africa" (SWN 33), encourages them to dream up spaces that permit a subjective expansion beyond the reduced scale imposed by Magona's "sad, small houses."

The values and narrative structure of the soap opera, however, never become that of Dike's play, despite its interest in consumerist luxuries and the romantic ups and downs of the friends' lives. At the final curtain, the sound of the Sisters' old signature tune, "The Chattanooga Choo Choo" fades out (appropriately, since they decide that it is not a good financial proposition to revive the old group) and the sound of the theme song of *The Bold and the Beautiful* is interrupted by gun-fire. Mercedes, the truly aspirational figure of the play (though named, ironically, after a luxury car) is left alone onstage, and she is no longer smiling. The future, or so this conclusion implies, is a serious matter, but whether it will turn out well or not is left unclear. Since the play avoids the familiar genres of both mass-mediated culture and of South African political writing, it presents no heroic or romantic resolution. The characters are neither the mothers, widows, and vic-tims of the emerging South African national allegory, nor are they the "Barbie dolls" (SWN 33) of the American soap opera. However, while less upright than Tlali's Muriel, they are similarly translator figures: they are contemporary cultural agents, who are able to bring the "experience-distant" and the "experience-near" aspects of their lives into productive, if at times confusing negotiation.[84] *So What's New?* consequently offers little fodder for the "alterity industry" that has tended to shape the interest of U.S. and European readers and audiences in the lives of (post)colonial women. But the play does something very important, especially in light of the reflections in this chapter. It foregrounds, while refusing to resolve, the problematic relationship between real empowerment and enhanced intellectual space on the one hand and the merely materialistic dreaming inspired by global consumer culture on the other. How this relationship will play out in years to come will be absolutely crucial for the quality of social, political, and intellectual life in South Africa's new democracy.

THE LOCATION OF POSTAPARTHEID CULTURE

A revolution that does not produce a
new space has not realized its full potential; indeed it has failed in that it has not
changed life itself, but has merely changed
ideological superstructures, institutions or
political apparatuses. A social transformation, to be truly revolutionary in character, must manifest a creative capacity in
its effects on daily life, on language, and
on space.

—Henri Lefebvre, *The Production of Space*

A Commitment to Territory

In his often-cited essay "The Tyranny of Place and Aesthetics," Es'kia Mphahlele
presents the reader with three passages of descriptive writing (by Neil Williams,
Can Themba, and Alex La Guma) he considers "typically expressive of the South
African ghetto atmosphere." He then reflects on their shared aesthetic qualities
in a manner that both registers and validates a certain kind of urban shock: "The
writer in South Africa tends to document his physical and human settings in
stark, grim detail, to document minute-to-minute experience. There is a specifically African drama in the ghettos that the writer cannot ignore. So he replays the
drama. He has got to stay with it. He must simply come to terms with the tyranny of place or grapple with it, because he *must* have place, because his writing
depends on his commitment to territory."[1] The prescriptive effect of Mphahlele's
comments, as I have already suggested in chapter 5, outweighs their descriptive
value. But it is worth asking why Mphahlele expresses himself with such intensity
(especially in that emphatic and rather ambiguous phrase, "he *must* have place").
Why must commitment necessarily express itself in the form of a literature of
referential and geographical immediacy? It seems to me that Mphahlele's position
is overdetermined by his long experience of exile. A careful reading of his essay
reveals that it is precisely a sense of dislocation combined with a burdensome
sense of responsibility to his native land that makes Mphahlele reluctant to "dare

question"—even after his return to South Africa—the idea that the "tyranny of place" is anything other than the committed writer's "salvation."[2] His strenuous rhetoric, one comes to suspect, is symptomatic of repression—and the reason for this repression emerges when one discovers, elsewhere in the essay, the signs that Mphahlele himself struggled to live up to the aesthetic he advocates. He confesses that when one is living abroad and far away from home, one's writing is far more likely to "register ideas" than to offer a "dramatization of concrete experience." If this is indeed the case, Mphahlele's belief that a literature of commitment should be tied to a raw and immediate record of the concrete details of place must have been an onerous and disempowering one for him to labor under during his many years abroad.

And such a belief was an increasingly onerous one for writers living in South Africa as well. It is no accident that Njabulo Ndebele included the melodramatic evocation of the black townships, predictably contrasted with the luxury of the white suburbs, in his list of the shopworn and "spectacular" features of antiapartheid writing.[3] By the mid-1980s, the image of matchbox houses in serried ranks had become an all too familiar and ready-made trope. It had, of course, a certain kind of usefulness in the repertoire of writer and filmmaker alike, as an instant icon of apartheid's stark geographical injustices. But as the geographers Sue Parnell and Owen Crankshaw have suggested, it is also possible that this image's very iconicity had an intellectually and politically numbing effect: its Orwellian grimness may have exaggerated the extent of state control over the lives of urban residents.[4] In so doing, the recreation of "ghetto atmosphere" may have unintentionally discouraged resistance instead of fostering it, as it was supposed to do.

It is therefore with a sense of striking newness that one discovers in the fiction of Zakes Mda a deliberate affirmation that neither the novelist nor his characters are compelled to "replay" the drama of the ghetto. They might, at times, quite simply *play*. This ludic sensibility does not equate with irresponsibility: on the contrary, Mda's work retains what we might call "a commitment to territory," but not in the stylistic and generic sense in which Mphahlele deploys the phrase. Both in his fiction and in his academic writing, Mda places impoverished and marginal communities at center stage and emphasizes the importance of a kind of territorial micropolitics to grassroots emancipation. But his work never shows the immediate material environment to have a determining, much less a tyrannical, effect on his characters. The experiences Mda recounts are neither spatially nor temporally confined, and the sites represented in his work—an urban shack settlement, a mountain village, a remote coastal hamlet, and so forth—are shown to be multidimensional and culturally porous. These richly imagined chronotopes also generate complex narrative structures rather than stark reportage. The plot of *Ways of Dying*, for example, with its proliferating flashbacks, anecdotes, and points of view, oscillates between country and city. The terrain the novel seeks to represent is not that of the ghetto so much as that of urbanization: a fluid terrain of hope, yearning, and memory. The plot of *The Heart of Redness*, by contrast, oscillates between historical and contemporary narratives. The setting is a single out-of-the-way village, but the cultural and experiential territory of that village is, in Mda's conception, both expansive and contested. It is affected by national and international centers of influence and is open to values, tastes, threats, and opportunities that arise in distant places. The village is a complex cultural locale, connected to the "Otherworld" of the ancestral spirits, to the historical world in which the ancestors were people of flesh and blood, and to the broad contemporary world that the characters have encountered or at least heard about—to distant cities like Cape Town and Johannesburg, and to even more distant countries like Russia and the United States.

In other words, Mda's work suggests that even the poorest of the poor live not only in the gut of the here and now but also in the spaces of the imagination. The point is readily demonstrated in a bravura passage midway through *Ways of Dying*. Mda describes how his protagonist, the artistic Toloki, covers the walls of his home-girl Noria's shack with pictures from old catalogues and *House and Garden* magazines. On some sections of the walls he pastes pictures of well-equipped kitchens, and on others pictures of elegant living rooms, dining rooms, and bedrooms. The remaining sections he covers with images of lavish exteriors—patios, formally landscaped gardens, and swimming pools. As he evokes this "wallpaper of sheer luxury," Mda's prose seems to mimic Toloki's collage: it becomes a pastiche of the effusive phraseology of the sales catalogue and the commercial magazine. The "kitchen scheme," the brand-new "music centre," and the verdant garden all seem "awash in a potpourri of color." And when night falls, Mda tells us, the landscape "comes to shimmering life with fireflies and moonbeams—courtesy of a combination of entrance, well, tier, globe, and mushroom lights" (WD 105).

The fantasy presented here is of course a consumerist one (and I will touch on Mda's attitudes to the culture of consumption at several points over the course of this chapter). But it is also an imaginative exploration of—and a claim to—places far beyond the confines of the tiny dwelling, which offers but fragile shelter in the unpredictable terrain of a South African shack settlement. Hand in hand, Toloki and Noria "stroll through the grandeur": they test out the king-size bed and fight with the "continental pillows"; they laugh at "idiotic American situation comedies on the wide-screen television set"; and they walk out of their "Mediterranean style mansion" to follow several of the pathways that twist and wind through the spacious garden (WD 103–104). While I would hesitate to describe the passage in terms of magical realism as other critics have done (it seems to me somewhat closer to the "capitalist realism" of advertising), it certainly reveals the optative and performative character of *Ways of Dying*: the temporality here is the present tense of the stage direction, and the characters, much like actors on a bare stage, create a new, if ephemeral, experiential space through their improvisations.[5] Far from merely "replaying" the actual circumstances of their lives, Toloki and Noria are here demonstrating that capacity "for imagining space where there is none," which, as we saw in chapter 5, is the indispensable artistry of the poor.[6]

The passage I have discussed, which ends with Noria thanking Toloki for teaching her "how to walk in the garden" (WD 106), captures one of the crucial elements of Mda's novelistic project. Like Njabulo Ndebele, he senses the need for a new aesthetic education, especially after the environmental deprivation and physical violence of the apartheid years.[7] As I will show in this chapter, Mda's fiction frequently addresses conceptions of the beautiful and the ugly: it is deeply concerned with aesthetic taste and, what is even more relevant to my interests, with the various sites in which judgments about beauty and ugliness are made. One might say that Mda's novels of the transition, *Ways of Dying* and *The Heart of Redness* in particular, map out the location of culture in postapartheid South Africa: they enable a meditation on the transformation of the country's cultural geography from the old landscapes of oppression to the new mediascapes of leisure and tourism, which have often subsumed the old sites of deprivation in a new logic of display. Township tours, for instance, are now a profitable business (some are even operated by former Umkhonto we Sizwe [MK] freedom fighters), the Robben Island prison and the Apartheid Museum have become must-sees for any visitor to the country, and images of "shack chic" (a new phrase we may retroactively attach to Toloki's form of survival artistry) are exhibited in art collections and coffee-table books.[8] It is the latter transformation—one that Mda seems to prefigure when he observes that Noria's shack "would certainly be at home in any museum of modern art" (WD 60)—that will be my overarching concern in this closing chapter.

A City of Crossings

In her magisterial study of South African drama, Loren Kruger describes Zakes Mda's plays of the 1970s and 1980s as "inhabiting a subjunctive place and time between the act of defiance and the future of a new society" while exposing "the future *im*perfect of postcolonial Africa."[9] This deft formulation is also applicable to Mda's first work of fiction, *Ways of Dying* (1996). With its semiallegorical *mise en scène* and its interest in the potential of the artistic imagination, the novel hovers between the referential and the wishful, between the era of apartheid and that of a new dispensation that, at the moment of narration, is still waiting in the wings.

Ways of Dying is forward-looking, insofar as it provides a springboard for speculations about the new urban subjectivities and semantic topographies that may emerge with apartheid's demise.[10] But the novel also looks to the past. While it is not conventionally realist (Mda refrains from providing proper names for locations and historical figures), *Ways of Dying* presents a surprisingly detailed and accurate overview of the major trends in the history of black South African urbanization over the last three decades.[11] In the course of its many reminiscences, orations, and editorializing asides, the novel gives an account of the failure of the apartheid government's policy of influx control. It describes the stubborn resilience of ordinary people who rebuilt their homes again and again in the face of bulldozers, and it celebrates the eventual result of their perseverance: an informal settlement that grows from a shantytown into a proper township, with streets and schools and shopping centers. The novel also records, through the various characters' experiences, the rise of an informal economic sector, with vendors operating in the central business districts and "spaza" shops taking off in the townships. It observes changes in the daily conditions of commuting: both positive changes, like the emergence of the privately owned minibus taxis that broke the monopoly of state-owned bus companies, and frightening changes, like the increasing levels of crime on trains and the murderous feuding among the various taxi organizations. *Ways of Dying* captures, furthermore, a new sense of social mobility, as black nouveaux riches procure houses in the posh white suburbs and ordinary people gain greater access to public spaces like beaches and malls. But it also depicts a dangerous fissuring of communities. It reminds us vividly of the rift created by the apartheid government between "illegal" and "legal" residents of shantytowns, and evokes in gruesome detail the subsequent polarization of hostel dwellers and township residents: the cause of the retaliatory violence that features so prominently in the novel's dilatory plot.[12]

The broad historical process outlined in *Ways of Dying* concerns the emergence of an unprecedented diversity in what was once, for unhappy reasons, a remarkably homogeneous black urban populace.[13] In the novel, as in the work of geographers and historians of the period, we may trace the story of how a group of people who were once tenants of the state, housed in identical boxes, and employed in menial jobs, came to be accommodated in increasingly varied structures and interpellated by an increasingly wide array of social forces—of which the state, finally, is but one. This is also a story of how the South African city, shaped by massive, precarious, and increasingly unplanned migration, as well as an ever-waxing informal economy, came to be less and less of an anomaly both in the African and the global context.[14]

In its interest in black urban space, *Ways of Dying* is not unique among recent South African novels: Sindiwe Magona's *Mother to Mother*, as we have seen in chapter 5, is another case in point. But I would argue that Mda's novel is remarkable for its minimal reliance on the evocation of "ghetto atmosphere" privileged by Mphahlele. A characteristic moment in the novel is the scene in which Toloki, performing his morning ablutions outside a shack in the squatter camp, is greeted by a stream of passers-by whose various journeys are catalogued for us: "domestic workers rushing to catch taxis that would take them to the kitchens of their madams in the suburbs, factory workers going to the industrial areas, and pickpockets and muggers going to ply their trade in the central business district" (WD 145). Even in the sole passage of the novel that does describe the squalor of the informal settlement, the emphasis is not on the inert setting itself but on Toloki's movement through it: "He walks among the shacks of cardboard, plastic, pieces of canvas, and corrugated iron. . . . Dirty children follow him. They dance about in their tattered clothes and spontaneously compose a song about him, which they sing with derisive gusto. Many mongrels follow him. . . . He ignores them all, and walks through a quagmire of dirty water and human ordure that runs through the streets of this informal settlement as the place is politely called, looking for Noria" (WD 42). The urban setting here serves neither as an objective correlative for the psychological state of the observer nor as an iconographic expression of the oppressiveness of the state. It is instead conceptualized in a way that one might expect in the work of a former theater practitioner like Mda: as a stage or intersection in a busy flow of human interactions and activities.

In this respect, Mda's novelistic practice seems congruent with some recent approaches to the study of third world cities. Faced with the difficulty of describing the social environments of the world's mushrooming informal settlements, some researchers have begun to see the need for a new methodology "to chart the flows of complicity, co-operation, and affiliation which come and go across the city and its neighbourhoods."[15] One way of realizing this methodology, according to AbdouMaliq Simone, is through a rediscovery of a sense of the city's original raison d'être as a port, railhead, or crossroads: as a node for a multiplicity of entries and exits. Places like docks and taxi ranks—both of which are important in *Ways of Dying*—have thus become crucial sites for the investigation of the intersecting stories of urban lives. So, too, has the experience of marginal citizens, especially survival entrepreneurs of the sort exemplified in Mda's novel by Toloki, the would-be professional mourner, and Shadrack, the settlement's taxi driver and "spaza" shop owner. In Simone's view, researchers can learn a great deal about urban processes from the quotidian experience of people like street vendors, whose occupations force them to be stationary. As stage managers of a small urban arena (and we may think here of the grave sites where Toloki plies his trade and learns about his community), such people have an acute understanding of the dynamics of a particular space, since they have to draw others to them and find ways to extract income from the little patch of terrain they control. Equally rich in practical knowledge, Simone argues, are city dwellers on the opposite end of the spectrum: folks who are constantly on the move, like delivery people, or teenage drifters, or even the many residents of the urban margins who have to walk very long distances to work every day.[16] The grand question of "where the African city is going," he posits with daring simplicity, may be answered "by taking a close look at where African urban residents are going." If one tracks these journeys and taps into these sources, Simone asserts, one will not be left with a sense of hopelessness or stasis: "Urban residents are not standing still. There is something going on, people are trying to come up with new ways of earning a living, of helping others out, of making interesting cities."[17]

Now: it is easy to draw connections between Mda's and Simone's conceptions of contemporary African urban space. Indeed, I would make the broad claim that Mda's shift away from the earlier poetics of a grim documentation of physical surroundings to a new, more fluid sense of black urban experience parallels a shift in South African urban studies from a nearly exclusive concern with the location of physical structures and the visible aspects of urban organization to a concern with the city as a dynamic entity. It is perhaps not all that surprising, therefore, that Mda's homage to the women of Noria's informal settlement should read as an echo of Simone's positive conclusions about the dynamic potentialities of urban life and the admirable sense of responsibility shown by the poor. The women of the settlement, Toloki notes, are "never still":

> They are cooking. They are sewing. They are outside scolding the children. They are at the tap drawing water. They are washing clothes. They are sweeping the floor in their shacks, and the ground outside. They are closing holes in the shacks with cardboard and plastic. They are loudly joking with their neighbors while they hang washing on the line. . . . Or they are fighting with their neighbours

about children who have beaten up their own children. They are preparing to go to the taxi rank to catch the taxis to the city to work in the kitchens of their madams. They are always on the move. They are always on the go. (WD 164)

Such activities—and their textual representations—can be seen to shape the city fully as much as they are shaped by it, especially if, like Jane Jacobs, we think of the city as an "ambiguation of the boundary separating social reality and the representation of social reality," and thus as an entity straddling the subjective and the objective.[18] It is for this reason that fictional works may serve a cognitive function by helping urbanists come to an understanding of the emergent spaces of the African city, just as literary critics, in turn, may arrive at a better account of the generic and characterological peculiarities of contemporary fiction by attending to recent work in urban studies.[19]

It is not surprising, then, that one of South Africa's more creative geographers, Jennifer Robinson, should have turned to *Ways of Dying* to articulate her ideas about the postapartheid city. In her essay "(Im)mobilizing Space—Dreaming of Change," Robinson cites the following passage as "one story of a changing space."[20]

> In the afternoon Toloki walks to the taxi rank, which is on the other side of the downtown area, or what is called the central business district. The streets are empty, as all the stores are closed. He struts like a king, for today the whole city belongs to him. He owns the wide tarmac roads, the skyscrapers, the traffic lights, and the flowers on the sidewalks. That is what he loves most about the city. It is a garden city, with flowers and well-tended shrubs and bushes growing at every conceivable place. In all seasons, blossoms fill the site. (WD 39–40)

Robinson argues that this passage illustrates the way spaces may transform subjects and subjects may transform spaces. Toloki, she points out, is making his way from one inauspicious place to another: from a waiting room in the docklands, where he parks a shopping trolley containing his few possessions, to the squatter camp where Noria lives. Yet his pleasure in the grand urban scene transforms him, momentarily, from "an old bum" (WD 109) into a *flâneur*. The transformation is, of course, comic and largely performative, but it has important implications if one considers the long history of colonial and apartheid discourses that depicted the black urban resident as an anomalous, if not a pathological, figure—as an essentially rural creature, out of place and dangerous in the city. Mda's image of the migrant enjoying the ordinary aesthetic pleasures of urban life quietly challenges this stereotype and sets aside this old baggage. It is instructive, in fact, to compare the difference between Toloki's proprietorial strutting and the servile, if ironic, movements of the lyric speaker of Mongane Serote's best-known poem, "City Johannesburg" (1974). No longer does the black subject's hand rear up in automatic "salute" to the white city; no longer is his expression "frozen"; no longer are his routines or trajectories in and out of the city fixed in relation to exploitative labor. Indeed, the social divisions so starkly expressed in Serote's image of "black and white and robotted roads" are no longer in evidence—at least not during the break from the city's weekday routines of which Toloki is taking advantage.[21]

Robinson's purpose in attending to this passage from *Ways of Dying*, however, is not so much to contrast the pre- and postapartheid city. Attentive to Henri Lefebvre's reflections on the way new potentialities may arise from the abstract space of power, she argues instead that the moment of transition allows us to recognize the extent to which the disciplinary spaces of apartheid were productive of ambivalences and fluid possibilities: "Just as the spaces of the apartheid city divided, they also generated crossings and interactions as people moved and lived and worked in different places; crossings as the memories and meanings of different places were carried with them; crossings as people imagined what those other places were like, places they'd never seen except on the TV or in magazines."[22] It is true, of course, that "one [was] one's address" under apartheid (especially in the case of "coloureds," where, as John Western puts it, the state tried to tackle the problem of a racially "ambiguous who's who" with the fixed "who's where" of the Groups Areas Act); and Robinson, whose earlier work relied on Foucault rather than Lefebvre, would not deny this.[23] But her aim in "(Im)mobilizing Space"—to put it simplistically—is to remind us that no one stays at home all the time: people move through different spaces, all of which elicit different subjective and subjunctive potentialities. At stake, ultimately, is a strategic methodology for discovering the dynamic potential that exists even in a city of division: a methodology in which urbanity is conceptualized not as a fixed and tyrannical topography but as what Simone has called a "productive modality for generating an incessant fluidity in the composition and relationship of people and things."[24]

We should note, further, that the dynamic potential of cities is expressed in and produced by not only the flows and connections made within them but also by the way they look outward: by their multiple links to "other cities, other places, and other times."[25] This point also seems to be implicit in the symbolic geography of *Ways of Dying*. With his many memories and fantasies, Mda's Toloki is nothing if not a figure of crossings and transitions: his name is an isiXhosa version of the Afrikaans word *tolk* ("translator"), and he is described by other characters as looking "like something that has come to fetch us to the next world" (WD 64). His life on the docks, to which he is drawn by the "thirst of a man for a concoction he has never tasted" (WD 10), is a life of poverty. But the waterfront is also a place where he can watch the ships arriving from or departing to far-flung ports, and where he can travel back in his imagination to the yellow-ochre landscape of his home village. The waterfront is, in other words, a place that permits Toloki a kind of imaginative expansion (call it "intellectual space," if you will) and allows him to stage new modes of self-invention. Toloki's conception of what it means to be a professional mourner—the vocation he founds and practices throughout the novel—is based on a pamphlet given to him by a "pink-robed devotee" who embarked one day from one of the ships in the harbor. It is by means of this little tract that Toloki is able to "transport" himself to the distant land of the *aghori sadhu*, where "he spends his sparse existence on the cremation ground, cooks his food on the fires of a funeral pyre, and feeds on human waste and human corpses"

(WD 10). An idea imported from far away thus transforms Toloki's experience of everyday life: it enables him to think of his poverty as a form of monkish austerity and to consider the shopping trolley in the smelly waiting room as his "headquarters"—the base of operations of a serious professional.

Ways of Dying includes several other instances of such imaginative reaching out to distant horizons, on the part of not only the rich, who acquire German and American cars and natter on about *Vogue* magazine and the latest Italian styles, but also the poor. In addition to Toloki, who imagines himself mourning in all the great cemeteries in the world, there are the migrant dock workers, who come home with exciting tales of a seafaring life they have never experienced, and even the prophet in Toloki's village, who awards himself the fancy degrees "B.A., M.Div., D.Theol. (U.S.A.)" to enhance his prestige (WD 97). The shack settlement's spaza shop fittingly operates from an old shipping container. Such details, which might seem quite fanciful and comic, are in fact not uncommon features in the lives of Africa's urban poor. Indeed, as AbdouMaliq Simone discovered in his fascinating research on cities like Cape Town, Johannesburg, Khartoum, and Dakar, it is the very vulnerability of such city dwellers that produces their need for extended networks of association, expanded circuits of movement, and imaginative affiliations that reach far and wide. A "small glimmer of cosmopolitanism," as Simone calls it, thus arises in surprisingly inauspicious contexts and serves as a reminder that the factories of poverty on the edges of cities are, in fact, both part and product of a global economy to which they may otherwise seem quite impenetrable.[26]

I would therefore take issue with Grant Farred's dismissal of *Ways of Dying* as "only locally resonant" and lacking in an "encompassing vision, an expansive sense of politics."[27] In protesting what he sees (incorrectly, I think) as the complete absence of the state from its purview, Farred fails to consider that the very point of the novel may be to offer a new frame of reference: that it tries to think through the imaginative geographies of the world's destitute, in which the rudimentary distinctions between the local and the global often fail to hold up, and where the state, as I have already suggested, is neither the sole nor the most determining factor in daily life. *Ways of Dying* represents a relinquishment of the strictly national optic that has been so crucial in South African literature to date, and the adoption of one that is at once broader and more minute. Mda's "encompassing vision," it seems to me, can be discovered in his insistence that we view the informal settlements as part of the creative urbanity of the city and in his demand that we begin to think of the South African experience in both an African and a global frame.

Grotesque Geographies

There is one respect in which Farred's complaint that the purview of *Ways of Dying* remains fixed on the micropolitics of the margins makes sense (though only up to a point, as my reading of the novel's conclusion will suggest). The novel's imagistic patterns do rely on a contrast rather than a continuity between the formal economy (the world of the central business district and the shopping mall) and the informal economy (the world of the shack settlement and the spaza shop). A telling scene, in this respect, is the novel's first funeral—a contentious affair, which concludes with a traffic jam involving two different processions trying to go in opposite directions. One is a funeral procession of bereaved shack dwellers with a scruffy taxi in the lead, and the other is a wedding parade headed by a fancy convertible and followed by a row of vehicles "embellished with colourful ribbons and balloons" (WD 6). In defiance of traditional custom and "funeral etiquette," the driver of the convertible insists that the wedding should be given precedence. "We are a procession of beautiful people, and many posh cars and buses," he brags, "while yours is an old skorokoro of a van and hundreds of ragged souls on foot" (WD 6). The driver's taunt sets up a symbolic antithesis, one that resonates throughout the novel, between the "beautiful" and the "ugly" and, by extension, between the "first world" of official power and prestige and the "second world" of the marginal and the destitute.[28]

The novel's sympathies are, of course, entirely with "ragged" funeral-goers, and its validation of the "ugly" over the "beautiful" may be read in sociogeographic terms. It is important to bear in mind that aesthetic questions have historically exerted an important influence on the attitudes of urban planners toward informal settlements both in South Africa and all over the developing world. An attachment to an idea of "the city beautiful" often meant that the informal sectors of the city came to be "stereotyped as unsightly, unattractive, or dangerous": "the activities of the common hawker, backyard artisan, or shebeener were viewed as contrary to official images of what constituted a 'modern' South African city."[29] *Ways of Dying* takes up this stereotyped discourse of beauty and ugliness and subjects it to a carnivalesque inversion. While the novel shows the city's poor to be the source of genuine creativity and a new democratic vision, it consistently mocks the high-and-mighty airs of the "beautiful" people. (An example of this satirical spirit is the treatment of the coffin maker Nefolovhodwe, the one migrant who actually makes it in the formal economy and who comes to think of himself as "civilized," "refined," and "cultured" [WD 192], in large measure because he is able to set himself up in a downtown office staffed with an army of white managers and to buy himself a house in the white suburbs, complete with security guards, Alsatians, electrical fences, and any number of stout doors.)

But the focal figure for the novel's grotesque humor is Toloki, Nefolovdwe's "ugly" counterpart, who, despite his strange face, his bad smell, and his eccentric dietary and dress codes, is nevertheless the novel's chief producer of aesthetic pleasure. The humor here is partly parodic: Toloki's notion that the ragged Dracula costume he wears to his performances, complete with battered top hat and cape, confers on him the dignity of a senior advocate proudly wearing his aged robe may be taken as a grotesque undermining of "first world" professional prestige. There is also an element of parody in the story of how Toloki manages to procure this costume. He first notices the silky outfit in a small shop next to the food court in an upscale city mall, where "genteel people" dine amid well-tended potted plants and flowers (WD 20). It is a site where the rules and the aesthetics of the formal economy hold sway, and Toloki's desire to own the "beautiful" costume is, of course, exactly the kind of longing the shopping mall is designed to produce.

But since Toloki is both penniless and jobless, his desire becomes grotesque: he sits for days and days drooling—literally—over the expensive silk costume, until the restaurant owners, whose customers find the sight of Toloki's slimy saliva distasteful, eventually buy him the costume simply to get rid of the ugly sight of him. Toloki's participation in the formal economy thus serves only to undermine its most fundamental rule: the businessmen end up having to consider something other than profit in order to protect the beautiful image of their enterprise. Toloki's gross materialization of consumerist cravings, in the form of what Mda calls "inzincwe, the gob of desire" (WD 22), thus exposes the vulgarity of consumption that the mall's self-congratulatory gentility carefully masks.

The critical energies brought into play by the novel's carnivalesque figurations ultimately invert all socially sanctioned designations and produce new possibilities for a creative urbanity. One must concede that Toloki's expulsion from the mall, comic as it is, marks the limits of the optimistic vision of a city of mobility and crossings: it serves as a salutary reminder of the fact that landscapes of exclusion will not evaporate overnight and that, as Jennifer Robinson also reminds us, some citizens' dreams of change may be the nightmares of others.[30] Nefolovhodwe's opulent self-imprisonment serves a similar purpose: for all its satirical exaggeration, it captures the very real threat that the "new" South Africa's security-obsessed suburbs and gated communities pose to the promise of a truly democratic public space. But the final scenes of *Ways of Dying* seem to figure the possibility of bridging social divides. Nefolovhodwe, surprisingly, plays an important part in this symbolic resolution. Plagued by dreams in which the spirit of Toloki's father Jwara, a talented blacksmith and sculptor, appears to him, Nefolovhodwe decides to return to his old mountain home; there he collects all the iron figurines Jwara made during his lifetime, and delivers them, in characteristically self-aggrandizing style, to Toloki and Noria's shack in the settlement. The meaning of the figurines and their sudden reemergence into narrative focus is open to several possible interpretations, all of which are relevant to the novel's symbolic geography and to its understanding of the location of culture in postapartheid South Africa.

The first and the simplest way of interpreting the figurines is in relation to their provenance. One might say that it is through these strange and sinister-looking artifacts that the village reasserts its presence in the life of the urban migrants. It is telling that Toloki and Noria decide to keep one of the figurines in their shack to "remind themselves where they came from" (WD 198). In accepting the strange bequest of the figurines from his father, Toloki is in effect learning to view his rural past in a more positive way. He is reconnecting with his artistic heritage in both a generational and in a more broadly cultural sense. Though presented as a difficult character who both envies and tries to stifle his "ugly" son's talents, Jwara must also be seen through the lens of Mda's positive conception of the precolonial artisan. For all the dismissals of any sort of romantic primordialism in his academic work, Mda imagines this figure as a cultural ideal: a person whose practical creativity combines the aesthetic and the utilitarian and does so in a context where there is little separation between artistic production and consumption (WPP 47–48). The arrival in the city of Jwara's figurines—compelling, half-forgotten figures from the past—implies that the new ways of living that need to be devised for the survival and pleasure of the urban resident need not be "Western" or rootless. The sculptures embody the possibility of "learning from the ancient wisdom of Africa"—to steal a phrase from the title of one of Mda's articles—and of celebrating the legacies and journeys that connect past and present, country and city.[31]

A second way of reading the meaning of the figurines is in relation to their great number, which is clearly intended as a tribute to the richness of popular creativity. The figurines fill up "a mountain of boxes" (WD 199) so high that it dwarfs Noria's small shack. They "occupy a space," as Mda emphatically puts it, "many times bigger than the shack, in height, breadth, and length" (WD 197). The insistence on the matter of scale is significant: the figurines require a shelter adequate to house the vast creative energies they embody. Associated by way of their grotesque appearance with the marginalized people of the funeral parade and the settlement, they represent a claim to dwelling spaces far ampler than those offered by existing homes—including the prized "four-roomed township match-box house" (WD 196). Toloki and Noria recognize the practical and imaginative challenge the figurines pose and begin to muse about building a giant shack in which they will display all the figurines and where the children of the settlement can come to laugh at the "comic monsters" at their pleasure.[32] They consider the possibility of creating what amounts to a local museum and, by extension, the possibility of shifting the privileged sites of consumption and aesthetic pleasure away from the city proper to the shack settlement, thus turning the urban margin into a cultural center.

A third way of reading the return of the figurines is in relation to their possible market value. Before delivering the figurines to the settlement, Nefolovhodwe has them appraised by two of his eminent friends, an art dealer and the director of a museum. The former considers the figurines to be kitschy, while the latter insists that they are folksy: inane judgments that Nefolovhodwe reiterates with ponderous self-importance. The two connoisseurs agree, however, that the figurines, once considered "worthless monsters" by Toloki's neglected mother, are likely to find a niche in the art market and bring in good money. It is here, of course, that the novel suddenly introduces what Appadurai has described as the global "traffic in criteria": the expertise of brokers who are more knowledgeable than producers are about the value of their own creations.[33]

Mda clearly intends to ridicule the official arbiters of taste, as well as their inane mimic, Nefolovhodwe. Even so, Toloki and Noria do not reject the sale of Jwara's figurines out of hand, leaving open the possibility of a new economic connection between the "first world" of the city and the "second world" of the informal settlement. Indeed, Toloki and Noria discuss the possibility of donating the money they might raise by selling the figurines to help support the child-care work of their friend MaDimbhaza, whose shack is known as the settlement's "dumping ground"—the most marginal and forgotten of all the city's marginal and forgotten spaces. The negotiations between the world of the poor people and the world of the rich could thus produce some beneficial results. But the sale of Jwara's "strange and sinister-looking" (WD 197) figurines would rob "ugliness" of its critical power. If sold, the grotesque objects would be incorporated into the world of the beautiful people and the official economy as commodities.

The question of where the figurines will end up is ultimately left undecided. If the second possibility I have described presents by far the most attractive denouement, the third possibility is the most realistic one—and, not insignificantly, the one most relevant to the situation of the novel and the novelist himself. Though Mda seems to posit a shift in the location and thus in the meaning of the museum as institution, he also acknowledges the institution's cultural authority. Noria's colorfully constructed shack, as I have already noted earlier, is validated as something that would "certainly be at home in any museum of modern art" (WD 60). Mda's criteria, it would seem, are not entirely separable from those of the metropolitan cognoscenti after all. We should also note that the novel's prose, with its many editorial asides and explanations, is not addressed to the marginal people it celebrates but to what Lewis Nkosi has called the "cross-border reader," who reads it to learn something about a community different from his or her own.[34] The question of the circulation and market value of Jwara's figurines thus raises analogous questions about the circulation and market position of Mda's novel. Mda is, of course, far from a marginal figure in contemporary South African culture, but on the level of global culture he shares the position of all so-called postcolonial writers, whose work occupies a metropolitan market niche of a very particular kind—one that academic readers have helped to define. In saying this, I do not wish to diminish the force of Mda's critique of the official centers of consumption, or to suggest that postcolonial writers and critics are inevitably and wholly complicit with exoticizing modes of cultural consumption. But I do think we need to ponder Graham Huggan's astute observation that *postcoloniality* (which he defines as a value regulating and essentially assimilative mechanism within the global late-capitalist system of commodity exchange) and *postcolonialism* (which he defines as a politics of value opposed to global processes of commodification) are more often than not entangled.[35] This entanglement confronts us again, and has still greater pertinence to questions of place, when we turn to Mda's third and perhaps richest novel, *The Heart of Redness*.

(Dis)locating Redness

I have argued that in *Ways of Dying*, Mda works to extend our conception of the South African city to include both the informal settlements at its margins and the cosmopolitan dreams and rural memories of its migrant inhabitants. This interest in imagining a newly expansive and fluid urban geography is also evident in *The Heart of Redness*: an ambitious novel that rivals the work of both Chinua Achebe, in its imaginative recreation of colonial history, and Ngugi wa Thiong'o, in its denunciation of a greedy emergent bourgeoisie. The novel's second chapter takes place in the Hillbrow area of Johannesburg, the most densely populated and most relentlessly modernist cityscape on the African continent and—in the novel as in actuality—a place of transience, "swarm[ing] with restless humanity" (HR 29). The chapter's *mise en scène* is a single high-rise building (a new chronotope, surely, in African literature): a site where journeys even greater than those of the migrants in *Ways of Dying* intersect.

This high-rise is the venue for two apparently contrasting gatherings. The first is a party of sophisticated exiles, recently returned from places like Tanzania, Sweden, Yugoslavia, and America, who are drinking in a nightclub called Giggles on the building's ground floor. The second is an assembly of "aged and forgotten" rural migrants (HR 307) who are attending a wake in a tattered tent on the building's roof, twenty floors above the street. This juxtaposition of "gigglers" and mourners would seem to harken back to the stark and grotesque oppositions of *Ways of Dying*. But in this case, Mda presents the two groups as having much in common, for all their differences. Both groups are made up of disaffected "rejects" (HR 28) who feel themselves to be ill-served by the postapartheid dispensation. The exiles, who are now exiles in their own country, complain about how they have to survive on mere crumbs from the tables of the "Aristocrats of the Revolution" (HR 36); while the mourners complain about how all the "fruits of liberation" (HR 34) seem to vanish into the mouths of returned exiles. But both groups seem out of place in Johannesburg, the center of cultural and political power in postapartheid South Africa, where members of the new national elite exert their control and enforce their values in the kinds of objects they buy and the kinds of people they hire.

The longtime exile Camagu is not one of these people: he does not dance the "freedom dance" (HR 31), an ability the new regime requires of all candidates for success.[36] In Johannesburg's new economy of signs, the usefulness of his American Ph.D. and his experience in international communications pales in comparison to the display value of "beautiful men and women" who are willing to be exhibited as emblems of black economic empowerment in the "glass affirmative action offices" of corporations (HR 33). If Camagu's talents are too cosmopolitan to find favor in the national metropolis, those of the deceased migrant Twin (whose wake Camagu decides on a whim to join) are too parochial. Twin's realistic carvings—though they were considered "wonders" by the residents of his village, and seemed perfectly desirable to the patrons of the trading store where they were sold as souvenirs—have not found favor with the "ungrateful" city's buyers (HD 30), who prefer their black artists to be "folksy" and who have a taste for distorted figures of "people who grew heads on their stomachs and eyes at the back of their heads" or "twisted lips at their feet" (HR 307).

As the Hillbrow chapter suggests, *Ways of Dying* is crucially concerned with the intersections of place, identity, and taste. It is, in fact, by attending to a number of different sites of aesthetic judgment that Mda is able to map out the shifting horizons of cultural production and consumption in postapartheid South Africa and to describe some of the ways new identities and identifications—new senses of belonging—are currently being negotiated. Camagu's response to the song of one of the mourners, a beautiful young woman from the countryside, is revealing in this respect: he thinks her voice "cries to be echoed by the green hills, towering cliffs and deep gullies of a folktale dream land" (HR 27). His longing for a proper rural context to match the young woman's "hearthly" beauty suggests something of the exile's own sense of incongruity and out-of-placeness; but he also seems alert to the comic appropriateness of singing the hymn "Nearer, My God, to Thee" on the top of a skyscraper. This ambivalence about proper places and contexts is characteristic of Mda's vision in the novel as a whole. In a world of traveling people and objects, it is hard to say what a "proper place" might be (and it is telling that the rural beauty turns out to bear the surprisingly cosmopolitan name of NomaRussia): all available contexts turn out to be shifty, and all judgments, especially judgments of taste, are shown to depend on the perceiver's location in the sometimes overlapping and sometimes disjunctive domains of local, national, and transnational culture. The key word "beautiful" (about which I will have quite a bit to say in the pages that follow) must therefore be understood as a semantic shifter—a translation term, in James Clifford's phrase.[37] It is not used ironically, since that would imply a consistent vantage, but is deployed, rather, in such a way as to draw our attention to the multiple cultural horizons that are traced out in the course of the novel.

A similarly shifty term is "redness," which refers—significantly, given the novel's preoccupation with the aesthetic—to the Xhosa custom of decorating the body and clothes with red ochre. This locally specific meaning does not diminish the novel's connection with Joseph Conrad's *Heart of Darkness*, which Mda provocatively establishes in his title. On the contrary: in the colonial discourse of the Eastern Cape, "redness" was virtually synonymous with "darkness."[38] Even as late as the 1960s, ethnographic literature still employed the term "red people" (as opposed to "school people") to refer to "uncivilized" pagans: that is, to traditionalists with strong ties to Xhosa custom who were resistant to the lure of "Western" culture. The term "redness" has thus played into what the anthropologist Steven Robins has called the "great divide" in colonial and apartheid discourse: the opposition between the urban and the rural, between the center and the periphery, and, more generally, between "progressive" modernity and traditional African custom.[39] The connection between *The Heart of Redness* and *Heart of Darkness* is therefore not a wholly ironic and adversarial one. For there is a sense in which one might see Camagu's journey to kwaXhosa in search of the beautiful NomaRussia as a journey into the heart of Xhosa "redness." The girl's hometown of Qolorha, as we soon learn, was the site of a dramatic eruption of anticolonial resistance in the mid–nineteenth century. It is the birthplace of Nongqawuse, the young girl who once brought the amaXhosa the compelling but ultimately disastrous message that if everyone killed their cattle and burned their crops, the ancestors would arise and sweep the colonists into the sea. This millenarian prophecy led to the starvation of thousands of people and to the eventual incorporation of the resistant tribes into the colonial economy as wage slaves. From a certain perspective—one held by some of the characters in the novel—Qolorha thus seems to be the historic epicenter of benightedness. But like *Heart of Darkness*, though in a less melodramatic vein, *The Heart of Redness* reveals the instability of the key terms in its title. All localizing strategies of containment (like that of confining savagery on the periphery) fail, and all moral and value judgments (like "darkness," "redness," "beauty," "civilization," and so forth) become ungrounded. If there is anything at the heart of *The Heart of Redness*, it is a debate over the meaning of the novel's translation terms.

As depicted in the novel, Qolorha conforms in certain respects to nostalgic ideas of village life. Despite historic divisions between the amaThamba and amaGogotya (the Believers and Unbelievers in Nongqawuse vision, and their traditionalist and modernist decedents, too), it is a real community. The entire village considers itself invited to any party that might be held, and everyone attends all the funerals—even the bitterest enemies. But Qolorha is by no means the bounded village of ethnographic fantasy.[40] Its daily life is connected to the world beyond by the movement of both commodities and people—like the schoolteacher, Xoliswa Ximiya, who has ventured as far as Athens, Ohio. There are herd boys, to be sure, as there are anywhere in rural Africa, but they often let the cattle stray while they watch TV on the veranda of the trading store. Even Qukezwa, a young girl devoted to traditional custom and named after an ardent nineteenth-century Believer, sports a Pierre Cardin beret and has a secret "yearning for the city" (HR 51). In this she is not alone: many of the villagers' names, especially those of women, express a desire for global connectedness. While names such as "Satellite" and "NoCellphone" (the names a corrupt chief selects for his children) strike some of the villagers as laughable signs of trendiness and venality, names like "NoEngland," and "NoPetticoat" pass without comment. The curious name "NomaRussia" turns out to be commonplace and even traditional. Its appeal dates back to the 1850s, when the amaXhosa, who had suffered a cruel defeat at the hands of the British in the War of Mlanjeni, got wind of Russian victories in the Crimea, concluded that these Russians must be black people or ancestral spirits who would come to the amaXhosa's assistance, and posted men on the hills near the ocean to look out for the arrival of Russian ships.

Qolorha, in short, is presented as having had metropolitan connections, both real and imagined, for well over a century. As a historic frontier and as a contemporary tourist destination, it is a contact zone, a place where "natives" and colonizers, dwellers and travelers encounter each other—and where the distinctions between such groups can at times be quite blurry.[41] The categories are straddled by intermediary figures like Camagu, the cosmopolitan umXhosa exile, who becomes a resident of Qolorha in the course of the novel, and John Dalton, the white trader, who (though descended from a settler who played a bloody part in the British conquest of the region) is in many ways more of a "native" than Camagu. Dalton has never traveled abroad, speaks perfect isiXhosa, was circumcised along with the local *abakwetha*, and is perceived by the village elite as "a raw umXhosa who still lives in darkness" (HR 75). The juxtaposition of these two anomalous characters serves to complicate any simple notion of dwelling and belonging. The intense debates between traditionalists and modernists over the legacy of Nongqawuse and, more immediately, over the possibility of a casino development in the village provide further evidence that social identity and culture are not solely defined by the place one is from. Even a small village like Qolorha cannot be viewed as an undifferentiated cultural site.

But *The Heart of Redness* also suggests that identity is never entirely separable from questions of place. Actual or imagined geographies invariably come into play in the novel's treatment of questions of aesthetics and style. We have already seen how the Johannesburg art dealers decided the fate of the unfortunate Twin and his carvings of "beautiful people who looked like real people" (HR 47). But the novel does not depict the city as the only locus of aesthetic judgment. On the contrary: we learn, for instance, that Xoliswa's austere beauty is not prized in her village. It is too much like that of the "hungry women who are referred to as supermodels in the fashion magazines" (HR 70) to appeal to local men, who like their women "plump and juicy" (HR 10). More is at stake, however, in the novel's aesthetic arguments than an opposition between the naïve country and the sophisticated city or, as was the case in *Ways of Dying*, between the "beautiful" and the "ugly." Whereas the grotesque thematics of the earlier novel required the latter opposition to be stark, in order to underscore the gulf between the world of wealth and the world of deprivation, *The Heart of Redness* is concerned with subtler and more culturally specific distinctions. These distinctions are still expressive of power and privilege; but in this novel, power and privilege tend to be expressed incrementally, and by degrees of mobility and access to metropolitan centers of consumption. For example, in terms of status in the village, the teacher Xoliswa, who has traveled to the United States, has the looks of a supermodel, and dresses in the most austere and up-to-date fashions, clearly outranks the receptionist Miss Vathiswa, who has also traveled, but only to Durban, where she modeled for an Indian trader's clothing catalogue, and who dresses in elaborate outfits that were in style a decade earlier.

There is, of course, a sense in which beauty is always a spatial matter. The beautiful thing—or its appraiser—may be harmoniously and authoritatively in place, or dramatically out of place. It is therefore with some justice that Bhonco, the most ardent modernist among the villagers, attributes Camagu's perception of Qolorha as the most "beautiful place on earth" to the fact that he is a tourist and has not been "forced to live [in the village] forever" (HR 69). The old man's observation is worth consideration, especially since tourism (both as source of income and as source of scopic pleasure) is such an important theme in the novel. A tourist is perhaps most usefully defined as someone who "takes a leap out of ordinary life."[42] As Jamaica Kincaid, for one, has insisted, such a leap tends to yield aesthetic pleasure at the cost of other kinds of perception. Tourists in her native Antigua, she notes, invariably find the island and its sunny weather beautiful: it means that they will enjoy the four days or so they have come to spend on the beach without worrying about the rain. But for the person who lives in Antigua year round, the constant sunshine can mean drought, lack of sanitation, and so forth.[43] Mda's take on tourism is not at odds with Kincaid's, but it is more nuanced. He makes it clear in *The Heart of Redness* that Camagu's appreciation of Qolorha's beauty is neither invalid nor necessarily self-serving: even Bhonco at one point lets "his eyes feast" on the "mountains of snow-white surf," the "green valleys," and the "beautiful houses painted pink, powder blue, yellow, and white" (HR 5). Nevertheless, Mda makes it clear that the perception of the valley as a landscape painting, "a canvas where blue and green dominate" (HR 61), is an effect of privilege and distance. It requires a bracketing not only of utilitarian concerns but also and more signally of the local meanings of the beautiful thing. To apprehend the pastel-colored rondavels as picturesque one must refrain from thinking about practical things (their vulnerability to termites and so forth) and be able to ignore, if only momentarily, the fact that different architectural styles (the rondavel, the hexagon, and the square *ixanga*) are signifiers in a highly fraught local discourse about tradition and modernity, in terms of which round houses—rondavels—are considered traditional, indigenous, and rural, while square houses, are considered modern, imported, and urban.[44]

A similar line of argument can be applied to fashion and styles of dress, a pervasive theme in *The Heart of Redness*. In one of the novel's historical sections, Mda allows us to see the arbitrariness of fashion and style as a system of signs: the nineteenth-century amaXhosa find the idea that "the way to the white man's heaven was through trousers and dresses" (HR 54) patently absurd. They cannot see that the convert, William Goliath, dressed in a suit discarded by the missionaries, is in any way superior to them in his physical appearance. In the novel's contemporary sections, however, the meaning of clothing is no longer arbitrary: it is densely but differentially encoded at every level of the social hierarchy. On the village level, the key figure is the formidable NoPetticoat, Bhonco's wife and Xoliswa's mother. She has never traveled: Centani, Butterworth, Bisho, Pretoria, and America are all for her simply distant places, with no particular cultural meaning or authority. As a result, she is able to fully enjoy the decorative traditions of Qolorha's *amahomba*, "those who look beautiful and who pride themselves on fashion" (HR 47), including the red-ochred *isikhakha* skirts, the broad *iqhiya* turbans, and the various kinds of traditional beadwork: the *uphlalaza*, *amatikiti*, *amacici*, and *icangci*. This elaborate vocabulary is foregrounded in the novel for good reason.[45] Traditional costume is for NoPetticoat "an art form," a language that she and the other *amahomba* use to "say something" about themselves (HR 47). Other styles of clothing are for her simply "soulless" (HR 300): they are signifiers in a language that NoPetticoat cannot translate—despite what her wonderfully inappropriate name might lead one to expect. (And I should probably note here that the prefix "No" does not mean "no" as in English but serves to mark a name as feminine.)

The elegant Xoliswa is also committed to "beautiful things," or, in her students' more negative view, is dismissive of people and things that do not meet her exacting aesthetic and cultural standards. Her fascination with a strange news story about a Taiwanese girl who stabbed her mother and mother-in-law because she felt that "they were not pretty enough to live" (HR 114) suggests Xoliswa's own radical intolerance. In contrast to NoPetticoat, she is almost painfully aware of being stuck in what she considers a marginal cultural location. She is prone to giving uninvited geography lessons to all and sundry, demonstrating her careful sense of the relative size and importance of Bisho, Pretoria, and New York—the latter is "ten times bigger than Johannesburg," she informs the bemused Camagu (HR 71). Her standards of beauty, not surprisingly, are not defined locally, but in America, which is for her a "fairytale country," the home of "beautiful people" like Eddie Murphy and Dolly Parton (HR 71). As a result, Xoliswa "hates to see her mother looking so beautiful" (HR 48)—beautiful, that is, in terms of a code that Xoliswa rejects as shameful. But the limits to her much-vaunted cosmopolitanism are slyly revealed in her examples of beautiful people, Dolly Parton in particular. The country singer's extravagant performance of beauty reflects her own marginal origins in American society: Parton's style, one might say, speaks with a regional accent and in this respect is not so unlike the local fashions of the *ama-homba*. Its dimension of ironic performance, moreover, is something that Xoliswa is much too parochial a cultural observer to detect.

Yet another set of visual and aesthetic codes defines the Johannesburg glitterati and the new national elite. Confident in their new social power and sufficiently removed from the historical stigmas that still attach to traditional Xhosa clothing on the local level, they are eager to buy such things as *isikhakha* skirts, shoulder bags, and beadwork. Far from marking them as backward, these items denote them as particularly *au courant* and responsive to the president's much publicized call for an "African Renaissance" (HR 185). But Mda's language makes it clear that the glitterati behave like tourists: they "condescendingly visit" the clothes of the *amaqaba* and wear these fashions as "curiosities" (HR 61) on special occasions—especially occasions like the opening of parliament, when they might appear on TV as embodiments of the spirit of the nation. But this sartorial "leap out of the ordinary" reveals the limits of the elite's cultural discrimination. Their everyday (and therefore more normative) clothing is in fact no less exotic than the traditional styles they adopt as a kind of ceremonial fancy dress. They like to wear embroidered dashikis and *bubus*—items of dress specific to West Africa, though, ironically, often made from fabrics woven in Germany or Java. The meaning of the glitterati's clothing is thus at odds with its origins: they deploy regional and local costumes to signify their status as national leaders, and sport thoroughly hybrid and imported fashion items to signify their "authentic" Africanness and their status as new players on the world stage.[46]

The cultural map I have just sketched out would seem to validate the most cosmopolitan character in the novel: Camagu, an expert in international communications and a former denizen of New York and Rome and Paris, who often brings an illuminating comparatist position to bear on local and national issues. Unlike Xoliswa, he is able, as he puts it, to distinguish between "civilization" and "western civilization" (HR 286): an ability that sets him free to appreciate the amaXhosa's "beautiful artistic heritage" (HR 184), which he is also—more problematically—in a position to market to collectors in the city. It is possible to view Camagu as an exemplary catalyst figure of the sort Mda describes in his academic writing on development issues (indeed, the character seems to echo Mda's own views on questions like primordialist concepts of culture and on the importance of grassroots participation in community affairs [WPP 47–48]). Yet the novel stops short of turning Camagu into an oracle. It never allows us to lose sight of the fact that it is his educational and cultural privilege that renders him invulnerable to the stigma of being called a "barbarian" (a word that might be attached to a less sophisticated man who, like Camagu, expresses an emotional attachment to his clan totem). There is at least one minor but telling scene in the novel in which a villager turns the tables on Camagu and subjects his cosmopolitan judiciousness to delightful mockery. The clever local girl Qukezwa uses the occasion of a village fundraising event (a concert at which one donates money in exchange for the right to compel any other audience member to do whatever one asks) to force Camagu to become a judge in a beauty contest. She "buys" the right to make Camagu decide who among the dozen or so NomaRussias in the audience—women of all shapes, sizes, and ages—is the most beautiful. Though he wisely makes a hefty donation to release himself of the obligation, Camagu's discomfiture, which exposes the skirt-chasing intentions that originally led him to Qolorha, allows the villagers a good laugh at his expense and undermines his authority as a cultural arbiter. Thus Mda is careful not to validate, albeit on a more global level, Xoliswa's assumption that judgments and tastes from afar are necessarily the most valid.[47]

But beauty is no laughing matter in *The Heart of Redness*. In the novel, aesthetic preconceptions and practices (among which we must include the scopic pleasures of sightseeing) are not the mere epiphenomena of taste, but are enmeshed in such grave political and economic matters as the control and ownership of valuable land, the meaning and uses of tradition, and the fate of a unique coastal ecosystem. There is, for instance, a clear danger in the inability of a village progressive like Bhonco to view the "bush" as anything other than a humiliating sign of backwardness. The old man's inability to appreciate anything local leads him to dismiss indigenous flora and fauna—cycads, rare lizards, and the like—as "ugly" (HR 106, 168), to consider exotics like blue gums and pines as "civilized trees," and to regard plantations, with their neatly planted rows, as "beautiful forests" (HR 169). Aesthetic judgments like these make the villagers vulnerable to exploitative projects like the proposed casino resort—especially when they hear about such projects not from the white developers themselves but from a "very handsome" black CEO in a new navy blue suit (HR 229).

In Mda's satirical description, the development consultants' plans for the proposed "tourist heaven" in Qolorha becomes a caricature of modernist aesthetics. Mr. Jones's dream of a splendid crystal casino, surrounded by amusement park rides, roller coasters, cable cars, and a lake for jet skis, captures something of the streamlined aesthetic of speed and mobility, but it does so in trivialized fashion, by envisioning a haven for mechanized play. Mr. Smith's vision of a retirement village for millionaires, with neatly landscaped English gardens, carefully surveyed roads, Olympic-size pools, and new—and pronounceable—names like "Willowbrook Grove" or something ending in "Close, Dell and Downs" (HR 234), expresses modernity's homogenizing logic, its rage for order. But the ill-fitting English toponyms underscore the neocolonial nature of the project. Mr. Smith is the trivial postmodern avatar of the novel's archvillain, Sir George Grey, the British governor of the Cape, also known by the amaXhosa as He-Who-Named-Ten-Rivers. The fact that the village progressives are blind to this resemblance and to the fact that they would, at best, experience the glitz and the exciting rides as spectators, would seem to underscore the need for a new kind of aesthetic education. It is no accident that the novel's first page raises, however comically, the idea of "crying over beautiful things" (HR 1) or that the romantic plot ends up rewarding Qukezwa, who, as Mda puts it, is free-spirited because she is not "burdened with beauty" (HR 175). Aesthetic prejudices can be divisive and destructive precisely because they are so ideologically malleable.

The Tourist's Gaze

The Heart of Redness is concerned not only with aesthetic judgment but also with the very practice of looking—specifically, with the problem of voyeurism implicit in the gaze of the tourist, appreciative though it may be. We have already seen, in the case of the resort, how Mda presents a certain kind of tourism as a figure of an invasive and homogenizing modernity. But the same also can be said, rather ironically, about the novel's more preservation-minded tourist operations, most notably the venture into "cultural tourism" sponsored by the trader John Dalton. In his ground-breaking study *The Tourist*, Dean MacCannell has argued that sightseeing is a quintessentially modern phenomenon. It is a response to the reification of all aspects of daily life, especially in the realm of production. The modern subject, MacCannell suggests, can only regain a sense of totality through voyeurism: specifically, by looking at and thus fetishizing the work of others.[48] This empowering perspective is not available to the person who is being looked at, and tourism thus inevitably relies on unequal relations of power—on precisely the kind of uneven modernity (or postmodernity) of a country like South Africa. MacCannell, it must be said, is not particularly attuned to the (neo)colonial character of the tourist's gaze. He writes, with considerable obtuseness, that "our" love for "primitives" has to do with their "innocent openness" to our gaze—with the fact that their social life is so unproblematically and totally "exposed to outsiders who happen to be present."[49]

Mda, by contrast, is sensitive to the questions of power that are at stake in looking. We have already seen the way the politics of voyeurism and display is introduced in the Hillbrow chapter of *The Heart of Redness*, in which Mda implicitly questions the efficacy of black economic empowerment as long as it remains a matter of displaying "beautiful" black employees in the "glass cases" of modern office buildings. Much as these tokens of tolerance might enjoy their luxury German sedans, housing allowances, and expense accounts, they are deprived of any real autonomy. The same argument applies, on a different socioeconomic level, to the two Qolorha women whose "work," as Mda puts it, "is to display amasiko—the customs and cultural practices of the amaXhosa" (HR 109) to the white tourists John Dalton escorts around the scenic valley in his four-wheel-drive bakkie. Predictably, but with some justice, the progressive Xoliswa Ximiya considers this spectacularization as disgraceful: for her, Dalton's cultural tourism is simply a display of "primitive practices" that turn her people into "monkeys in a zoo" (HR 110). But Mda makes it clear that being looked at is in fact quite a complicated matter. NoVangeli and NoManage are perfectly aware that they are performers, and Dalton himself thinks of his employees as "actors" (HR 285). Their divining is a charade, as is their samp grinding, laying of cow-dung floors, and the like. If the tourists who view their show have "leapt out of the ordinary," so, too, in a sense, have the two Xhosa women: they would never go about their real domestic work in the cumbersome regalia of the *amahomba*. The very inauthenticity of their performance is, one might say, its saving grace: there is, in Irwin Goffman's terms, the possibility of a "back region" of "intimate reality" to their public and commercial "front."[50]

But the scopic, reifying dimensions of tourism are not so easily contained, as the novel shows in relation to NoPetticoat's experience with tourists. The old woman is outraged when a family of English tourists, who hired her as a nanny, asks her to speak into their camcorder, so that they can preserve a record of her "clicky language" as a curiosity (HR 163). The colonial resonances of this effort to "turn her into a bioscope" (HR 226) are clear: the tourists' prurient and patronizing interest recalls the specter of Sir George Grey, vaunted pacifier of Kaffraria, who collected the relics of the amaXhosa and recorded their grammar, in the secure conviction that these outlandish savages were on their way to cultural extinction. The tourists' video of NoPetticoat is not identical, of course, to the "souvenirs" of heads and ears and private parts of South African indigenes that have ended up in European museums, and which are a recurrent topic of conversation in the novel. But there are clearly some similarities between them: at stake in both instances is the assumption that the whole lives and persons of cultural others—of "primitives," in MacCannell's term—should be open to the gaze of the modern or, as the case may be, postmodern man. If NoPetticoat's treatment is less cruel than, say, that meted out to the Xhosa King Hintsa by the British governor Sir Benjamin D'Urban (who sent the chieftain's ears and head to a museum in Scotland), it is more compromising and therefore in a sense more invasive. While Hintsa did not consent to his own harsh treatment, NoPetticoat knows that she must oblige the English tourists or run the risk of being dismissed from her job at the hotel. Besides, as John Dalton points out to Bhonco, who is ready to fight for her honor, she is compromised by the fact that she sings in the weekly show the hotel employees put on for the tourists. Her position as nanny, moreover, means that she already appears to the tourists in a menial role: as someone whose thoughts are of little consequence and whose "clicky language" is therefore not worthy of attention insofar as it expresses her own experiences but only insofar as it reminds them, by association, of their own. NoPetticoat's situation makes it difficult to distinguish between public ("front") and private ("back") spaces: her position in a globalizing economy is one that tends to blur the differences between servant, entertainer, and exotic object.

Click! Click!

The conclusion of The Heart of Redness is arguably a happy one. But if so, the happiness seems precarious. The paradoxical "laughter of sadness" (HR 271) with which Bhonco is afflicted toward the end of the novel is perhaps a fitting response to its evocation of postapartheid South Africa. Qolorha is saved from environmental destruction through the intervention of the Department of Arts, Culture, and Heritage, which decides to declare the village an official national heritage site on the basis of its connection to Nongqawuse and her prophecies. The scene in which John Dalton, brandishing the department's decree, arrives on the resort's proposed building site and orders the surveyor to stop his work is dramatic, even stagy, and is open to obvious symbolic readings. The figure of the surveyor with his tellurometer, a device that can pinpoint location with perfect accuracy, is the very embodiment of an invasive and homogenizing modernity. The surveyor (if I may push the allegory a little) is pitted against and defeated by the shade of Nongqawuse, the embodiment of the regional past, with her perpetual air of disorientation and her potent, if dangerous, message of resistance to the modern and colonial world order. But Mda makes it clear that Qolorha's victory may be short-lived: it is entirely possible that the powers-that-be will decide before too long that a "gambling city," in which they or their proxies would have controlling interests, is in the national interest after all. Clearly the postcolonial nation is far from incompatible with the globalizing forces of modernity and postmodernity.

The victory of the environmentalists, moreover, has dubious results, even in the very short term. Not only is the dispute between the Believers and the Unbelievers left smoldering, and Bhonco's desire for a glamorous urbanity left unassuaged, but the environmentalist party is also divided, their enterprises devoted to very different notions of conservation. Each of these enterprises is beset with ironies. Dalton's tourist operation is expanded to include a "cultural village," employing several young men and women in addition to NoVangeli and NoManage. Unlike Qolorha itself, this village does fulfill the ethnographer's dream of a bounded site: it is a place where, as Dalton puts it, "various aspects of the people's culture can be shown in one place" (HR 285). This very deliberate localization of tradition for the sake of display is necessarily a misrepresentation. In real life, as Camagu angrily points out, the *abakwetha* initiates would be in seclusion, away from the village. They would never be standing around with their ochre faces or fighting with sticks right there in the village for all to see—especially not next to the place where the village maidens, or *amagqiyazana*, are dancing. Culture cannot be put "in one place" without wrenching things out of place, or so Mda implies.

By displaying only markedly "ethnic" or "traditional" things, the "cultural village" also has the effect of suggesting that contemporary life somehow fails to merit the designation "culture."[51] Dalton's tourist operation thus renders him a thoroughly ambiguous character. Because he helps protect and conserve Qolorha, he would seem to be symbolically aligned with Nongqawuse, her Believers, and the village traditionalists. Yet Mda's description of Dalton's triumph over the developers is followed all too closely in the novel by a final, nightmarish description of Sir George Gray riding wildly through kwaXhosa and exulting over his victory: "Finally, I have pacified Xhosaland" (HR 312). The reader is left to wonder if Dalton's ethnic village does not represent a postmodern version of pacification: a domestication and commercialization of otherness, and a collapse of both time and space.

Camagu's rival operation, the backpacker's holiday camp, where tourists are considered to be the guests of the amaGcaleka clan, is at first glance considerably less retrograde. Run as a collective, it would seem to be an example of a more sensitive, grassroots form of economic development. Unlike Dalton, Camagu avoids the problematic position of cultural impresario. But he is nevertheless a middleman and, as NoPetticoat's experience suggests, the realities of a tourist economy inevitably make it difficult to preserve one's dignity and autonomy: the lines between the roles of host, servant, entertainer, and spectacle are not easy to draw.

Moreover, though the ecotourism that Camagu sponsors requires neither costumes or nor acting, it is not entirely devoid of an element of exotic display. The holiday camp eventually incorporates the novel's symbolic site of local tradition and cultural continuity: the compound of the staunch traditionalist, Zim, as well as his giant wild fig tree full of *amahobohobo* or weaver bird's nests, finally becomes an attraction for sightseers. It proves to be as commodifiable, almost, as the handicrafts on display in one of the traditional hexagonal houses. Selling nature, moreover, is not all that easy to separate from selling culture. Camagu, as he finally admits to Dalton, uses the name of Nongqawuse whenever he advertises the camp in glossy travel magazines, and he seems somewhat regretful that the prophet was not actually buried in Qolorha. Marketed as a shrine, as a *lieu de mémoire*, in Pierre Nora's phrase, his tourist site would be even more profitable.[52]

The historical irony implicit here is deepened by the novel's penultimate flashback to the nineteenth century, one that seems to foreshadow Nongqawuse's twentieth-century fate, even as it gives us a brief glimpse into her personal tragedy. This fragment is presented from the point of view of the white woman who took Nongqawuse and Nonkosi, another girl prophet, into her care—fickle care, as it turns out, since the girls are soon shipped off to the Pauper's Lodge in Cape Town. She tries to teach them to play English games, keeps them cleanly scrubbed, dresses them in colorful clothes, and, most significantly, takes them to a photographer's studio to have their pictures taken. In Mda's re-creation of the scene, the white woman urges the prophetesses to smile for the camera. But they remain sullen, as if to resist their incorporation as icons of "redness" in a culture of visual display. Their resistance, however, is in vain, since even on the boat that ferries them to the dumping ground of the colony's female criminals and transportees, they are a "show piece": "Everyone wants to take a good look at them" (HR 318). Thus begins the process in which Camagu, for all his good intentions, is enmeshed, and which neither the author nor the reader can fully escape, as we are reminded by the fact that the photograph of Nongqawuse and Nonkosi is reprinted on the inside cover of the South African edition of the novel. We are, we hope, cultural consumers of a different kind from the English tourists, who tried to capture the cultural oddity of NoPetticoat and her "clicky" language with their camcorder, but we are consumers and gazers nevertheless.

In the novel's concluding collage, however, Mda seems to be gesturing toward a mode of recollection that is unavailable for commodification and display. Here Qukezwa—the nineteenth-century Qukezwa, that is (though her identity in these final passages is clearly intended to blend into that of her contemporary namesake)—is described as singing "in colors." "She sings in glaring colors. In violent colours. Colours of gore. Colours of today and of yesterday. Dreamy colours. . . . She haunts yesterday's reefs and ridges with redness" (HR 312). Creating paintings of pure song, she conjures a vision of "prophetesses walking in the mist" (HR 319). But what we are to think of these prophetesses is left appropriately open. In the final fragment, Qukezwa is playing on the beach with her son Heitsi, who has been named for the Khoi prophet and savior Heitsi Eibib, who brought his people to safety while leaving their enemies to drown in the mighty waters of the Gariep. Impatient with the boy's fear of the ocean—his reluctance, as she sees it, to "carry out the business of saving his people" (HR 319)—Qukezwa drags the child into the sea; but Heitsi flees from the waves, shouting: "No mama no, this boy does not belong in the sea, this boy belongs in the man village!" (HR 320). It is a curious assertion of belonging, and its placement in the novel's very last sentence might tempt us to read it as offering redemptive possibilities. But if so, they are far from being unambiguous. The idea of belonging, the idea of the bounded village, and the idea of salvation: these are precisely the notions that Mda's narrative has worked to complicate.

A Clearing in the Bush

I would like to conclude this chapter by stepping away for a moment from Mda's fictional tourist haven in order to attend to a real one: the luxurious game lodge to which the writer and critic Njabulo Ndebele once paid a visit and which he subsequently decoded in an excellent essay—just as good, for my money, as anything in Barthes's *Mythologies*.[53] The game lodge, Ndebele suggests, has always been a mythic space and, as such, has impeded new ways of thinking about Africa as "a transforming historical phenomenon."[54] But it is not without its own semiotic mutations. In colonial times, the game lodge—quintessentially a clearing in the bush—functioned as an arrogant celebration of the extent of colonial power, of its ability to provide safety and even comfort in inimical terrain. In the postcolony, however, it has become something more nostalgic. It is now "a place where those who have lost power go to regain a sense of its possession."[55] Ndebele's description of the lodge's topography seems uncannily familiar. It is reminiscent, in fact, of the description J. M. Coetzee gives us in *Life and Times of Michael K* of the ideal sociogeographic arrangement imagined by apartheid's beneficiaries: a scenario in which all the workers could be placed in some distant camp, from which they would "come in on tiptoe in the middle of the night like fairies and do their work, dig their gardens, wash their pots, and be gone in the morning leaving everything nice and clean" (LT 82). At the game lodge, Ndebele observes, the privileged are relieved to find that "everything . . . is still in place":

> The measured conveniences [are there], of course, but also the faceless black workers, behaving rather meekly, who clear the rooms, wash the dishes, make the fire, baby sit the children and make sure that in the morning the leisure refugees find their cars clean. Living somewhere "out there," beyond the neatly clipped frontier, the black workers come into the clearing to serve. And then they disappear again. In their comings and goings, they are as inscrutable as the dense bush from which they emerge and to which they return.[56]

Ndebele's point is not that nothing has changed in postapartheid South Africa. The game park, as he makes quite clear, is fenced off from the country as a whole, and it misrepresents the broader relations of power. But in the passage I have cited, Ndebele reminds us that the remapping of the terrain of the gaze has remained incomplete—despite the rainbow nation's very deliberate self-display in the eyes of the rest of the world. The workers still remain invisible, relegated to the periphery "out there." And so the black tourist, though he can now book himself a luxurious space in the clearing, still finds himself in an awkward and contradictory position. He is, as Ndebele, puts it, "paying to be the viewer who has to be viewed." At the campsite he feels as though he is adding color to the experience of the white guests, and when out viewing game he finds it difficult, or so Ndebele confesses, to repress the thought that "in the total scheme of things," he should be "out there with the animals," being stared and marveled at through binoculars.[57]

Far from being a small matter, a problem of the privileged few, the discomfort of the black tourist is for Ndebele symptomatic of a serious condition. It points to the limits of the black majority's cultural power and compels us to attend to a neglected aspect of freedom, namely, the liberation of leisure: something that can only be fully realized once the gap between the everyday experiences and expectations of the workers and the tourists begins to narrow. Ndebele's essay also identifies an unexpected new structure of feeling. It is a pervasive anxiety, reminiscent in certain ways of the disquieting sensation of the uncanny that Lars Engle diagnosed in South African writing, but with the signal difference that it afflicts not guilty whites but newly liberated blacks. Struggling to make sense of their lives, Ndebele writes, black South Africans feel at times "like people who have awoken in an enormous vacation house which is now supposed to be theirs but which they do not quite recognize."[58] This sensation gives rise to troubling new forms of national consciousness, which replicate the old topographies of inclusion and exclusion on an international level. Anxious to survive in the global economy and to market South Africa as a haven of safety and success on a troubled continent, the country runs the risk, as Ndebele judges, of becoming one big game lodge from which its citizens may view the rest of Africa as onlookers, gazing out, in self-congratulatory fashion, at the chaos to the north.

Ndebele's meditations home in on the central dilemma of the postcolonial nation-state in an era of globalization. As Jean and John Comaroff have observed, the new democracies that emerged with the collapse of the Berlin Wall and the Soviet Union have differed from the earlier postcolonies in one crucial respect: they have had to confront the challenge of creating a modern nation in a postmodern era—in an age of fluid markets, electronic media, and a triumphal neoliberal capitalist economy. In this context, the Comaroffs argue, the state becomes essentially "a business in the business of attracting business," and its citizens, no longer bound by the "deep horizontal fraternity" of nationalism, become stakeholders, who desire simultaneously to be global citizens and to have a maximum share in the nation's wealth.[59] In this context, national borders become contradictory and contentious things, simultaneously essential and detrimental to national prosperity. As global markets erode the distinctive riches of individual nations, notions such as "heritage" become both more elusive and more important: a sense of patrimony is redefined in a rather zealous but also entrepreneurial fashion (of the sort evident in the ecofriendly tourist developments in *The Heart of Redness*). The culture of the new postcolonies, or so the Comaroffs suggest, becomes essentially an exotic commodity "to be patented, made into intellectual property, merchandised, consumed."[60]

It is not insignificant that these broad cultural and political issues should arise from a meditation about nature, wildlife, and the bush. In their essay "Naturing the Nation," the Comaroffs specifically discuss the paradox of national borders in relation to nature or, more precisely, to *naturalization*, a word they use with a full sense of its ambiguities. Their essay analyzes the way the wildfires that blazed in the Cape in January 2000, devastating vast tracks of *fynbos* (the region's unique, delicate, and diverse flora), seemed to trigger a discourse of invasion. The fires were blamed, accurately enough, on the presence of alien plants—exotic acacia and hakea species—which fueled flames of great intensity, far more devastating than those the fynbos itself can sustain and by which it would normally be renewed. The Comaroffs' point is not to deny the valid ecological concerns raised by this event; but they do wish to imply that the ecological discourse about the natural and autochthonous is overdetermined. It is no accident, or so they argue, that the fear of invader species seemed to arise at a time when anxieties about illegal migrants—human aliens from elsewhere in Africa—were on the rise in South Africa. All the media talk about indigeneity and invasion provided an indirect means of voicing anxieties about outsiders in a new nation officially opposed to all forms of discrimination and racism.

The shape of the Comaroffs' intriguing (if somewhat vulnerable) argument is not unfamiliar to students of South Africa literature.[61] In Nadine Gordimer's novel *The Conservationist*, the discourse of ecological preservation is also exposed as an alibi for territorial possession and policies of exclusion: it offers a way in which the white landowner can express his anxiety about black trespassers and encroaching townships without seeming to be as crudely racist as his less aesthetically attuned Afrikaans neighbors. The Comaroffs, one might say, transpose Gordimer's critique of the ideology of conservation onto a grand international scale, one appropriate to an era of globalization.

All of these considerations lead us back to Zakes Mda and *The Heart of Redness*. Qukezwa, a fierce environmentalist who at one point in the novel runs into trouble for chopping down the exotic inkberry trees that, as she puts it, "kill the plants of [her] forefathers" (HD 102), presents her argument for conservation in ways that would seem to mark *The Heart of Redness* as a quintessential work of the year 2000. The novel deploys the very same discourses and touches on the very same themes—of indigeneity, heritage, and the paradoxes of belonging—that the Comaroffs trace back to the ambivalent politics of naturalization in the new postcolony: a politics that is attentive to the world at large but profoundly ethnocentric nevertheless. How exactly are we then to judge Mda's engagement with these emerging South African discourses? Is his work symptomatic, or is it critical of the pervasive anxieties about cultural and natural patrimonies in an age of porous borders and the aggressive commodification of the world's picturesque margins?

The question is not, I think, an easy one to answer. Though Mda, having learnt from Brecht, presents all of these matters in the context of local debates in which different arguments are staged, the romantic plot clearly validates Qukezwa and her notion of autochthonous heritage. And yet, as we have seen, this is a novel that at its very outset presents us with the fluid terrain of contemporary Hillbrow: a place of transients where, as one character puts it, "everyone . . . comes from somewhere else" (HR 39). The very idea that a funeral might be staged in a tent on top of a modern building seems to be an ironic comment on the recurrent trope of burial in South African literature, in which the black South African—most notably the dead city slicker of Gordimer's otherwise revolutionary novel *The Conservationist*—is characteristically returned to rural soil. Any nostalgia for proper places, homecoming, and unproblematic belonging seems to be mocked, even before the protagonist of *The Heart of Redness* embarks on his journey to his ethnic heartland, by the migrant mourners who, as we have seen, sing the all too fitting hymn "Nearer, My God to Thee" on top of a twenty-story high-rise (HR 27). Mda's novel of the millennium thus seems poised between an acceptance of a kind of postmodern nomadism—of a world of exiles, tourists, and migrants—and a desire to recover a sense of local belonging and indigeneity in a way that is utterly characteristic of the postcolony in an age of globalization. Mda, it seems fair to say, derives his novelistic energies precisely from what Ndebele describes as the "split personality" of the new nation, a condition that, he predicts, is likely to generate its own forms of creativity.[62] *The Heart of Redness*, therefore, might be said to resemble *Heart of Darkness* at least in this one respect: its enduring cultural and literary interest may lie precisely in its undecidable and contradictory ideological stance.

NOTES

Introduction

1. John Western, *Outcast Cape Town* (Minneapolis: University of Minnesota Press, 1981), 8.

2. While one certainly understands the cultural, linguistic, and generic reasons for this separateness (apartheid has made it difficult to conceptualize a national literature), it seems to me that the postapartheid situation requires a greater effort on the part of literary critics to place the work of South African authors of diverse ethnicities in dialogue. I therefore see Michael Chapman's controversial *Southern African Literatures* (Harlow, Essex, England: Longman, 1996), which tries to do precisely this, as a courageous and innovative contribution.

3. Rob Nixon, *Homelands, Harlem, and Hollywood: South African Culture and the World Beyond* (New York: Routledge, 1994), 5 and throughout.

4. Jacques Derrida, "Racism's Last Word," and Anne McClintock and Rob Nixon, "No Names Apart: The Separation of Word and History in Derrida's 'Le Dernier Mot du Racisme,'" and Derrida, "But, beyond . . . (Open Letter to Anne McClintock and Rob Nixon)," both in *"Race," Writing, and Difference*, ed. Henry Louis Gates, Jr. (Chicago: University of Chicago Press), 329–369. See also Lars Engle's provocative essay "The Novel without the Police," *Pretexts* 3 (1991): 111.

5. J. M. Coetzee, "The Great South African Novel," *Leadership SA* 2 (1983): 74.

6. For helpful overviews of the importance of space in cultural and literary theory, see Tony Pinckney, "Space: The Final Frontier," *Notes from Nowhere* 8 (autumn 1990): 10–28,

and Caren Kaplan, "Reconfigurations of Geography and Historical Narrative: A Review Essay," *Public Culture* 3 (Fall 1990): 25–27.

7. Timothy Mitchell, *Colonizing Egypt* (Cambridge, England: Cambridge University Press, 1991), 35.

8. Edward W. Said, *Culture and Imperialism* (New York: Vintage, 1994), 7.

9. The remark was first reported in the *Johannesburg Star* on 3 April 1973. It has since been cited by David M. Smith, in "Race-Space Inequality in South Africa: A Study in Welfare Geography," *Antipode* 6 (1974): 42; by John Western, in *Outcast Cape Town*, 69; and by Peter Jackson, in "Geography, Race, and Racism," in *New Models in Geography: The Political-economy Perspective*, ed. Richard Peet and Nigel Thrift (London: Unwin Hyman, 1989), 180.

10. Leonard Thompson, *The Political Mythology of Apartheid* (New Haven: Yale University Press, 1985), 191.

11. Jeremy Cronin, *Inside* (London: Jonathan Cape, 1987), 9.

12. Glenn Mills, "Space and Power in South Africa: The Township as a Mechanism of Control," *Ekistics* 56 (January/February–March/April 1989): 65.

13. Ibid., 66–67.

14. Ibid., 72.

15. Michel Foucault, "Of Other Spaces," *Diacritics* 16 (Spring 1986): 23–24.

16. Mtutuzeli Matshoba, "Getting Back to Writing," interview with James Munnick and Geoffrey V. Davis, in *Southern African Writing: Voyages and Explorations*, ed. Geoffrey V. Davis (Amsterdam: Rodopi, 1994), 123–132. The brutal murders of commuters by Inkatha thugs in the months preceding the elections of 1994 make sense only if one recognizes the political dimension of trains and combi-taxis as "mobile meeting places."

17. Glenn Mills makes the same point with regard to the townships ("Space and Power in South Africa," 73).

18. Annamaria Carusi, "Post, Post, Post; Or Where Is South African Literature in All This?" *Ariel* 20 (October 1989): 80–81. See also Anne McClintock, "The Angel of Progress: Pitfalls of the Term 'Post-colonialism,'" in *Colonial Discourse and Post-colonial Theory: A Reader*, ed. Patrick Williams and Laura Chrisman (New York: Columbia University Press, 1994), 291–304.

19. Vijay Mishra and Bob Hodge, "What Is Post(-)colonialism?" in Williams and Chrisman, *Colonial Discourse and Post-colonial Theory*, 289.

20. Achille Mbembe, "Prosaics of Servitude and Authoritarian Civilities," *Public Culture* 5 (Fall 1992): 144.

21. See Sarah Nuttall, "City Forms and Writing the 'Now' in South Africa," *Journal of Southern African Studies* 30: 4 (December 2004): 731–748.

Chapter 1

1. To understand the redirection of critical energy implicit in this epigraph, we must bear in mind that to many South African critics Coetzee seems by now to be completely "domesticated by international criticism," to the point that he functions, as Louise Bethlehem puts it, as a "convenient point of reference through which to hone by now predictable aspects of postcolonial theory in its metropolitan guises." See Bethlehem, "In the Between: Time, Space, Text in Recent South African Literary Theory," *English in Africa* 27 (May 2000): 153. Stephen Gray makes the point even more strongly in a 2000 interview: "What J. M. Coetzee does," he argues, "is almost not South African at all; it is an exercise conducted in the powerful intellectual forums of Europe and America." See Ulrike Ernst,

From Anti-apartheid to African Renaissance: Interviews with South African Writers and Critics on Cultural Politics beyond the Cultural Struggle (Hamburg: LIT Verlag, 2001), 73.

2. Interview with Folke Rhedin, *Kunapipi* 6 (1984): 10.

3. J. M. Coetzee, "The Novel Today," *Upstream* 6 (Summer 1988): 2.

4. Edward W. Soja, *Postmodern Geographies: The Reassertion of Space in Critical Social Theory* (New York: Verso, 1989), especially chapter 1, "History, Geography, Modernity," 10–42. We may consider, further, the fact that neoliberal urban policy, not unlike apartheid, relies on the physical and symbolic displacement of the poor in order to enable gentrification and encourage investment in the city center. See Jane Schneider and Ida Susser, eds., *Wounded Cities: Destruction and Reconstruction in a Globalized World* (New York: Berg, 2003), 6. For a brief defense of the expanded application of the term "apartheid," see Salih Booker and William Minter, "Global Apartheid," *Nation*, 9 July 2001, and for an analysis from a South African vantage, see Patrick Bond, *South Africa and Global Apartheid: Continental and International Policies and Politics* (Uppsala: NAI, 2004).

5. Cited in Soja, *Postmodern Geographies*, 22.

6. The geographer Alan Mabin, among others, has noted that spatially determined inequality has proved difficult to resist, even after the rescinding of the Group Areas Act. Grassroots responses to oppressive spatial conditions during the transition years (invasions of open land next to cities, squatting, and the like) have tended to reinforce, rather than challenge, the segregated geography of cities. For the most part, land invaders and squatters have established themselves next to the peripheral residential areas, so that the poorest people are still, in effect, remote and invisible. The conditions Coetzee describes here have been ameliorated, but they have not yet disappeared. See Mabin, "Dispossession, Exploitation and Struggle: An Historical Overview of South African Urbanization," in *The Apartheid City and Beyond: Urbanization and Social Change in South Africa*, ed. David M. Smith (New York: Routledge, 1992), 21–22.

7. Louise Bethlehem, "'Under the Protea Tree, at Daggaboersnek': Stephen Gray, Literary Historiography and the Limit Trope of the Local," *English in Africa* 24 (October 1997): 29. Southern African scholarly works on the intersections of literature and critical human geography and landscape theory include John Noyes, *Colonial Space* (Philadelphia: Harwood, 1992); Kate Darien-Smith, Liz Gunner, and Sarah Nuttall, eds., *Text, Theory, Space: Land, Literature and History in South Africa and Australia* (New York: Routledge, 1996); Hilton Judin and Ivan Vladislavić, eds., *Blank_____: Architecture, Apartheid, and After* (Cape Town: David Phillips, 1999), which includes articles by several prominent South African writers, including Marlene van Niekerk, Karel Schoeman, Achmat Dangor, and Vladislavić himself; and, most recently, Hein Viljoen, Chris van der Merwe, and Minnie Lewis, eds., *Storyscapes: South African Perspectives on Literature, Space, and Identity* (New York: Peter Lang, 2004). A useful overview of an "iconology of South African landscape," which comments on both Gray and Coetzee, is offered by Kathrin Wagner in *Rereading Nadine Gordimer* (Bloomington: Indiana University Press, 1994), 167–174. See also David Bunn, "Relocations: Landscape Theory, South African Landscape Practice, and the Transmission of Political Value," *Pretexts* 4 (Summer 1993): 44–67.

8. Gray's essay appears in *A Sense of Place in the New Literatures in English*, ed. Peggy Nightingale (London: University of Queensland Press, 1986), 5–12.

9. Ibid., 8.

10. Ibid.

11. Gray also projects, albeit somewhat vaguely, a fourth phase of writing, expressive of a new kind of postnational, multicultural, and critically potent marginality, but he cites only the Australian writer David Malouf as a possible example—no South Africans. The case of Malouf is interesting, and it is no wonder that he is mentioned only as a coda: the novel

Gray mentions, *An Imaginary Life*, is not set in Australia but on the fringes of the ancient Roman Empire. "A Sense of Place," 1–12.

12. For a critique of Gray on the grounds of his rhetorical investment in the tropes of colonial mapping, as well as his nationalistic homogenization of the geographic experience of white and black South Africans, see Bethlehem, "'Under the Protea Tree.'" Bethlehem seizes on a moment in the essay when Gray, on a trip to Stratford, pretends to experience a sense of *heimwee* for the girl he had left behind, "standing there, talking ethnic, under the protea tree, at Daggaboersnek, with a sjambok . . . in her freckled arms" (6). Bethlehem relentlessly unpacks this line, tracking down etymologies, excoriating essentialisms, and so forth, in order to reveal, somewhat predictably, that Gray's trope of the local is already complicit with the "systematization of spatiality through which Europe produces the place of the colony" (36). As I see it, the problem with Gray's lame joke (one he could only have gotten away with outside South Africa) is not that he makes his claims for a deterritorialized English through a territorial trope. It is rather that he figures his colonial identity by (mis)appropriating (and stereotyping) an Afrikaans cultural identity—this despite the fact that his essay entirely represses the importance of Afrikaans and, indeed, any language other than English—in the formation of a national literary tradition. The figure under the "protea tree" (proteas actually grow on bushes) is recognizable to any South African as a version of "Sarie Marais": a figure unlikely to be speaking English, however "ethnic."

13. We may consider, for example, Graham Huggan's argument that the rapid rise of postcolonial studies in the United States, the United Kingdom, and Europe cannot be separated from a newly fashioned desire for the exotic, created by what he calls the "alterity industry." See *The Post-colonial Exotic: Marketing the Margins* (New York: Routledge, 2001), vii and throughout.

14. See Ernst, *From Anti-apartheid to African Renaissance*, 74, 82.

15. Gray, "A Sense of Place," 7.

16. One might also point out that a "place," or a "setting," is by no means inertly material but socially and discursively produced. A concept like "landscape" makes the point particularly well: the word, as John Barrell has pointed out, was used in the realm of aesthetic representation (to describe a kind of painting) well before landscapes came to be observed in the "real world," before the word began to apply to a given tract of land; moreover, aesthetic and social concepts have frequently driven modifications of the actual shape of the land. Landscapes, in short, are always forms of a "second nature"; "place" and "setting" are never empirical, never separate from forms of writing. See John Barrell, *The Idea of Landscape and the Sense of Place, 1730–1840: An Approach to the Poetry of John Clare* (Cambridge, England: Cambridge University Press, 1972), especially chap. 1.

17. Stephen Watson, "Colonialism in the Novels of J. M. Coetzee," *Research in African Literatures* 17 (1986): 374.

18. Teresa Dovey, *The Novels of J. M. Coetzee: Lacanian Allegories* (Johannesburg: Ad Donker, 1988), 52. Though now inevitably dated in its range of reference, it seems to me that Dovey's work is still worthy of critical scrutiny, since it has, in its insistently theoretical and poststructuralist emphasis, given impetus to many subsequent responses to Coetzee.

19. Dovey adopts the hermit crab as the central metaphor of her Lacanian reading of Coetzee, using as an epigraph the following passage from *In the Heart of the Country*: "It is the hermit crab, I remember from a book, that as it grows migrates from one empty shell to another. . . . Whose shell I presently skulk in does not matter, it is the shell of a dead creature. What matters is that my anxious softbodied self should have a refuge from the predators of the deep" (HC 43–44). The passage from Barthes that Dovey alludes to reads as follows: "L'atopie—Atopia. Pigeonholed: I am pigeonholed, assigned to an (intellectual) site, to a residence in a caste (if not in a class). Against which there is only one internal doc-

trine: that of atopia (of a drifting habitation). Atopia is superior to utopia (utopia is reactive, tactical, literary, it proceeds from meaning and governs it." It is interesting that while for Dovey the word "atopia" means something very similar to the Derridean *différance*, it actually has a political meaning in Barthes's text (and one that is particularly pressing in the South African context): it addresses the problem of the class position/allegiance of the intellectual. See *Roland Barthes by Roland Barthes*, trans. Richard Howard (New York: Hill and Wang, 1977), 49.

20. Dovey, *The Novels of J. M. Coetzee*, 9.

21. This point is also addressed by Peter Strauss in "Coetzee's Idylls: The Ending of *In the Heart of the Country*," in *Momentum: On Recent South African Writing*, ed. M. J. Daymond, J. U. Jacobs, and Margaret Lenta (Pietermaritzburg: University of Natal Press, 1984), 123–128.

22. See the epigraph to *July's People*: "The old is dying and the new cannot be born; in this interregnum there arises a great diversity of morbid symptoms." Coetzee's interest in this condition is evident in the title of *Waiting for the Barbarians*, and there are several explicit statements on this condition to found elsewhere in his oeuvre. In his review of Vincent Crapanzano's book *Waiting: The Whites of South Africa*, for instance, Coetzee quotes with assent the author's characterization of this experience: "Wittingly or unwittingly, the whites wait for something, anything, to happen. They are caught in the peculiar, paralytic, time of waiting. . . . Waiting—the South African experience—must be appreciated in all its banality. Therein lies its pity—and its humanity." See J. M. Coetzee, "Listening to the Afrikaners— Waiting," *New York Times Book Review*, 14 April 1985, 3. In *Life and Times of Michael K*, which presents actual South African conditions in a futuristic allegory, we find a similar meditation: "War-time is a time of waiting. . . . What was there to do in camp but wait, going through the motions of living, fulfilling one's obligations, keeping an ear tuned all the time to the hum of the war beyond the walls, listening for its pitch to change?" (MK 158).

23. Richard Begam's essay "Silence and Mut(e)ilation: White Writing in J. M. Coetzee's *Foe*," *South Atlantic Quarterly* 93 (Winter 1994): 111–130, is an example of a critique that avoids this rigidity, that is fully conscious of the condition of what Said has called "traveling theory." Begam observes that in Coetzee's work the Derridean opposition of speech and writing comes to be recoded in a locally—and politically—relevant manner: "speech" is associated with blackness, with the colonized, and "writing" with the white settler. See also David Attwell, "The Problem of History in the Fiction of J. M. Coetzee," in *Rendering Things Visible*, ed. Martin Trump (Athens: Ohio University Press, 1990), 99, for more general discussion of the need for this kind of contextual redefinition.

24. Attwell, "The Problem of History," 113.

25. Dovey, *Lacanian Allegories*, 288.

26. Ibid.

27. J. M. Coetzee, "The White Man's Burden," *Speak* 1 (1977): 4–7.

28. It is worth offering an anecdotal observation here: I have often heard Afrikaners commend Pauline Smith as the one English writer "who got us right," which is to say (as Coetzee would observe) that her work represents us according to our own flattering myth of ourselves.

29. The names of these soaps, standard fare on Springbok radio during my childhood, often referred to family farms, such as *Die Du Plooys van Soetmelksvlei* (The Du Plooys of Sweetmilk Valley), or *Die Geheim van Nantes* (The Secret of Nantes). While in *White Writing* Coetzee does not mention these subliterary examples of the South African pastoral, they confirm its thoroughly ideological status.

30. In *Doubling the Point*, Coetzee seems to question the value of demystificatory readings on the grounds that they actually privilege mystification. He describes himself

as having become "suspicious of such suspiciousness" (DP 106). But this kind of critical practice is essential to much of his earlier work—as is only confirmed by this apparent recantation.

31. *In the Heart of the Country* offers a number of ironic five-finger exercises in many of the varieties of landscape poetry Coetzee discusses in his critical volume. It even presents a grotesque enactment of one of these: the strange scenes at the end of the novel, where Magda tries to spell out her enigmatic messages in painted stones for the benefit of mysterious Spaniards who seem to pass overhead in airplanes, are legible as her literalization of the romantic notion that to represent Africa one needs to speak a language that is indigenous to and at one with the land. Magda's signifiers are literally and absurdly part of the land. In an interview with Attwell, Coetzee also discusses the fantasy of a putatively natural congruence of language and land (DP 377).

32. There is much evidence in support here: Dick Penner uses as an epigraph for his book a remark that Coetzee made at a writers' workshop in Kentucky in 1984: "In the kind of game that I am talking about, you can change the rules if you are good enough. You can change the rules for everybody if you are good enough. You can change the game." See *Countries of the Mind: The Fiction of J. M. Coetzee* (Westport, Conn.: Greenwood Press, 1989). In *Doubling the Point* David Attwell describes one of the presuppositions on which Coetzee's fiction is based in a similar way: "If authority is ultimately a function of power, then it ought to be possible, through the rediscovery of fiction's capacity to reconfigure the rules of discourse, to find a position outside current power relations from which to speak. This is the sense in which Coetzee speaks . . . of the imperative to 'imagine the unimaginable'" (DP 11).

33. Attwell, "The Problem of History," 94, and DP 12.

34. Coetzee's affinity with Adorno seems all the more striking if one considers that these remarks assume that we have become accustomed to the kind of modern music Adorno favored: Coetzee's example is the "substantial silence structured by tracings of sound" created by Webern (WW 81).

35. Strauss, "Coetzee's Idylls," 128.

36. The response of South African critics to *Life and Times of Michael K* suggests that Coetzee's cautiousness with regard to what can be said in the present is well founded. In an essay on South African fiction in the 1980s, Stephen Clingman has dismissively noted that Coetzee seems to leave us, by the end of *Michael K* with the moral learned by Candide: *Il faut cultiver notre jardin*. "Is Coetzee simply returning us to this Voltairean dictum without any sense of irony?" he asks with ironic incredulity. The sense of scandal implicit in Clingman's question is of course shaped by the immediate connection of the idea of the cultivation of the garden with an individualistic escape—from "what would normally count as political." But it seems to me that Coetzee wants us to question this kind of antipastoral automatism: we should at least be allowed to ask why an interest in the pastoral should no longer appear possible, and why the values traditionally associated with the pastoral (Raymond Williams cited among these the idea of a natural way of life: of peace, innocence, and simple virtue) should no longer, apparently, be desired. See Clingman, "Revolution and Reality: South African Fiction in the 1980s," in Trump, *Rendering Things Visible*, 48.

37. The argument about *Disgrace* and global homogenization is made by Derek Attridge in "Age of Bronze, State of Grace: Music and Dogs in Coetzee's *Disgrace*," *Novel* 34 (2001): 98–121.

38. Zoë Wicomb, "Translations in the Yard of Africa," *Journal of Literary Studies* 18 (2002): 209–223. From this perspective, the perfective form of the verb (the grammatical construct Coetzee is most concerned with in the novel) represents something to

be desired: an arrival at the "target language/culture" or "the site where the original is effaced and the time system of a new language takes over" (210, 215), as well as the completed process of "crossing over to democracy" (222). In Wicomb's grim reading, where plot and grammar seem to become figures for each other, the novel's lack of a politically satisfactory closure, as well as Lurie's ineffectual brooding on the perfective, are taken as signs that the "progressive transition has come to a stuttering halt" (222). Mark Sanders's reading of the novel, by contrast, suggests that "grammar will, in the end, trump narrative" and any simplistic idea of history and temporality. In Coetzee's avoidance of the certainties of the perfective, Sanders sees an open-endedness that the utilitarian moral economy of present-day South Africa would deny. A possibility of grace (which cannot fully be thematized or expressed in the plot) thus inheres for him in the novel's textual fabric and in its very lack of closure. See Sanders, "Disgrace," *Interventions* 4 (2002): 372.

39. In *Boyhood*, the young John is embarrassed by the simultaneous objectification and elevation implicit in a servant addressing him as "die kleinbaas" ("the little master") (B 82), just as the fictional Magda is confounded by being addressed as "die Mies" ("the mistress") (HC 30). At stake in John's horror of this grammatical form is a stubborn resistance to his possible interpellation into the alternative subject positions of either mastery or docile servility that the language seems to him to impose on its users.

40. For a fuller discussion of the linguistic aspects of the novel, see my essay "*Disgrace* and the South African Pastoral," *Contemporary Literature* 44 (Summer 2003): 199–224.

41. Wicomb, "Translation," 216.

42. It is interesting, especially considering Zoë Wicomb's reading of *Disgrace*, to note that Coetzee defines "white writing" as a state of imperfect translation: "it is generated by the concerns of people no longer European, not yet African" (WW 11).

43. For a more detailed reading of this phrase, which alludes to the final act of Goethe's *Faust* and the possibility of religious redemption, see my essay "*Disgrace* and the South African Pastoral," 217–219.

44. Ampie Coetzee, "My Birthright Gives Me a Servitude on This Land: The Farm Novel within the Discourse on Land," *Journal of Literary Studies* 12: 1 and 2 (1996): 133.

45. I find Attridge's discussion of singularity in his essay on *The Master of Petersburg* helpful in explicating this scene, especially the quotation from Derrida's book *The Gift of Death* that he brings into focus: "I am responsible to the other as other, I answer to him and I answer for what I do before him. But of course, what binds me thus in my singularity to the absolute singularity of the other, immediately propels me into the space or risk of absolute sacrifice. There are also others, an infinite number of them, the innumerable generality of others to whom I should be bound by the same responsibility, a general and universal responsibility (what Kierkegaard calls the ethical order). I cannot respond to the call, the request, the obligation, or even the love of another without sacrificing the other other, the other others." See Attridge, "Expecting the Unexpected in Coetzee's *Master of Petersburg* and Derrida's Recent Writings," in *Applying—To Derrida*, ed. John Brannigan, Ruth Robbins, and Julian Wolfreys (London: Macmillan, 1996), 30.

Chapter 2

1. Among the few critics who have emphasized the metafictional character of Gordimer's work is Dominic Head, *Nadine Gordimer* (Cambridge, England: Cambridge University Press, 1994), chap. 5; Johan U. Jacobs also addresses Gordimer's narrative self-reflexivity and connects it to the recurrent images of mirrors in her work; "Finding a Safe House of

Fiction in Nadine Gordimer's *Jump and Other Stories*," in *Telling Stories: Postcolonial Short Fiction in English*, ed. Jacqueline Bardolph (Amsterdam: Rodopi, 2001), 204.

2. Louis Althusser, "Ideology and Ideological State Apparatuses (Notes towards an Investigation)," in *Lenin and Philosophy and Other Essays*, trans. Ben Brewster (New York: Monthly Review, 1971), 127–186.

3. In addition to the first chapter of *The Lying Days*, from which I quote here, see also Gordimer's autobiographical essay "What Being a South African Means to Me," *South African Outlook* 107 (July 1977): 88, and several of her interviews, including those with Studs Terkel (1962) and with E. G. Burrows (1970), in *Conversations with Nadine Gordimer*, ed. Nancy Topping Bazin and Marilyn Dallman Seymour (Jackson: University Press of Mississippi, 1990), 14–15 and 49.

4. John Western, *Outcast Cape Town* (Minneapolis: University of Minnesota Press, 1981), 3.

5. See Jacobs, "Finding a Safe House," 204, and "A New Nation in Africa: Homecoming in Nadine Gordimer's *None to Accompany Me*, in Winnifred Bogaards, *Literature of Region and Nation: Proceedings of the Sixth International Literature of Region and Nation Conference* (Saint John, New Brunswick, Canada: Social Sciences and Humanities Research Council of Canada, 1998), 333. See Head, *Nadine Gordimer*, 26–32, and for a retrospective formulation, "Gordimer's *None to Accompany Me*: Revision and Interregnum," where he asserts—quite rightly, in my view—that one of Gordimer's major preoccupations, beginning with her first novel, has been "to examine the control of space (both rural and urban) as an index of repression . . . and as an index of political resistance." *Research in African Literatures* 26 (Winter 1995): 47.

6. Homi K. Bhabha, "The World and the Home," *Social Text* 31–32 (1992): 145. See also chap. 1 of *The Location of Culture* (New York: Routledge, 1994), 1–18.

7. I am thinking here especially of John Cooke, *The Novels of Nadine Gordimer: Private Lives/Public Landscapes* (Baton Rouge: Louisiana State University Press, 1985), and Kathrin Wagner, *Rereading Nadine Gordimer* (Bloomington: Indiana University Press, 1994), 166–216. Cooke structures his book in terms of a movement from detachment ("landscapes as outward signs") to identification ("landscapes inhabited in the imagination"), the latter phrase expressing for him a linkage between "private lives" and "public landscapes." Though his study offers many meticulous close readings, it seems to me that the stable opposition between public and private, between character and landscape that is Cooke's starting point needs to be problematized. (If character, or subjectivity, is determined by place, it is, in a sense, always already public.) So, too, does the rather romantic, untheorized conception of "landscape's power" (165)—of the "veld" as a kind of African sublime—that becomes increasingly important in the latter part of his book. Wagner's reading has a theoretical advantage over Cooke's, in that she fully recognizes the ideological and historical character of the idea of landscape. But, unfortunately, this recognition produces in her work a rather ungenerous hermeneutics of suspicion: Gordimer's simple insistence that Africa belongs to black people is seen as "a late version of the old stereotype of the exotic," and her commitment to a new South Africa is seen as an inversion of "the old colonial trope of 'going native'" (215). Moreover, Wagner's tendency to equate the idea of "place" with "landscape" leads her to ignore the rather minute examination of sociospatial relations one finds in a novel like *July's People*. She thus asserts (incorrectly, it seems to me) that an interest in "place" survives in the later novels only in attenuated fashion (214).

8. It is worth bearing in mind here Homi Bhabha's early difficulties in accounting for a novel like V. S. Naipaul's *A House for Mr. Biswas* in terms of the traditions of Anglo-American criticism of the liberal novel: "The sovereignty of the concept of character, grounded as it is in the aesthetic discourse of cultural authenticity and the practical ethics of individual

freedom, bore little resemblance to the overdetermined, unaccommodated postcolonial figure of Mr. Biswas" ("The World and the Home," 142). My suggestion in this chapter is that, despite her ties to the novelistic tradition of E. M. Forster and the like, Gordimer becomes increasingly "postcolonial" in the sense Bhabha suggests here.

9. Stephen Clingman, *The Novels of Nadine Gordimer: History from the Inside*, 2nd ed. (Amherst: University of Massachusetts Press, 1992), especially chap. 1.

10. Irene Gorak, "Libertine Pastoral: Nadine Gordimer's *The Conservationist*," *Novel* (1992): 242.

11. This is a story that some critics have regarded as establishing the narrative and thematic formula for much of Gordimer's work. See Clingman, *The Novels of Nadine Gordimer*, 210–212; Cooke, *The Novels of Nadine Gordimer*, 128–129; Abdul R. JanMohamed, *Manichean Aesthetics: The Politics of Literature in Colonial Africa* (Amherst: University of Massachusetts Press, 1983), 87–88.

12. Interview with Jill Fullerton-Smith (1988), in Bazin and Seymour, *Conversations with Nadine Gordimer*, 303.

13. For various formulations of the idea, see Jameson, *Postmodernism, or The Cultural Logic of Late Capitalism* (Durham, N.C.: Duke University Press, 1990), especially 51–54; "Marxism and Postmodernism," *New Left Review* no. 176 (1989): 44–45; "Cognitive Mapping," in *Marxism and the Interpretation of Culture*, ed. Cary Nelson and Larry Grossberg (Urbana: University of Illinois Press, 1988), 347–360.

14. The Eurocentric character of Jameson's thought, which is evident even when he theorizes the work of what he calls "Third World" writers, has evoked strong protest on the part of postcolonial critics. See his essay "Third World Literature in the Era of Multinational Capitalism," *Social Text* 15 (Fall 1986): 65–88, and Aijaz Ahmad's impassioned response, "Jameson's Rhetoric of Otherness and the 'National Allegory,'" *Social Text* 17 (Fall 1987): 3–25. But since my immediate purpose is to evoke the racist epistemology constructed by apartheid, its Eurocentric bias is precisely what makes Jameson's general conception so applicable.

15. Jameson, "Modernism and Imperialism," in *Nationalism, Colonialism and Literature: A Field Day Pamphlet*, no. 14 (Lawrence Hill, Derry, England: Field Day Theater Company, 1988), 11.

16. Jameson, "Cognitive Mapping," 349–350.

17. One might certainly argue that Jameson exaggerates the extent to which the otherness of colonial life and the facts of colonial exploitation are unconscious in European modernism in the same way, perhaps, that the disappearance of "Nature" and the "Third World" is exaggerated in his work on postmodernism. Massively suggestive though it always is, Jameson's work is often vulnerable to J. M. Coetzee's observation that a "demystifying criticism privileges mystifications" (DP 106).

18. Lars Engle, "The Political Uncanny: The Novels of Nadine Gordimer," *Yale Journal of Criticism* 2 (1989): 101–128.

19. Jameson in fact allows for the possibility that his hypotheses about the relationship between modernism and the representational dilemmas of the imperial world system could be "verified" by thinking through their applications in the contexts of certain "experimental variations": for instance, in circumstances where colonial and metropolitan conditions simultaneously apply. The "variation" he has in mind is James Joyce's Ireland, but I would suggest that the experiential world of the privileged South African (especially from 1948 to 1976) might offer another such variation. A difference one might immediately observe, then, is that Gordimer's work does not merely symptomatically register but in fact thematizes the epistemological and geographical difficulties Jameson describes. See Jameson, "Modernism and Imperialism," 19.

20. Interview with Diana Cooper-Clark (1983), in Bazin and Seymour, *Conversations with Nadine Gordimer*, 218.

21. Ibid., 223–224.

22. Interview with John Barkham (1962), in Bazin and Seymour, *Conversations with Nadine Gordimer*, 9.

23. In a 1954 autobiographical essay, Gordimer describes the house in which she grew up in almost identical terms: "Ours was a bungalow-type house with two bow windows and a corrugated-iron roof, like almost all the other houses that were built in the Witwatersrand gold-mining towns during the twenties and early thirties." "A South African Childhood: Allusions in a Landscape," *New Yorker*, 16 October 1954, 114.

24. Engle sees Verwoerd's moralistic political rhetoric, in particular, as a way of fictionalizing racial domination as charitable and in the best interest of all parties. In apartheid, Engle argues, the "'*Heimlichkeit*' of an enclosure of persons of like background was appropriated . . . in the most extreme form, as totalizing racial discrimination, and has thus been rendered '*unheimlich*.'" Though in Engle's essay the idea of the home is used figuratively as a metaphor of the mind and, more generally, of dominant interpretive paradigms, the relevance of his work to the spatial politics of South African literature is obvious. See Engle, "The Political Uncanny," 101–105, 110–116.

25. Gordimer, "What Being a South African Means to Me," 88.

26. See Althusser, "Ideology and Ideological State Apparatuses," 127–186.

27. See, for example, Cooke, *The Novels of Nadine Gordimer*, 48; and Clingman, *The Novels of Nadine Gordimer*, 41.

28. This is true also of the description I quoted from "The Termitary." The "house face" with the "bow-window eyes" and the "front-door mouth," though it might at first not seem so obviously gendered, eventually becomes connected with the face of the narrator's mother: the *genius loci* and, ultimately, the prisoner of the family home.

29. Judie Newman, *Nadine Gordimer* (New York: Routledge, 1988), 17–21. Head's reading of the novel also suggests that it offers a critique of the conventional *Bildungsroman*. See *Nadine Gordimer*, 35–36, 41, 45–46.

30. Robin Visel, "Othering the Self: Nadine Gordimer's Colonial Heroines," *Ariel* 19 (1988): 37.

31. Michel Foucault, "Of Other Spaces," *Diacritics* 16 (Spring 1986): 24–25. Head also uses this notion with regard to Gordimer's work, but argues that the idea is present only embryonically in *The Lying Days* (*Nadine Gordimer*, 29–32, 43).

32. Engle, "The Political Uncanny," 112.

33. Several of the stories in this collection are relevant to the question of domestic and interpretative enclosures, and to the thematics of the political uncanny. In addition to "The Life of the Imagination," there is also "An Intruder" (first published as "Out of the Walls"), "Abroad," "Inkalamu's Place," "Open House," and "No Place Like."

34. Maurice Blanchot defines everyday life, the time/space where social relations are reproduced, in exactly these terms: "Nothing happens: this is the everyday." For Blanchot there is in this assertion something of the doubleness one associates with the uncanny: the disappointment with "nothing," the recognition of boredom, implicitly carries the hope of discovering that, in fact, "something essential might be allowed to happen." "Everyday Speech," *Yale French Studies* 73 (1987): 15.

35. This passage evokes intertextual resonances that further satirize its confident and banal assertions. There is, for instance, an ironic allusion to the house of Lionel Burger, the archrevolutionary from *Burger's Daughter*: an anomalous space (and marked as such by the reiterated phrase "in that house"), where the political is as ordinary as breakfast cornflakes and where a little boy does, in fact, drown in the swimming pool. The idea of the "abso-

lutely trustworthy" servant has already been exploded by the complicated figure of July in *July's People*: a man who, as I will show, cannot be fully known in a context like the one "Once Upon a Time" describes.

36. Tony Pinkney has argued that one can chart in the work of current critical theorists and geographers two divergent modes of rethinking social space. It is conceptualized, first, as an ideological structure to be critiqued, and second, as a utopian rupture of spatial and social confines. In the first category one might place such critics as Fredric Jameson, Edward Soja, and David Harvey, while in the second category one might place Lefebvre, the Situationists, Kristen Ross's work on the spatial practices of the Paris Commune, and so forth. The distinction, Pinkney suggests, corresponds to what Ernst Bloch has termed the warm and cold currents of Marxism. Both currents can, I think, be distinguished in Gordimer's work. See Pinkney, "Space: The Final Frontier," *Notes from Nowhere* 8 (autumn 1990): 24.

37. See, for example, Rosemarie Bodenheimer, "The Interregnum of Ownership in *July's People*," in *The Later Fiction of Nadine Gordimer* (New York: St. Martin's Press, 1993), 108; and Newman, *Nadine Gordimer*, 85. Dominic Head's discussion of the novel is focused mainly on the idea of the construction of identity; but he does make some fine observations regarding the way this matter is implicated in the control of space (*Nadine Gordimer*, 133–134).

38. Defamiliarization provides, as Jameson puts it, "that distance from immediacy which is at length characterized as historical perspective" (*Postmodernism*, 284).

39. Walter Benjamin, "N [Theoretics of Knowledge; Theory of Progress]," trans. Leigh Hafrey and Richard Sieburth, *Philosophical Forum* 15 (Fall–Winter 1983–84): 21.

40. See Viktor Shklovsky, "Art as Technique," in *Russian Formalist Criticism*, ed. T. Lemon (Lincoln: University of Nebraska Press, 1984), 12–15. It is also interesting to recall, considering the concerns of this chapter, that Shklovsky's chief example of those habits that require defamiliarization is taken from Tolstoy's comments about one's daily movements in one's home: "I was cleaning a room, and meandering about, approached the divan and couldn't remember whether or not I had dusted it. Since these movements are habitual and unconscious, I could not remember and felt that it was impossible to remember—so that if I had dusted it and forgot—that is, had acted unconsciously, then it was the same as if I had not."

41. Even the editorial form of the first person plural pronoun comes to be marked in the novel by scare quotes: "Yet how was that absolute nature of intimate relationships arrived at? Who decided? 'We' (Maureen sometimes harked back) understand the sacred power and rights of sexual love as formulated in master bedrooms, and motels with false names in the register" (JP 65).

42. Sheila Roberts, in an article exploring what she sees as the gothic devices in the novel, emphasizes the "unhomeliness" of the hut in which the Smales family is so uncomfortably accommodated. She cites, as an example, the following description: "a stamped mud and dung floor, above her, cobwebs stringy with dirt dangling from the rough wattle steeple that supported the frayed gray thatch. Stalks of light poked through. A rim of shady light where the mud walls did not meet the eaves; nests glued there of a brighter-coloured mud— wasps or bats" (JP 2). Roberts's point is well taken, but I am not convinced that Gordimer's sense of the uncanny is usefully thought of in terms of the gothic: Engle's application of the idea of the uncanny seems more productive. "Sites of Paranoia and Taboo: Lessing's *The Grass Is Singing* and Gordimer's *July's People*," *Research in African Literatures* (1994): 80.

43. On mirrors as heterotopic, see Jacobs, "Finding a Safe House of Fiction," 204.

44. In a good close reading of this passage, Cooke has also noted its emphasis on what is "not seen." But I would go further than Cooke does and suggest that once the element

of the visual is lost, the term "landscape," with its origins firmly in the tradition of the pictorial, also loses its usefulness (*Novels of Nadine Gordimer*, 167). I find it curious, then, that Wagner should complain that the landscape in *July's People* has become "annexed . . . to the ideological programme" of the novel (*Rereading Nadine Gordimer*, 214). The strength of *July's People* lies precisely in the seriousness with which it tries to imagine and represent a *transitional* ideological position—a problematic "imaginary relation to the real"—at the moment of a fundamental shift in power, as is evident in descriptive passages such as the one I have cited.

45. Bodenheimer, "Interregnum," 112.

46. It is interesting, however, that Bodenheimer should call the novel "a materialist fable." Ibid., 108.

47. Bhabha, "The World and the Home," 143, 150. See also chap. 1 of *The Location of Culture*.

48. On the "political sublime," see Engle, "The Political Uncanny," 108–110.

49. Wagner, for example, has argued that the mass funeral scene in this novel "cannot escape an element of the banal and the clichéd," and that Gordimer here recapitulates some of the timeworn themes of the antiapartheid struggle (*Rereading Nadine Gordimer*, 223).

50. Head, "Revision and Interregnum," 47.

51. Marlene van Niekerk, "Take Your Body Where It Has Never Been Before," in *Blank _____: Architecture, Apartheid, and After,* ed. Hilton Judin and Ivan Vladislavić (Cape Town: David Phillips, 1999), 321–329.

52. Lindsay Bremner, "Crime and the Emerging Landscape of Post-Apartheid Johannesburg," in Judin and Vladislavić, *Blank _____*, 58. The seedy and variegated cosmopolitanism of the emerging city seems to have taken Gordimer by surprise, to judge by a 1997 interview with Karen Lazar. Though she again affirms in her responses the importance of a hybrid public space and public visibility, she also expresses her amazement at its international character. "A year ago," she declares, "who would have thought that we would have the problem of illegal immigration which we now have—that we'd have Koreans selling watches in the streets, Zaireans talking French in the streets. Who would have thought this? It's something we couldn't possibly have imagined." "'A Feeling of Realistic Optimism': An Interview with Nadine Gordimer," *Salmagundi* 113 (Winter 1997): 163.

53. Bremner, "Crime," 62.

54. Ibid., 59.

55. Ibid., 62.

56. Ibid.

57. See especially Ivan Vladislavić, *The Exploded View* (Johannesburg: Ravan, 2004).

58. Jacobs sees the novel's denouement as marking a "narrative tenancy" on Gordimer's part: a metafictional recognition that her old novelistic forms and strategies may no longer be serviceable ("A New Nation in Africa," 338).

Chapter 3

1. For an excellent postapartheid account of this master narrative about land, see Cherryl Walker, "Relocating Restitution," *Transformation* 44 (2000): 1–16. Walker, who served as a researcher for the Surplus People's Project in the 1980s and later as a land rights commissioner in Kwazulu-Natal, presents a useful synopsis of the key elements of this narrative, as well as a measured assessment of its contemporary implications: "The narrative," she insists, "is compelling in its dramatic authenticity and authoritative in its moral and political power. As a political fable it worked extremely well in mobilizing opposition

to apartheid both at home and abroad" (2). But she also analyzes, in thoughtful detail, the various respects in which this broad narrative, which organizes a multiplicity of individual stories of suffering and loss, has proven too simplistic to be of much help with the nitty-gritty task of delivering on the thousands of land claims with which the new democratic government was presented during the 1990s. I will return to these sobering considerations at the end of this chapter.

2. The "dynamic third decade" was so termed by Minister M. C. Botha. Cited in Cosmas Desmond, O.F.M., *The Discarded People: An Account of African Resettlement in South Africa* (Harmondsworth, Middlesex, England: Penguin, 1971), 25.

3. Cited in Laurine Platzky and Cherryl Walker, *The Surplus People: Forced Removals in South Africa* (Johannesburg: Ravan Press, 1985), 64.

4. Ibid., 79.

5. Cited in Desmond, *The Discarded People*, 18.

6. Walker, "Relocating Restitution," 10.

7. Rob Nixon cites, as an example of apartheid's misleading and self-justificatory anticolonial rhetoric, the words of G. F. van L. Froneman, chairman of the Bantu Affairs Commission. Speaking in 1968, Froneman declared that "separate development" was "not a policy of discrimination on the ground of race or colour, but a policy of differentiation on the ground of nationhood . . . granting to each self-determination within the borders of their homelands." See *Homelands, Harlem, and Hollywood: South African Culture and the World Beyond* (New York: Routledge, 1994), 240. This justificatory rhetoric of national "self-determination" also informed the Nationalists' mythic historiography: Afrikaner historians typically interpreted the Great Trek (the nineteenth-century expansion of white settlers into the interior of Southern Africa) as the first indigenous anticolonial movement on the African continent.

8. Desmond, *The Discarded People*, 21.

9. John Dugard, "Denationalization: Apartheid's Ultimate Plan," *Africa Report* (July–August 1983), cited in Platzky and Walker, *The Surplus People*, 16.

10. Solomon Tshekisho Plaatje, *Native Life in South Africa*, ed. Brian Willan (Harlow, Essex, England: Longman, 1987), 7.

11. Cited in Nixon, *Homelands, Harlem and Hollywood*, 240.

12. Following De Certeau, I am using the term "urbanistic" here in a somewhat metaphorical sense; however, my assertion has literal validity as well. The contributors to David M. Smith's collection *The Apartheid City and Beyond: Urbanization and Social Change in South Africa* (London: Routledge, 1992) take it as axiomatic that apartheid, as legislated racial separation, was inextricably bound up with urbanization. Moreover, as Alan Mabin observes, country and city are inseparable in the South African context: behind almost every form of urbanization lies a brutal history of rural dispossession. See his "Dispossession, Exploitation and Struggle: An Historical Overview of South African Urbanization," in Smith, *The Apartheid City and Beyond*, 15–17 and 22.

13. Michel de Certeau, *The Practice of Everyday Life* (Berkeley: University of California Press, 1984), 94–96; see also 34–39, on the idea of "strategy."

14. See Elaine Unterhalter, *Forced Removals: The Division, Segregation and Control of the People of South Africa* (London: International Defense and Aid Fund, 1987), 93.

15. It is important to note, however, that on some freehold farms, such as Cremin, not far from Roosboom, an influx of tenants had begun to intensify residential settlement and to cause a decline in agricultural output long before the community's forced removal. I mention this to qualify somewhat the idea that colonialism created a clean rupture in idyllic ways: rural life in South Africa must always be understood in relation to broader economic formations and especially to the significant but always incomplete proletarianiza-

tion of the black population during the nineteenth and twentieth centuries. For more on Cremin, see Cherryl Walker, "'We Are Consoled': Reconstructing Cremin," *South African Historical Journal* 51(2004): 199–223.

16. This continued to be the case in the 1990s, when many victims were finally able to petition the ANC government's Land Claims office for the restitution of their property. Cherryl Walker refers, for example, to the story of a woman who wished, thirty years after the fact, to find redress for a small but clearly unassuaged loss: "When we had to leave Umkumbane I lost my sewing machine and my cat for which I was not compensated" ("Relocating Restitution," 3). Members of the Cremin community, likewise, vividly recalled the emotions they experienced when their community was removed twenty-five years earlier: "To see your house being demolished in a minute—you feel like cracking yourself." Cited in Cherryl Walker, "'We Are Consoled': Reconstructing Cremin," 209.

17. Cited in Desmond, *The Discarded People*, 45.

18. Cited in Platzky and Walker, *The Surplus People*, 51.

19. Speech reported in the Johannesburg *Star*, 21 November 1969; cited in Desmond, *The Discarded People*, 18.

20. One might argue that in this respect the Nationalist government was not so different from other colonial regimes. As Raymond Williams has observed, the English "idealization of the peasant was not extended, when it might have mattered, to the peasants, the plantation-workers, and the coolies of colonized societies." See *The Country and the City* (New York: Oxford University Press, 1973), 286.

21. The quoted words are those of the chairman of the Elandslaagte Farmers' Association in northern Natal, at a meeting in 1954. Cited in Platsky and Walker, *The Surplus People*, 109.

22. Boningkosi Ndlovu Bafanyana, "Viva Pen of Culture!" (1989), cited and discussed in David Maughan Brown, "'An Unfinished Mourning': Echo Poems from Pietermaritzburg," in *On Shifting Sands: New Art and Literature from South Africa*, ed. Kirsten Holst Petersen and Anna Rutherford (Portsmouth, N.H.: Heinemann, 1992), 53–55.

23. De Certeau, *The Practice of Everyday Life*, 95, 34.

24. Achille Mbembe remarks not only on the literal waste evident in a landscape of mine dumps, and the extravagant expenditure evident in the luxurious lifestyles of the rich, but also on the cruel waste of black people, who were both indispensable and expendable under apartheid. "Because native life was seen as excessive and naturally doomed to self-destruction, it constituted a wealth that could be lavishly spent," Mbembe observes. See his essay "Aesthetics of Superfluity," *Public Culture* 16 (2004): 381.

25. Lars Engle, "The Political Uncanny: The Novels of Nadine Gordimer," *Yale Journal of Criticism* 2 (1989): 101–125. "We have been thrown away" is a phrase that Father Desmond heard time and time again as he visited the victims of forced removals. See *The Discarded People*, 18. I have in mind here, however, the words of Mr. Makodi, the leader of the Machabestad community, which was eventually removed to Rooigrond in Bophuthatswana. His statement is strikingly relevant, as my reading in this chapter will imply, to Gordimer's concerns in *The Conservationist*: "We have been thrown away. We feel very much grieved. When I talk of our land I mean the land of our forefathers, the land where our forefathers' graves are. I would like to pose the question: Who are the foreigners? I can say that my people were there to accept the foreigners when they came. It is so painful that those people are the ones who are now telling us to go. We grieve for our forefather's graves which have been ploughed over." Cited in Platzky and Walker, *The Surplus People*, 79.

26. In a 1982 interview, Gordimer comments on the problem of white South Africans' claim to the land, which, as in Mehring's case, is based essentially on "a piece of paper—a deed of sale." "And what is a deed of sale," she asks, "when people have first of all taken

a country by conquest? Tenure is a very interesting concept, morally speaking. When you come to think of it, what is tenure? What is 'legal' tenure? Blacks take the land for granted, it's simply there. It's theirs, although they've been conquered; they were always there. They don't have this necessity to say, 'Well I love this land because it's beautiful.'" In Nancy Topping Bazin and Marilyn Dallman Seymour, eds., *Conversations with Nadine Gordimer* (Jackson: University Press of Mississippi, 1990), 188.

27. Desmond, *The Discarded People*, xvii.

28. Ibid., xv–xvi.

29. Gordimer refers explicitly to Britain and the United States, countries that have "profited, by long tradition, from the exploitation of South Africa's natural resources and underpaid labor." She emphasizes, in a quotation from Sartre, the moral connection between privileged whites (both in South Africa and in these countries) and the victims of resettlement: "It is enough that they show us what we have made of them for us to realize what we have made of ourselves" (Desmond, *The Discarded People*, xvi). The emphasis on self-knowledge we see here is also a significant idea in *The Conservationist*: Mehring's problem, ultimately, is that he refuses to know himself.

30. "Graphism," Mbembe explains, "consisted foremost in tracing marks on the body and on the territory. It also entailed various acts of coding and inscription, and, above all, legislative efforts to define the various races and enforce the separate use, occupation, and ownership of critical resources. It was enacted through small gestures of everyday life, such as the public contexts of walking, or more generally, pass laws. . . . Territorial segmentation was a key form of the state's inscription of power onto the landscape. But the main site of this inscription was the black body itself." All of these aspects of graphism—of apartheid's "tattooed desert"—are relevant to my reading of Gordimer's novel. See Mbembe, "Aesthetics of Superfluity," 390.

31. A significant development in Gordimer's work is marked by the fact that in *The Conservationist* the buried body of the black man is no longer associated with the infernal shades of the classical and Christian traditions, as in *The Lying Days*, but with the Zulu ancestral spirits.

32. This correlation, as I argue in this chapter, is symbolically expressed in the novel and especially in the final scene. For Gordimer's comments on the "unitary South Africa," see, for example, the interviews with Nesta Wyn Ellis (1978) and Diana Loercher (1979), in Bazin and Seymour, *Conversations with Nadine Gordimer*, 88 and 100.

33. J. M. Coetzee, *Doubling the Point: Essays and Interviews* (Cambridge: Harvard University Press, 1992), 61. The pastoral, Coetzee notes, "defines and isolates a space in which whatever cannot be achieved in the wider world (particularly the city) can be achieved."

34. *The Conservationist* is not the first novel about a Southern African farm to recall *The Waste Land*. Doris Lessing's novel *The Grass Is Singing*, which has always seemed to me to be almost as important to the pastoral tradition in South Africa as Schreiner's *Story of an African Farm*, takes both its title and its epigraph from the poem's final section, "What the Thunder Said." Gordimer's use of Eliot is far more implicit, and far more thoroughly assimilated. Michael Thorpe has also, albeit only in passing, connected *The Waste Land* and *The Conservationist*. See "The Motif of the Ancestor in *The Conservationist*," in *Critical Essays on Nadine Gordimer*, ed. Rowland Smith (Boston: G. K. Hall, 1990), 117.

35. Stephen Clingman makes a similar point with regard to the novel's oblique, prophetic character. See *The Novels of Nadine Gordimer: History from the Inside* (Amherst: University of Massachusetts Press, 1992), 163.

36. Abdul JanMohamed, *Manichean Aesthetics: The Politics of Literature in Colonial Africa* (Amherst: University of Massachusetts Press, 1983), 117. Consider also JanMohamed's dis-

tinctly Lukácsian complaint about "the imbalance between subjective and objective narratives" in the novel (124).

37. Irene Gorak, "Libertine Pastoral: Nadine Gordimer's *The Conservationist*," *Novel* 24 (1992): 251, 248. In contrast to the crude assimilation of Lukács's antimodernist stance we see in Gorak and JanMohamed, one might profitably consider Clingman's nuanced application of Lukácsian ideas to the novel. *The Conservationist*, Clingman argues, uses stream-of-consciousness techniques to signify a historically specific, rather than a universal, crisis of subjectivity. Mehring's pathological condition—as a modernist character of the sort Lukács would have disapproved of—is not shared by Gordimer or endorsed by the novel. See *The Novels of Nadine Gordimer*, 153–155.

38. Gorak, "Libertine Pastoral," 243, 241. Gorak's comments are grounded on the unexamined and hierarchical opposition between space and time—an opposition that (as we saw in chapter 1) has until recently dominated critical social theory. "Space," as Michel Foucault puts it, has been "treated as the dead, the fixed, the undialectical, the immobile," while time, on the contrary, has signified "richness, fecundity, life, dialectic." See his "Questions on Geography," in *Power/Knowledge: Selected Interviews and Other Writings, 1972–1977*, ed. Colin Gordon (New York: Pantheon, 1980), 70.

39. Interview with Diana Cooper-Clark (1983), in Bazin and Seymour, *Conversations with Nadine Gordimer*, 225.

40. De Certeau, *The Practice of Everyday Life*, 31–32.

41. Williams, *The Country and the City*, 296.

42. Though rather more pessimistic with regard to the power of the "overall structure," Gordimer's conception here has connections with De Certeau's discussion of the relations between landlord and tenant and between the architecture of a given construct and the way individuals may use it. See *The Practice of Everyday Life*, especially xii, 30–32.

43. Ibid., 30–39.

44. Ibid., 35–36.

45. Mehring's privileged urban experience stands in striking contrast to that of one of the black children from the farm, who manages one day to hitch a ride into Johannesburg in a manure hawker's cart. Unable to claim Mehring's privileged vantage, the child experiences a kind of urban shock after "seeing the buildings, enormous, jolting all round as if about to topple with the movement of the frightened horse and uneven axles in the traffic" (C 86).

46. Though Mehring's international travel and his Mercedes do not grant him absolute freedom, one must resist the urge to romanticize the "rootedness" of the black workers on the farm. In this respect as, in many others, Gordimer's insights into the relation between rural and urban areas jibe with those of Williams's *The Country and the City*. For instance, Williams excoriates T. S. Eliot's celebration of the settled character of rural communities as an idealization of the lack of mobility and economic options available to the rural poor. Such sentiments express, Williams argues, "an insolent indifference to most people's needs." "Settlement is indeed easy, is positively welcome, for those who can settle in a reasonable independence. For those who cannot . . . it can become a prison: a long disheartening and despair, under an imposed rigidity of conditions." See *The Country and the City*, 84–85.

47. Ibid., 284. For Williams, the structure of relations between the colonies (or former colonies) and the metropolitan powers reiterates the old structure of relations between country and city on a global scale. The idea of "development" functions in this vast new system as essentially an alibi for exploitation. It is interesting to note that Williams specifically mentions South Africa and the work of Ezekiel Mphahlele in his chapter on the new imperial metropolis to suggest that the issues he traces in his study, especially the uprooting of rural communities, have by no means been relegated to the past (286). For a discussion

of the idea of development in South Africa, see At Fischer, "Whose Development? The Politics of Development and the Development of Politics in South Africa," in *South African Keywords: The Uses and Abuses of Political Concepts*, ed. Emile Boonzaaier and John Sharp (Cape Town: David Philip, 1988), 122–135.

48. Gordimer's most obvious dig at the moral deficiency of an aestheticizing sensibility can be found in a passage describing Mehring's response to the sight of a baby who suffers from malnutrition: "Children going towards the compound have not greeted him. There's a baby being carried among them that has light yellow-reddish hair—very ugly. He doesn't remember ever seeing it before; God knows how many people move into that compound" (C 109).

49. Interview with Margaret Walters (1987), in Bazin and Seymour, *Conversations with Nadine Gordimer*, 287; interview with Hermione Lee (1986), in Bazin and Seymour, *Conversations with Nadine Gordimer*, 244–245.

50. Interview with Margaret Walters, 298. Gordimer's comments are worth citing in full: "South Africa has been a kind of exclusive club for white people. The beaches, the parks—they all belonged only to whites, which meant that they were tremendously underused. So now people throw up their hands and say, can you imagine how crowded, how dirty everything is going to be, because the whole population will be using what was a private domain. Well, the country club is closing down, because the whole country is going to belong to the people."

51. Roland Barthes, *Mythologies* (New York: Noonday Press, 1991), 142–145.

52. Mary Douglas, *Purity and Danger: An Analysis of Concepts of Pollution and Taboo* (New York: Praeger, 1966), introduction and chap. 7. The motifs of trespassing and trash also feature in the work of other South African writers, like Fugard and Coetzee.

53. Though he does not comment on this curious scene, Clingman has emphasized the importance of puns in his excellent chapter on *The Conservationist*: "Puns in *The Conservationist* (as in Freudian theory) refer to a 'subconscious' level of the surface text, and on this level Mehring's future fate is present beneath his slightest word" (*The Novels of Nadine Gordimer*, 158).

54. Ibid., 153–154.

55. See, for example, Clingman, *The Novels of Nadine Gordimer*, 162–163; and Judie Newman, *Nadine Gordimer* (London: Routledge, 1988), 55–57.

56. See, for example, Michael Wade, *Nadine Gordimer* (London: Evans, 1978), 220, and Clingman, *The Novels of Nadine Gordimer*, 139–140.

57. John Cooke, *The Novels of Nadine Gordimer: Private Lives/Public Landscapes* (Baton Rouge: Louisiana State University Press, 1985), 150. The scene in question is often misread. JanMohamed seems to think that Mehring dies or is attacked by thugs in this scene. Irene Gorak also (though she apparently has read Gordimer's impatient comments about those critics who think that Mehring has died when in fact he makes a telephone call in the very last section of the novel) asserts that "to all intents and purposes Mehring dies, the victim of an interracial attack." Also troubling in this reading is the identification of the hitchhiker in stereotypical terms as a "fast-talking colored." In fact there is no evidence that this racial identification is anything other than Mehring's paranoid projection. See JanMohamed, *Manichean Aesthetics*, 123–124; Gorak, "Libertine Pastoral," 251.

58. Engle, "The Political Uncanny," 118.

59. I see Mehring's fate as parallel to that of the supposedly artistic woman in the roughly contemporaneous story "The Life of the Imagination" who ends up terrified, just like any other white suburban housewife, that *tsotsis* will break into her home and murder her in her bed.

60. Gorak, "Libertine Pastoral," 56 and throughout.

61. Kathrin Wagner makes a similar point in her chapter "Landscape Iconography," in *Rereading Nadine Gordimer* (Bloomington: Indiana University Press, 1994). "The body discovered in the pasture," she observes, "is that of a township man, a stranger to the workers on the farm, but, as we have seen, their acceptance of their brotherhood with and responsibility towards this anonymous figure significantly elides the theoretical gap between the rural and urban black experience, and attests to their common brotherhood in oppression" (209).

62. Interview with Jannika Hurwitt (1979 and 1980), in Bazin and Seymour, *Conversations with Nadine Gordimer*, 150.

63. Walker's research has shown that the Roosboom community's storybook return was not without difficulties: relationships between former tenants and former owners have proven problematic, thus demonstrating the extent to which the broad categories of black and white obscure more nuanced class stratifications, and that land reform policies—like many other postapartheid improvements—have often served the interests of a relatively privileged class.

64. The creators of the volume are well aware that they are capturing a special moment, one that might neither last nor be predictive of a new trend but nevertheless requires documentation. "History," they observe, "does not often witness such intense celebration of the land—a sense of release possibly only equaled by those rare seasons when our southern droughts are broken, if only temporarily." See Marlene Winberg, Paul Weinberg, and Achmat Dangor, *Back to the Land* (Johannesburg: Porcupine Press, 1996), 6.

65. Seremane is cited in George Packer, "Politics in Apartheid's Shadow," *Vogue* (June 1995): 116.

66. In her careful analysis of the White Paper's historical intervention and its rhetoric, Jennifer Wenzel observes further that while "racial or ethnic terms are used throughout . . . to describe past history," "class-inflected terms like 'disadvantaged,' 'landless,' 'landowner,' or 'commercial farmer' are used to describe the present and look towards the future. The language of this document performs the process of deracialization that it aims to realize in land policy." Of course, narrative, symbolic, and rhetorical changes are easier to create than changes on the ground. See Wenzel, "The Pastoral Promise and the Political Imperative: The *Plaasroman* Tradition in an Era of Land Reform," *Modern Fiction Studies* 46 (Spring 2000): 98.

67. The most compelling reason such a reversal of the percentages is unlikely lies in the geographical realities of South Africa's climate and territory. Only 12 percent of the country's land is arable, and only the eastern and southern coastlines are blessed with reasonable rainfall. Most of the arable land is already densely populated. The Northern Cape, the largest province by area and the most sparsely populated, might, as Walker notes, "appear on paper as a prime location for a major resettlement programme for black farmers—except that much of it is, officially, desert" (see "The Limits to Land Reform: Rethinking 'The Land Question,'" *Journal of Southern African Studies* 13 [December 2005]: 822). Walker's warning that scholars cannot repeat the old formulae like mantras is apt: "Memory, power, the politics of place, and identity are all themes that are relevant to a seriously engaged politics of land reform and to understanding the constraints and challenges enmeshed in that. But to be useful as analytical concepts, they have to be grounded, linked to actual places and projects, and not remain abstractions, floating like balloons over exotic landscape." See her "Relocating Restitution," 15.

68. Ibid., 10–11.

69. Ibid., 16.

70. The same ethic is articulated in Gordimer's story "Spoils," from the 1992 collection *Jump*. See my essay "The Final Safari: On Nature, Myth, and the Literature of the Emer-

gency," in *Writing South Africa: Recent Literature and Its Challenges*, ed. Derek Attridge and Rosemary Jolly (Cambridge, England: Cambridge University Press, 1998), 130.

71. Patrick Laurence's comment is apt: "Anyone appraising the efficacy of land reform in South Africa should heed the counsel of the African nationalist leader, Amilcar Cabral: 'claim no easy victories.'" See Laurence, "Struggle for Land: A Crucial New Chapter," *Focus* 28 (fourth quarter 2002): 6; available at the Web site of the Helen Suzman Foundation: www.hsf.org.za.

Chapter 4

1. Lars Engle, "The Novel without the Police," *Pretexts* 3 (1991): 116–117.

2. This is not to say that Gordimer and Coetzee have not come in for criticism too, or that Fugard's reputation with the theater-going public and with some academics is not extremely high. The most recent full-length study of Fugard's work, Albert Wertheim, *The Dramatic Art of Athol Fugard: From South Africa to the World* (Bloomington: Indiana University Press, 2000), is largely hagiographic. But there is also a significant body of work excoriating Fugard for the inadequacy of his liberal solutions to South Africa's political problems. See, for instance, Mshengu (Robert Kavanaugh), "Political Theater in South Africa and the Work of Athol Fugard," *Theater Research International* 7 (Spring 1982): 160–179; Hilary Seymour, "*Sizwe Bansi Is Dead*: A Study of Artistic Ambivalence," *Race and Class* 21 (1980): 273–289; and, from a later period, Nicholas Visser, "Drama and Politics in a State of Emergency: Athol Fugard's *My Children! My Africa!*" *Twentieth Century Literature* 39 (1993): 486–502, and Jean Colleran, "Athol Fugard and the Problematics of the Liberal Critique," *Modern Drama* 38 (1995): 389–407. In her magisterial study *The Drama of South Africa: Plays, Pageants and Publics since 1910* (London: Routledge, 1999), Loren Kruger is not hostile to Fugard, exactly, but she does tend to treat his drama as "literature," and therefore as being of less interest and importance than the work of more politicized theater practitioners in the process of radicalizing the institutions of theatre and creating an alternative public sphere. Black playwrights also tend to be dismissive: Zakes Mda, for one, distinguishes Fugard's work, which he categorizes as "Theater of Protest" appealing to guilty whites, from the work of black South African writers, which he categorizes as "Theater as Resistance" appealing to a mass audience. It should be said that these last distinctions are not entirely tenable, given the many fertile exchanges across racial boundaries. I am more inclined to agree with Michael Chapman, who describes both Fugard and Mda as originators of "black theater." See Chapman, *Southern African Literatures* (London: Longman, 1996), 360–365.

3. See, for example, Athol Fugard, "Recent Notebook Entries," *Twentieth Century Literature* 38 (Winter 1993): 530.

4. Address to architecture students at University of Port Elizabeth, cited in "Don't Forget the Past," *Eastern Province Herald*, 24 April 1992, 2.

5. See Colleran, "Athol Fugard and the Problematics of the Liberal Critique," Visser, "'Drama and Politics in a State of Emergency,'" and Myles Holloway, "*Playland*: Fugard's Liberalism," *UNISA English Studies* 31 (April 1993): 36–42, for persuasive critiques of these plays.

6. Athol Fugard, "Recent Notebook Entries," 528.

7. See Breyten Breytenbach, "Andersheid en Andersmaak: Oftewel die Afrikaner as Afrikaan (Berig gerig aan Frederick van Zyl Slabbert)," *Fragmente* 4 (1999): 26–44.

8. Athol Fugard, "On Henry David Thoreau's *Walden*," in *Text and Teaching: The Search for Human Excellence*, ed. Michael J. Collins and Francis J. Ambrosio (Washington: Georgetown University Press, 1991): 112–113.

9. Ibid., 120.

10. Fugard's interest in this passage also makes biographical sense: its theme of individual responsibility resonates with the challenges confronting a recovering alcoholic such as himself. In fact, he refers elsewhere in the address to the "massive renewal" that he had recently undergone. This "renewal" is reflected elsewhere in his work of the period, for example, in *A Place with the Pigs*, which Stephen Gray describes as "a gruelling atonement for years of addiction to booze." See Gray's "'Between Me and My Country': Fugard's *My Children! My Africa!* at the Market Theater, Johannesburg," *New Theatre Quarterly* 6 (1990): 25.

11. The problem with these assertions is evident when one juxtaposes them with a comment made by the playwright Maishe Maponja when asked how he felt about the response of white audiences to his work: "Yes, some whites come to my plays, to our kind of theatre, I'm not rejecting the whites. But then they go home, and the black servant brings the coffee in on a tray and goes out to her small room at the back and has her coffee there." The place of reception, both in the theatre and in the social spaces surrounding it, makes a difference to the larger meaning of drama. Maponja is cited in Dennis Walder, "South African Drama and Ideology: The Case of Athol Fugard," in *Altered State? Writing and South Africa*, ed. Elleke Boehmer, Laura Chrisman, and Kenneth Parker (Sydney: Dangaroo, 1994), 121.

12. Another such exercise was connected to the creation of *The Island*. Kani and Ntshona recount: "We did one exercise on the lawn, calling it a sacred ground. We explored its space, stood in the center, walked to the edge, and kept halving it until there was only room for the two of us." Cited in Mary Benson, "Keeping an Appointment with the Future: The Theater of Athol Fugard, *Theater Quarterly* 28 (1977–78): 86.

13. Athol Fugard, "On Henry David Thoreau's *Walden*," 114.

14. See Sheila Roberts, "Fugard in the Seventies: Inner and Outer Geography," in *Athol Fugard*, ed. Stephen Gray (Johannesburg: McGraw-Hill, 1982), 224, and Barrie Hough, "Fugard's *Boesman and Lena* in Perspective," *Inspan* 1 (1978): 96. A useful, if mainly thematic, early essay on Fugard's geographies is Chris Wortham, "A Sense of Place: Home and Homelessness in the Plays of Athol Fugard," in *Olive Schreiner and After: Essays on Southern African Literature in Honour of Guy Butler*, ed. Malvern van Wyk Smith and Don Maclennan (Cape Town: David Philip, 1983): 165–183.

15. See Cosmas Desmond, O.F.M., *The Discarded People: An Account of African Resettlement in South Africa* (Harmondsworth, Middlesex, England: Penguin, 1971), xvii.

16. Several critics have related the play to apartheid's geographical schemes. See, for example, Martin Orkin, *Drama and the South African State* (Manchester: Manchester University Press, 1991), 142–145. Fugard's attention to the forced removals was, if anything, even more intense and detailed than it seems to be in Orkin's cogent reading. In a notebook entry from April 1969, for example, Fugard refers to a newspaper photograph of and story about the demolition of a squatter camp at Missionvale (one of the places mentioned in *Boesman and Lena*): "The picture—shacks demolished, a pile of twisted corrugated-iron, packing case wood, etc. etc. and the people standing 'staring at the pieces'"(N 182).

17. Surprisingly ambiguous, that is, from the perspective provided by Engle. But from the point of view of the history of drama, this ambivalence is not so surprising. Una Chaudhuri has argued that modern drama may be viewed as a "century-long struggle with the problem of place": as a "geopathology," which "unfolds as an incessant dialogue between belonging and exile, home and homelessness." The figure of home is therefore almost invariably a contradictory one: "its status as both shelter and prison, security and entrapment" is essential to its dramatic meaning. See Chaudhuri, *Staging Place: The Geography of Modern Drama* (Ann Arbor: University of Michigan Press, 1995), 8, 14–15.

18. Michael Issacharoff, "Comic Drama," in *The Theatrical Space*, ed. James Redmond (Cambridge, England: Cambridge University Press, 1987), 188.

19. Ibid., and Issacharoff, "Space and Reference in Drama," *Poetics Today* 2 (1981): 211. In the latter essay, Issacharoff defines mimetic space as "that which is made visible to an audience and represented on stage," while diegetic space is "*described*, that is, referred to by the characters" (215).

20. On the indexical creation of dramatic worlds, see Keir Elam, *The Semiotics of Drama and Theatre* (London: Routledge, 2003), 88–102 and 130–131.

21. Homi Bhabha, "How Newness Enters the World: Postmodern Space, Postcolonial Times and the Trials of Cultural Translation," in *The Location of Culture* (London: Routledge, 1994), 224.

22. See, for instance, Robert Kavanagh, *Theatre and Cultural Struggle in South Africa* (London: Zed, 1984); Anne Fuchs, *The Market Theatre: Johannesburg 1976–1986* (Amsterdam: Rodopi, 2002); Loren Kruger, "Staging South Africa," *Transition* 59 (1993): 120–129; David Graver and Loren Kruger, "South Africa's National Theatre: The Market or the Street," *New Theatre Quarterly* 19 (August 1988): 272–281.

23. I would like to offer an initial definition of my use of the term "translation," especially since its usage in contemporary literary criticism and theory has been so capacious, ranging, as Bella Brodzki has observed, "from the most benign to the most venal." Translation may encompass the idea of colonial political inscription (an argument made in Eric Cheyfitz, *The Poetics of Imperialism*), as well as the undoing of such inscription, as in Derek Walcott's poetry, which in Bhabha's reading "shifts the focus from the nominalism of imperialism to the emergence of another sign of agency and identity." See Brodzki, "History, Cultural Memory, and the Tasks of Translation in T. Obinkaram Echewa's *I Saw the Sky Catch Fire*," *PMLA* 114 (1999): 207; Cheyfitz, *The Poetics of Imperialism: Translation and Colonization from "The Tempest" to "Tarzan"* (Philadelphia: University of Pennsylvania Press, 1987), and Bhabha, *The Location of Culture*, 231. In contemporary theory, translation functions as a highly ambivalent mechanism of mediation. As such, it is somewhat analogous to photography in Fugard's work, which can be a mechanism for surveillance and subjection or a means of performative self-affirmation and survival. Though I am attentive to the more oppressive definitions, especially in Cheyfitz's work, I do view "the space of translation" in a positive light: my term refers both to the interpretive space that must be traversed between the real world and the "elsewhere" of drama and to the space of critical and creative mediation: to the "epic gap" of performance that the poet Jeremy Cronin evokes in one of his "Pollsmoor Sketches," in *Inside* (London: Jonathan Cape, 1987), 25. As such, we may see "translation" as virtually equivalent to the word "consciousness," as it is used in one of Fugard's most revealing observations: "Without consciousness we become victims instead of actors—even if it is still only a question of acting victims" (N 107).

24. On this last point, see Kruger, *The Drama of South Africa*, 160–161.

25. Don Maclennan, "A Tribute to Fugard at Sixty," *Twentieth Century Literature* 39 (Winter 1993): 522.

26. See Georg Lukács, "Narrate or Describe," *Writer and Critic and Other Essays*, ed. Arthur Kahn (London: Merlin, 1978), 110–148.

27. The name "Tsotsi" is, in this respect, reminiscent of Bloke Modisane's moniker, which, as he explains in his Sophiatown memoir, was something he picked up by watching Hollywood movies. It, too, is the sign of what Modisane calls "depersonalization"—or, as Fugard puts it, "the name, in a way, of all men." See *Blame Me on History* (New York: Simon and Schuster, 1986), 166–167. Modisane, an associate of Fugard since the days of *No-Good Friday* (1958), who also played the part of Outa in the 1971 production of *Boesman and Lena*

in London, understood the idea of the "violence of immediacy" extremely well: he once observed that the "specialty of the poor is that they have no privacy" (N 191).

28. "What does this 'me' really consist of? Memory?" Fugard once wrote in his notebook. "Our lives, our special and utterly unique 'selves,' just a memory in action" (N 102).

29. In recent years, Fugard has come to describe the Karoo, his most beloved landscape, as "a landscape where man is always the right size." See, for example, Mary Benson, "Encounters with Fugard: Native of the Karoo," *Twentieth Century Literature*, 39 (Winter 1993): 460. This lyrical celebration of a desert landscape—for which the Afrikaans adjective *onherbergsaam* (weakly translatable as "inhospitable") is an apt descriptor—does not accord well with the experience of, say, the destitute woman, evicted from a Karoo farm, whom Fugard and his friends once found walking along the vast and barren plains near Cradock with all her belongings piled on her head (N 123–124). For this woman, the Karoo was surely too vast and unaccommodating, and her burdened body too small. Fugard's later aesthetic generalization conflicts with the moving details of South African social life to which he was so attentive in the 1960s and 1970s.

30. *Tsotsi* records, for instance, the image of a group of children pretending to drive "to-hell-and-gone" in the rusted-out wreck of a car (T 134): a fantasy of mobility that is explored further in *The Blood Knot* (1960). It also includes an incident in which a migrant worker poses for a deceptively happy photograph to send back to his family in the homelands, a scenario that was to become the germ of *Sizwe Bansi Is Dead* (1972). More generally, *Tsotsi* reveals Fugard's perennial interest in what he came to call, after Oscar Lewis, "the culture of poverty" (C 32). It shows his keen awareness of the trajectories of people's movements, the humble routines of daily life, and the expressive, almost ritual function of certain commodities. The description of how the migrant, Gumboot Dhlamini, walks to the city for weeks and weeks in his bare feet and only puts on his precious shoes when he sees the skyline of Johannesburg in the distance looks ahead to many such small acts of celebration and survival in Fugard's plays.

31. Orkin, *Drama and the South African State*, 142.

32. For reflections on the shifting impact of *Boesman and Lena* in performance, both before and after the end of apartheid, see Marcia Blumberg, "Re-staging Resistance, Reviewing Women: 1990s Productions of Fugard's *Hello and Goodbye* and *Boesman and Lena*," in *Staging Resistance: Essays on Political Theater*, ed. Jeanne Colleran and Jenny S. Spence (Ann Arbor: University of Michigan Press, 2001), 131–142.

33. Chaudhuri, *Staging Place*, 8.

34. See, for instance, Kruger, *The Drama of South Africa*, 155.

35. Jeremy Cronin, "No Unnecessary Noises Allowed, OK?" *Ingolovane* 2 (1989): 9.

36. Kracauer is quoted in Susan Buck-Morss, "Walter Benjamin—Revolutionary Writer (1)," *New Left Review* (September 1982): 74–75. We might also note here that Fugard often feels compelled to find the unloved beautiful. In response to the faces of the poor, he remarks: "Always, I first think 'how beautiful.' A really living thing always is—a living thing marked, scarred or broken by life even more so" (N 63). The aloe's beauty, one might say, is of this battered sort.

37. Quoted in Mel Gussow, "Profiles: Witness," *New Yorker*, 20 December 1982, 79.

38. For a discussion of Coetzee's review, see chapter 1.

39. Benjamin, "The Task of the Translator," in *Illuminations: Essays and Reflections*, ed. Hannah Arendt (New York: Schocken, 1969), 80–81.

40. Cheyfitz's discussion of such definitions is highly relevant to my concerns in this chapter, especially since he points out that "the very idea of metaphor seems to find its ground in a kind of territorial imperative." He cites, among other commentators, George Puttenham, who defines "*Metaphora*, or the Figure of transporte," as "a kinde of wrest-

ing of a single word from its own right signification, to another not so naturall, but yet of some affinities or convenience with it," and Roland Barthes, who argues that the division of a proper and a figurative language cannot be separated from the division "national/foreign" (*national/étranger*) and "familiar/strange" (*normal/étrange*). See Cheyfitz, *The Poetics of Imperialism*, 36–37. The *Oxford English Dictionary* definition of "translation" ("transference; removal or conveyance from one person, place, or condition to another") is also helpful, given its emphasis on the spatial and transformative connotations of the word.

41. J. M. Coetzee, "The Great South African Novel," *Leadership SA* (1983): 75.

42. Cheyfitz's key example of a translation that represses its rhetoricity and operates on the assumption of unproblematic similitude is the translation of Native American lands into "property" so that the title of this property could then be legally transferred to the United States government. (The repressed difference is, of course, that between private and communal ownership.) This example supports Cheyfitz's observation, relevant to my present reflections, that "all theories of translation" are "dependent on a notion of place." See *The Poetics of Imperialism*, 167.

43. See also Athol Fugard, interview with Barrie Hough, *Theoria* 55 (1980): 44. Fugard here comments as follows: "Am I in fact trying to suggest that, although I'm writing in English, this is actually something taking place in Afrikaans. . . . I suppose one of the problems I had, specifically with a play like *Boesman and Lena*, was that I think I was conscious all the way through it that I was trying to do a very difficult thing—which was to tell the story of these two people in the English language, when in a sense Afrikaans would have been possibly a richer medium."

44. It is interesting to note that for Benjamin quotation is just as defamiliarizing as translation, since both involve an unstable dialectic between text and context: "Quotations in my works," he declares, "are like robbers by the roadside who make an armed attack and relieve an idler of his convictions" (*Illuminations*, 38).

45. See Patrice Pavis, *Theatre at the Crossroads of Culture* (London: Routledge, 1992), and George Steiner, *After Babel: Aspects of Language and Translation* (Oxford: Oxford University Press, 1992), 27–29.

46. Dennis Walder has linked this line of thinking to Brecht, whose work has had a profound influence on Fugard: "If racialism and exploitation seem natural as 'the growth of leaves in spring,' then it is in the capacity of art to show us that this is not so. As Brecht said, to make the ordinary extraordinary." See Walder, *Athol Fugard* (London: Macmillan, 1984), 10–11.

47. Ibid., 119.

48. See Coetzee, *White Writing*, 7–11 and chap. 7.

49. W. B. Worthen, "'Homeless Words': Field Day and the Politics of Translation," *Modern Drama* 38 (1995): 23, and Gayatri Chakravorty Spivak, "The Politics of Translation," in *Outside in the Teaching Machine* (New York: Routledge, 1993), 181.

50. It is telling that Piet's final silence in *A Lesson from Aloes* follows on the revelation of a dangerous slippage in the meaning of "naming." The blustering Afrikaner learns to his sorrow that the word "naming" does not only refer to the act of identifying and humanizing one's world but can also refer to the act of betraying one's comrades: to the act of "naming names" as Steve Daniels has done, and as Piet himself is also suspected of doing. Fugard's conclusion in no way attempts to resolve this disjuncture but allows the uncomfortable semantic slippage, one that brings to mind the adage "Traddutore, traditore," to resonate—even perhaps beyond the final curtain.

51. See, for instance, Albert Wertheim, who pushes the comparison, at times *ad absurdum*: "Like the South African aloes, [Piet] remains to face the drought that is South Africa. And like those succulents, he must rely on his tough skin and his ability to go without

nurture for long periods" (*The Dramatic Art of Athol Fugard*, 134). But we should recall the careful way Fugard's dialogue brings up the question of survival without suggesting any simplistic identity of man and plant:

GLADYS: Is that the price of survival in this country? Thorns and bitterness.
PIET: For the aloe it is. Maybe there's some sort of lesson for us there.
GLADYS: What do you mean?
PIET: We need survival mechanisms too.

(AL 16)

It is worth bringing to mind here Wertheim's own reading of the collaborative plays *Sizwe Bansi Is Dead* and *Statements*, where he links survival with acting. I am arguing that the rhetoric of *A Lesson from Aloes* and especially its metatheatrical scenes advocate that linkage as well, though implicitly and as much by negation as by positive demonstration.

52. We may compare Fugard's observation, made back in 1963, that "South Africa's tragedy is the small, meager portions of love in the hearts of the men who walk this beautiful land" (N 82), with Coetzee's even harsher judgment in 1987: "At the heart of the unfreedom of the hereditary masters of South Africa is a failure of love. To be blunt, their love is not enough today and has not been enough since they arrived on the continent" (DP 97). Though Fugard may seem to come off rather badly in Coetzee's sardonic 1977 review of *The Guest*, Fugard's writings have also, it would seem, held some lessons for the novelist.

53. Kani and Ntshona have described the origins of the play in precisely these terms: "Athol came up with the idea that there is a place we never talk about, no one can write about, the press cannot talk about, not even white South Africans, free as they are, can talk about." Cited in Benson, "Keeping an Appointment," 86. My understanding of *The Island* is enriched by Dennis Walder's excellent comments on the limits of witness in "South African Drama and Ideology," 124–133.

54. Northrop Frye, "Conclusion to a Literary History of Canada," in *The Bush Garden: Essays on the Canadian Imagination* (Toronto: Anansi, 1971), 220. The situation Frye describes corresponds to the situation that John and Jean Comaroff (as I will show in greater detail in chapter 6) have defined as the particular dilemma of the second wave of postcolonial nations, those of the 1990s (including, of course, South Africa). These states face the dilemma of having to forge a new national identity and manage a national economy in which their citizens can be stakeholders at a time when neoliberal global forces, the worldwide movement of labor, capital, and goods, are increasingly making national frontiers more porous. In these conditions, the border is a "double bind because national prosperity appears to demand, but is simultaneously threatened by, *both* openness and closure." See the Comaroffs' "Naturing the Nation: Aliens, Apocalypse, and the Postcolonial State," *Journal of South African Studies* 27 (September 2001): 636, and their "Millennial Capitalism: First Thoughts on a Second Coming," in Jean Comaroff and John L. Comaroff, eds., *Millennial Capitalism and the Culture of Neoliberalism*, special issue, *Public Culture* 12 (Spring 2000): 291–343.

55. Elam argues that "spatial deixis finally takes priority over the temporal. It is above all the physical 'here' represented by the stage and its vehicles that the utterance must be anchored." He also cites Alessandro Serpieri's claim that the shifter is the "founding semiotic unit of dramatic representation at large." See Elam, *Semiotics of Theatre*, 127–128.

56. William Shakespeare, *Anthony and Cleopatra* (New York: Penguin, 1999), 110.

57. Issacharoff, "Comic Space," 187.

58. For a graceful theorization of these matters, see Chaudhuri's twist on Benjamin's essay "The Storyteller: Reflections on the Work on Nikolai Leskov." Drama, she argues,

partakes of both the rootedness and orality of the story and the geographical freedom of the novel: a tension she describes in terms of the "platiality" and the "spatiality" of drama, respectively. Chaudhuri, *Staging Place*, 267.

59. See Loren Kruger, "Apartheid on Display: South Africa Performs for New York," *Diaspora* 1 (1991): 191–209, and Jeanne Colleran, "Athol Fugard and the Problematics of the Liberal Critique." Colleran notes how the bare stage of *My Children! My Africa!* is quite different in its effect from those of the earlier plays (where the staging was both a pragmatic response to "limited and endangered production resources" and a metaphorical expression of dispossession). Though she cautiously notes that the bare stage does not exactly impose ahistoricity, it does, especially in American productions, render the context for the play's debate about the value of education neutral—which it certainly was not during the years of Bantu education (395–396).

60. On Fugard's confessed debt to Faulkner, see Hough, *Interview with Athol Fugard*, 42–43, or *Cousins*, 49. Faulkner's famous statement is first recorded in *Lion in the Garden: Interviews with William Faulkner, 1926–1962*, ed. James B. Meriwether and Michael Millgate (New York: Random House, 1968), 255.

Chapter 5

1. Antjie Krog, *Country of My Skull: Guilt, Sorrow, and the Limits of Forgiveness in the New South Africa* (New York: Times Books, 1999), 51–52.

2. Ibid., 52.

3. Ibid., 58.

4. Ibid., 54.

5. Ibid., 55.

6. For a critical discussion of the TRC's iconography of victims and mothers in the creation of a new national history (including that offered in Krog's book), see Ntabiseng Motsemme, "Gendered Experiences of Blackness in Post-apartheid South Africa," *Social Identities* 8 (2002): 650–651. On the history of the "mother of the nation" icon in South African literature and politics and the way it suppresses the private and personal self, see Desirée Lewis, "Black South African Women and Biography under Apartheid," in *Apartheid Narratives*, ed. Nahem Yousaf (Amsterdam: Rodopi, 2001), 170 and throughout.

7. Mamphela Ramphele, *A Bed Called Home: Life in the Migrant Labour Hostels of Cape Town* (David Philip: Cape Town, 1993). Other fictional works on the changing spaces of the South African transition to democracy include Ivan Vladislavić, *The Restless Supermarket* (Cape Town: David Philip, 2001), and *The Exploded View* (Cape Town: David Philip, 2004), along with the novels of Zakes Mda, which I discuss in chapter 6. Among the academic works concerned with space, I would list most prominently Hilton Judin and Vladislavić's imaginative and capacious collection *Blank _____: Architecture, Apartheid, and After* (Cape Town: David Philip, 2000).

8. Ramphele was the lover of the murdered activist Steve Biko and was pregnant with his child at the time of his death. She has commented rather scathingly, both in her autobiography and in her academic essays, on the apparent need South Africans feel to define her primarily in terms of this role—despite all of her own personal achievements. See Mamphela Ramphele, "Political Widowhood in South Africa: The Embodiment of Ambiguity," *Daedalus* 125 (Winter 1996): 99–118.

9. Though Ramphele is not a particularly belle-lettristic writer, it seems to me that her treatment of space is congenial to students of literature: her idea of the "locale" as a fusion of time and space, for instance, is readily related to the Bakhtinian concept of the

chronotope. It is interesting to note that Bachelard's highly imaginative work *The Poetics of Space* was a decisive influence on her thinking. See Mamphela Ramphele, *Across Boundaries: The Journey of a South African Woman Leader* (New York: Feminist Press, 1995), 171.

10. Ramphele, *A Bed Called Home*, 23. Ramphele also refers to the observations of the former political prisoner Neville Alexander about the importance of the imagination in situations of confinement. On Robben Island, Alexander recalls, "one created imaginary boundaries around oneself. Body language is an important part of the strategies used. Just turning one's shoulder slightly establishes private conversation space" (*A Bed Called Home*, 23). These observations are also relevant, as will become clear, to Miriam Tlali's analysis of the boundaries that are set up by the black workers to protect their dignity and freedom of speech in the rather carceral space of the radio shop that is the setting for her novel *Muriel at Metropolitan*.

11. Ibid., 134. Ramphele's emphasis on psychological space marks her ongoing allegiance to certain aspects of Black Consciousness, especially its emphasis on self-affirmation and psychological decolonization. When I discussed the issues raised in this chapter with her in May 2003, she responded in a way I found both characteristic and endearing: she pointed to her head and said, "The most important place to liberate is in here."

12. Ibid., 3. Ramphele is here drawing on the work of Anthony Giddens.

13. Ibid. One might think of the poetics of Jeremy Cronin as an attempt to link the space of literary performance with political space, or "room for strategic maneuver." On Cronin's thinking about the poetic creation of "liberated zones," analogous to the rural areas that served the MPLA and FRELIMO as bases of operation in the anticolonial struggles in Angola and Mozambique, see my essay "Speaking Places: Prison, Poetry and the South African Nation," *Research in African Literatures* 32 (Fall 2001): 155–176.

14. Ramphele, *A Bed Called Home*, 6.

15. Ibid., 13.

16. Appadurai further describes the capacity to aspire as a "highly specific way of connecting what Clifford Geertz long ago called the 'experience-near' and the 'experience-distant' aspects of life." This capacity must be distinguished from the universalizing and idealistic conception of self-renewal I criticized in Fugard's Georgetown address: just like "intellectual space," the "capacity to aspire" must be understood as materially contingent and far from universally developed or available to all people. Appadurai writes: "If the map of aspirations (continuing the navigational metaphor) is seen to consist of a dense combination of nodes and pathways, relative poverty means a smaller number of aspirational nodes and a thinner, weaker sense of the pathways from concrete wants to intermediate contexts to general norms and back again. Where these pathways do exist for the poor, they are likely to be more rigid, less supple, and less strategically valuable, not because of any cognitive deficit on the part of the poor but because the capacity to aspire like any complex cultural capacity thrives and survives on practice, repetition, exploration, conjecture, and refutation. Where the opportunities for such conjecture and refutation in regard to the future are limited (and this may well be one way to define poverty) it follows that the capacity itself remains relatively less developed." See Arjun Appadurai, "The Capacity to Aspire: Culture and the Terms of Recognition," unpublished paper presented at the University of the Witwatersrand Institute for Social and Economic Research's International Visitors Lecture Series, 29 August 2002, 7–8.

17. Louise Bethlehem, "'A Primary Need as Strong as Hunger': The Rhetoric of Urgency in South African Literature under Apartheid," *Poetics Today* 22:2 (Summer 2002): 373.

18. Ibid., 367.

19. Ibid., 369.

20. Cited in Bethlehem, "'A Primary Need,'" 367. If one considers Mzamane's article as a whole, the emphasis on an unmediated realism is, in fact, combined with other aesthetic agendas and theories, which Bethlehem tends to ignore. These include his emphasis on the connection between the traditional *izibongo* or *lithoko* and the Soweto poets and on the humanist aspiration fostered by their work: these poets, he insists, "are engaged in the re-creation of black dignity and identity." Mbulele V. Mzamane, "New Poets of the Soweto Era: Van Wyk, Johennesse, and Madingoane," *Research in African Literatures* 19 (1998): 10. This is not to say that Mzamane's elision of the divide between the literary and the real should escape critique. Mikhail Bakhtin puts the problem well: "If I relate (or write about) an event that has just happened to me, then I as the teller (or writer) of this event am already outside the time and space in which the event occurred. It is just as impossible to forge an identity between myself, my own 'I,' and that 'I' that is the subject of my stories as it is to lift myself up by my own hair. The represented world, however realistic and truthful, can never be chronotopically identical with the real world it represents, where the author and creator of the literary world is to be found." *The Dialogic Imagination: Four Essays*, ed. Michael Holquist (Austin: University of Texas Press, 1981), 256.

21. Bethlehem, "'A Primary Need,'" 367.

22. Nkosi, "Fiction by Black South Africans," in *Home and Exile and Other Selections* (New York: Longman, 1983), 110.

23. Lewis Nkosi, "South African Fiction Writers at the Barricades," *Third World Book Review* 2 (1986): 43. For Bethlehem's deconstructive reading of Nkosi as still complicit in the tropes he criticizes, see "'A Primary Need,'" 369–373.

24. André Brink, *A Dry White Season* (New York: Penguin, 1984), 167. The fact that a white writer should assume the trope of pressing immediacy and constriction seems to me to emphasize all the more the hegemonic influence of the "rhetoric of urgency." For similar images in the work of a black writer, see Sindiwe Magona, *Mother to Mother*, where a crowded bus is described in a similarly distasteful metaphor: as "a tube, a giant sausage casing and we, minced meat, stuffed piecemeal down it. . . . Everywhere, everywhere, something takes up room. Fills the gap, arrests all circulation" (MTM 25).

25. Es'kia Mphahlele, "The Tyranny of Place and Aesthetics: The South African Case," in *Race and Literature/Ras en Literatuur*, ed. Charles Malan, Sensal Publications no. 15 (Pinetown: Owen Burgess, 1987), 54.

26. It should be said that, while this particular quotation is very pertinent to Bethlehem's argument, the Mphahlele essay from which she draws here is diffuse and desultory: the realist, antiliterary rhetoric does not emerge quite as strongly from the piece as a whole as Bethlehem leads us to believe. See "South African Literature vs. The Political Morality (1)," *English Academic Review* 1 (1983): 8–28, and Bethlehem, "'A Primary Need,'" 369.

27. This is what happens in some of the "Soweto poetry" from the 1970s, for example, Fhazel Johennesse's "Living in a Flat in Eldorado Park," of which I cite only a sampling:

the drunk trying to mount the steps
swearing as he skids in predecessors' vomit . . .
the occasional tinkle of glass
as a stone is hurled through a window
and the grating calling of a mother
shouting for her child and
the rich pong of gas exuding from
the slowly rotting garbage in dustbins
and the throaty gurgle of pipes
as someone else's crap passes through

my flat and the infuriating
tap tap tap on the ceiling as some brat upstairs explores the
mysteries of his floor with a hammer

The effect here—of a kind of emotionally souped-up naturalism rather than documentary—is not atypical, though it must be said that the loose designation of "Soweto" or "township poetry" has been applied to a very divergent body of work. See Fhazel Johennesse, *The Rainmaker* (Johannesburg: Ravan Press, 1979): 75.

28. Ramphele, *A Bed Called Home*, 19–20.

29. Bethlehem, "'A Primary Need,'" 368.

30. Margaret Daymond has suggested that one may work somewhat against the grain of Tlali's declared commitments to realistic protest writing in order to uncover her relation to older modes of orality, evident in the way she draws on vernacular speech patterns and communal tales. "Inventing Gendered Traditions: The Short Stories of Bessie Head and Miriam Tlali," in *South African Feminisms: Writing Theory and Criticism, 1990–1994*, ed. Daymond (New York: Garland, 1996), 223–240. My reading of Tlali here is quite different from Daymond's, partly because I am focusing on Tlali's first novel rather than her later stories. But I believe that we share the understanding that Tlali at times avails herself of a hegemonic critical discourse that does not entirely describe some of her creative work.

31. Miriam Tlali, interview with Mineke Schipper, in *Unheard Words: Women and Literature in Africa, the Arab World, Asia, the Caribbean and Latin America*, ed. Schipper (London: Allison and Busby, 1985): 68.

32. Virginia Woolf, *A Room of One's Own* (New York: Harcourt, Brace, 1929): 9. I am indebted to Pamela Ryan's article "Black Women Do Not Have Time to Dream: The Effect of the Politics of Time and Space on Black Women's Writing in South Africa," *Tulsa Studies in Women's Literature* 11: 1 (1992): 95–102, for drawing my attention to the connections between Woolf and Tillie Olsen's important feminist interventions and South African women's writing.

33. Woolf, *A Room of One's Own*, 103.

34. Tillie Olsen, *Silences* (New York: Delacorte Press, 1978), 33.

35. Miriam Tlali, interview with Mineke Schipper, 59.

36. Miriam Tlali, interview with Jeanette Dean, *New Literatures Review* (Summer 1994): 46.

37. Cited in Raoul Granqvist and John Stotesbury, eds., *African Voices: Interviews with Thirteen African Writers* (Sydney: Dangaroo Press, 1989: 77). The most extreme South African variation on the room-of-one's-own theme is Gcina Mlhope's short story "The Toilet," in which a woman living illegally in her sister's maid's room and working in a factory discovers just enough space to write in a clean public toilet in one of the city parks. On Mlhope, see Ryan, "Black Women," 100–101.

38. Miriam Tlali, interview with Jeanette Dean, 49. It is interesting to note that while the conventional roles of women often prevent them from becoming writers (as Olsen so amply documents), Tlali produced *Muriel at Metropolitan* partly because of her obligations as wife and daughter-in-law. Her mother-in-law suffered from a terminal illness, and it was during the years when Tlali stayed at home to nurse her that she was able to complete the manuscript (Miriam Tlali, interview with Mineke Schipper, 61).

39. Miriam Tlali, "Quagmires and Quicksands," *Index on Censorship* 17 (May 1988): 95.

40. Tlali even uses the same digestive metaphor we have seen in Mphahlele, Nkosi, and Magona to express the impact of external circumstances: "In South Africa today, the colonial and neocolonial structures are fused together to form quagmires and quicksands

to befuddle and *consume* the African writer and reader alike." "Quagmire and Quicksands," 95. The South African edition of her *Soweto Stories* appeared under the title *Footprints in the Quag.*

41. See, for example, Kelwyn Sole, "The Days of Power: Depictions of Politics and Community in Four Recent South African Novels," *Research in African Literatures* 19 (Spring 1988): 65–88. Cecily Lockett, to some extent, argues against the view of Tlali as a producer of formless, journalistic writings, but nevertheless describes the digressive interludes of the novel as "a loosely-woven rendering of the fabric of the black experience" or "segments of lived experience whose importance is generated by their context and historical specificity." "The Fabric of Experience: A Critical Perspective on the Writing of Miriam Tlali," in *Women and Writing in South Africa: A Critical Anthology*, ed. Cherry Clayton (Marshalltown, South Africa: Heinemann, 1989): 279. Eva Hunter defends Tlali's deployment of the trope of the mother in her feminist stories—a strategy I continue to find problematic and one that Tlali avoids in her best novel, *Muriel at Metropolitan.* See "'A Mother Is Nothing but a Backbone': Women, Tradition and Change in Miriam Tlali's *Footprints in the Quag*," *Current Writing* 5 (1991) 60–75.

42. For example, Marie Dyer, cited in Lockett, "Fabric of Experience," 287.

43. Mehlaleng Mosotho, "Metropolitan Miriam," *Tribute* (August 1987): 38.

44. Miriam Tlali, interview with Rosemary Jolly, in *Writing South Africa: Literature, Apartheid, and Democracy, 1970–1995*, ed. Derek Attridge and Rosemary Jolly (Cambridge, England: Cambridge University Press, 1997): 144.

45. The project of reading South African cultural history in terms of creolization—a project that only becomes possible in the postapartheid era—has not been uncontroversial. But I find myself persuaded by Sarah Nuttall's arguments in its favor in her essay "City Forms and Writing the 'Now' in South Africa," *Journal of Southern African Studies* 30: 4 (December 2004): 731–748.

46. N. Chabani Manganyi, "Architecture: A View from Outside," in *Looking through the Keyhole: Dissenting Essays on the Black Experience* (Johannesburg: Ravan Press, 1981), 140. A preoccupation with "inner space," he argues, "is the subjective response to the standardization of the communal environment." See also his essay "Soweto on My Mind," in *Looking*, 155. I use the word "spectacular" in the sense developed by Njabulo Ndebele. See his *South African Literature and Culture: The Rediscovery of the Ordinary* (Manchester: Manchester University Press, 1994), 41–59.

47. In the view of Tom de Koning, "The greatest effect on blacks [of commercial TV] will be the raising of their cultural aspirations. They will see other blacks with cars, houses, and so on and ask, 'Why can't I have that?' In a real sense there will be a westernization of blacks because of television. And their political claims will escalate as a result." Cited in Rob Nixon, "The Devil in the Black Box: The Idea of America and the Outlawing of TV," in *Homelands, Harlem, and Hollywood* (New York: Routledge, 1994): 65.

48. Nixon, *Homelands, Harlem, and Hollywood*, 63.

49. It is worth remembering, however, how the SABC weather report with its familiar litany of place names ("Port Shepstone to the Tugela Mouth . . . the Tugela Mouth to Kosi Bay" and so forth) helped the political prisoner Jeremy Cronin to re-create a sense of social geography and ultimately a revolutionary poetics in the confines of his cell at Pretoria Central. See Cronin, *Inside* (London: Jonathan Cape, 1987), 9.

50. Nixon, *Homelands, Harlem, and Hollywood*, 65.

51. This view is put forward by Manganyi, who remarks on the fact that humble four-roomed matchbook houses in the townships were often full to capacity with expensive furniture, of a quality comparable to those in the mansions of South Africa's white suburbs. A psychologist by training, he sees this practice as an example of how the "material

artifacts of culture" may signify a person's innermost desire, which, in the case of South Africa's township residents, included an enormous need to give the imagination free play and to express individual identity in the context of a rigidly standardized, dehumanizing environment ("Architecture," 140).

52. A. N. Pelzer, ed., *Verwoerd Speaks: Speeches 1948–1966* (Johannesburg: APB, 1966) 155–156. I am indebted to Alice Brittan for drawing my attention to this fascinating passage. For an imaginative discussion of the question of scale—of "diminution" and "amplification"—in South African cultural history and literature, see chap. 3 of her "Writing and Portage: The Post-settlement Novel and the Movement of Things," Ph.D. diss., University of Pennsylvania, 2002.

53. Sandra Klopper has recorded an ongoing tendency to celebrate bigness as a mark of physical desirability and beauty even among middle-class and wealthy black South Africans today. This persistent linkage of physical size and social standing (as opposed to the Western validation of thinness amid abundance) could be explained, at least in part, as a legacy of the physical, psychological, and political diminution of black people under colonialism and apartheid. See her essay "Re-dressing the Past: The Africanisation of Sartorial Style in Contemporary South Africa," in Avtar Brah and Annie E. Coombes, eds., *Hybridity and Its Discontents: Politics, Science, Culture* (New York: Routledge, 2000): 224–226.

54. Brittan, "Writing and Portage," 123. See Monica Hunter, *Reaction to Conquest: Effects of Contact with Europeans on the Pondo of South Africa* (New York: Oxford University Press, 1961), 446, for an early description of a township living room crowded with prized secondhand furniture.

55. Liz Gunner has argued that this practice occurred even on the state's ideological apparatus Radio Bantu, where some writers of radio dramas were able to find an outlet for their creativity and for the articulation of an incipient black nationalism. "Supping with the Devil: Zulu Radio Drama under Apartheid—The Case of Alexius Buthelezi," *Social Identities* 11: 2 (March 2005): 161–169.

56. On the "severance scene," a recurrent feature of black women's writing in the 1980s, in which the focal female character or the female author separates from her husband and family, and moves toward greater autonomy, see Margaret Lenta, "Goodbye Lena, Goodbye Poppie: Post-apartheid Black Women's Writing," *Ariel* 29 (October 1998): 111. It is tempting to read a political dimension into this severance scene: Muriel's departure from Metropolitan arguably parallels Tlali's own movement away from an interest in the poetics and politics of creolization (a particularly urban form of the "contestation of spaces") toward a position closer to that of Black Consciousness, with its strategic racial separations.

57. Can Themba, *The Will to Die* (Cape Town: David Philip, 1985): 107; Ulf Hannerz, "Sophiatown: The View from Afar," *Journal of Southern African Studies* 20 (June 1994): 192–193.

58. Hannerz, "Sophiatown," 191.

59. Ibid., 190–191.

60. Ibid., 182–183, 189–190.

61. Ibid., 190. For a reading of postapartheid Johannesburg from a perspective very similar to Hannerz's, see Achille Mbembe and Sarah Nuttall, "Writing the World from an African Metropolis," *Public Culture* 12 (2004): 347–372.

62. On the "concept-city," see chapter 3.

63. For an excellent discussion of excremental tropes in colonial and postcolonial contexts, see Joshua Esty, "Excremental Postcolonialism," *Contemporary Literature* 40 (Spring 1999): 26–34. I use the idea of the "abject" here in Julia Kristeva's sense, as a discursive phenomenon that is associated with defiled matter and that "disturbs identity, system, order."

See Kristeva, *Powers of Horror: An Essay on Abjection*, trans. Leon S. Roudiez (New York: Columbia University Press, 1982), 4.

64. It is quite comical to see how the whites in the novel try to reduce the politics of the newly decolonized African states to matters of furniture, as, for example, in their scornful references to a politician (the name Nkrumah, of course, eludes them) who wastes his country's wealth on a golden bed, and to a bunch of black parliamentarians who argued so much about who should sit at the head of the table that they ended up having to buy a round one (MM 28–29).

65. Margaret Lenta, "Intimate Knowledge and Willful Ignorance: White Employers and Black Employees in South African Fiction," in *Women and Writing in South Africa: A Critical Anthology*, ed. Cherry Clayton (Johannesburg: Heinemann, 1989): 241–242.

66. Miriam Tlali, interview with Jeanette Dean, 50.

67. Tlali herself, I should note, has not published anything since her *Soweto Stories* (1989), and in an interview with Rosemary Jolly during the mid-1990s reported on a failed workshop for aspirant writers at the Windybrow Theater in Johannesburg: "Notices had been sent out asking aspirant writers to come for help with their short stories and so on. I sat there for two hours, but there was nobody. Nobody turned up. Because there are other factors which are pertinent which have to be dealt with, and which have not received attention. It's not enough to say just sit down there and write a story. How can you say that to a person who is concerned about how to survive, where to get the next meal. It's still fighting against the odds. You have to remove all these problems that prevent people from sitting down, reading the books, appreciating them and developing their own writing" (Miriam Tlali, interview with Rosemary Jolly, 148).

68. Reproduced in Yoon Jung, Joanne Fedler, and Zubeida Dangor, eds. *Reclaiming Women's Spaces: New Perspectives on Violence against Women and Sheltering in South Africa* (Johannesburg: Nisaa Institute for Women's Development, 2000), 154.

69. Olusola Olufemi and Dory Reeves, "Lifeworld Strategies of Women Who Find Themselves Homeless in South Africa," *Planning Theory and Practice* 5 (March 2004): 71.

70. Sean Jacobs, "Reading Politics, Reading Media," in *Shifting Selves: Post-apartheid Essays on Mass Media, Culture, and Identity*, ed. Herman Wasserman and Sean Jacobs (Cape Town: Kwela Books, 2003): 36–37.

71. Allister Sparks, *Beyond the Miracle: Inside the New South Africa* (Chicago: University of Chicago Press, 2003), 52.

72. Francis Wilson and Mamphela Ramphele, *Uprooting Poverty: The South African Challenge,* Report for the Second Carnegie Inquiry into Poverty and Development in Southern Africa (New York: Norton, 1989), 44. Sparks, curiously, claims their insight as his own.

73. Achille Mbembe, "Aesthetics of Superfluity," *Public Culture* 16: 3 (2004): 381.

74. Sparks, *Beyond the Miracle*, 52–53.

75. There has been a revival of popular protest around the privatization of electricity and water (as documented by scholars like Patrick Bond, Hein Marais, and Ashwin Desai) and there is no question that the struggle to secure more affordable services for the very poor will continue to galvanize activists. However, it is quite safe to say (even if this means damning with faint praise) that the ANC government has fared considerably better than its successor in making electricity provision a policy priority.

76. For discussion of the manuscript, which is in the collection of the National English Literary Museum in Grahamstown, see Sarah Nuttall, "Literature and the Archive: The Biography of Two Texts," in *Refiguring the Archive*, ed. Carolyn Hamilton, Verne Harris, Jane Taylor, Michele Pickover, Graeme Reid, and Razia Saleh (Cape Town: David Philip, 2002).

77. While one is reluctant to make grand claims based on individual testimony or endorse any simplistic view of the positive effect of "role models" in the media, it is nevertheless interesting to consider here Ntabiseng Motsemme's interview with a black woman called Lydia who grew up speaking only Afrikaans in a "coloured" community and was always made to feel inferior because of her darker complexion. Lydia attests to the powerful impact the integration of the broadcast media, in the wake of the 1994 election, had on her life: "Amazingly when the channels opened up in my community, people's attitude about black people . . . changed. . . . Suddenly people could see beauty in you, because of role models on TV, they'll compliment you or say you look like that presenter or that presenter. . . . You've become accepted. . . . I'm telling you, its unbelievable but true. . . . [The media] opened up . . . a position [in] coloured communities which wasn't there before. . . . okay, it was always mostly this trying to be white. All of a sudden it wasn't that any more, suddenly it was striving to be black because they could see successful black people on TV" (quoted in Motsemme, "Gendered Experiences," 657).

78. Motsemme has begun to demonstrate the vastly different experiences of "blackness" in postapartheid South Africa. "Placing a heavy reliance solely on race," she asserts, "will only add in masking other forms of power relationships which find their expression through racialized notions of beauty, femininity, and sexuality" ("Gendered Experiences," 657).

79. Magona, *Mother to Mother* (Cape Town: David Philip, 1998), 27.

80. We might contrast this thoroughgoing and exculpatory determinism not only with, say, Fugard's redemptive, albeit at times sentimental, treatment of his characters who are exposed to poverty (like Lena in *Boesman and Lena*) but also with the position of Ramphele, who, while emphasizing throughout the importance of environmental influences on the human capacity for aspiration and change, nevertheless refuses to abandon moral responsibility. She refers to Wole Soyinka's caution, in *A Play of Giants*, against simplistic analyses of power relations like Magona's: "Unlike many commentators on power and politics, I do not know how monsters come to be, only that they are, and in defiance of place, time and pundits . . . no one has ever satisfactorily explained why near identical socioeconomic conditions should produce on one hand, Julius Nyerere and on the other, an Idi Amin" (*A Bed Called Home*, 13–14).

81. For an interesting discussion of the extent to which representations of black women's lives were directed to an international audience, "allow[ing] non–South Africans to experience the urgency of South African politics," see Desirée Lewis, "Constructive Lives: Black South African Women and Biography under Apartheid," in *Apartheid Narratives*, ed. Nahem Yousaf (Amsterdam: Rodopi, 2001): 163.

82. *The Bold and the Beautiful* has in fact been enormously popular with black South Africans of all genders, to the point where some taxi drivers in Johannesburg have scheduled their work in such a way as to allow themselves to watch the soap at 5:30 p.m. and the reruns at 9 a.m. A study of the viewing experiences of black urban fans has revealed that the pleasures provided by *The Bold and the Beautiful* lie not only in the viewers' fascination with the lavish lifestyles represented in the soap but also in the discussions and debates it generates (people seldom watch it alone). The study also suggests that black South African viewers find the predicaments of the American characters quite applicable to their lives, rather than strange (women often have to cope with infidelity, which is a prominent theme in the soap opera, and viewers of both genders like the focus on a single extended family). Most interesting, in the light of my discussion of intellectual space, viewers seem to seek out rather intellectual pleasures in their approach to the utterly conventional saga: what they enjoy most is criticizing the show, or the satisfaction of having their predictions about how the plot will turn out confirmed. They enjoy the show's silliness, in other words,

because it allows them to be experts. See Michelle Tager, "Identification and Interpretation: *The Bold and the Beautiful*," *Critical Arts Journal* 11 (1997): 95–115. ·

83. In a revealing interview with Ijeoma Akunyili, Dike describes the play as distinctly "postapartheid," even though she wanted to write something along these lines as far back as 1976. "That was the era when I was living the life of the women described in that play. That was when it was born in my heart. But I could not write it then because there was something much more urgent. There was the struggle, we had to write for the struggle. All my previous plays were for the struggle. When in 1990 Mandela came out of prison I finally felt it was the right time. During the struggle I kept asking myself what I was going to write about when the change did come. I kept *So What's New?* at the back of my mind and decided that it would be my first play when the South African situation changed." These comments emphasize the constraints of the rhetoric of urgency and the way De Klerk's historic announcement of February 1990 almost instantly enlarged the political and cultural "room for maneuver" in South Africa. See Akunyili, "Interviews with South African and Other African Writers," honors thesis, University of Pennsylvania, 2000, 65–66.

84. The terms "experience-near" and "experience-distant" are Clifford Geertz's, quoted in Appadurai, "The Capacity to Aspire," 8. See note 16.

Chapter 6

1. Es'kia Mphahlele, "The Tyranny of Place and Aesthetics: The South African Case," in *Race and Literature/Ras en Literatuur*, ed. Charles Malan (Pinetown: Owen Burgess, 1987), 54.

2. Ibid., 58.

3. Njabulo S. Ndebele, "The Rediscovery of the Ordinary," in *South African Literature and Culture: The Rediscovery of the Ordinary* (Manchester: Manchester University Press, 1994), 41.

4. Owen Crankshaw and Susan Parnell, "Interpreting the 1994 African Township Landscape," in *Blank _____: Architecture, Apartheid, and After*, ed. Hilton Judin and Ivan Vladislavić (Cape Town: David Philip, 1999), 439.

5. See Jennifer Robinson, "(Im)mobilizing Space—Dreaming of Change," in Judin and Vladislavić, *Blank _____*, 164, and Margaret Mervis, "Fiction for Development: Zakes Mda's *Ways of Dying*," *Current Writing* 10 (1998): 42. The term "capitalist realism" is Michael Schudson's. See his *Advertising, the Uneasy Persuasion: Its Dubious Impact on American Society* (New York: Basic Books, 1984), 214–218.

6. I am referring here to a comment made by a resident of one of the *favelas* of Rio de Janeiro quoted in Mamphela Ramphele, *A Bed Called Home: Life in the Migrant Labour Hostels of Cape Town* (Cape Town: David Philip, 1993), 23. For a discussion of this idea, see chapter 5.

7. See Ndebele, "The Rediscovery of the Ordinary," in *South African Literature and Culture*, throughout.

8. On the logic of touristic display, see, for example, Steve Robins, "City Sites," in *Senses of Culture: South African Cultural Studies*, ed. Sarah Nuttall and Cheryl-Ann Michael (Cape Town: Oxford University Press, 2000), 408–425; Craig Fraser, *Shack Chic: Art and Innovation in South African Shack-Lands* (Cape Town: Quivertree, 2002); and Annie Coombes, *History after Apartheid: Visual Culture and Public Memory in a Democratic South Africa* (Durham: Duke University Press, 2003), especially 179–195, where Coombes discusses the MuseuMAfrica's exhibition "Birds in a Cornfield," featuring a display of reconstructed dwellings from Thokoza township, as well as the photographs of Zwelethu Mthethwa, depicting posed subjects in their exuberantly decorated shacks.

9. Loren Kruger, *The Drama of South Africa: Plays, Pageants and Publics since 1910* (New York: Routledge, 1999), 185.

10. For some comments on these new subjectivities, see my essay "On Laughter, the Grotesque, and the South African Transition: Zakes Mda's *Ways of Dying*," *Novel* 37 (Summer 2004): 280–282.

11. While the port city would seem to resemble Cape Town and the mountain village would seem to be in Lesotho, where Mda lived for many years, he avoids any specific identifications. Certainly the carnival described at the end of the novel reminds one of Cape Town's annual "Klopse" or "Coon Carnival," but black residents of the city settlements would be unlikely to participate in this traditionally "Malay" or "coloured" event. Moreover, while there was some feuding between hostel dwellers and township residents in the Cape Flats during the 1970s and 1980s, the battle lines fell out in somewhat different ways from those described in the novel: the influence of a "tribal chief" was far more palpable in the struggles between migrants and township residents in the Gauteng townships of Thokoza and Boitpatong, where Buthelezi's Inkhatha Freedom Party had a strong following. So Mda seems to be creating a condensed and composite South African city. The mountain village, likewise, is best grasped as what Johan van Wyk has termed a "Pan-African village": it is effectively dislocated by the use of isiXhosa, Sesotho, and tsiVenda words and names. It is therefore best to read the novel as allegorical rather than realist, and to see its setting as being like that of Mda's play *We Will Sing for the Fatherland*, which could take place in any postcolonial African country. See Van Wyk, "Catastrophe and Beauty: *Ways of Dying*, Zakes Mda's Novel of the Transition," *Literator* 18: 3 (1997): 79.

12. For another discussion of the novel's overview of South African historical geography, see Van Wyk, "Catastrophe and Beauty," 81.

13. For a discussion of the contrast between the uniform townships of "high apartheid" and the heterogeneous urban landscape of apartheid's decline, see Crankshaw and Parnell, "Interpreting," in Judin and Vladislavić, *Blank* _____, 439–443.

14. On the demise of the exceptionalism of the South African city, see C. M. Rogerson, "The Absorptive Capacity of the Informal Sector in the South African City," in *The Apartheid City and Beyond: Urbanization and Social Change in South Africa*, ed. David M. Smith (London: Routledge, 1992), 162 and Allister Sparks, *The Mind of South Africa* (New York: Ballantine Books, 1990), 373–375.

15. AbdouMaliq Simone, "Globalization and the Identity of African Urban Practices," in Judin and Vladislavić, *Blank* _____, 186.

16. Ibid., 186–188. See also Robinson, who usefully summarizes these trends and discusses in particular the work of the Latin American urbanists Arturo Escobar and Sonia Alvarez, who have called for "a cultural theory of social movement" and have demonstrated the inadequacy of the dominant categories of the social sciences to express the great variety of popular practices. "(Im)mobilizing Space," 164.

17. Simone, "Globalization," 197. "How unfortunate it is," Simone adds, "that this inspiring sense of responsibility found in Africa today meets with such an irresponsible reaction in the rest of the world."

18. Jacobs is cited in AbdouMaliq Simone, "Urban Processes and Change in Africa" (Dakar: Codesria, 1998), 2.

19. I offer as an example of literary criticism inflected by urban studies my own speculations on the new "prosaics" of the informal economy, in "On Laughter," 179–182, and Sarah Nuttall's commentary on migrant subjectivities in "City Forms and Writing the 'Now' in South Africa," *Journal of Southern African Studies* 30 (December 2004): 740–747.

20. Robinson, "(Im)mobilizing Space," 163.

21. Mongane Wally Serote, *Yakhal'inkomo* (Johannesburg: Renoster, 1974), 4–5.

22. Robinson, "(Im)mobilizing Space," 164.

23. John Western, "Knowing One's Place: 'The Coloured People' and the Group Areas Act in Cape Town," 305; Jennifer Robinson, "Power, Space, and the City: Historical Reflections on Apartheid and Post-apartheid Orders," in *The Apartheid City and Beyond*, ed. David M. Smith (New York: Routledge, 1992), 292–302.

24. Simone, "Urban Processes," 3.

25. Robinson, "(Im)mobilizing Space," 170.

26. Simone, "Globalization," 178.

27. Grant Farred, "Mourning the Postapartheid State Already? The Poetics of Loss in Zakes Mda's *Ways of Dying*," *Modern Fiction Studies* 46 (Spring 2000): 195.

28. The distinction between the official world and the "second world" of carnival derives, of course, from Bakhtin's work on the grotesque. See Mikhail Bakhtin, *Rabelais and His World*, trans. Hélène Iswolsky (Bloomington: Indiana University Press, 1984), 6–11.

29. Rogerson, "The Absorptive Capacity of the Informal Sector," 163. This attitude seems to have persisted well into the postelection period. AbdouMaliq Simone writes about how debates in the Johannesburg city council about a new urban vision and a new strategy for development seemed to get bogged down because of an obsession with cleanliness: "The predominant feeling amongst the councilors is that if only people would stop hanging their laundry on apartment balconies, stop selling vegetables on the streets, or putting notices and posters on walls, Johannesburg would be able to attract the foreign investment necessary to improve the lives of urban dwellers" ("Urban Processes," 56).

30. Robinson, "(Im)mobilizing Space," 171.

31. Zakes Mda, "Learning from the Ancient Wisdom of Africa in the Creation and Distribution of Messages," *Current Writing* 6 (1994): 139–140.

32. I use the phrase "comic monster" to underscore the connections between Mda's novel and Bakhtin's account of the psycho-symbolic meaning of the carnivalesque transformation of fear into laughter: in the carnival mock-up of hell, Bakhtin suggests, "the awesome becomes a 'comic monster'" (91). Similarly, Jwara's "monsters who make people happy" (WD 212) enable Mda's characters, especially the children, to laugh fear away and to turn their gaze from the horrors of the past to the future. For further discussion of the connection between Bakhtin and Mda, see my essay "On Laughter," 285–289.

33. Arjun Appadurai, ed., *The Social Life of Things: Commodities in Perspective* (Cambridge, England: Cambridge University Press, 1986), 54.

34. Nkosi argues that a constitutive principle in South African literature—including black protest writing—is its "narratee," or implied reader. That this reader is often imagined as metropolitan and white is evident, not only in the fact that writers choose to write in English but also in their detailed descriptions of South African scenes and explanations of its political life, which strike Nkosi as "signals that the ignorant foreign reader is targeted." "Constructing the Cross-border Reader," in *Altered State? Writing and South Africa*, ed. Elleke Boehmer, Laura Chrisman, and Kenneth Parker (Sydney: Dangaroo Press, 1994), 45. This essay strikes me as essential reading for anyone interested in the location of contemporary South African culture.

35. Graham Huggan, *The Postcolonial Exotic: Marketing the Margins* (London: Routledge, 2001), 6.

36. There are several focal characters in this novel, but if we read *The Heart of Redness* as what Mervis calls "fiction for development" (a promising perspective, though not the one I adopt here), Camagu is clearly the chief protagonist, the one best qualified to serve as a catalyst in the Qolorha community, since he offers the necessary critical distance, or "heterophily," that Mda discusses at some length in his work on community theatre (WPP 85–87).

37. James Clifford defines a "translation term" as a "word of apparently general application and usefulness, that is used for the sake of comparison in a strategic and contingent way." See his *Routes: Travel and Translation in the Late Twentieth Century* (Cambridge, Mass.: Harvard University Press, 1997), 39.

38. In fact, one of the village modernists, Bhonco, merges the two terms when he disparagingly refers to "the darkness of our redness" (HR 79).

39. Steven Robins, "Bodies out of Place: Crossroads and the Landscapes of Exclusion," in Judin and Vladislavić, *Blank _____*, 58–59. See also Iona and Phillip Mayer, *Townsmen or Tribesmen: Conservatism and the Process of Urbanization in a South African City* (Cape Town: Oxford University Press, 1971).

40. See Clifford, *Routes*, 20–21.

41. Clifford defines contact zones as "places of hybrid possibility and political negotiation, sites of exclusion and struggle," in *Routes*, 212. See also Mary Louise Pratt, *Imperial Eyes: Travel Writing and Transculturation* (London: Routledge, 1992), 6–7.

42. See Pierre L. van den Berghe, *The Quest for the Other: Ethnic Tourism in San Cristóbal, Mexico* (Seattle: University of Washington Press, 1994), 5.

43. Jamaica Kincaid, *A Small Place* (New York: Farrar, Straus, and Giroux, 1988), 4–5, 13.

44. On the discourse of modernity and traditionalism as pertaining to the forms of South African domestic architecture, see Rayda Becker, "Homesteads and Headrests," in Judin and Vladislavić, *Blank _____*, 79–81.

45. I should note here that Mda chooses not to italicize any of the isiXhosa words he uses in the novel. The decision makes sense to me: he refuses to mark these words as strange or foreign and thereby declines to adopt an outsider's point of view on the local culture he presents in the novel. Since I myself am not a speaker of isiXhosa, I have decided to follow the usual custom of italicizing "foreign" words, except, of course, where I specifically quote Mda.

46. For an academic essay exploring the significance of ethnic dress along similar lines as Mda, see Sandra Klopper, "Re-dressing the Past: The Africanisation of Sartorial Style in Contemporary South Africa," in Avtar Brah and Annie E. Coombes, *Hybridity and Its Discontents: Politics, Science, Culture* (New York: Routledge, 2000): 216–231. It is interesting to note that the cultural commodity that seems to have the widest circulation is a poster of a naked African mother and child that is sold on the street in every village in South Africa and is displayed by John Dalton's wife on their living room wall. Though Mda refrains from explicitly calling it kitschy, he makes it clear that Dalton (himself far from a sophisticate) finds the image to be rather embarrassing. Its appeal, however, is as understandable in the social world of the novel as it is politically suspicious. By representing the mother and child as naked, the image simply dispenses with complicated questions about style and social identity, and sells a primitivist and universalist fantasy about Africa and the family of man.

47. If anything, Mda endorses a grassroots perspective and favors local interests over institutional power on the national and global level. His novel is revealing in this regard when it addresses the lack of real local representation, given the centralized power wielded by a ruling party that tends to simply nominate candidates in rural elections. The same geography of power that we see in the novel's aesthetic debates thus plays out in other areas of life as well.

48. Dean MacCannell, *The Tourist: A New Theory of the Leisure Class* (New York: Schocken, 1976), 6–9.

49. Ibid., 49.

50. Cited in ibid., 92.

51. Mda makes this same point about the fascination with primordial culture in his work on theatre and development (WPP 47–48).

52. Pierre Nora, "Between Memory and History: *Les Lieux de Mémoire*," *Representations* (Spring 1989): 7–25.

53. Ndebele is in fact an astute reader of *Mythologies*. See the discussion of Barthes's essay on wrestling in "The Rediscovery of the Ordinary," in *South African Literature and Culture*, 41.

54. Njabulo Ndebele, "Game Lodges and Leisure Colonialists," in Judin and Vladislavić, *Blank _____*, 119.

55. Ibid., 120.

56. Ibid.

57. Ibid., 121. I use the masculine pronoun here, since the model black tourist Ndebele imagines is obviously himself.

58. Ibid., 122.

59. Jean Comaroff and John L. Comaroff, "Naturing the Nation: Aliens, Apocalypse and the Postcolonial State," *Journal of Southern African Studies* 27 (September 2001): 634, 636.

60. Ibid., 634.

61. The most obvious vulnerability, it seems to me, lies in the fact that the anxieties about invader species and about invader people were not necessarily felt or expressed by the same people.

62. Ndebele, "Game Lodges," 122.

INDEX